Microsoft®
Training &
Certification

2279B: Planning, Implementing, and Maintaining a Microsoft® Windows® Server 2003 Active Directory® Infrastructure

Released: 05/2003

Microsoft®

Course Number: 2279B
Part Number: X09-90403
Released: 05/2003

END-USER LICENSE AGREEMENT FOR MICROSOFT OFFICIAL CURRICULUM COURSEWARE –STUDENT EDITION

PLEASE READ THIS END-USER LICENSE AGREEMENT ("EULA") CAREFULLY. BY USING THE MATERIALS AND/OR USING OR INSTALLING THE SOFTWARE THAT ACCOMPANIES THIS EULA (COLLECTIVELY, THE "LICENSED CONTENT"), YOU AGREE TO THE TERMS OF THIS EULA. IF YOU DO NOT AGREE, DO NOT USE THE LICENSED CONTENT.

1. **GENERAL.** This EULA is a legal agreement between you (either an individual or a single entity) and Microsoft Corporation ("Microsoft"). This EULA governs the Licensed Content, which includes computer software (including online and electronic documentation), training materials, and any other associated media and printed materials. This EULA applies to updates, supplements, add-on components, and Internet-based services components of the Licensed Content that Microsoft may provide or make available to you unless Microsoft provides other terms with the update, supplement, add-on component, or Internet-based services component. Microsoft reserves the right to discontinue any Internet-based services provided to you or made available to you through the use of the Licensed Content. This EULA also governs any product support services relating to the Licensed Content except as may be included in another agreement between you and Microsoft. An amendment or addendum to this EULA may accompany the Licensed Content.

2. **GENERAL GRANT OF LICENSE.** Microsoft grants you the following rights, conditioned on your compliance with all the terms and conditions of this EULA. Microsoft grants you a limited, non-exclusive, royalty-free license to install and use the Licensed Content solely in conjunction with your participation as a student in an Authorized Training Session (as defined below). You may install and use one copy of the software on a single computer, device, workstation, terminal, or other digital electronic or analog device ("Device"). You may make a second copy of the software and install it on a portable Device for the exclusive use of the person who is the primary user of the first copy of the software. A license for the software may not be shared for use by multiple end users. An "Authorized Training Session" means a training session conducted at a Microsoft Certified Technical Education Center, an IT Academy, via a Microsoft Certified Partner, or such other entity as Microsoft may designate from time to time in writing, by a Microsoft Certified Trainer (for more information on these entities, please visit www.microsoft.com). WITHOUT LIMITING THE FOREGOING, COPYING OR REPRODUCTION OF THE LICENSED CONTENT TO ANY SERVER OR LOCATION FOR FURTHER REPRODUCTION OR REDISTRIBUTION IS EXPRESSLY PROHIBITED.

3. **DESCRIPTION OF OTHER RIGHTS AND LICENSE LIMITATIONS**

   3.1   *Use of Documentation and Printed Training Materials.*

   3.1.1   The documents and related graphics included in the Licensed Content may include technical inaccuracies or typographical errors. Changes are periodically made to the content. Microsoft may make improvements and/or changes in any of the components of the Licensed Content at any time without notice. The names of companies, products, people, characters and/or data mentioned in the Licensed Content may be fictitious and are in no way intended to represent any real individual, company, product or event, unless otherwise noted.

   3.1.2   Microsoft grants you the right to reproduce portions of documents (such as student workbooks, white papers, press releases, datasheets and FAQs) (the "Documents") provided with the Licensed Content. You may not print any book (either electronic or print version) in its entirety. If you choose to reproduce Documents, you agree that: (a) use of such printed Documents will be solely in conjunction with your personal training use; (b) the Documents will not republished or posted on any network computer or broadcast in any media; (c) any reproduction will include either the Document's original copyright notice or a copyright notice to Microsoft's benefit substantially in the format provided below; and (d) to comply with all terms and conditions of this EULA. In addition, no modifications may made to any Document.

   Form of Notice:

   © 2003. Reprinted with permission by Microsoft Corporation. All rights reserved.

   Microsoft and Windows are either registered trademarks or trademarks of Microsoft Corporation in the US and/or other countries. Other product and company names mentioned herein may be the trademarks of their respective owners.

   3.2   *Use of Media Elements.* The Licensed Content may include certain photographs, clip art, animations, sounds, music, and video clips (together "Media Elements"). You may not modify these Media Elements.

   3.3   *Use of Sample Code.* In the event that the Licensed Content includes sample code in source or object format ("Sample Code"), Microsoft grants you a limited, non-exclusive, royalty-free license to use, copy and modify the Sample Code; if you elect to exercise the foregoing rights, you agree to comply with all other terms and conditions of this EULA, including without limitation Sections 3.4, 3.5, and 6.

   3.4   *Permitted Modifications.* In the event that you exercise any rights provided under this EULA to create modifications of the Licensed Content, you agree that any such modifications: (a) will not be used for providing training where a fee is charged in public or private classes; (b) indemnify, hold harmless, and defend Microsoft from and against any claims or lawsuits, including attorneys' fees, which arise from or result from your use of any modified version of the Licensed Content; and (c) not to transfer or assign any rights to any modified version of the Licensed Content to any third party without the express written permission of Microsoft.

3.5   *Reproduction/Redistribution Licensed Content.* Except as expressly provided in this EULA, you may not reproduce or distribute the Licensed Content or any portion thereof (including any permitted modifications) to any third parties without the express written permission of Microsoft.

4.   **RESERVATION OF RIGHTS AND OWNERSHIP.** Microsoft reserves all rights not expressly granted to you in this EULA. The Licensed Content is protected by copyright and other intellectual property laws and treaties. Microsoft or its suppliers own the title, copyright, and other intellectual property rights in the Licensed Content. You may not remove or obscure any copyright, trademark or patent notices that appear on the Licensed Content, or any components thereof, as delivered to you. **The Licensed Content is licensed, not sold.**

5.   **LIMITATIONS ON REVERSE ENGINEERING, DECOMPILATION, AND DISASSEMBLY.** You may not reverse engineer, decompile, or disassemble the Software or Media Elements, except and only to the extent that such activity is expressly permitted by applicable law notwithstanding this limitation.

6.   **LIMITATIONS ON SALE, RENTAL, ETC. AND CERTAIN ASSIGNMENTS.** You may not provide commercial hosting services with, sell, rent, lease, lend, sublicense, or assign copies of the Licensed Content, or any portion thereof (including any permitted modifications thereof) on a stand-alone basis or as part of any collection, product or service.

7.   **CONSENT TO USE OF DATA.** You agree that Microsoft and its affiliates may collect and use technical information gathered as part of the product support services provided to you, if any, related to the Licensed Content. Microsoft may use this information solely to improve our products or to provide customized services or technologies to you and will not disclose this information in a form that personally identifies you.

8.   **LINKS TO THIRD PARTY SITES.** You may link to third party sites through the use of the Licensed Content. The third party sites are not under the control of Microsoft, and Microsoft is not responsible for the contents of any third party sites, any links contained in third party sites, or any changes or updates to third party sites. Microsoft is not responsible for webcasting or any other form of transmission received from any third party sites. Microsoft is providing these links to third party sites to you only as a convenience, and the inclusion of any link does not imply an endorsement by Microsoft of the third party site.

9.   **ADDITIONAL LICENSED CONTENT/SERVICES.** This EULA applies to updates, supplements, add-on components, or Internet-based services components, of the Licensed Content that Microsoft may provide to you or make available to you after the date you obtain your initial copy of the Licensed Content, unless we provide other terms along with the update, supplement, add-on component, or Internet-based services component. Microsoft reserves the right to discontinue any Internet-based services provided to you or made available to you through the use of the Licensed Content.

10.   **U.S. GOVERNMENT LICENSE RIGHTS.** All software provided to the U.S. Government pursuant to solicitations issued on or after December 1, 1995 is provided with the commercial license rights and restrictions described elsewhere herein. All software provided to the U.S. Government pursuant to solicitations issued prior to December 1, 1995 is provided with "Restricted Rights" as provided for in FAR, 48 CFR 52.227-14 (JUNE 1987) or DFAR, 48 CFR 252.227-7013 (OCT 1988), as applicable.

11.   **EXPORT RESTRICTIONS.** You acknowledge that the Licensed Content is subject to U.S. export jurisdiction. You agree to comply with all applicable international and national laws that apply to the Licensed Content, including the U.S. Export Administration Regulations, as well as end-user, end-use, and destination restrictions issued by U.S. and other governments. For additional information see <http://www.microsoft.com/exporting/>.

12.   **TRANSFER.** The initial user of the Licensed Content may make a one-time permanent transfer of this EULA and Licensed Content to another end user, provided the initial user retains no copies of the Licensed Content. The transfer may not be an indirect transfer, such as a consignment. Prior to the transfer, the end user receiving the Licensed Content must agree to all the EULA terms.

13.   **"NOT FOR RESALE" LICENSED CONTENT.** Licensed Content identified as "Not For Resale" or "NFR," may not be sold or otherwise transferred for value, or used for any purpose other than demonstration, test or evaluation.

14.   **TERMINATION.** Without prejudice to any other rights, Microsoft may terminate this EULA if you fail to comply with the terms and conditions of this EULA. In such event, you must destroy all copies of the Licensed Content and all of its component parts.

15.   **DISCLAIMER OF WARRANTIES. TO THE MAXIMUM EXTENT PERMITTED BY APPLICABLE LAW, MICROSOFT AND ITS SUPPLIERS PROVIDE THE LICENSED CONTENT AND SUPPORT SERVICES (IF ANY)** *AS IS AND WITH ALL FAULTS,* **AND MICROSOFT AND ITS SUPPLIERS HEREBY DISCLAIM ALL OTHER WARRANTIES AND CONDITIONS, WHETHER EXPRESS, IMPLIED OR STATUTORY, INCLUDING, BUT NOT LIMITED TO, ANY (IF ANY) IMPLIED WARRANTIES, DUTIES OR CONDITIONS OF MERCHANTABILITY, OF FITNESS FOR A PARTICULAR PURPOSE, OF RELIABILITY OR AVAILABILITY, OF ACCURACY OR COMPLETENESS OF RESPONSES, OF RESULTS, OF WORKMANLIKE EFFORT, OF LACK OF VIRUSES, AND OF LACK OF NEGLIGENCE, ALL WITH REGARD TO THE LICENSED CONTENT, AND THE PROVISION OF OR FAILURE TO PROVIDE SUPPORT OR OTHER SERVICES, INFORMATION, SOFTWARE, AND RELATED CONTENT THROUGH THE LICENSED CONTENT, OR OTHERWISE ARISING OUT OF THE USE OF THE LICENSED CONTENT. ALSO, THERE IS NO WARRANTY OR CONDITION OF TITLE, QUIET ENJOYMENT, QUIET POSSESSION, CORRESPONDENCE TO DESCRIPTION OR NON-INFRINGEMENT WITH REGARD TO THE LICENSED CONTENT. THE ENTIRE RISK AS TO THE QUALITY, OR ARISING OUT OF THE USE OR PERFORMANCE OF THE LICENSED CONTENT, AND ANY SUPPORT SERVICES, REMAINS WITH YOU.**

16.   **EXCLUSION OF INCIDENTAL, CONSEQUENTIAL AND CERTAIN OTHER DAMAGES. TO THE MAXIMUM EXTENT PERMITTED BY APPLICABLE LAW, IN NO EVENT SHALL MICROSOFT OR ITS SUPPLIERS BE LIABLE FOR ANY SPECIAL, INCIDENTAL, PUNITIVE, INDIRECT, OR CONSEQUENTIAL DAMAGES WHATSOEVER (INCLUDING, BUT NOT**

LIMITED TO, DAMAGES FOR LOSS OF PROFITS OR CONFIDENTIAL OR OTHER INFORMATION, FOR BUSINESS INTERRUPTION, FOR PERSONAL INJURY, FOR LOSS OF PRIVACY, FOR FAILURE TO MEET ANY DUTY INCLUDING OF GOOD FAITH OR OF REASONABLE CARE, FOR NEGLIGENCE, AND FOR ANY OTHER PECUNIARY OR OTHER LOSS WHATSOEVER) ARISING OUT OF OR IN ANY WAY RELATED TO THE USE OF OR INABILITY TO USE THE LICENSED CONTENT, THE PROVISION OF OR FAILURE TO PROVIDE SUPPORT OR OTHER SERVICES, INFORMATION, SOFTWARE, AND RELATED CONTENT THROUGH THE LICENSED CONTENT, OR OTHERWISE ARISING OUT OF THE USE OF THE LICENSED CONTENT, OR OTHERWISE UNDER OR IN CONNECTION WITH ANY PROVISION OF THIS EULA, EVEN IN THE EVENT OF THE FAULT, TORT (INCLUDING NEGLIGENCE), MISREPRESENTATION, STRICT LIABILITY, BREACH OF CONTRACT OR BREACH OF WARRANTY OF MICROSOFT OR ANY SUPPLIER, AND EVEN IF MICROSOFT OR ANY SUPPLIER HAS BEEN ADVISED OF THE POSSIBILITY OF SUCH DAMAGES. BECAUSE SOME STATES/JURISDICTIONS DO NOT ALLOW THE EXCLUSION OR LIMITATION OF LIABILITY FOR CONSEQUENTIAL OR INCIDENTAL DAMAGES, THE ABOVE LIMITATION MAY NOT APPLY TO YOU.

17.   LIMITATION OF LIABILITY AND REMEDIES. NOTWITHSTANDING ANY DAMAGES THAT YOU MIGHT INCUR FOR ANY REASON WHATSOEVER (INCLUDING, WITHOUT LIMITATION, ALL DAMAGES REFERENCED HEREIN AND ALL DIRECT OR GENERAL DAMAGES IN CONTRACT OR ANYTHING ELSE), THE ENTIRE LIABILITY OF MICROSOFT AND ANY OF ITS SUPPLIERS UNDER ANY PROVISION OF THIS EULA AND YOUR EXCLUSIVE REMEDY HEREUNDER SHALL BE LIMITED TO THE GREATER OF THE ACTUAL DAMAGES YOU INCUR IN REASONABLE RELIANCE ON THE LICENSED CONTENT UP TO THE AMOUNT ACTUALLY PAID BY YOU FOR THE LICENSED CONTENT OR US$5.00. THE FOREGOING LIMITATIONS, EXCLUSIONS AND DISCLAIMERS SHALL APPLY TO THE MAXIMUM EXTENT PERMITTED BY APPLICABLE LAW, EVEN IF ANY REMEDY FAILS ITS ESSENTIAL PURPOSE.

18.   APPLICABLE LAW. If you acquired this Licensed Content in the United States, this EULA is governed by the laws of the State of Washington. If you acquired this Licensed Content in Canada, unless expressly prohibited by local law, this EULA is governed by the laws in force in the Province of Ontario, Canada; and, in respect of any dispute which may arise hereunder, you consent to the jurisdiction of the federal and provincial courts sitting in Toronto, Ontario. If you acquired this Licensed Content in the European Union, Iceland, Norway, or Switzerland, then local law applies. If you acquired this Licensed Content in any other country, then local law may apply.

19.   ENTIRE AGREEMENT; SEVERABILITY. This EULA (including any addendum or amendment to this EULA which is included with the Licensed Content) are the entire agreement between you and Microsoft relating to the Licensed Content and the support services (if any) and they supersede all prior or contemporaneous oral or written communications, proposals and representations with respect to the Licensed Content or any other subject matter covered by this EULA. To the extent the terms of any Microsoft policies or programs for support services conflict with the terms of this EULA, the terms of this EULA shall control. If any provision of this EULA is held to be void, invalid, unenforceable or illegal, the other provisions shall continue in full force and effect.

Should you have any questions concerning this EULA, or if you desire to contact Microsoft for any reason, please use the address information enclosed in this Licensed Content to contact the Microsoft subsidiary serving your country or visit Microsoft on the World Wide Web at http://www.microsoft.com.

Si vous avez acquis votre Contenu Sous Licence Microsoft au CANADA :

DÉNI DE GARANTIES. Dans la mesure maximale permise par les lois applicables, le Contenu Sous Licence et les services de soutien technique (le cas échéant) sont fournis *TELS QUELS ET AVEC TOUS LES DÉFAUTS* par Microsoft et ses fournisseurs, lesquels par les présentes dénient toutes autres garanties et conditions expresses, implicites ou en vertu de la loi, notamment, mais sans limitation, (le cas échéant) les garanties, devoirs ou conditions implicites de qualité marchande, d'adaptation à une fin usage particulière, de fiabilité ou de disponibilité, d'exactitude ou d'exhaustivité des réponses, des résultats, des efforts déployés selon les règles de l'art, d'absence de virus et d'absence de négligence, le tout à l'égard du Contenu Sous Licence et de la prestation des services de soutien technique ou de l'omission de la 'une telle prestation des services de soutien technique ou à l'égard de la fourniture ou de l'omission de la fourniture de tous autres services, renseignements, Contenus Sous Licence, et contenu qui s'y rapporte grâce au Contenu Sous Licence ou provenant autrement de l'utilisation du Contenu Sous Licence. PAR AILLEURS, IL N'Y A AUCUNE GARANTIE OU CONDITION QUANT AU TITRE DE PROPRIÉTÉ, À LA JOUISSANCE OU LA POSSESSION PAISIBLE, À LA CONCORDANCE À UNE DESCRIPTION NI QUANT À UNE ABSENCE DE CONTREFAÇON CONCERNANT LE CONTENU SOUS LICENCE.

EXCLUSION DES DOMMAGES ACCESSOIRES, INDIRECTS ET DE CERTAINS AUTRES DOMMAGES. DANS LA MESURE MAXIMALE PERMISE PAR LES LOIS APPLICABLES, EN AUCUN CAS MICROSOFT OU SES FOURNISSEURS NE SERONT RESPONSABLES DES DOMMAGES SPÉCIAUX, CONSÉCUTIFS, ACCESSOIRES OU INDIRECTS DE QUELQUE NATURE QUE CE SOIT (NOTAMMENT, LES DOMMAGES À L'ÉGARD DU MANQUE À GAGNER OU DE LA DIVULGATION DE RENSEIGNEMENTS CONFIDENTIELS OU AUTRES, DE LA PERTE D'EXPLOITATION, DE BLESSURES CORPORELLES, DE LA VIOLATION DE LA VIE PRIVÉE, DE L'OMISSION DE REMPLIR TOUT DEVOIR, Y COMPRIS D'AGIR DE BONNE FOI OU D'EXERCER UN SOIN RAISONNABLE, DE LA NÉGLIGENCE ET DE TOUTE AUTRE PERTE PÉCUNIAIRE OU AUTRE PERTE

DE QUELQUE NATURE QUE CE SOIT) SE RAPPORTE DE QUELQUE MANIÈRE QUE CE SOIT À L'UTILISATION DU CONTENU SOUS LICENCE OU À L'INCAPACITÉ DE S'EN SERVIR, À LA PRESTATION OU À L'OMISSION DE LA 'UNE TELLE PRESTATION DE SERVICES DE SOUTIEN TECHNIQUE OU À LA FOURNITURE OU À L'OMISSION DE LA FOURNITURE DE TOUS AUTRES SERVICES, RENSEIGNEMENTS, CONTENUS SOUS LICENCE, ET CONTENU QUI S'Y RAPPORTE GRÂCE AU CONTENU SOUS LICENCE OU PROVENANT AUTREMENT DE L'UTILISATION DU CONTENU SOUS LICENCE OU AUTREMENT AUX TERMES DE TOUTE DISPOSITION DE LA U PRÉSENTE CONVENTION EULA OU RELATIVEMENT À UNE TELLE DISPOSITION, MÊME EN CAS DE FAUTE, DE DÉLIT CIVIL (Y COMPRIS LA NÉGLIGENCE), DE RESPONSABILITÉ STRICTE, DE VIOLATION DE CONTRAT OU DE VIOLATION DE GARANTIE DE MICROSOFT OU DE TOUT FOURNISSEUR ET MÊME SI MICROSOFT OU TOUT FOURNISSEUR A ÉTÉ AVISÉ DE LA POSSIBILITÉ DE TELS DOMMAGES.

<u>LIMITATION DE RESPONSABILITÉ ET RECOURS.</u>   MALGRÉ LES DOMMAGES QUE VOUS PUISSIEZ SUBIR POUR QUELQUE MOTIF QUE CE SOIT (NOTAMMENT, MAIS SANS LIMITATION, TOUS LES DOMMAGES SUSMENTIONNÉS ET TOUS LES DOMMAGES DIRECTS OU GÉNÉRAUX OU AUTRES), LA SEULE RESPONSABILITÉ 'OBLIGATION INTÉGRALE DE MICROSOFT ET DE L'UN OU L'AUTRE DE SES FOURNISSEURS AUX TERMES DE TOUTE DISPOSITION DEU LA PRÉSENTE CONVENTION EULA ET VOTRE RECOURS EXCLUSIF À L'ÉGARD DE TOUT CE QUI PRÉCÈDE SE LIMITE AU PLUS ÉLEVÉ ENTRE LES MONTANTS SUIVANTS : LE MONTANT QUE VOUS AVEZ RÉELLEMENT PAYÉ POUR LE CONTENU SOUS LICENCE OU 5,00 $US. LES LIMITES, EXCLUSIONS ET DÉNIS QUI PRÉCÈDENT (Y COMPRIS LES CLAUSES CI-DESSUS), S'APPLIQUENT DANS LA MESURE MAXIMALE PERMISE PAR LES LOIS APPLICABLES, MÊME SI TOUT RECOURS N'ATTEINT PAS SON BUT ESSENTIEL.

À moins que cela ne soit prohibé par le droit local applicable, la présente Convention est régie par les lois de la province d'Ontario, Canada. Vous consentez Chacune des parties à la présente reconnaît irrévocablement à la compétence des tribunaux fédéraux et provinciaux siégeant à Toronto, dans de la province d'Ontario et consent à instituer tout litige qui pourrait découler de la présente auprès des tribunaux situés dans le district judiciaire de York, province d'Ontario.

Au cas où vous auriez des questions concernant cette licence ou que vous désiriez vous mettre en rapport avec Microsoft pour quelque raison que ce soit, veuillez utiliser l'information contenue dans le Contenu Sous Licence pour contacter la filiale de succursale Microsoft desservant votre pays, dont l'adresse est fournie dans ce produit, ou visitez écrivez à : Microsoft sur le World Wide Web à http://www.microsoft.com

Contents

About This Course

This section provides you with a brief description of the course, audience, suggested prerequisites, and course objectives.

Description

This five-day instructor-led course includes self-paced and instructor-facilitated components. It provides students with the knowledge and skills to successfully plan, implement, and troubleshoot an Active Directory® directory service infrastructure in Microsoft® Windows® Server 2003. The course focuses on a Windows Server 2003 directory service environment, including forest and domain structure, Domain Name System (DNS), site topology and replication, organizational unit structure and delegation of administration, Group Policy, and user, group, and computer account strategies.

Audience

The target audience for this course includes individuals who are either employed or seeking employment as a systems engineer in medium, large, or enterprise organizations.

Students should meet one of the following criteria:

- Career entrants: Individuals new to technology. This audience includes nontechnical people who currently work in roles outside of IT who want to obtain and validate engineering-level technical job skills for the purpose of changing professions.

- Career enhancers: Experienced individuals who currently work as entry-level IT professionals and who are new to Windows server engineering-level functions. These individuals includes Tier 2 systems administrators or support professionals in Windows, UNIX, or Novell NetWare environments who lack the depth or breadth of knowledge and engineering skills that are required to implement and troubleshoot a network based on Windows Server 2003 Server Active Directory technology.

- Professionals who are preparing for Microsoft Certified Professional Exam 70-294, *Planning, Implementing, and Maintaining a Microsoft Windows Server 2003 Active Directory Infrastructure*, which is a core requirement for the Microsoft Certified Systems Engineer (MCSE) certification credential.

At the completion of this course, students will possess the technical skills to perform the tasks in Active Directory as defined in this course.

Note Audiences that are not targeted for Course 2279A include experienced Windows NT®, Windows 2000, UNIX/Linux, or Novell NetWare systems engineers, software developers and programmers, business end-users, and home users.

Student prerequisites

This course requires that students complete Course 2278: *Planning and Maintaining a Windows Server 2003 Network Infrastructure*, or have the equivalent knowledge and skills.

Note Completion of CompTIA A+ and Network + training or equivalent knowledge and skills are a prerequisite for the core Windows curriculum. A+ Certification and Network+ Certification are recommended, but not required. For A+ and Network+ Certification exam requirements, visit http://www.comptia.org.

Course objectives

After completing this course, the student will be able to:

- Describe the logical and physical components of Active Directory.
- Create and configure a forest and domain structure by using an Active Directory infrastructure design.
- Plan and implement an organizational unit structure.
- Plan and implement Active Directory user, group, and computer accounts.
- Plan and implement a Group Policy strategy to centrally manage users and computers in an enterprise.
- Deploy, manage, and troubleshoot software that is deployed by using Group Policy.
- Implement sites to manage and monitor Active Directory replication.
- Plan and implement the placement of domain controllers, global catalog servers, and DNS servers that are integrated with Active Directory.
- Plan and manage operations masters.
- Back up, restore, and maintain Active Directory.
- Plan and implement an Active Directory infrastructure that is based on a directory service design that an enterprise architect provides.

Student Materials Compact Disc Contents

The Student Materials compact disc contains the following files and folders:

- *Autorun.exe*. When the compact disc is inserted into the CD-ROM drive, or when you double-click the **Autorun.exe** file, this file opens the compact disc and allows you to browse the Student Materials compact disc.

- *Autorun.inf*. When the compact disc is inserted into the compact disc drive, this file opens Autorun.exe.

- *Default.htm*. This file opens the Student Materials Web page. It provides you with resources pertaining to this course, including additional reading, review and lab answers, lab files, multimedia presentations, and course-related Web sites.

- *Readme.txt*. This file explains how to install the software for viewing the Student Materials compact disc and its contents and how to open the Student Materials Web page.

- *Addread*. This folder contains additional reading pertaining to this course.

- *Appendix*. This folder contains appendix files for this course.

- *Flash*. This folder contains the installer for the Macromedia Flash 6.0 browser plug-in.

- *Fonts*. This folder contains fonts that may be required to view the Microsoft Word documents that are included with this course.

- *Labfiles*. This folder contains files that are used in the hands-on labs. These files may be used to prepare the student computers for the hands-on labs.

- *Media*. This folder contains files that are used in multimedia presentations for this course.

- *Mplayer*. This folder contains the setup file to install Microsoft Windows Media® Player.

- *Webfiles*. This folder contains the files that are required to view the course Web page. To open the Web page, open Windows Explorer, and in the root directory of the compact disc, double-click **Default.htm** or **Autorun.exe**.

- *Wordview*. This folder contains the Word Viewer that is used to view any Word document (.doc) files that are included on the compact disc.

Document Conventions

The following conventions are used in course materials to distinguish elements of the text.

Convention	Use
Bold	Represents commands, command options, and syntax that must be typed exactly as shown. It also indicates commands on menus and buttons, dialog box titles and options, and icon and menu names.
Italic	In syntax statements or descriptive text, indicates argument names or placeholders for variable information. Italic is also used for introducing new terms, for book titles, and for emphasis in the text.
Title Capitals	Indicate domain names, user names, computer names, directory names, and folder and file names, except when specifically referring to case-sensitive names. Unless otherwise indicated, you can use lowercase letters when you type a directory name or file name in a dialog box or at a command prompt.
ALL CAPITALS	Indicate the names of keys, key sequences, and key combinations—for example, ALT+SPACEBAR.
`monospace`	Represents code samples or examples of screen text.
[ ]	In syntax statements, enclose optional items. For example, [*filename*] in command syntax indicates that you can choose to type a file name with the command. Type only the information within the brackets, not the brackets themselves.
{ }	In syntax statements, enclose required items. Type only the information within the braces, not the braces themselves.
|	In syntax statements, separates an either/or choice.
►	Indicates a procedure with sequential steps.
...	In syntax statements, specifies that the preceding item may be repeated.
. . .	Represents an omitted portion of a code sample.

Microsoft®
Training &
Certification

Introduction

Contents

Introduction

- Name
- Company affiliation
- Title/function
- Job responsibility
- Networking experience
- Windows experience
- Expectations for the course

Course Materials

- Name card
- Student workbook
- Student Materials compact disc
- Course evaluation
- Evaluation software

The following materials are included with your kit:

- *Name card.* Write your name on both sides of the name card.

- *Student workbook.* The student workbook contains the material covered in class, in addition to the hands-on lab exercises.

- *Student Materials compact disc.* The Student Materials compact disc contains the Web page that provides you with links to resources pertaining to this course, including additional readings, review and lab answers, lab files, multimedia presentations, and course-related Web sites.

    Note   To open the Web page, insert the Student Materials compact disc into the CD-ROM drive, and then in the root directory of the compact disc, double-click **Autorun.exe** or **Default.htm**.

- *Assessments.* There are assessments for each lesson, located on the Student Materials compact disc. You can use them as pre-assessments to identify areas of difficulty, or you can use them as post-assessments to validate learning.

- *Course evaluation.* To provide feedback about the course, training facility, and instructor, you will have the opportunity to complete an online evaluation near the end of the course.

- Evaluation software: An evaluation copy of the Microsoft® Windows® Server 2003 software is provided for your personal use only.

    To provide additional comments or inquire about the Microsoft Certified Professional program, send e-mail to mcphelp@microsoft.com.

Additional Reading from Microsoft Press

Microsoft Windows Server 2003 books from Microsoft Press can help you do your job—from the planning and evaluation stages through deployment and ongoing support—with solid technical information to help you get the most out of the Windows Server 2003 key features and enhancements. The following titles supplement the skills taught in this course.

Title	ISBN
Microsoft® Windows® Server 2003 Admin Pocket Consultant	0-7356-1354-0
Active Directory® Services for Microsoft® Windows® Server 2003 Technical Reference	0-7356-1577-2
Microsoft® Windows® Server 2003 Administrator's Companion	0-7356-1367-2
Microsoft® Windows® Server 2003 Deployment Kit	0-7356-1486-5
Migrating from Microsoft® Windows NT® Server 4.0 to Microsoft® Windows® Server 2003	0-7356-1940-9
Microsoft® Windows® Server 2003 Security Administrator's Companion	0-7356-1574-8

Prerequisites

Completion of Course 2278: *Planning and Maintaining a Microsoft Windows Server 2003 Network Infrastructure*, or equivalent knowledge and skills

This course requires that you complete Course 2278: *Planning and Maintaining a Microsoft Windows Server 2003 Network Infrastructure*, or that you possess the equivalent knowledge and skills.

Note   Completion of CompTIA A+ and Network + training or equivalent knowledge and skills are a prerequisite for the core Windows curriculum. A+ Certification and Network+ Certification are recommended, but not required. For A+ and Network+ Certification exam requirements, visit http://www.comptia.org.

Course Outline

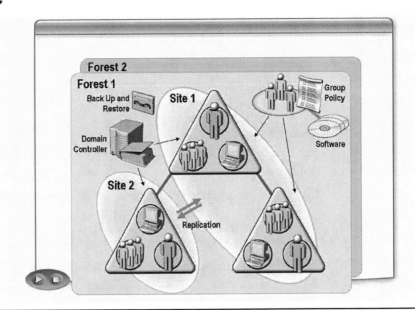

Module 1, "Introduction to Active Directory Infrastructure," introduces students to the Active Directory® directory service infrastructure, its logical and physical structure, and its function as a directory service. The module also introduces the Microsoft Management Console (MMC) snap-ins and command-line tools that you can use to examine the components of Active Directory and the Active Directory design, planning, and implementing process.

Module 2, "Implementing an Active Directory Forest and Domain Structure," discusses Active Directory installation requirements, how to create a forest and domain structure by using the Active Directory Installation Wizard, and the post-installation tasks that you must perform. It also explains how to configure Domain Name System (DNS) in an Active Directory environment, raise forest and domain functional levels, and create trust relationships.

Module 3, "Implementing an Organizational Unit Structure," provides students with the knowledge and skills necessary to create organizational units, delegate common administrative tasks, customize the delegation of administrative tasks for an organizational unit, and plan the implementation of an organizational unit structure.

Module 4, "Implementing User, Group, and Computer Accounts," provides students with the knowledge and skills required to plan and implement Active Directory user, group, and computer accounts. The module explains how to create and manage multiple user and computer accounts and how to implement User Principle Name suffixes.

Module 5, "Implementing Group Policy," provides students with the knowledge and skills necessary to plan and implement a Group Policy strategy to centrally manage users and computers in an enterprise.

Module 6, "Deploying and Managing Software Using Group Policy," explains how to deploy and manage software by using Group Policy. The module focuses on basic concepts of deploying, configuring, maintaining software, troubleshooting deployed software, and planning software deployment.

Module 7, "Implementing Sites to Manage Active Directory Replication," provides students with the knowledge and skills necessary to implement sites in order to manage and monitor replication in Active Directory. The module presents basic concepts of replication and sites in Active Directory, specifically: creating, configuring, and managing sites; monitoring and troubleshooting replication failures; and planning a site strategy.

Module 8, "Implementing the Placement of Domain Controllers," introduces students to the placement of domain controllers. The module focuses on planning the placement of domain controllers, which include global catalog servers and DNS servers that are integrated with Active Directory. The module also discusses guidelines for caching universal group membership information for a site.

Module 9, "Managing Operations Masters," introduces students to managing operations masters in Active Directory. It explains the purpose of each of the five types of operations masters, how to transfer and seize operations master roles, and how to plan a strategy for placing operations masters.

Module 10, "Maintaining Active Directory Availability," explains basic concepts about maintaining Active Directory availability, including how to defragment, move, back up, restore, and monitor an Active Directory database.

Module 11, "Planning and Implementing an Active Directory Infrastructure," provides students with the skills to plan and implement an Active Directory service infrastructure based on the business requirements of a fictitious organization.

Setup

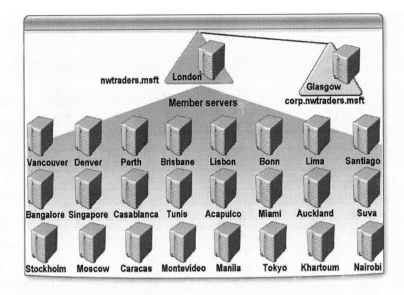

Course files

The files that are associated with the labs in this course are located in the folder \MOC\2279\Labfiles on the student computers. The Windows Server 2003 distribution files are located in the shared folder \\London\OS.

Classroom setup

The classroom is configured as a single forest with two domains, as shown in the slide.

Each student computer in the classroom has Windows Server 2003 installed as a member server of the nwtraders.msft domain. Each student computer has one of the following TCP/IP addresses: $192.168.x.1 - 192.168.x.24$, where x is the classroom network number, in order from left to right in the slide.

The primary instructor computer, London, is a domain controller for the forest root domain, nwtraders.msft. Its TCP/IP address is $192.168.x.200$ and runs Windows Internet Name Service (WINS), Dynamic Host Configuration Protocol (DHCP), and DNS services for the classroom environment. It also contains the Microsoft PowerPoint® slides and shared folders for the lab files.

The secondary instructor computer is Glasgow. It has a TCP/IP address of $192.168.x.201$. It is a domain controller for the child domain corp.nwtraders.msft. Its main purpose is to support instructor demonstrations and labs.

The necessary administrative and support tools are installed on both of the instructor computers. Only the support tools are installed on the student computers. Students will install the administrative tools on their computers during Module 1.

In Module 2, the domain structure changes. In contrast to the structure described previously, the new structure has separate forests for each pair of student computers. Each pair will be a forest root and a child domain. The domain structure will change again in Module 7 so that each pair of student computers will be domain controllers for the same domain. These changes are necessary to support and reinforce the labs.

Microsoft Official Curriculum

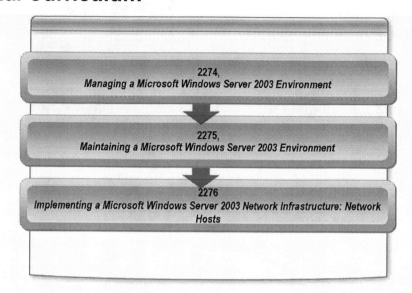

Introduction

Microsoft Training and Certification develops Microsoft Official Curriculum (MOC), including MSDN® Training, for computer professionals who design, develop, support, implement, or manage solutions by using Microsoft products and technologies. These courses provide comprehensive skills-based training in instructor-led and online formats.

Additional recommended courses

Each course relates in some way to another course. A related course may be a prerequisite, a follow-up course in a recommended series, or a course that offers additional training.

It is recommended that you take the following courses in this order:

- 2274, *Managing a Microsoft Windows Server 2003 Environment*
- 2275, *Maintaining a Microsoft Windows Server 2003 Environment*
- 2276, *Implementing a Microsoft Windows Server 2003 Network Infrastructure: Network Hosts*

Microsoft Official Curriculum *(continued)*

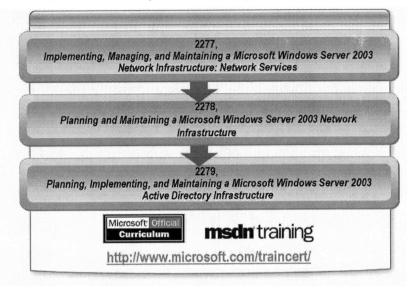

- 2277, *Implementing, Managing, and Maintaining a Microsoft Windows Server 2003 Network Infrastructure: Network Services*

- 2278, *Planning and Maintaining a Microsoft Windows Server 2003 Network Infrastructure*

- 2279, *Planning, Implementing, and Maintaining a Microsoft Windows Server 2003 Active Directory Infrastructure*

Other related courses may become available in the future, so for up-to-date information about recommended courses, visit the Training and Certification Web site.

Microsoft Training and Certification information

For more information, visit the Microsoft Training and Certification Web site at http://www.microsoft.com/traincert/.

Microsoft Certified Professional Program

Exam number and title	Core exam for the following track	Elective exam for the following track
70-294: *Planning, Implementing, and Maintaining a Microsoft® Windows® Server 2003 Active Directory® Infrastructure*	MCSE	N/A

Microsoft
C E R T I F I E D
Professional

http://www.microsoft.com/traincert/

Introduction

Microsoft Training and Certification offers a variety of certification credentials for developers and IT professionals. The Microsoft Certified Professional program is the leading certification program for validating your experience and skills, keeping you competitive in today's changing business environment.

Related certification exam

This course helps students to prepare for 70-294: *Planning, Implementing, and Maintaining a Microsoft Windows Server 2003 Active Directory Infrastructure.*

Exam 70-294 is a core exam for the Microsoft Certified Systems Engineer (MCSE) certification.

MCP certifications

The Microsoft Certified Professional program includes the following certifications.

- MCSA on Microsoft Windows Server 2003

  The Microsoft Certified Systems Administrator (MCSA) certification is designed for professionals who implement, manage, and troubleshoot existing network and system environments based on Microsoft Windows 2000 platforms, including the Windows Server 2003 family. Implementation responsibilities include installing and configuring parts of the systems. Management responsibilities include administering and supporting the systems.

- MCSE on Microsoft Windows Server 2003

  The Microsoft Certified Systems Engineer (MCSE) credential is the premier certification for professionals who analyze the business requirements and design and implement the infrastructure for business solutions based on the Microsoft Windows 2000 platform and Microsoft server software, including the Windows Server 2003 Server family. Implementation responsibilities include installing, configuring, and troubleshooting network systems.

- MCAD

  The Microsoft Certified Application Developer (MCAD) for Microsoft .NET credential is appropriate for professionals who use Microsoft technologies to develop and maintain department-level applications, components, Web or desktop clients, or back-end data services or work in teams developing enterprise applications. The credential covers job tasks ranging from developing to deploying and maintaining these solutions.

- MCSD

  The Microsoft Certified Solution Developer (MCSD) credential is the premier certification for professionals who design and develop leading-edge business solutions with Microsoft development tools, technologies, platforms, and the Microsoft Windows DNA architecture. The types of applications MCSDs can develop include desktop applications and multi-user, Web-based, N-tier, and transaction-based applications. The credential covers job tasks ranging from analyzing business requirements to maintaining solutions.

- MCDBA on Microsoft SQL Server® 2000

  The Microsoft Certified Database Administrator (MCDBA) credential is the premier certification for professionals who implement and administer Microsoft SQL Server databases. The certification is appropriate for individuals who derive physical database designs, develop logical data models, create physical databases, create data services by using Transact-SQL, manage and maintain databases, configure and manage security, monitor and optimize databases, and install and configure SQL Server.

- MCP

  The Microsoft Certified Professional (MCP) credential is for individuals who have the skills to successfully implement a Microsoft product or technology as part of a business solution in an organization. Hands-on experience with the product is necessary to successfully achieve certification.

- MCT

  Microsoft Certified Trainers (MCTs) demonstrate the instructional and technical skills that qualify them to deliver Microsoft Official Curriculum through Microsoft Certified Technical Education Centers (Microsoft CTECs).

Certification requirements

The certification requirements differ for each certification category and are specific to the products and job functions addressed by the certification. To become a Microsoft Certified Professional, you must pass rigorous certification exams that provide a valid and reliable measure of technical proficiency and expertise.

For More Information   See the Microsoft Training and Certification Web site at http://www.microsoft.com/traincert/.

You can also send e-mail to mcphelp@microsoft.com if you have specific certification questions.

Acquiring the skills tested by an MCP exam

Microsoft Official Curriculum (MOC) and MSDN Training can help you develop the skills that you need to do your job. They also complement the experience that you gain while working with Microsoft products and technologies. However, no one-to-one correlation exists between MOC and MSDN Training courses and MCP exams. Microsoft does not expect or intend for the courses to be the sole preparation method for passing MCP exams. Practical product knowledge and experience is also necessary to pass the MCP exams.

To help prepare for the MCP exams, use the preparation guides that are available for each exam. Each Exam Preparation Guide contains exam-specific information, such as a list of the topics on which you will be tested. These guides are available on the Microsoft Training and Certification Web site at http://www.microsoft.com/traincert/.

Facilities

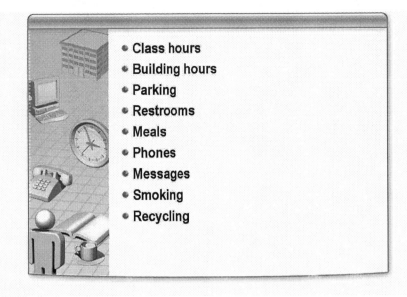

- Class hours
- Building hours
- Parking
- Restrooms
- Meals
- Phones
- Messages
- Smoking
- Recycling

Module 1: Introduction to Active Directory Infrastructure

Overview

- The Architecture of Active Directory
- How Active Directory Works
- Examining Active Directory
- The Active Directory Design, Planning, and Implementation Processes

Introduction

This module introduces the logical and physical structure of the Active Directory® directory service and its function as a directory service. The module also introduces the snap-ins, the command-line tools, and the Windows Script Host that you can use to manage the components of Active Directory and the Active Directory design, planning, and implementing processes.

Objectives

After completing this module, you will be able to:

- Describe the architecture of Active Directory.
- Describe how Active Directory works.
- Use administrative snap-ins to examine the components of Active Directory.
- Describe the Active Directory design, planning, and implementation processes.

Lesson: The Architecture of Active Directory

* What Does Active Directory Do?
* Multimedia: The Logical Structure of Active Directory
* Multimedia: The Physical Structure of Active Directory
* What Are Operations Masters?

Introduction

Active Directory consists of components that constitute its logical and physical structure. You must plan both the logical and physical structures of Active Directory to meet your organization's requirements. To manage Active Directory, you must understand the purpose of these components and how to use them.

Lesson objectives

After completing this lesson, you will be able to:

- Describe the function of Active Directory.
- Describe the logical structure of Active Directory.
- Describe the physical structure of Active Directory.
- Describe the operations master roles.

What Does Active Directory Do?

- Centralizes control of network resources
- Centralizes and decentralizes resource management
- Stores objects securely in a logical structure
- Optimizes network traffic

Introduction

Active Directory stores information about users, computers, and network resources and makes the resources accessible to users and applications. It provides a consistent way to name, describe, locate, access, manage, and secure information about these resources.

The function of Active Directory

Active Directory provides the following functions:

- *Centralizes control of network resources.* By centralizing control of resources such as servers, shared files, and printers, only authorized users can access resources in Active Directory.

- *Centralizes and decentralizes resource management.* Administrators can manage distributed client computers, network services, and applications from a central location by using a consistent management interface, or they can distribute administrative tasks by delegating the control of resources to other administrators.

- *Stores objects securely in a logical structure.* Active Directory stores all of the resources as objects in a secure, hierarchical logical structure.

- *Optimizes network traffic.* The physical structure of Active Directory enables you to use network bandwidth more efficiently. For example, it ensures that, when users log on to the network, they are authenticated by the authentication authority that is nearest to the user, thus reducing the amount of network traffic.

Multimedia: The Logical Structure of Active Directory

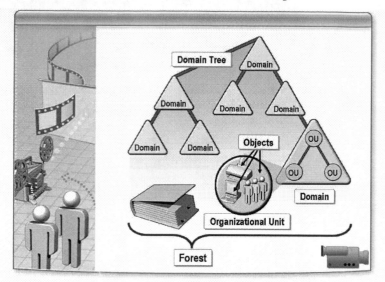

File location

To view the presentation, *The Logical Structure of Active Directory*, open the Web page on the Student Materials compact disc, click **Multimedia**, and then click the title of the presentation. Do not open this presentation unless the instructor tells you to.

Objectives

At the end of this presentation you will be able to:

- Define the elements of the logical structure of Active Directory.

- Discuss the purposes of those elements.

Key points

Active Directory provides secure storage of information about objects in its hierarchical logical structure. Active Directory *objects* represent users and resources, such as computers and printers. Some objects are containers for other objects. By understanding the purpose and function of these objects, you can complete a variety of tasks, including installing, configuring, managing, and troubleshooting Active Directory.

The logical structure of Active Directory includes the following components:

- *Objects.* These are the most basic components of the logical structure. *Object classes* are templates or blueprints for the types of objects that you can create in Active Directory. Each object class is defined by a group of *attributes*, which define the possible values that you can associate with an object. Each object has a unique combination of attribute values.

- *Organizational units.* You use these container objects to arrange other objects in a manner that supports your administrative purposes. By arranging objects by organizational unit, you make it easier to locate and manage objects. You can also delegate the authority to manage an organizational unit. Organizational units can be *nested* in other organizational units, which further simplifies the management of objects.

- *Domains.* The core functional units in the Active Directory logical structure, domains are a collection of administratively defined objects that share a common directory database, security policies, and trust relationships with other domains. Domains provide the following three functions:

  - An administrative boundary for objects

  - A means of managing security for shared resources

  - A unit of replication for objects

- *Domain trees.* Domains that are grouped together in hierarchical structures are called domain trees. When you add a second domain to a tree, it becomes a *child* of the tree root domain. The domain to which a child domain is attached is called the *parent domain.* A child domain may in turn have its own child domain.

  The name of a child domain is combined with the name of its parent domain to form its own unique Domain Name System (DNS) name such as corp.nwtraders.msft. In this manner, a tree has a *contiguous namespace.*

- *Forests.* A forest is a complete instance of Active Directory. It consists of one or more trees. In a single two-level tree, which is recommended for most organizations, all child domains are made children of the forest root domain to form one contiguous tree.

  The first domain in the forest is called the *forest root domain.* The name of that domain refers to the forest, such as nwtraders.msft. By default, the information in Active Directory is shared only within the forest. This way, the forest is a security boundary for the information that is contained in the instance of Active Directory.

Multimedia: The Physical Structure of Active Directory

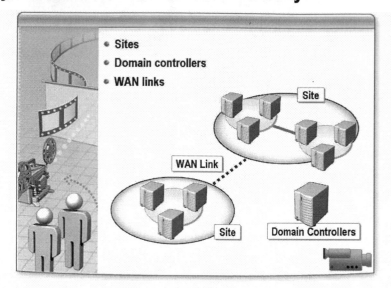

File location

To view the presentation, *The Physical Structure of Active Directory*, open the Web page on the Student Materials compact disc, click **Multimedia**, and then click the title of the presentation. Do not open this presentation unless the instructor tells you to.

Objectives

At the end of this presentation, you will be able to:

- Define the elements of the physical structure of Active Directory.
- Discuss the purpose of those elements.

Key points

In contrast to the logical structure, which models administrative requirements, the physical structure of Active Directory optimizes network traffic by determining when and where replication and logon traffic occur. To optimize Active Directory's use of network bandwidth, you must understand the physical structure. The elements of the Active Directory physical structure are:

- *Domain controllers.* These computers run Microsoft® Windows® Server 2003 or Windows 2000 Server, and Active Directory. Each domain controller performs storage and replication functions. A domain controller can support only one domain. To ensure continuous availability of Active Directory, each domain should have more than one domain controller.

■ *Active Directory sites.* These sites are groups of well-connected computers. When you establish sites, domain controllers within a single site communicate frequently. This communication minimizes the *latency* within the site; that is, the time required for a change that is made on one domain controller to be replicated to other domain controllers. You create sites to optimize the use of bandwidth between domain controllers that are in different locations.

Note For more information about Active Directory sites, see Module 7, "Implementing Sites to Manage Active Directory Replication" in Course 2279: *Planning, Implementing, and Maintaining a Microsoft Windows Server 2003 Active Directory Infrastructure.*

■ *Active Directory partitions.* Each domain controller contains the following Active Directory partitions:

  • The *domain partition* contains replicas of all of the objects in that domain. The domain partition is replicated only to other domain controllers in the same domain.

  • The *configuration partition* contains the forest topology. *Topology* is a record of all domain controllers and the connections between them in a forest.

  • The *schema partition* contains the forest-wide schema. Each forest has one schema so that the definition of each object class is consistent. The configuration and schema partitions are replicated to each domain controller in the forest.

  • Optional *application partitions* contain objects that are unrelated to security and that are used by one or more applications. Application partitions are replicated to specified domain controllers in the forest.

Note For more information about Active Directory partitions, see Module 7, "Implementing Sites to Manage Active Directory Replication," in Course 2279: *Planning, Implementing, and Maintaining a Microsoft Windows Server 2003 Active Directory Infrastructure.*

What Are Operations Masters?

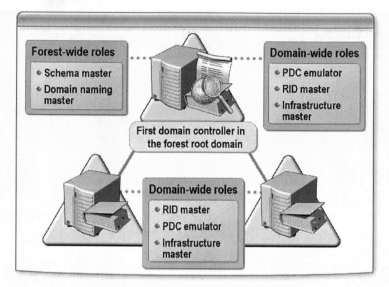

Introduction

When a change is made to a domain, the change is replicated across all of the domain controllers in the domain. Some changes, such as those made to the schema, are replicated across all of the domains in the forest. This replication is called *multimaster replication*.

Single master operations

During multimaster replication, a replication conflict can occur if originating updates are performed concurrently on the same object attribute on two domain controllers. To avoid replication conflicts, you use *single master replication*, which designates one domain controller as the only domain controller on which certain directory changes can be made. This way, changes cannot occur at different places in the network at the same time. Active Directory uses single master replication for important changes, such as the addition of a new domain or a change to the forest-wide schema.

Operations master roles

Operations that use single-master replication are arranged together in specific roles in a forest or domain. These roles are called *operations master roles*. For each operations master role, only the domain controller that holds that role can make the associated directory changes. The domain controller that is responsible for a particular role is called an *operations master* for that role. Active Directory stores information about which domain controller holds a specific role.

Active Directory defines five operations master roles, each of which has a default location. Operations master roles are either forest-wide or domain-wide.

- *Forest-wide roles.* Unique to a forest, forest-wide roles are:
  - *Schema master.* Controls all updates to the schema. The schema contains the master list of object classes and attributes that are used to create all Active Directory objects, such as users, computers, and printers.
  - *Domain naming master.* Controls the addition or removal of domains in the forest. When you add a new domain to the forest, only the domain controller that holds the domain naming master role can add the new domain.

  There is only one schema master and one domain naming master in the entire forest.

- *Domain-wide roles.* Unique to each domain in a forest, the domain-wide roles are:
  - *Primary domain controller emulator* (PDC). Acts as a Windows NT PDC to support any backup domain controllers (BDCs) running Microsoft Windows® NT within a *mixed-mode domain*. This type of domain has domain controllers that run Windows NT 4.0. The PDC emulator is the first domain controller that you create in a new domain.
  - *Relative identifier master.* When a new object is created, the domain controller creates a new security principal that represents the object and assigns the object a unique security identifier (SID). This SID consists of a domain SID, which is the same for all security principals created in the domain, and a relative identifier (RID), which is unique for each security principal created in the domain. The RID master allocates blocks of RIDs to each domain controller in the domain. The domain controller then assigns a RID to objects that are created from its allocated block of RIDs.
  - *Infrastructure master.* When objects are moved from one domain to another, the infrastructure master updates object references in its domain that point to the object in the other domain. The object reference contains the object's globally unique identifier (GUID), distinguished name, and a SID. Active Directory periodically updates the distinguished name and the SID on the object reference to reflect changes made to the actual object, such as moves within and between domains and the deletion of the object.

  Each domain in a forest has its own PDC emulator, RID master, and infrastructure master.

Note For more information about operations master roles see, Module 9, Managing Operations Masters in Course 2279: *Planning, Implementing, and Maintaining a Microsoft Windows Server 2003 Active Directory Infrastructure.*

Lesson: How Active Directory Works

- **What Is a Directory Service?**
- **What Is a Schema?**
- **What Is the Global Catalog?**
- **What Are Distinguished and Relative Distinguished Names?**
- **Multimedia: How Active Directory Enables a Single Sign-On**

Introduction

This lesson introduces the function of Active Directory as a directory service. Understanding how Active Directory works will help you manage resources and troubleshoot problems with accessing resources.

Lesson objectives

After completing this lesson, you will be able to:

- Describe the function of Active Directory as a directory service.
- Define the purpose of the Active Directory schema and how it is used.
- Define the purpose of the global catalog.
- Determine the distinguished name and relative distinguished name of an Active Directory object.
- Describe how Active Directory enables single sign-on.

What Is a Directory Service?

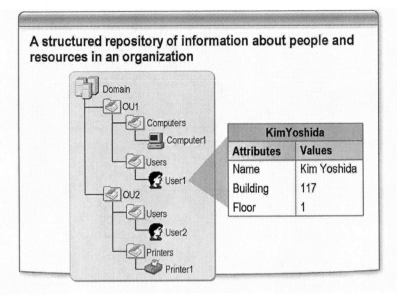

Introduction

Resources in large networks are shared by many users and applications. To enable users and applications to access these resources and information about them, you require a consistent way to name, describe, locate, access, manage, and secure information about these resources. A directory service performs this function.

What is a directory service?

A directory service is a structured repository of information about people and resources in an organization. In a Windows Server 2003 network, the directory service is Active Directory.

Capabilities of Active Directory

Active Directory has the following capabilities:

- *Enables users and applications to access information about objects.* This information is stored in the form of attribute values. You search for objects on the basis of their object class, attributes, attribute values, their location within the Active Directory structure, or any combination of these values.

- *Makes the physical network topology and protocols transparent.* This way, a user on a network can access any resource, such as a printer, without knowing where the resource is or how it is physically connected to the network.

■ *Permits the storage of a very large number of objects.* Because it is organized in partitions, Active Directory can expand as an organization grows. For example, a directory can expand from a single server with a few hundred objects to thousands of servers and millions of objects.

■ *Can run as a non-operating system service.* Active Directory in Application Mode (AD/AM) is a new capability of Microsoft Active Directory that addresses certain deployment scenarios related to directory-enabled applications. AD/AM runs as a non-operating system service and, as such, does not require deployment on a domain controller. Running as a non-operating system service means that multiple instances of AD/AM can run concurrently on a single server, with each instance being independently configurable.

Note   For more information about AD/AM, see "Introduction to Active Directory in Application Mode" at http://www.microsoft.com/windowsserver2003/techinfo/overview/adam.mspx.

What Is a Schema?

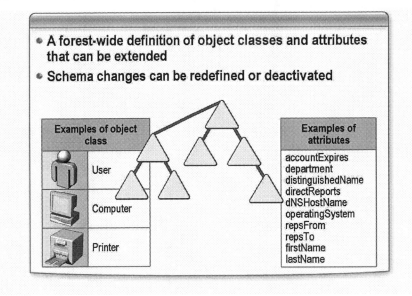

Introduction

The Active Directory schema defines the kinds of objects, the types of information about those objects, and the default security configuration for those objects that can be stored in Active Directory.

What is the Active Directory schema?

The Active Directory *schema* contains the definitions of all objects, such as users, computers, and printers that are stored in Active Directory. On domain controllers running Windows Server 2003, there is only one schema for an entire forest. This way, all objects that are created in Active Directory conform to the same rules.

The schema has two types of definitions: object classes and attributes. *Object classes* such as user, computer, and printer describe the possible directory objects that you can create. Each object class is a collection of attributes.

Attributes are defined separately from object classes. Each attribute is defined only once and can be used in multiple object classes. For example, the **Description** attribute is used in many object classes, but is defined only once in the schema to ensure consistency.

Active Directory schema and extensibility

You can create new types of objects in Active Directory by extending the schema. For example, for an e-mail server application, you could extend the user class in Active Directory with new attributes that store additional information, such as users' e-mail addresses.

Note For more information about extending the Active Directory schema, see Extending the Schema in the MSDN Library online reference.

Schema changes and deactivation

On Windows Server 2003 domain controllers, you can reverse schema changes by deactivating them, thus enabling organizations to better exploit Active Directory's extensibility features.

You may also redefine a schema class or attribute. For example, you could change the Unicode String syntax of an attribute called SalesManager to Distinguished Name.

What Is the Global Catalog?

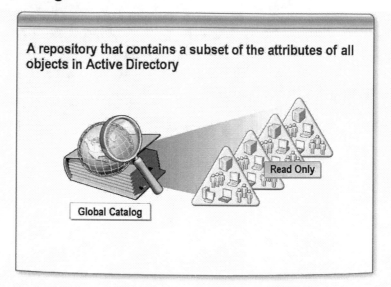

Introduction

Resources in Active Directory can be shared across domains and forests. The global catalog feature in Active Directory makes searching for resources across domains and forests transparent to the user. For example, if you search for all of the printers in a forest, a global catalog server processes the query in the global catalog and then returns the results. Without a global catalog server, this query would require a search of every domain in the forest.

What is the global catalog?

The *global catalog* is a repository of information that contains a subset of the attributes of all objects in Active Directory. Members of the Schema Admins group can change which attributes are stored in the global catalog, depending on an organization's requirements. The global catalog contains:

- The attributes that are most frequently used in queries, such as a user's first name, last name, and logon name.

- The information that is necessary to determine the location of any object in the directory.

- A default subset of attributes for each object type.

- The access permissions for each object and attribute that is stored in the global catalog. If you search for an object that you do not have the appropriate permissions to view, the object will not appear in the search results. Access permissions ensure that users can find only objects to which they have been assigned access.

What is a global catalog server?

A *global catalog server* is a domain controller that efficiently processes intraforest queries to the global catalog. The first domain controller that you create in Active Directory automatically becomes a global catalog server. You can configure additional global catalog servers to balance the traffic for logon authentication and queries.

Functions of the global catalog

The global catalog enables users to perform two important functions:

- Find Active Directory information anywhere in the forest, regardless of the location of the data.
- Use universal group membership information to log on to the network.

Note For more information about the global catalog, see Module 8, "Implementing the Placement of Domain Controllers," in Course 2279: *Planning, Implementing, and Maintaining a Microsoft Windows Server 2003 Active Directory Infrastructure.*

What Are Distinguished and Relative Distinguished Names?

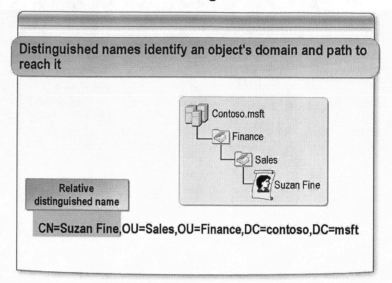

Distinguished names identify an object's domain and path to reach it

Contoso.msft
Finance
Sales
Suzan Fine

Relative distinguished name

CN=Suzan Fine,OU=Sales,OU=Finance,DC=contoso,DC=msft

Introduction

Client computers use the Lightweight Directory Access Protocol (LDAP) protocol to search for and modify objects in an Active Directory database. LDAP is a subset of X.500, an industry standard that defines how to structure directories. LDAP uses information about the structure of a directory to find individual objects, each of which has a unique name.

Definition

LDAP uses a name that represents an Active Directory object by a series of components that relate to the logical structure. This representation, called the *distinguished name* of the object, identifies the domain where the object is located and the complete path by which the object is reached. A distinguished name must be unique in an Active Directory forest.

The *relative distinguished name* of an object uniquely identifies the object in its container. No two objects in the same container can have the same name. The relative distinguished name is always the first component of the distinguished name, but it may not always be a common name.

Example of a Distinguished Name

For a user named Suzan Fine in the Sales organizational unit in the Contoso.msft domain, each element of the logical structure is represented in the following distinguished name:

```
CN=Suzan Fine,OU=Sales,DC=contoso,DC=msft
```

- CN is the common name of the object in its container.

- OU is the organizational unit that contains the object. There can be more than one OU value if the object resides in a nested organizational unit.

- DC is a domain component, such as "com" or "msft". There are always at least two domain components, but possibly more if the domain is a child domain.

The domain components of the distinguished name are based on the Domain Name System (DNS).

Example of a Relative Distinguished Name

In the following example, Sales is the relative distinguished name of an organizational unit that is represented by this LDAP naming path:

```
OU=Sales,DC=contoso,DC=msft
```

① What is the hierarchy of the AD logical structure?
forest, Domain tree, Domain, organizational unit and objects

② What are the components used to build the physical structure of Active Directory?
Sites (made up of subnets) and Domain controllers.

③ What are the forest and domain operations master roles?
Schema and Domain Naming are forest-wide masters.
PDC emulator, RID and Infrastructure are domain-wide masters.

④ What protocol is used for communication with AD?
LDAP

Multimedia: How Active Directory Enables a Single Sign-on

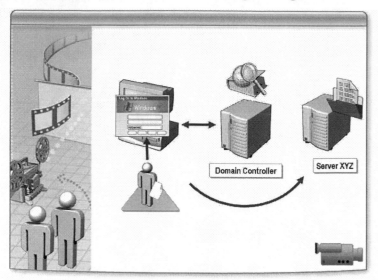

File location

To view the presentation, *How Active Directory Enables a Single Sign-on*, open the Web page on the Student Materials compact disc, click **Multimedia**, and then click the title of the presentation. Do not open this presentation unless the instructor tells you to.

Objectives

At the end of this presentation, you will be able to:

- Describe the process by which Active Directory enables a single sign-on.

- Discuss the importance of a single sign-on.

Key points

By enabling a single sign-on, Active Directory makes the complex processes of authentication and authorization transparent to the user. Users do not need to manage multiple sets of credentials.

A single sign-on consists of:

- *Authentication*, which verifies the credentials of the connection attempt.

- *Authorization*, which verifies that the connection attempt is allowed.

As a systems engineer, you must understand how these processes work in order to optimize and troubleshoot your Active Directory structure.

Lesson: Examining Active Directory

- Active Directory Management
- Active Directory Administrative Snap-ins and Tools
- How to Examine Active Directory

Introduction

Windows Server 2003 provides administrators with snap-ins and command-line tools to manage Active Directory. This lesson introduces these snap-ins and command-line tools and explains how you use them to examine the logical and physical structure of Active Directory.

Lesson objectives

After completing this lesson, you will be able to:

- Explain how Active Directory is designed to enable centralized and decentralized management.

- Describe common Active Directory administrative snap-ins and command-line tools.

- Examine the logical and physical structure of Active Directory.

Active Directory Management

Centralized management

- Enables a single administrator to centrally manage resources
- Enables administrators to locate information and group objects
- Uses Group Policy to specify settings and control the user environment

Decentralized management

- Enables delegation of network administrative responsibilities for specific organizational units to other administrators
- Enables delegation of specific tasks across organizational units

Introduction

By using Active Directory, you can manage large numbers of users, computers, printers, and network resources from a central location, using the administrative snap-ins and tools in Windows Server 2003. Active Directory also supports decentralized administration. An administrator with the proper authority can delegate a selected set of administrative privileges to other users or groups in an organization.

How Active Directory supports centralized management

Active Directory includes several features that support centralized management:

- *It contains information about all objects and their attributes.* The attributes contain data that describes the resource that the object identifies. Because information about all network resources is stored in Active Directory, one administrator can centrally manage and administer network resources.

- *You can query Active Directory by using protocols such as LDAP.* You can easily locate information about objects by searching for selected attributes of the object, using tools that support LDAP.

- *You can arrange objects that have similar administrative and security requirements into organizational units.* Organizational units provide multiple levels of administrative authority, so that you can apply Group Policy settings and delegate administrative control. This delegation simplifies the task of managing these objects and enables you to structure Active Directory to fit your organization's requirements.

- *You can specify Group Policy settings for a site, a domain, or an organizational unit.* Active Directory then enforces these Group Policy settings for all of the users and computers within the container.

How Active Directory supports decentralized management

Active Directory also supports decentralized management. You can assign permissions and grant user rights in very specific ways. For example, you can delegate administrative privileges for certain objects to the sales and marketing teams in an organization.

You can delegate the assigning of permissions:

- For specific organizational units to different domain local groups. For example, delegating the permission Full Control for the Sales organizational unit.

- To modify specific attributes of an object in an organizational unit. For example, assign the permission to change the name, address, and telephone number and to reset passwords on a user account object.

- To perform the same task, such as resetting passwords, in all organizational units of a domain.

Active Directory Administrative Snap-ins and Tools

- **Administrative MMC snap-ins**
  - Active Directory Users and Computers
  - Active Directory Domains and Trusts
  - Active Directory Sites and Services
  - Active Directory Schema
- **Command-Line Administrative Tools**
  - Dsadd
  - Dsmod
  - Dsquery
  - Dsmove
  - DSrm
  - DSget
  - CSVDE
  - LDIFDE
- **Windows Script Host**

Introduction

Windows Server 2003 provides a number of snap-ins and command-line tools to manage Active Directory. You can also manage Active Directory by using Active Directory Service Interfaces (ADSI) objects from Windows Script Host scripts. ADSI is a simple yet powerful interface to Active Directory for creating reusable scripts to manage Active Directory.

Administrative snap-ins

The following table describes some common administrative snap-ins for managing Active Directory.

Snap-in	Description
Active Directory Users and Computers	A Microsoft Management Console (MMC) that you use to manage and publish information in Active Directory. You can manage user accounts, groups, and computer accounts, add computers to a domain, manage account policies and user rights, and audit policy.
Active Directory Domains and Trusts	An MMC that you use to manage domain trusts and forest trusts, add user principal name suffixes, and change the domain and forest functional levels.
Active Directory Sites and Services	An MMC that you use to manage the replication of directory data.
Active Directory Schema	An MMC that you use to manage the schema. It is not available by default on the Administrative Tools menu. You must add it manually.

Note You can also use the ADSI Editor to view, create, modify, and delete objects in Active Directory. ADSI Editor is not installed by default. To install the ADSI Editor, install the Windows Server 2003 support tools from the \Support\Tools folder on the product compact disc.

You can customize administrative consoles to match the administrative tasks that you delegate to other administrators. You can also combine all of the consoles required for each administrative function into one console.

Command-line administrative tools

The following table describes some common command-line tools to use when you manage Active Directory.

Tool	Description
Dsadd	Adds objects, such as computers, users, groups, organizational units, and contacts, to Active Directory.
Dsmod	Modifies objects, such as computers, servers, users, groups, organizational units, and contacts, in Active Directory.
Dsquery	Runs queries in Active Directory according to specified criteria. You can run queries against servers, computers, groups, users, sites, organizational units, and partitions.
Dsmove	Moves a single object, within a domain, to a new location in Active Directory, or renames a single object without moving it.
Dsrm	Deletes an object from Active Directory.
Dsget	Displays selected attributes of a computer, contact, group, organizational unit, server, or user in Active Directory.
Csvde	Imports and exports Active Directory data by using comma-separated format.
Ldifde	Creates, modifies, and deletes Active Directory objects. Can also extend the Active Directory schema, export user and group information to other applications or services, and populate Active Directory with data from other directory services.

Note For more information about command-line tools provided by Windows Server 2003, see "Managing Active Directory from the command-line" in Help and Support.

Windows Script Host

Although Windows Server 2003 provides a number of snap-ins and command-line tools to manage Active Directory, they are not suited to doing batch operations to perform changes in Active Directory that involve complex conditions. In such cases, you can make changes more quickly by using scripts. For example, you can change the first digit of the telephone extension number from 3 to 5 and from 4 to 5 for all employees who had moved to building 5.

You can create Windows Script Host scripts that use ADSI to perform the following tasks:

- Retrieve information about Active Directory objects
- Add objects to Active Directory
- Modify attribute values for Active Directory objects
- Delete objects form Active Directory
- Extend the Active Directory schema

ADSI uses the LDAP protocol to communicate with Active Directory.

How to Examine Active Directory

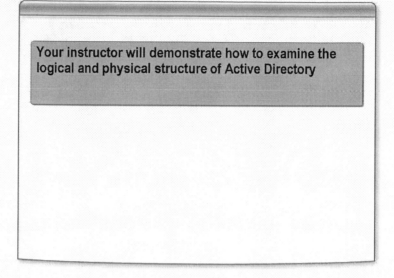

Your instructor will demonstrate how to examine the logical and physical structure of Active Directory

Introduction

You can view the logical and physical structure of Active Directory by using Active Directory Users and Computers, Active Directory Sites and Services, and Active Directory Domains and Trusts.

Procedure

To view the Active Directory logical and physical structure, perform the following steps:

1. Open Active Directory Users and Computers and view the organizational units in Active Directory. To do so, perform the following steps:

   a. Click **Start**, point to **All Programs**, point to **Administrative Tools**, and then click **Active Directory Users and Computers**.

   b. In the console tree, expand **Active Directory Users and Computers**.

   c. In the console tree, expand the domain for which you want to view the organizational units.

   d. Display the **Properties** page for each container in the console tree.

   e. Determine the object type by using the Object class information on the **Object** tab. The Object class for organizational units is *Organizational Unit*.

2. Open Active Directory Domains and Trusts to view the logical structure of Active Directory. To do so, perform the following steps:

   a. Click **Start**, point to **All Programs**, point to **Administrative Tools**, and then click **Active Directory Domains and Trusts**.

   b. In the left pane, expand the node that represents the forest-root domain to view the domains that make up the logical structure of Active Directory.

3. Open Active Directory Sites and Services and view the physical structure of Active Directory. To do so, perform the following steps:

   a. Click **Start**, point to **All Programs**, point to **Administrative Tools**, and then click **Active Directory Sites and Services**.

   b. In the console tree, expand **Sites**, and then expand the folder that represents the site for which you want to view a list of servers.

   c. Click **Servers** to view a list of servers in the right pane.

Note For more information about examining Active Directory, see "How to Examine Active Directory" in Module 1 in the Appendices on the Student Materials compact disc.

Practice: Examining the Active Directory Structure

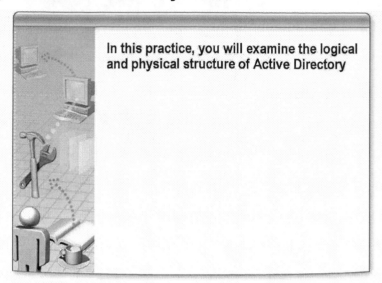

In this practice, you will examine the logical and physical structure of Active Directory

Objectives

In this practice, you will examine the logical and physical structure of Active Directory.

Scenario

Today is your first day as a systems engineer at Northwind Traders. Your manager has asked you to study the logical and physical structure of Active Directory at Northwind Traders.

Practice

▶ **Examine the default structure of Active Directory objects by using Active Directory Users and Computers**

1. Log on as **nwtraders**_ComputerName_**User** with a password of **P@ssw0rd**

2. Install the Windows Server 2003 Administration Tools Pack. To do so, perform the following steps:

   a. Click **Start**, right-click **Command Prompt**, and then click **Run as**.

   b. In the **Run As** dialog box, click **The following user**, type a user name of **nwtraders\\administrator** and a password of **P@ssw0rd** and then click **OK**.

   c. At the command prompt, type **\\London\OS\i386\Adminpak.msi** and then press ENTER.

   d. In the **File Download** dialog box, click **Open**, and then complete the installation.

   e. Close the command prompt window.

3. Open Active Directory Users and Computers.

4. Enable Advanced Features.

5. Expand **nwtraders.msft**, and locate the Locations object. What is the object type?

   organizational unit

6. Expand **Locations**. What are the object types in the folder?

   _ou_

7. The objects in the Locations folder represent geographical locations in an organization. Each location contains three objects. What is the purpose for these objects?

   Computer, group, user

8. Open any of the containers that represent a location, and then open the Users container.

   What do you observe about the objects that are located in this container?

   they are all disabled

▶ **Examine the default structure of Active Directory by using Active Directory Sites and Services**

1. Open Active Directory Sites and Services.

2. Expand **Sites**, right-click **Default-First-Site-Name**, and then click **Properties**.

3. On the **Security** tab, view the permissions for the Domain Admins group. What are the permissions?

    _____ *read* _____

    _____ *special permission* _____

4. View the permissions that are assigned to the Domain Admins group for the **Default-First-Site-Name \Servers\London** object. What do you observe?

    _____ *read, write, create child* _____

    _____ *open connector queue, special permissions* _____

▶ **Examine the default structure of Active Directory by using Active Directory Domains and Trusts**

1. Open Active Directory Domains and Trusts.

2. Expand **nwtraders.msft**, and then view the properties for nwtraders.msft. What do you observe?

    _____ *parent* _____

3. Choose to manage the corp.nwtraders.msft domain. What do you notice happens?

    _____ *special permissions required* _____

Lesson: The Active Directory Design, Planning, and Implementation Processes

- Overview of Active Directory Design, Planning, and Implementation
- The Active Directory Design Process
- The Active Directory Planning Process
- The Active Directory Implementation Process

Introduction

This lesson provides an overview of the Active Directory design, planning, and implementation processes.

Lesson objective

After completing this lesson, you will be able to:

- Differentiate between Active Directory design, planning, and implementation.
- Describe the phases of the Active Directory design process.
- Describe the phases of the Active Directory planning process.
- Describe the phases of the Active Directory implementation process.

Overview of Active Directory Design, Planning, and Implementation

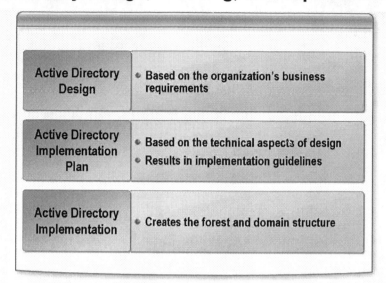

Introduction

The implementation of Active Directory begins with the creation of the Active Directory design. You use the design to plan the implementation of Active Directory and then implement Active Directory.

Active Directory design

One or more systems architects create the Active Directory design, based on the business requirements of an organization. These business requirements determine the functional specifications for the design.

Active Directory implementation plan

The Active Directory implementation plan determines how the Active Directory design is implemented based on the hardware infrastructure of the organization. For example, the Active Directory design may specify the number of domain controllers for each domain on the basis of a specific server configuration. However, if this configuration is not available, in the planning phase, you may decide to alter the number of servers to meet the business requirements of the organization.

After you implement Active Directory, you must manage and maintain it to ensure availability, reliability, and network security. This course describes the planning and implementation phases. The detailed design of Active Directory is beyond the scope of this course.

Active Directory implementation

During deployment of Active Directory, systems engineers:

- Create the forest and domain structure and deploy the servers.
- Create the organizational unit structure.
- Create the user and computer accounts.
- Create the security and distribution groups.
- Create Group Policy objects (GPOs) and apply them to domains, sites, and organizational units.
- Create software distribution policies.

The Active Directory Design Process

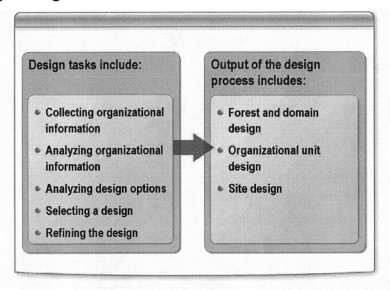

Introduction

An Active Directory design includes several tasks, each of which defines the functional requirements for a component of an Active Directory implementation.

Tasks in the Active Directory Design process

The Active Directory design process includes the following tasks:

- *Collecting organizational information.* This first task defines the need for the directory service and the business requirements for the project. Examples of organizational information include a high-level organizational profile, geographic locations of the organization, technical and network infrastructure, and plans for change in the organization.

- *Analyzing organizational information.* You analyze the collected information to assess its relevance and value to the design process. You determine the most important information and which components of the Active Directory design the information will affect. Be prepared to apply that information throughout the design process.

- *Analyzing design options.* When you analyze specific business requirements, several design options may satisfy the business requirements. For example, an administrative requirement may be met with either a domain design or an organizational unit structure. Each choice that you make affects the other components of the design, so stay flexible in your approach to the design throughout the entire process.

- *Selecting a design.* Develop several Active Directory designs and then compare their strengths and weaknesses. When you select a design, examine conflicting business requirements and consider their effects on your design choices. There may not be a clear winner among the design choices. Choose the design that meets most of your business requirements and presents the best overall choice.

- *Refining the design.* The first version of your design plan is likely to change before the pilot phase of the implementation. The design process is iterative because you must consider so many variables when you design an Active Directory infrastructure. Review and refine each design concept several times to accommodate all of the business requirements.

Output of the Active Directory Design process

The output of the Active Directory design phase includes the following elements:

- *The forest and domain design.* The forest design includes information such as the number of forests required, the guidelines for creating trusts, and the fully qualified domain name (FQDN) for the forest root domain for each forest. The design also includes the forest change control policy, which identifies the ownership and approval processes for configuration changes that have a forest-wide impact. Identify who is responsible for determining the forest change control policy for each forest in the organization. If multiple forests are in your design plan, you can assess if forest trusts are necessary to share network resources across forests.

  The domain design indicates the number of domains required in each forest, which domain will be the forest root domain for each forest, and the domain hierarchy if there are multiple domains in the design. The domain design also includes the DNS name for each domain and any trust relationships between domains.

- *The organizational unit design.* Specifies how you will create the organizational units for each domain in the forest. Include a description of the administrative authority that will apply to each organizational unit and to whom that administrative authority will be delegated. Finally, include the strategy for applying Group Policy to the organizational unit structure.

- *The site design.* Specifies the number and location of sites in the organization, the necessary site links, and the cost of the links.

The Active Directory Planning Process

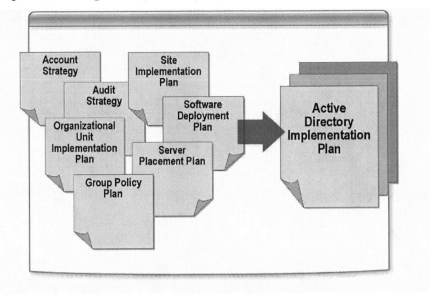

Introduction

The output of the planning process is the Active Directory implementation plan. This plan consists of several plans that define the functional requirements for a specific component of an Active Directory implementation.

Components of an Active Directory plan

An Active Directory plan includes the following components:

- *Account strategy*. Includes information, such as the guidelines for account naming and lockout policy, the password policy, and the guidelines for setting security on objects.

- *Audit strategy*. Determines how to monitor modifications to Active Directory objects.

- *Organizational unit implementation plan*. Defines how and which organizational units to create. For example, if the organizational unit design specifies that organizational units will be created geographically and organized by business unit within each geographical area, the organizational unit implementation plan defines the organizational units to implement, such as sales, human resources, and production. The plan also provides guidelines for the delegation of authority.

- *Group Policy plan*. Determines who creates, links, and manages Group Policy objects, and how Group Policy will be implemented.

- *Site plan*. Specifies the sites, site links, and the link schedule. It also specifies the replication schedule and interval and the guidelines for securing and configuring the replication between sites.

- *Software deployment plan.* Specifies how you will use Group Policy to deploy new software and upgrades to software. For example, it can specify whether software upgrades are mandatory or optional.

- *Server placement plan.* Specifies the placement of domain controllers, global catalog servers, Active Directory-integrated DNS servers, and operations masters. It also specifies whether you will enable universal group membership caching for sites that do not have a global catalog server.

After each component plan is complete, you combine them to form the complete Active Directory implementation plan.

The Active Directory Implementation Process

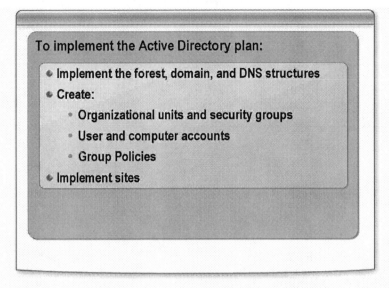

Introduction

After the Active Directory implementation plan is in place, you can begin to implement Active Directory in accordance with your design plan.

The implementation process

You perform the following tasks when you implement Active Directory:

- *Implement the forest, domain, and DNS structure.* Create the forest root domain, domain trees, and any child domains that make up the forest and domain hierarchy.

- *Create organizational units and security groups.* Create the organizational unit structure for each domain in each forest, create security groups, and delegate administrative authority to administrative groups in each organizational unit.

- *Create user and computer accounts.* Import user accounts into Active Directory.

- *Create Group Policy objects.* Create GPOs based on the Group Policy strategy, and then link them to sites, domains, or organizational units.

- *Implement sites.* Create sites according to the site plan, create site links, set site link schedules, and deploy domain controllers, global catalog servers, DNS servers, and operations masters in sites.

Microsoft®
Training &
Certification

Module 2: Implementing an Active Directory Forest and Domain Structure

Contents

Overview

- Creating a Forest and Domain Structure
- Examining Active Directory Integrated DNS
- Raising Forest and Domain Functional Levels
- Creating Trust Relationships

Introduction

This module presents installation requirements for the Active Directory® directory service and explains how to create a forest and domain structure by using the Active Directory Installation Wizard. The module also provides the knowledge and skills required to examine Domain Name System (DNS) in an Active Directory environment, raise forest and domain functional levels, and create trust relationships.

Objectives

After completing this module, you will be able to:

- Create a forest and domain structure.
- Examine Active Directory integrated DNS.
- Raise the functional level of a forest and a domain.
- Create trust relationships between domains.

Lesson: Creating a Forest and Domain Structure

* Requirements for Installing Active Directory
* The Active Directory Installation Process
* How to Create a Forest and Domain Structure
* How to Add a Replica Domain Controller
* How to Rename a Domain Controller
* How to Remove a Domain Controller from Active Directory
* How to Verify the Active Directory Installation
* How to Troubleshoot the Installation of Active Directory

Introduction

This lesson provides you with the skills and knowledge necessary to create a forest and domain structure. You will learn how to verify a successful installation of Active Directory, identify common problems that may arise during Active Directory installation, and resolve these problems.

Lesson objectives

After completing this lesson, you will be able to:

- Identify the requirements for installing Active Directory.
- Describe the Active Directory installation process.
- Create a forest and domain structure.
- Add a replica domain controller to a domain.
- Rename a domain controller.
- Remove a domain controller from Active Directory.
- Verify an Active Directory installation.
- Troubleshoot the installation of Active Directory.

Requirements for Installing Active Directory

- A computer running Windows Server 2003
- Minimum disk space of 250 MB and a partition formatted with NTFS
- Administrative privileges for creating a domain
- TCP/IP that is installed and configured to use DNS
- An authoritative DNS server that supports SRV resource records

Introduction

Before you install Active Directory, you must ensure that the computer that is to be configured as a domain controller meets certain hardware and operating system requirements. In addition, the domain controller must be able to access a DNS server that meets certain requirements to support integration with Active Directory.

Requirements for domain controllers

The following list identifies the requirements for an Active Directory installation:

- A computer running Microsoft® Windows® Server 2003 Standard Edition, Enterprise Edition, or Datacenter Edition. The Windows Server 2003, Web Edition, does not support Active Directory.

- A minimum of 250 megabytes (MB) of disk space—200 MB for the Active Directory database and 50 MB for the Active Directory database transaction log files. File size requirements for the Active Directory database and log files depend on the number and type of objects in the domain. Additional disk space is required if the domain controller is also a global catalog server.

- A partition or volume that is formatted with the NTFS file system. The NTFS partition is required for the SYSVOL folder.

- The necessary administrative privileges for creating a domain if you are creating one in an existing Windows Server 2003 network.

- TCP/IP installed and configured to use DNS.
- A DNS server that is authoritative for the DNS domain and supports the requirements listed in the following table.

Requirement	Description
SRV resource records (Mandatory)	Service locator resource (SRV) records are DNS records that identify computers that host specific services on a Windows Server 2003 network. The DNS server that supports Active Directory deployment must also support SRV resource records. If it does not, you must configure DNS locally during the Active Directory installation process or configure DNS manually after Active Directory is installed.
Dynamic updates (Optional)	Microsoft highly recommends that DNS servers also support dynamic updates. The dynamic update protocol enables servers and clients in a DNS environment to add and modify records in the DNS database automatically, which reduces administrative efforts. If you use DNS software that supports SRV resource records but does not support the dynamic update protocol, you must enter the SRV resource records manually in the DNS database.
Incremental zone transfers (Optional)	In an incremental zone transfer, changes made to a zone on a master DNS server must be replicated to the secondary DNS servers for that zone. Incremental zone transfers are optional, but they are recommended because they save network bandwidth by allowing only new or modified resource records to be replicated between DNS servers, instead of the entire zone database file.

Note For more information about SRV resource records, dynamic updates, and incremental zone transfers, see "Windows 2000 DNS" under "Additional Reading" on the Student Materials compact disc.

The Active Directory Installation Process

The installation process

- Starts the security protocol and sets the security policy
- Creates the:
  - Active Directory partitions, database, and log files
  - Forest root domain
  - SYSVOL folder
- Configures the site membership of the domain controller
- Enables security on the directory service and the file replication folders
- Applies the password for restore mode

Introduction

To start the Active Directory installation process, run the Active Directory Installation Wizard. The installation process makes a number of changes to the Windows Server 2003 server on which Active Directory is installed. Understanding these changes will help you troubleshoot problems that may arise post-installation.

The installation process

The installation process performs the following tasks:

- *Starts the Kerberos version 5 authentication protocol*

- *Sets the Local Security Authority (LSA) policy.* The setting indicates that this server is a domain controller.

- *Creates Active Directory partitions.* A directory partition is a portion of the directory namespace. Each directory partition contains a hierarchy, or subtree, of directory objects in the directory tree. During installation, the following partitions are created on the first domain controller in a forest:

  - schema directory partition

  - configuration directory partition

  - domain directory partition

  - the forest DNS zone

  - the domain DNS zone partition

  The partitions are then updated through replication on each subsequent domain controller that is created in the forest.

Note For more information about directory partitions, see Module 7, "Implementing Sites to Manage Active Directory Replication," in Course 2279, *Planning, Implementing, and Maintaining a Microsoft Windows Server 2003 Active Directory Infrastructure.*

■ *Creates the Active Directory database and log files.* The default location for the database and log files is systemroot\Ntds.

> **Note** For best performance, place the database and log files on separate hard disks. This way, Read and Write operations that are made to the database and log files are not competing for input and output resources.

■ *Creates the forest root domain.* If the server is the first domain controller on the network, the installation process creates the forest root domain, and then assigns operations master roles to the domain controller, including:

- primary domain controller (PDC) emulator
- relative identifier (RID) operations master
- domain-naming master
- schema master
- infrastructure master

> **Note** You can assign the operations master roles to another domain controller when you add replica domain controllers to the domain.

■ *Creates the shared system volume folder.* This folder structure is hosted on all Windows Server 2003 domain controllers and contains the following folders:

- The SYSVOL shared folder, which contains Group Policy information.
- The Net Logon shared folder, which contains logon scripts for computers not running Windows Server 2003.

■ *Configures the membership of the domain controller in an appropriate site.* If the IP address of the server that you are promoting to a domain controller is within the range for a given subnet defined in Active Directory, the wizard configures the membership of the domain controller in the site that is associated with that subnet.

If no subnet objects are defined or if the IP address of the server is not within the range of the subnet objects present in Active Directory, the server is placed in the *Default-First-Site-Name* site—the first site set up automatically when you create the first domain controller in a forest.

The Active Directory Installation Wizard creates a *server object* for the domain controller in the appropriate site. The server object contains information required for replication. The server object contains a reference to the computer object in the Domain Controllers organizational unit that represents the domain controller being created.

> **Note** If a server object for this domain controller already exists in the Servers container in the site in which you are adding the domain controller, the wizard deletes it and then re-creates it because it assumes that you are reinstalling Active Directory.

- *Enables security on the directory service and the file replication folders.* This enables you to control user access to Active Directory objects.

- *Applies the user-provided password for the administrator account.* You use the account to start the domain controller in Directory Services Restore Mode.

How to Create a Forest and Domain Structure

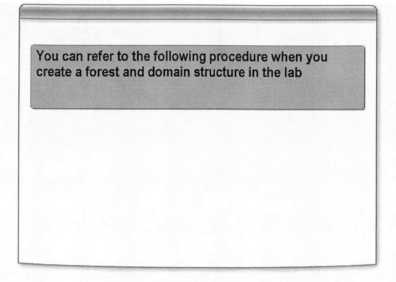

You can refer to the following procedure when you create a forest and domain structure in the lab

Introduction

You use the Active Directory Installation Wizard to create a forest and domain structure. When you install Active Directory for the first time in a network, you create the forest root domain. After you create the forest root domain, you use the wizard to create additional trees and child domains.

Procedure for creating the forest root domain

The Active Directory Installation Wizard guides you through the installation process and prompts you for information, which varies according to the options that you select.

To create the forest root domain, perform the following steps:

1. Click **Start**, click **Run**, and then type **dcpromo** as the name of the program.

   The wizard verifies that:

   - The user currently logged on is a member of the local Administrators group.

   - The computer is running an operating system that supports Active Directory.

   - A previous installation or removal of Active Directory has not occurred without your restarting the computer, or that an installation or removal of Active Directory is not in progress.

   If any of these four verifications fail, an error message appears and you exit the wizard.

2. On the **Welcome** page, click **Next**.

3. On the **Operating System Compatibility** page, click **Next**.

Caution   The Operating System Compatibility page contains information about early Windows operating system compatibility. Windows Server 2003 implements a higher level of security than Windows 2000. You must install the Active Directory client on Windows 95 and Microsoft Windows NT® (with service pack 3) to enable authentication by a Windows Server 2003 domain controller.

---

4. On the **Domain Controller Type** page, click **Domain controller for a new domain**, and then click **Next**.

5. On the **Create New Domain** page, click **Domain in a new forest**, and then click **Next**.

6. On the **New Domain Name** page, type the full DNS name for the new domain, and then click **Next**.

7. On the **NetBIOS Domain Name** page, verify the NetBIOS name, and then click **Next**.

   The NetBIOS name identifies the domain to client computers running earlier versions of Windows and Windows NT. The wizard verifies that the NetBIOS domain name is unique. If it is not, it prompts you to change the name.

8. On the **Database and Log Folders** page, specify the location in which you want to install the database and log folders, and then click **Next**.

9. On the **Shared System Volume** page, type the location in which you want to install the SYSVOL folder, or click **Browse** to choose a location, and then click **Next**.

10. On the **DNS Registration Diagnostics** page, verify if an existing DNS server will be authoritative for this forest or, if necessary, click **Install and configure the DNS server on this computer, and set this computer to use this DNS server as its preferred DNS server**, and then click **Next**.

11. On the **Permissions** page, specify whether to assign the default permissions on user and group objects that are compatible with servers running earlier versions of Windows or Windows NT, or only with servers running Windows Server 2003.

12. When prompted, specify the password for the Directory Services Restore Mode.

    Windows Server 2003 domain controllers maintain a small version of the Microsoft Windows NT 4.0 account database. The only account in this database is the Administrator account and this account is required for authentication when starting the computer in Directory Services Restore mode, as Active Directory is not started in this mode.

Note   For information about how to change the Directory Services Restore Mode password, see "Ntdsutil: Command-line reference" in Windows Server 2003 Help and Support.

---

13. Review the **Summary** page, and then click **Next** to begin the installation.

14. When prompted, restart the computer.

Procedure for creating a child domain

The procedure for creating a child domain by using the Active Directory Installation Wizard is similar to that of creating the forest root domain. The following table lists the steps you perform during the installation.

Active Directory Installation Wizard page	New step to perform
Create New Domain	Click **Child domain in an existing domain tree**.
Network Credentials	Type the user name, password, and user domain of the user account you want to use for this operation. The user account must be a member of the Enterprise Admins group.
Child Domain Installation	Verify the parent domain, and then type the new child domain name.

When you use the Active Directory Installation Wizard to create or remove a child domain, it contacts the domain-naming master and requests the addition or deletion. The domain-naming master is responsible for ensuring that the domain names are unique. If the domain-naming master is unavailable, you cannot add or remove domains.

Procedure for creating a tree

The procedure for creating a tree by using the Active Directory Installation Wizard is similar to that of creating the forest root domain. The following table lists the steps you perform during the installation.

Active Directory Installation Wizard page	New step to perform
Create New Domain	Click **Domain tree in an existing forest**.
Network Credentials	Type the user name, password, and user domain of the user account you want to use for this operation. The user account must be a member of the Enterprise Admins group.
New Domain Tree	Type the full DNS name for the new domain.

How to Add a Replica Domain Controller

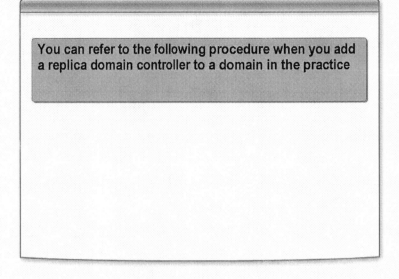

You can refer to the following procedure when you add a replica domain controller to a domain in the practice

Introduction

To enable fault tolerance in the event that a domain controller goes offline unexpectedly, you must have at least two domain controllers in a single domain. Because all domain controllers in a domain replicate their domain-specific data to one another, installing multiple domain controllers in the domain automatically enables fault tolerance for the data that is stored in Active Directory. If a domain controller fails, the remaining domain controllers will provide authentication services and access to objects in Active Directory, so that the domain operates as usual.

Procedure

Before you begin the installation, determine whether you will perform the initial replication of Active Directory over the network from a nearby domain controller or from backed-up media.

Choose to replicate Active Directory over the network if the replica domain controller will be installed:

- In a site where another domain controller exists.
- In a new site that is connected to an existing site by a high-speed network.

Choose to replicate Active Directory from backup media when you want to install the first domain controller in a remote site for an existing domain.

When you copy domain information from restored backup files, you must first back up the system state data of a domain controller running Windows Server 2003 from the domain in which this member server will become an additional domain controller. Then, you must restore the system state backup on the server on which you are installing Active Directory.

Important If a domain controller that was backed up contains an application directory partition, this partition will not be restored on the new domain controller. If the domain controller from which you restored the system state data was a global catalog server, you will have the option to make this new domain controller a global catalog server.

To install a replica domain controller, perform the following steps:

1. Run **dcpromo**. To install an additional domain controller from restored backup files, run **dcpromo** with the **/adv** option.

2. On the **Domain Controller Type** page, select the **Additional domain controller for an existing domain** checkbox.

   Or, if you run the Active Directory Installation Wizard with the **/adv** option, on the **Copying Domain Information** page, choose one of the following options:

   - **Over the network**.

   - **From these restored backup files**, and then specify the location of the restored backup files.

3. On the **Network Credentials** page, type the user name, password, and user domain of the user account that you want to use for this operation.

   The user account must be a member of the Domain Admins group for the target domain.

4. On the **Database and Log Folders** page, type the location in which you want to install the database and log folders, or click **Browse** to choose a location.

5. On the **Shared System Volume** page, type the location in which you want to install the SYSVOL folder, or click **Browse** to choose a location.

6. On the **Directory Services Restore Mode Administrator Password** page, type and confirm the Directory Services Restore Mode password, and then click **Next**.

7. Review the **Summary** page, and then click **Next** to begin the installation.

8. When prompted, restart the computer.

Note For more information about backing up and restoring Active Directory, see Module 10, "Maintaining Active Directory" in Course 2279, *Planning, Implementing, and Maintaining a Microsoft Windows Server 2003 Active Directory Infrastructure*.

How to Rename a Domain Controller

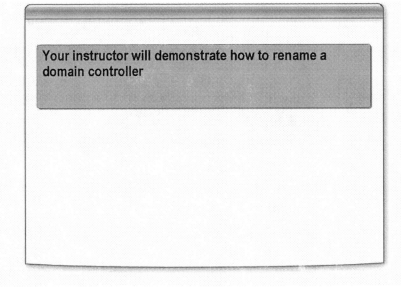

Your instructor will demonstrate how to rename a domain controller

Introduction

In Windows Server 2003, you can rename a domain controller after it has been installed. To rename a domain controller, you must have Domain Admin rights. When you rename a domain controller, you must add the new domain controller name and remove the old name from both the DNS and the Active Directory database. Renaming a domain controller is only possible if the domain functional level is set to Windows Server 2003.

Procedure

To rename a domain controller, perform the following steps:

1. In the Control Panel, double-click **System**.
2. In the **System Properties** dialog box, on the **Computer Name** tab, click **Change**.
3. When prompted, confirm that you want to rename the domain controller.
4. Enter the full computer name (including the primary DNS suffix), and then click **OK**.

Note Renaming this domain controller may cause it to become temporarily unavailable to users and computers.

You can change the Primary DNS suffix for a domain controller when you rename the domain controller. However, changing the Primary DNS suffix does not move the domain controller to a new Active Directory domain. For example, if you rename the dc2.nwtraders.msft server dc1.contoso.msft, the computer remains a domain controller for the nwtraders.msft domain, even though its Primary DNS suffix is contoso.msft. To move a domain controller to another domain, you must first demote the domain controller and then promote it to a domain controller in the new domain.

How to Remove a Domain Controller from Active Directory

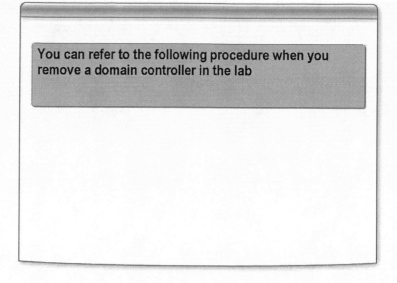

You can refer to the following procedure when you remove a domain controller in the lab

Introduction

In Windows Server 2003, you can remove a domain controller that is no longer required or that has been damaged by natural disaster. If the domain controller is the last domain controller in its domain, removing the domain controller will remove this domain from the forest. If this domain is the last domain in the forest, removing the domain controller will delete the forest.

Procedure for removing a domain controller that is online

To remove a domain controller that is online and is no longer required, perform the following steps:

1. Open the Active Directory Installation Wizard.

2. On the **Remove Active Directory** page, if this is the last domain controller for the domain, select the **This server is the last domain controller in the domain** check box, and then click **Next**.

3. On the **Administrator Password** page, in the **New Administrator Password** and **Confirm password** dialog boxes, type your new administrator password, and then click **Next**.

4. On the **Summary** page, review the summary, and then click **Next**.

Procedure for removing a domain controller that is damaged

To remove a domain controller that is damaged and cannot be started from Active Directory, restart the domain controller in directory services restore mode, and run the **ntdsutil** command by using the metadata cleanup option. To do so, perform the following steps:

1. At the command prompt, type the following command, and then press ENTER.

   ```
   Ntdsutil: metadata cleanup
   ```

2. At the Metadata cleanup prompt, type the following command, and then press ENTER.

   ```
   Metadata cleanup: connections
   ```

3. At the Server connections prompt, type the following sequence of commands to connect to a domain controller in the domain that contains the damaged domain controller:

   ```
   Server connections: Connect to server ServerName FQDN
   Server connections: quit
   ```

4. At the Metadata cleanup prompt, select the operations target by typing the following command:

   ```
   Metadata cleanup: select operations target
   ```

5. At the Select operations target prompt, type the following sequence of commands to identify and select the damaged domain controller:

   ```
   Select operations target: list sites
   Select operations target: select site number
   Select operations target: list servers in site
   Select operations target: select server number
   Select operations target: quit
   ```

6. At the Metadata cleanup prompt, type the following command to remove the damaged domain controller from Active Directory:

   ```
   Metadata cleanup: remove selected server
   Metadata cleanup: quit
   ```

Important   When you remove a domain controller that is a global catalog server, you must ensure that another global catalog is available to users before you demote the domain controller. Also, if the domain controller holds an operations master role, you must transfer that role to another domain controller before removing it. For information about transferring an operations master role to another domain controller, see Module 9, "Managing Operations Masters," in Course 2279, *Planning, Implementing, and Maintaining a Microsoft Windows Server 2003 Active Directory Infrastructure*.

How to Verify the Active Directory Installation

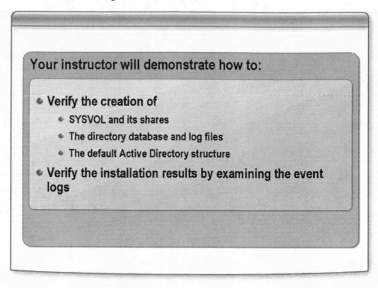

Your instructor will demonstrate how to:

● **Verify the creation of**
  ● SYSVOL and its shares
  ● The directory database and log files
  ● The default Active Directory structure

● **Verify the installation results by examining the event logs**

Introduction

The Active Directory installation process creates a number of default objects in the Active Directory database. It also creates the shared system folder and the database and log files. Verify the installation of Active Directory after the wizard completes the installation and the new domain controller restarts.

Verifying the creation of SYSVOL and its shares

You must verify that the SYSVOL folder structure was created, and then verify that the necessary shared folders were created. If the SYSVOL folder is not created correctly, data in the SYSVOL folder, such as Group Policy and scripts, will not be replicated between domain controllers.

To verify that the folder structure was created, perform the following step:

■ Click **Start**, click **Run**, type **%systemroot%\sysvol** and then click **OK**.

  Windows Explorer displays the contents of the SYSVOL folder, which should include the subfolders domain, staging, staging areas, and sysvol.

To verify that the necessary shared folders were created, perform the following step:

- At the command prompt, type **net share** and then press ENTER.

The following list of shared folders should appear on the computer.

Share name	Resource	Remark
NETLOGON	%systemroot%\SYSVOL\sysvol\domain\ SCRIPTS	Logon server share
SYSVOL	%systemroot%\SYSVOL\sysvol	Logon server share

Verifying the creation of the Active Directory database and log files

To verify that the Active Directory database and log files were created, perform the following step:

- Click **Start**, click **Run**, type **%systemroot%\ntds** and then click **OK**.

Windows Explorer displays the contents of the Ntds folder, which should include the following files:

- Ntds.dit. This is the directory database file.
- Edb.*. These are the transaction logs and the checkpoint files.
- Res*.log. These are the reserved log files.

Note If you changed the location of the directory database and log files during the installation, replace **%systemroot%** with the correct location.

Verifying the creation of the default Active Directory structure

During the installation of Active Directory on the first domain controller in a new domain, several default objects are created. These objects include containers, users, computers, groups, and organizational units.

View these default objects by using the Active Directory Users and Computers snap-in. The following table describes the purpose of some of the default objects.

Object	Description
Builtin	Holds the default built-in security groups.
Computers	Is the default location for computer accounts.
Domain Controllers	Is an organizational unit and is the default location for domain controller computer accounts.
ForeignSecurityPrincipals	Holds security identifiers (SIDs) from external, trusted domains.
Users	Is the default location for user and group accounts.
Lost and Found	Is the default container for orphaned objects.
NTDS Quotas	Stores quota specifications. Quota objects determine the number of directory objects that a security principal can own in Active Directory.
Program Data	Is the default location for storing application data.
System	Stores built-in system settings.

Examining the event logs for errors

After you install Active Directory, examine the event logs for any errors that may have occurred during the installation process. Error messages that are generated during the installation are recorded in the System, Directory Service, DNS Server, and File Replication service logs.

How to Troubleshoot the Installation of Active Directory

Symptom	Possible causes
Access denied when creating or adding a domain controller	• You are not logged on using an account in the Local Administrators group • Your credentials are not from a user account that is a member of the Domain Admins or Enterprise Admins group
DNS or NetBIOS domain names are not unique	• Another domain has the same DNS or NetBIOS name
Domain cannot be contacted	• Network error • DNS error
Insufficient disk space	• Available disk space is less than the minimum required to install Active Directory

Introduction

When installing Active Directory, you may encounter problems. These problems could result from improper security credentials, the use of names that are not unique, an unreliable network, or insufficient resources.

Common installation problems

The following table describes some common problems that you may encounter while installing Active Directory, and some strategies for resolving them.

Problem	Solution
Access denied while creating or adding domain controllers	Log off and then log on using an account that belongs to the Local Administrators group. Supply credentials of a user account that is a member of the Domain Admins group or the Enterprise Admins group.
DNS or NetBIOS domain names are not unique	Change the name to a unique name.
The domain cannot be contacted	Check that there is network connectivity between the server you are promoting to a domain controller and at least one of the domain controllers in the domain. Use the ping command from the command prompt to test connectivity with any domain controller in the domain. Verify that DNS provides name resolution to at least one domain controller in the domain by connecting to a domain controller by using its DNS name. To do so, at the command prompt, type the fully qualified domain name (FQDN) of the domain controller. If DNS is configured correctly, you will be able to connect to the domain controller. You can also check whether DNS has been configured properly by verifying the A records that the domain controllers register in the DNS database.
Insufficient disk space	Increase partition size, or install Active Directory database and log files on separate partitions.

Practice: Creating a Child Domain

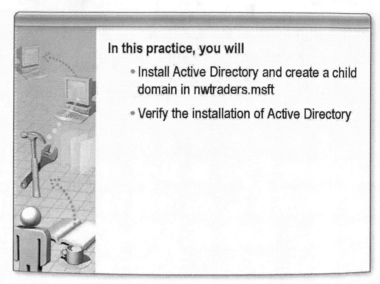

In this practice, you will

* Install Active Directory and create a child domain in nwtraders.msft

* Verify the installation of Active Directory

Objectives

In this practice, you will install Active Directory and create a child domain in the forest root domain nwtraders.msft. After installing Active Directory, you will verify the creation of the shared system volume folder, and the database and log files.

Scenario

Northwind Traders is opening offices at new locations. You must create new domains in the nwtraders.msft domain for each new office.

Practice

▶ **Install Active Directory and create the child domain**

1. Log on as **Nwtraders***ComputerName***User** with a password of **P@ssw0rd** (where *ComputerName* is the name of the computer you are working on).

2. Click **Start**, right-click **Command Prompt**, and then click **Run as**.

3. In the **Run As** dialog box, click **The following user**, type a user name of **Nwtraders\Administrator** and a password of **P@ssw0rd** and then click **OK**.

4. At the command prompt, type **dcpromo** and press ENTER.

5. On the **Welcome to the Active Directory Installation Wizard** page, click **Next**.

6. On the **Operating System Compatibility** page, click **Next**.

7. On the **Domain Controller Type** page, click **Domain controller for a new domain**, and then click **Next**.

8. On the **Create New Domain** page, click **Child domain in an existing domain tree**, and then click **Next**.

9. On the **Network Credentials** page, type **Administrator** for the user name, **P@ssw0rd** for the password, ensure that **nwtraders.msft** is the domain, and then click **Next**.

10. On the **Child Domain Installation** page, verify that the parent domain is nwtraders.msft, type a child domain name of **corp***x* where *x* is the last number from your IP address, and then click **Next**.

11. On the **NetBIOS Domain Name** page, verify the NetBIOS name of corp*x*, and then click **Next**.

12. On the **Database and Log Folders** page, accept the default selection, and then click **Next**.

13. On the **Shared System Volume** page, accept the default location to install the SYSVOL folder, and then click **Next**.

14. On the **DNS Registration Diagnostics** page, verify that the DNS configuration settings are accurate, and then click **Next**.

15. On the **Permissions** page, click **Permissions compatible only with Windows 2000 or Windows Server 2003 operating systems**, and then click **Next**.

16. On the **Directory Services Restore Mode Administrator Password** page, type and confirm a password of **P@ssw0rd** and then click **Next**.

17. Review the **Summary** page, click **Next** to begin the installation, and then click **Finish**.

18. When prompted, restart the computer.

Lesson: Examining Active Directory Integrated DNS

- DNS and Active Directory Namespaces
- What Are Active Directory Integrated Zones?
- What Are SRV Resource Records?
- SRV Records Registered by Domain Controllers
- How to Examine the Records Registered by a Domain Controller
- Multimedia: How Client Computers Use DNS to Locate Domain Controllers and Services

Introduction

Windows Server 2003 requires that a DNS infrastructure is in place before you install Active Directory. Understanding how DNS and Active Directory are integrated and how client computers use DNS during logon will help you resolve problems related to DNS, such as client logon problems.

This lesson describes the format of SRV (service) resource records—the DNS records that the domain controllers register—and explains how Active Directory uses SRV records to locate resource providers.

Lesson objectives

After completing this lesson, you will be able to:

- Describe the relationship between DNS and Active Directory namespaces.
- Explain the purpose of Active Directory integrated zones.
- Describe the purpose of SRV records.
- Describe the SRV records that are registered by domain controllers.
- Examine the DNS records registered by a domain controller.
- Describe how client computers use DNS to locate domain controllers and services.

DNS and Active Directory Namespaces

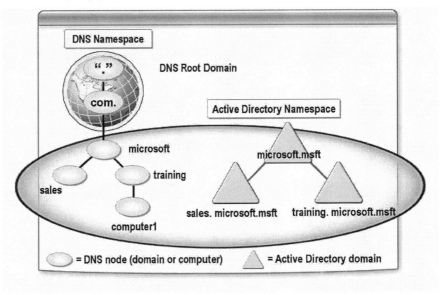

Introduction	DNS domains and Active Directory domains use identical domain names for different namespaces. By using identical domain names, computers in a Windows Server 2003 network can use DNS to locate domain controllers and other computers that provide Active Directory services.

Relationship between the DNS namespace and the Active Directory namespace

Domains and computers are represented by resource records in the DNS namespace and by Active Directory objects in the Active Directory namespace.

The DNS host name for a computer is the same name as that used for the computer account that is stored in Active Directory. The DNS domain name— also called the *primary DNS suffix*—has the same name as the Active Directory domain that the computer belongs to. For example, a computer named Computer1 that belongs to the Active Directory domain named training.microsoft.msft has the following FQDN:

computer1.training.microsoft.msft

Integration of DNS and Active Directory

The integration of DNS and Active Directory is essential because a client computer in a Windows Server 2003 network must be able to locate a domain controller so that users can log on to a domain or use the services that Active Directory provides. Clients locate domain controllers and services by using *A resource records* and *SRV records*. The A resource record contains the FQDN and IP address for the domain controller. The SRV record contains the FQDN of the domain controller and the name of the service that the domain controller provides.

What Are Active Directory Integrated Zones?

Active Directory Integrated Zones

- **Are primary and stub DNS zones that are stored as objects in the Active Directory database**
- **Can be stored in an application or a domain partition**
- **Offer the following benefits**
  - Multimaster replication
  - Secure dynamic updates
  - Standard zone transfers to other DNS servers

Introduction

One benefit of integrating DNS and Active Directory is the ability to integrate DNS zones into an Active Directory database. A zone is a portion of the domain namespace that has a logical grouping of resource records, which allows zone transfers of these records to operate as one unit.

Active Directory integrated zones

Microsoft DNS servers store information that is used to resolve host names to IP addresses and IP addresses to host names in a database file that has the extension .dns for each zone.

Active Directory integrated zones are primary and stub DNS zones that are stored as objects in the Active Directory database. You can store zone objects in an Active Directory application partition or in an Active Directory domain partition. If zone objects are stored in an Active Directory application partition, only domain controllers that subscribe to the application partition will participate in the replication of this partition. However, if zone objects are stored in an Active Directory domain partition, they are replicated to all domain controllers in the domain.

Benefits of Active Directory integrated zones

Active Directory integrated zones offer the following benefits.

- *Multimaster replication.* When you configure Active Directory integrated zones, dynamic updates to DNS are conducted based on a multimaster update model. In this model, any authoritative DNS server, such as a domain controller running a DNS server, is designated as a primary source for the zone. Because the master copy of the zone is maintained in the Active Directory database, which is fully replicated to all domain controllers, the zone can be updated by the DNS servers operating at any domain controller for the domain.

  In the multimaster update model of Active Directory, any of the primary servers for the directory integrated zone can process requests from DNS clients to update the zone, as long as a domain controller is available on the network.

- *Secure dynamic updates.* Because DNS zones are Active Directory objects in Active Directory integrated zones, you can set permissions on records within those zones to control which computers can update their records. This way, updates that use the dynamic update protocol can come from only authorized computers.

- *Standard zone transfers to other DNS servers.* Performs standard zone transfers to DNS servers that are not configured as domain controllers. It also performs standard zone transfers to DNS servers that are in other domains, which is the required method for replicating zones to DNS servers in other domains.

Note For more information about Active Directory integrated zones and DNS replication, see "What Are Active Directory Integrated Zones?" in Module 2 on the Appendices page on the Student Materials compact disc.

What Are SRV Resource Records?

- SRV resource records are DNS records that map a service to the computer that provides the service
- Format of SRV records

  Service.Protocol.Name Ttl Class SRV Priority Weight Port Target

- Example

  _ldap._tcp.contoso.msft 600 IN SRV 0 100 389 london.contoso.msft

Introduction

For Active Directory to function properly, client computers must be able to locate servers that provide specific services, such as authenticating logon requests and searching for information in Active Directory. Active Directory stores information about the location of the computers that provide these services in DNS records known as *SRV resource records*.

The purpose of SRV records

SRV resource records link a service to the DNS computer name of the computer that offers the service. For example, an SRV record can contain information to help clients locate a domain controller in a specific domain or forest.

When a domain controller starts, it registers SRV records and an A resource record, which contains its DNS computer name and its IP address. A DNS client computer later uses this combined information to locate the requested service on the appropriate domain controller.

Format of SRV records

All SRV records use a standard format, which consists of fields that contain the information that Active Directory uses to map a service to the computer that provides the service. SRV records use the following format:

Service.Protocol.Name Ttl Class SRV Priority Weight Port Target

The following table describes each field in an SRV record.

Field	Description
_Service	Specifies the name of the service, such as Lightweight Directory Access Protocol (LDAP) or Kerberos, provided by the server that registers this SRV record.
_Protocol	Specifies the transport protocol type, such as TCP or User Datagram Protocol (UDP).
Name	Specifies the domain name that the resource record references.
Ttl	Specifies the Time to Live (TTL) value in seconds, which is a standard field in DNS resource records that specifies the length of time that a record is considered valid.
Class	Specifies the standard DNS resource record class value, which is almost always "IN" for the Internet system. This is the only class that is supported by Windows Server 2003 DNS.
Priority	Specifies the priority of the server. Clients attempt to contact the host that has the lowest priority.
Weight	Denotes a load balancing mechanism that clients use when selecting a target host. When the priority field is the same for two or more records in the same domain, clients randomly choose SRV records that have higher weights.
Port	Specifies the port where the server is listening for this service.
Target	Specifies the FQDN, which is also called the full computer name, of the computer that provide the service.

Note For more information about priority and weight, including how to configure them, see "What Are SRV Resource Records?" in Module 2 on the Appendices page on the Student Materials compact disc.

Example

The following example shows an SRV record of a computer:

_ldap._tcp.contoso.msft 600 IN SRV 0 100 389 london.contoso.msft

The SRV record indicates that the computer has the following services or characteristics:

- Provides the LDAP service

- Provides the LDAP service by using the TCP transport protocol

- Registers the SRV record in the contoso.msft DNS domain

- Has a time to live (TTL) of 600 seconds or 10 minutes

- Has an FQDN of london.contoso.msft

SRV Records Registered by Domain Controllers

* Domain controllers running Windows Server 2003 register SRV records in the _msdcs subdomain in the following format:

  _Service._Protocol.DcType._**msdcs**.DnsDomainName

* Examples

  _**ldap._tcp**.DnsDomainName

  _**ldap._tcp**.SiteName._**sites.dc**

  _**msdcs**.DnsDomainName

  _**gc._tcp**.DnsForestName

  _**gc._tcp**.SiteName._**sites**.DnsForestName

  _**kerberos._tcp**.DnsDomainName

  _**kerberos._tcp**.SiteName

  _**sites**.DnsDomainName

Introduction

SRV resource records are registered by computers that provide an Active Directory service. In Windows Server 2003, domain controllers and global catalog servers register services with DNS.

How services are registered with DNS

When a domain controller starts, the Net Logon service running on the domain controller uses dynamic updates to register SRV resource records in the DNS database. These SRV resource records map the name of the service that the domain controller provides to the DNS computer name for that domain controller.

Services registered with DNS

To enable a computer to locate a domain controller, domain controllers running Windows Server 2003 register SRV resource records by using the following format:

_Service._Protocol.DcType._**msdcs**.DnsDomainName or DnsForestName

The _msdcs component denotes a subdomain in the DNS namespace that is specific to Microsoft, which allows computers to locate domain controllers that have functions in the domain or forest in Windows Server 2003.

The possible values for the DCType component, which is a prefix to the _msdcs subdomain, specify the following server roles types:

■ **dc** for a domain controller

■ **gc** for global catalog server

The presence of the _msdcs subdomain means that domain controllers running Windows Server 2003 also register the following SRV resource records:

_ldap._tcp.dc._msdcs.*DnsDomainName*

_ldap._tcp.*SiteName.***_sites.dc._msdcs.***DnsDomainName*

_ldap._tcp.gc._msdcs.*DnsForestName*

_ldap._tcp.*SiteName.***_sites.gc._msdcs.***DnsForestName*

_kerberos._tcp.dc._msdcs.*DnsDomainName*

_kerberos._tcp.*SiteName.***_sites.dc._msdcs.***DnsDomainName*

The following table lists some of the SRV resource records that are registered by domain controllers and defines the search criteria that each record supports.

SRV record	Enables a computer to find
_ldap._tcp.*DnsDomainName*	An LDAP server in the domain named by *DnsDomainName*. All domain controllers register this record.
_ldap._tcp.*SiteName.***_sites.dc._msdcs.***DnsDomainName*	A domain controller in the domain named by *DnsDomainName* and in the site named by *SiteName*. *SiteName* is the relative distinguished name of the site object that is stored in Active Directory. All domain controllers register this record.
_gc._tcp.*DnsForestName*	A global catalog server in the forest named by *DnsForestName*. *DnsForestName* is the domain name of the forest root domain. Only domain controllers that are configured as global catalog servers register this record.
_gc._tcp.*SiteName.***_sites.***DnsForestName*	A global catalog server in the forest named *DnsForestName* and in the site named by *SiteName*. Only domain controllers that are configured as global catalog servers register this record.
_kerberos._tcp.*DnsDomainName*	A Key Distribution Center (KDC) server for the domain named by *DnsDomainName*. All domain controllers running the Kerberos version 5 authentication protocol register this record.
_kerberos._tcp.*SiteName.***_sites.***DnsDomainName*	A KDC server for the domain named by *DnsDomainName* in the site named by *SiteName*. All domain controllers running the Kerberos version 5 protocol register this record.

How to Examine the Records Registered by a Domain Controller

Your instructor will demonstrate how to examine the records registered by a domain controller by using the DNS console or the NSLookup utility

Introduction

You can use either the DNS console or the Nslookup utility to view the SRV resource records that domain controllers register.

Procedure for viewing SRV records by using the DNS console

To view the SRV resource records that are registered by using the DNS console, perform the following steps:

1. Open DNS from the **Administrative Tools** menu.

2. Double-click *Server* (where *Server* is the name of your DNS server), double-click **Forward Lookup Zones**, and then double-click *domain* (where *domain* is the domain name).

3. Open the following folders in the *domain* folder to view the registered SRV resource records:

   • _msdcs.*DomainName*

   • _sites

   • _tcp

   • _udp

Procedure for viewing SRV records by using Nslookup

To view the list of SRV resource records that are registered by using the **Nslookup** command, perform the following steps:

1. Open a command prompt window, and run the Nslookup utility.

2. Type **ls –t SRV** *domain* (where *domain* is the domain name), and then press ENTER.

   The registered SRV resource records are listed. To save the results of this list to a file, type **ls –t SRV** *domain* > *filename* (where *filename* is any name you give to the file).

Note If you do not have a reverse lookup zone configured, Nslookup will report time-outs when you first run the utility. Reporting occurs because Nslookup generates a reverse lookup to determine the host name of the DNS server based on its IP address. The **ls –t** command performs a zone transfer. You must ensure that zone transfers are enabled before running the command.

Multimedia: How Client Computers Use DNS to Locate Domain Controllers and Services

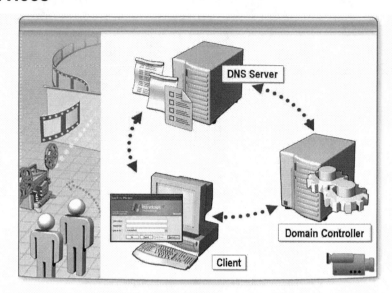

File location

To view the presentation, *How Client Computers Use DNS to Locate Domain Controllers and Services*, open the Web page on the Student Materials compact disc, click **Multimedia**, and then click the title of the presentation. Do not open this presentation unless the instructor tells you to.

Objectives

At the end of this presentation, you will be able to explain how client computers use DNS to locate domain controllers and services.

Process for using DNS to locate a domain controller

The following steps describe the process of how a client uses DNS to locate a domain controller:

1. A service on the client computer collects information about the client and the requested service.

2. The client service sends the collected information as a DNS query to a DNS server.

3. The DNS server returns a list of SRV records for domain controllers that provide the required service in the specified domain and site.

4. The client service reviews the SRV records and selects one according to the priority and weight that is assigned to the SRV record.

5. The client service sends a second DNS query that requests the IP address for the specific domain controller.

6. The DNS server returns the Host record for the domain controller, which contains the domain controller's IP address.

7. The client uses the IP address to contact the domain controller and initiate communication with the requested service.

   If the client cannot contact the domain controller, it selects another record from the returned SRV records to find an alternative domain controller.

8. The client service then caches the name of the domain controller and information about the services that it provides. Subsequent client requests use the cached information.

Note   For information about site coverage, see "How Client Computers Use DNS to Locate Domain Controllers and Services" in Module 2 on the Appendices page on the Student Materials compact disc.

Practice: Verifying SRV Records

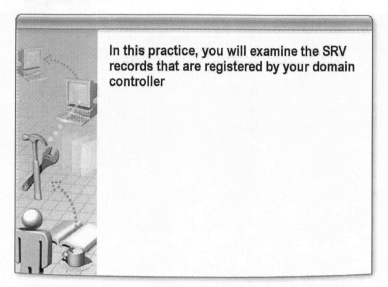

In this practice, you will examine the SRV records that are registered by your domain controller

Objectives

In this practice, you will examine the SRV records registered by your domain controller by using the DNS console.

Scenario

You have just created a child domain on your network. You want to verify that your domain controller has registered its SRV resource records with Active Directory.

Practice

▶ **View the SRV resource records registered by your domain controller**

1. Log on as **Corp*x*\Administrator** with a password of **P@ssw0rd**

2. Click **Don't display this page at logon**, and then close the **Manage Your Server** page.

3. Click **Start**, select **Administrative Tools**, and then click **Domain Controller Security Policy**.

4. In the console tree, expand **Local Policies**, and then click **User Rights Assignment**.

5. In the details pane, double-click **Allow log on locally**.

6. In the **Allow log on locally Properties** dialog box, click **Add User or Group**.

7. In the **Add User or Group** dialog box, type **Nwtraders*ComputerName*User** (where *CoumputerName* is the name of the computer you are working on), and then click **OK**.

8. In the **Allow log on locally Properties** dialog box, click **OK**.

9. Click **Start**, click **Run**, type **gpupdate** and then click **OK**.

10. Log off and then log on as **Nwtraders*ComputerName*User** with a password of **P@ssw0rd**

11. On the **Administrative Tools** menu, point to **DNS**, press and hold SHIFT, right-click, and then click **Run as**.

12. In the **Run As** dialog box, click **The following user**, type a user name of **Nwtraders\Administrator** and a password of **P@ssw0rd** and then click **OK**.

13. In the **Connect to DNS Server** dialog box, click **The following computer**, type **LONDON** and then click **OK**.

14. Expand London, expand **Forward Lookup Zones**, expand **nwtraders.msft**, and then open the following folders in the corp*x* folder to view the SRV resource records that are registered:

   - _msdcs
   - _sites
   - _tcp
   - _udp

15. Close the DNS console.

Lesson: Raising Forest and Domain Functional Levels

* What Is Forest and Domain Functionality?
* Requirements for Enabling New Windows Server 2003 Features
* How to Raise the Functional Level

Introduction

Forest and domain functionality determines what Active Directory features are enabled. This lesson introduces those features and explains how to raise the functionality of a forest and a domain.

Lesson objectives

After completing this lesson, you will be able to:

- Describe forest and domain functionality.
- Describe the requirements for raising the forest and domain functional levels.
- Raise the functional level of a forest and a domain.

What Is Forest and Domain Functionality?

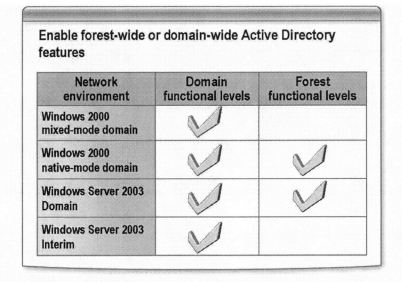

Network environment	Domain functional levels	Forest functional levels
Windows 2000 mixed-mode domain	✓	
Windows 2000 native-mode domain	✓	✓
Windows Server 2003 Domain	✓	✓
Windows Server 2003 Interim	✓	

Introduction

In Windows Server 2003, forest and domain functionality provides a way to enable forest-wide or domain-wide Active Directory features in your network environment. Different levels of forest functionality and domain functionality are available, depending on your environment.

What is domain functionality?

Domain functionality enables features that will affect the entire domain and that domain only. Four domain functional levels are available:

- *Windows 2000 mixed.* This is the default functional level. You can raise the domain functional level to either Windows 2000 native or Windows Server 2003. Mixed-mode domains can contain Windows NT 4.0 backup domain controllers but they cannot use universal security groups, group nesting, or security identifier (SID) history capabilities.

- *Windows 2000 native.* You can use this functional level if the domain contains only Windows 2000 and Windows Server 2003 domain controllers. Although domain controllers running Windows 2000 Server are not aware of domain functionality, Active Directory features, such as universal security groups, group nesting, and security identifier (SID) history capabilities, are available.

- *Windows 2003 Server.* This is the highest functional level for a domain. You can use it only if all of the domain controllers in the domain are running Windows Server 2003. All Active Directory features for the domain are available for use.

- *Windows 2003 interim.* This functional level is a special functional level that supports Windows NT 4.0 and the Windows 2003 Server domain controllers.

What is forest functionality?

Forest functionality enables features across all the domains within your forest. Two forest functional levels are available: Windows 2000 and Windows Server 2003. By default, forests operate at the Windows 2000 functional level. You can raise the forest functional level to Windows Server 2003, which enables features that are not available at the Windows 2000 functional level, including:

- Forest trusts
- Improved replication

Note For a complete list of the features that are enabled for each domain and forest functional level, see "Domain and forest functionality" in online Help and Support.

Important You cannot lower the functional level of the domain or forest after it has been raised.

Requirements for Enabling New Windows Server 2003 Features

Requirement	Domain	Forest
Domain controllers must run:	Windows Server 2003	Windows Server 2003
Domain functional level must be:	Raised to Windows Server 2003	Able to be raised to Windows Server 2003
Administrator:	Domain administrator to raise domain functional level	Enterprise administrator to raise forest functional level

Introduction

In addition to the basic Active Directory features on individual domain controllers, new forest-wide and domain-wide Active Directory features are available when certain conditions are met.

Requirements for enabling new domain-wide features

To enable the new domain-wide features, all domain controllers in the domain must be running Windows Server 2003, and the domain functional level must be raised to Windows Server 2003. You must be a domain administrator to raise the domain functional level.

Requirements for enabling new forest-wide features

To enable new forest-wide features, all domain controllers in the forest must be running Windows Server 2003, and the forest functional level must be raised to Windows Server 2003. You must be an enterprise administrator to raise the forest functional level.

How to Raise the Functional Level

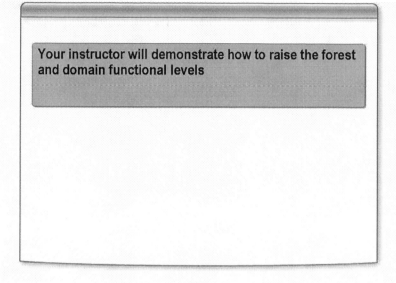

Your instructor will demonstrate how to raise the forest and domain functional levels

Introduction

Raising the forest and domain functionality to Windows Server 2003 enables certain features, such as forest trusts, that are not available at other functional levels. You can raise forest and domain functionality by using Active Directory Domains and Trusts. *ot Users + Computers*

Procedure for raising the domain functional level

To raise the domain functional level, perform the following steps:

1. Open Active Directory Domains and Trusts.

2. In the console tree, right-click the node for the domain whose functional level you want to raise, and then click **Raise Domain Functional Level**.

3. In **Select an available domain functional level** dialog box, select the functional level, and then click **Raise**.

Procedure for raising the forest functional level

To raise the forest functional level, perform the following steps:

1. In Active Directory Domains and Trusts, in the console tree, right-click **Active Directory Domains and Trusts**, and then click **Raise Forest Functional Level**.

2. In **Select an available forest functional level** dialog box, select **Windows Server 2003**, and then click **Raise**.

Note   You must raise the functional level of all domains in a forest to Windows 2000 native or higher before you can raise the forest functional level.

Practice: Raising the Domain Functional Level

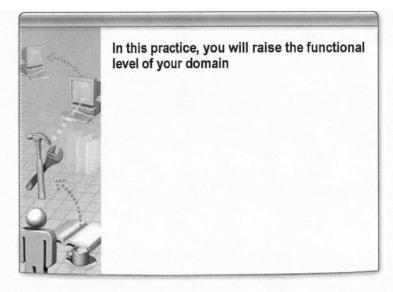

In this practice, you will raise the functional level of your domain

Objectives

In this practice, you will raise the domain functional level from Windows 2000 mixed to Windows Server 2003.

Scenario

You have just created a child domain by installing Active Directory on your Windows Server 2003 computer. You will prepare for cross-forest trusts by raising the functional level of your domain.

Practice

▶ **Raise the functional level of your domain controller from Windows 2000 mixed to Windows Server 2003**

1. Log on as **Nwtraders***ComputerName***User** with a password of **P@ssw0rd**

2. Open Active Directory Domains and Trusts as Nwtraders\Administrator by using **Run as**.

3. Examine the functional level of your domain, and then raise it to Windows Server 2003.

4. Close Active Directory Domains and Trusts.

Lesson: Creating Trust Relationships

- Types of Trusts
- What Are Trusted Domain Objects?
- How Trusts Work in a Forest
- How Trusts Work Across Forests
- How to Create Trusts
- How to Verify and Revoke a Trust

Introduction

Active Directory provides security across multiple domains and forests by using domain and forest trusts. This lesson explains the types of trusts; how trusts work; and how to create, verify, and revoke trust relationships.

Lesson objectives

After completing this lesson, you will be able to:

- Describe the types of trusts that you can establish between domains.
- Explain the purpose of trusted domain objects.
- Describe how trusts work within a forest.
- Describe how trusts work across forests.
- Create a trust.
- Verify and revoke a trust.

Types of Trusts

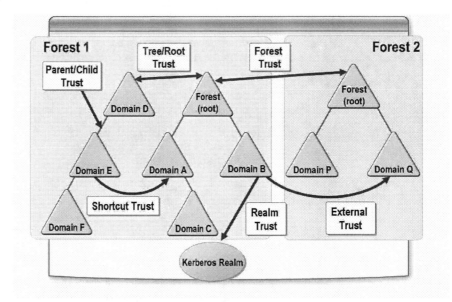

Introduction

Trusts are the mechanism that ensures that a user who is authenticated in his own domain can access resources in any trusted domain. In Windows Server 2003, there are two types of trusts—transitive trusts and nontransitive trusts.

Transitive vs. nontransitive trusts

A transitive trust is one in which the trust relationship that is extended to one domain is automatically extended to all other domains that trust that domain. For example, domain D directly trusts domain E, which directly trusts domain F. Because both trusts are transitive, domain D indirectly trusts domain F and vice versa. Transitive trusts are automatic. An example of transitive trust is a parent/child trust. Nontransitive trusts are not automatic and must be set up. An example of a nontransitive trust is an external trust, such as the trust between a domain in one forest and a domain in another forest.

Trust direction

In Windows Server 2003, there are three trust directions: one-way incoming, one-way outgoing, and two-way. If in domain B, you set up a one-way incoming trust between domain B and domain Q, users in domain B can be authenticated in domain Q. If you set up a one-way outgoing trust between domain B and domain Q, users in domain Q can be authenticated in domain B. A two-way trust means that both domains can authenticate users from the other domain.

Types of Trusts

Windows Server 2003 supports the following types of trusts, in the transitive and nontransitive categories.

Type	Transitivity	Use when you want to
Shortcut	Partially transitive	Reduce Kerberos authentication hops.
Forest	Partially transitive	Enable authentication between forests.
External	Nontransitive	Set up a trust relationship between a domain in one forest with a domain in another forest.
Realm	Transitive or nontransitive user choice	Trust an external Kerberos realm.

A *realm* is a set of security principles in a non-Windows environment that are subject to Kerberos authentication.

Note   For more information about Kerberos realms, see "Interoperability with RFC-1510 Kerberos implementations" in online Help and Support.

Shortcut trusts are only partially transitive because trust transitivity is extended only down the hierarchy from the trusted domain—not up the hierarchy. For example, because a shortcut trust exists between domain E and domain A, Active Directory extends the trust to the child domain, domain C, but not up the hierarchy to the forest root domain. Users in domain E can access only resources in the forest root domain through the parent/child trust with domain D and through the tree/root trust that domain D has with the forest root domain.

Forest trusts are also only partially transitive because forest trusts can only be created between two forests and they cannot be implicitly extended to a third forest. For example, if forest 1 trusts forest 2, and forest 2 trusts forest 3, domains in forest 1 transitively trust domains in forest 2, and domains in forest 2 transitively trust domains in forest 3. However, forest 1 does not transitively trust forest 3.

What Are Trusted Domain Objects?

> **Trusted domain objects**
>
> - Represent each trust relationship in a particular domain
> - Store information such as transitivity and trust type

Introduction

When you set up trusts between domains within the same forest, across forests, or with an external realm, information about these trusts is stored in Active Directory so that the information can be retrieved when required.

Trusted domain objects

Each trust relationship in a domain is represented by an object known as the trusted domain object (TDO). The TDO stores information about the trust, such as the trust transitivity and trust type. Whenever you create a trust, a new TDO is created and stored in the System container in the trust's domain.

Forest trust TDOs store additional information to identify all of the trusted namespaces from its partner forest. When you establish a forest trust, each forest collects all of the trusted namespaces in its partner forest and stores the information in a TDO. This information includes:

- the domain tree names

- service principal name (SPN) suffixes

- security ID (SID) namespaces

SPNs are structures that help identify the computer that a service is running on.

When a workstation requests a service and the service cannot be located in the domain or the forest in which the workstation is a member, TDOs locate the service in all trusted forests.

How Trusts Work in a Forest

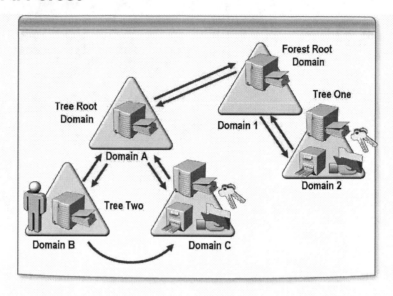

Introduction

Trusts enable users from one domain access to resources in another domain. Trust relationships can be transitive or non-transitive.

How trusts enable users to access resources in a forest

When a user attempts to access a resource in another domain, the Kerberos version 5 authentication protocol must determine whether the *trusting* domain—that is, the domain that contains the resource that the user is trying to access—has a trust relationship with the *trusted* domain—that is, the domain that the user is logging on to.

To determine this relationship, the Kerberos version 5 protocol travels the trust path utilizing the Trusted Domain Object (TDO) to obtain a referral to the target domain's domain controller. The target domain controller issues a service ticket for the requested service. The *trust path* is the shortest path in the trust hierarchy.

When the user in the trusted domain attempts to access the resource in the other domain, the user's computer first contacts the domain controller in its domain to get authentication to the resource. If the resource is not in the user's domain, the domain controller uses the trust relationship with its parent and refers the user's computer to a domain controller in its parent domain.

This attempt to locate a resource continues up the trust hierarchy, possibly to the forest root domain, and down the trust hierarchy until contact occurs with a domain controller in the domain where the resource is located.

How Trusts Work Across Forests

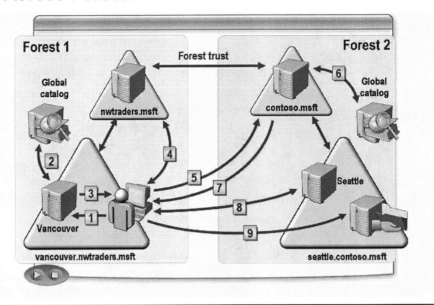

Introduction

Windows Server 2003 supports cross-forest trusts, which allow users in one forest to access resources in another forest. When a user attempts to access a resource in a trusted forest, Active Directory must first locate the resource. After the resource is located, the user can be authenticated and allowed to access the resource. Understanding how this process works will help you troubleshoot problems that may arise with cross-forest trusts.

How a resource is accessed

The following is a description of how a Windows 2000 Professional or Windows XP Professional client computer locates and accesses a resource in another forest that has Windows 2000 Server, or Windows Server 2003 servers.

1. A user who is logged on to the domain vancouver.nwtraders.msft attempts to access a shared folder in the contoso.msft forest. The user's computer contacts the KDC on a domain controller in vancouver.nwtraders.msft and requests a service ticket by using the SPN of the computer on which the resource resides. An SPN can be the DNS name of a host or domain, or it can be the distinguished name of a service connection point object.

2. The resource is not located in vancouver.nwtraders.msft, so the domain controller for vancouver.nwtraders.msft queries the global catalog to see if the resource is located in another domain in the forest.

   Because a global catalog only contains information about its own forest, it does not find the SPN. The global catalog then checks its database for information about any forest trusts that are established with its forest. If the global catalog finds one, it compares the name suffixes that are listed in the forest trust TDO to the suffix of the target SPN. After it finds a match, the global catalog provides routing information about how to locate the resource to the domain controller in vancouver.nwtraders.msft.

3. The domain controller in vancouver.nwtraders.msft sends a referral for its parent domain, nwtraders.msft, to the user's computer.

4. The user's computer contacts a domain controller in nwtraders.msft for a referral to a domain controller in the forest root domain of the contoso.msft forest.

5. Using the referral that the domain controller in the nwtraders.msft domain returns, the user's computer contacts a domain controller in the contoso.msft forest for a service ticket to the requested service.

6. The resource is not located in the forest root domain of the contoso.msft forest, so the domain controller contacts its global catalog to find the SPN. The global catalog finds a match for the SPN and sends it to the domain controller.

7. The domain controller sends the user's computer a referral to seattle.contoso.msft.

8. The user's computer contacts the KDC on the domain controller in seattle.contoso.msft and negotiates a ticket for the user to gain access to the resource in the domain seattle.contoso.msft.

9. The user's computer sends the server service ticket to the computer on which the shared resource is located, which reads the user's security credentials and constructs an access token, which gives the user access to the resource.

Note Cross-forest trusts allow users in one forest to gain access to resources in another forest. Active Directory secures cross-forest trusts by using SID filtering. For information about SID filtering, see "How Trusts Work Across Forests" in Module 2 on the Appendices page on the Student Materials compact disc.

How to Create Trusts

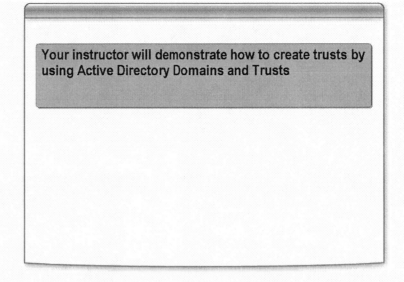

Your instructor will demonstrate how to create trusts by using Active Directory Domains and Trusts

Introduction

You can use Active Directory Domains and Trusts to create trust relationships between forests or between domains in the same forest. You can also use it to create shortcut trusts.

Before you create a forest trust, you must create a secondary lookup zone on the DNS server in each forest that points to the DNS server in the other forest. Creating a secondary lookup zone ensures that the domain controller in the forest where you create the forest trust can locate a domain controller in the other forest and set up the trust relationship.

Procedure

To create a trust, perform the following steps:

1. Open Active Directory Domains and Trusts.

2. In the console tree, perform one of the following steps:

   - To create a forest trust, right-click the domain node for the forest root domain, and then click **Properties**.

   - To create a shortcut trust, right-click the domain node for the domain that you want to establish a shortcut trust with, and then click **Properties**.

   - To create an external trust, right-click the domain node for the domain that you want to establish a trust with, and then click **Properties**.

   - To create a realm trust, right-click the domain node for the domain you want to administer, and then click **Properties**.

3. On the **Trust** tab, click **New Trust**, and then click **Next**.

4. On the **Welcome** page of the New Trust Wizard, click **Next**.

5. On the **Trust Name** page, perform one of the following steps:

   - If you are creating a forest trust, type the DNS name of the second forest, and then click **Next**.

   - If you are creating a shortcut trust, type the DNS name of the domain, type and confirm the trust password, and then click **Next**.

   - If you are creating an external trust, type the DNS name of the domain, and then click **Next**.

   - If you are creating a realm trust, type the realm name for the target realm, and then click **Next**.

6. On the **Trust Type** page, perform one of the following steps:

   - If you are creating a forest trust, click **Forest trust**, and then click **Next**.

   - If you are creating a shortcut trust, skip to step 7.

   - If you are creating an external trust, click **External trust**, and then click **Next**.

   - If you are creating a realm trust, click **Realm trust**, and then click **Next**. On the **Transitivity of Trust** page, do one of the following:

     - To form a trust relationship with the domain and the specified realm, click **Nontransitive**, and then click **Next**.

     - To form a trust relationship with the domain and the specified realm and all trusted realms, click **Transitive**, and then click **Next**.

7. On the **Direction of Trust** page, perform one of the following steps:

   - To create a two-way trust, click **Two-way**, and then follow the wizard instructions.

   - To create a one-way incoming trust, click **One-way: incoming**, and then follow the wizard instructions.

   - To create a one-way outgoing trust, click **One-way: outgoing**, and then follow the wizard instructions.

How to Verify and Revoke a Trust

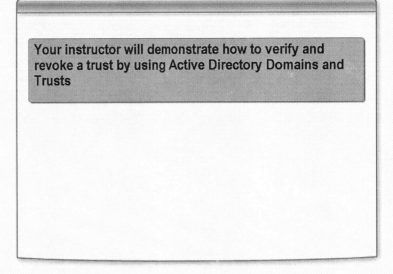

Your instructor will demonstrate how to verify and revoke a trust by using Active Directory Domains and Trusts

Introduction

When you create nontransitive trusts, you sometimes need to verify and revoke the trust paths that you created. You verify a trust to make sure it can validate authentication requests from other domains. You revoke a trust to prevent that authentication path from being used during authentication. You can use Active Directory Domains and Trusts or the **netdom** command to verify and revoke trust paths.

Procedure for verifying Trusts

To verify a trust by using Active Directory Domains and Trusts, perform the following steps:

1. In Active Directory Domains and Trusts, in the console tree, right-click one of the domains in the trust that you want to verify, and then click **Properties**.

2. On the **Trusts** tab, under **Domains trusted by this domain (outgoing trusts)** or **Domains that trust this domain (incoming trusts)**, click the trust that you want to verify, and then click **Properties**.

3. Click **Validate**, click **No, do not validate the incoming trust**.

4. Repeat steps 1 through 3 to verify the trust for the other domain in the relationship.

To verify a trust by using **netdom**, perform the following step:

■   At the command prompt, type the following command, and then press ENTER.

```
NETDOM TRUST trusting_domain_name
/Domain:trusted_domain_name /Verify
```

Procedure for revoking trusts

To revoke a trust by using Active Directory Domains and Trusts, perform the following steps:

1. In Active Directory Domains and Trusts, in the console tree, right-click one of the domains in the trust that you want to revoke, and then click **Properties**.

2. On the **Trusts** tab, under **Domains trusted by this domain (outgoing trusts)** or **Domains that trust this domain (incoming trusts)**, click the trust that you want to remove, and then click **Remove**.

3. Repeat steps 1 and 2 to revoke the trust for the other domain in the trust relationship.

To revoke a trust by using **netdom**, perform the following step:

- At the command prompt, type the following command, and then press ENTER.

```
NETDOM TRUST trusting_domain_name
/Domain:trusted_domain_name /Remove
```

Practice: Creating a Shortcut Trust

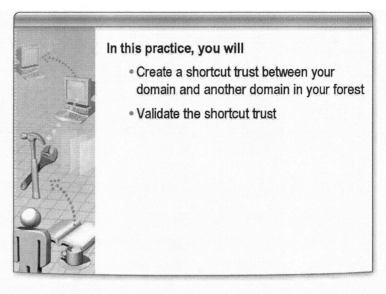

In this practice, you will

- Create a shortcut trust between your domain and another domain in your forest
- Validate the shortcut trust

Objectives

In this practice, you will create a shortcut trust between your domain and another domain in your forest, and then validate the trust.

Scenario

You have created a child domain in the nwtraders.msft forest. Sales managers in another domain need access to sales resources in your domain and vice versa. You need to set up a two-way shortcut trust between the two domains.

Instructions

You will work with a partner, whom your instructor will assign to you. You will create the shortcut trust between your domain and your partner's domain.

Practice: Creating the shortcut trust

▶ **Create the shortcut trust**

1. Log on as **Nwtraders***ComputerName***User** with a password of **P@ssw0rd**

2. Open Active Directory Domains and Trusts as **Nwtraders\Administrator** by using **Run As**.

3. Create a two-way trust to your partner's domain. Use a password of **P@ssw0rd** for the trust, and accept the default selections.

Practice: Validating the shortcut trust

▶ **Validate the shortcut trust**

1. On the **Trust** tab of the **Properties** page, click the trust that you created with your partner's domain, and then click **Properties**.

2. On the **Properties** page, click **Validate**.

3. Click **No, do not validate the incoming trust**, and then click **OK**.

   If the trust is valid, a validation message appears. If you perform the validation test before your partner sets up a two-way shortcut trust with your domain, you will receive a message.

4. Close all dialog boxes and then close Active Directory Domain and Trusts.

Lab A: Implementing Active Directory

- Removing a Child Domain from Active Directory
- Creating an Active Directory Forest Root Domain
- Creating an Active Directory Child Domain
- Raising Domain and Forest Functional Level
- Creating a Forest Trust

Objectives

After completing this lab, you will be able to:

- Remove a child domain from Active Directory.
- Create a forest root domain.
- Verify the forest and domain functional levels.
- Raise the functional level of a domain and a forest.
- Create a child domain in an existing forest.
- Create and verify forest trusts.

Prerequisites

Before working on this lab, you must have:

- Knowledge about the components that make up the logical and physical structure of Active Directory.
- Knowledge about how Active Directory integrated zones and DNS work.
- The knowledge about forest functional levels.
- The knowledge about forest trusts.

Scenario

You are a systems engineer for Northwind Traders. In response to a series of mergers with several smaller companies, Northwind Traders has decided to consolidate its Active Directory infrastructure. The individual organizations must maintain their Active Directory structure, yet they must also be able to communicate among all of the subsidiaries. You will provide the infrastructure necessary to support this goal by using multiple forests and trusts, as appropriate, between them.

Estimated time to complete this lab: 60 minutes

Exercise 1
Removing a Child Domain from Active Directory

In this exercise, you will remove Active Directory from your domain controller to prepare for the creation of an Active Directory forest and domain structure.

Scenario

Northwind Traders must implement Active Directory in several locations. The IT management team has asked the engineering group to implement Active Directory by using separate forests. You will work independently as the local administrator of the office that you have been assigned to. You will use the servers at your site to create a Active Directory forest root domain and a child domain. But first, you must demote your domain controller.

Tasks	Specific instructions
1. Remove Active Directory from your domain controller.	a. Log on as **Nwtraders**_ComputerName_**User**. b. Use **Run as** to start a command prompt and run **dcpromo** as Nwtraders\\Administrator.
2. Verify that Active Directory has been removed from your server.	a. Log on as **Administrator** with a password of **P@ssw0rd** b. Verify that the NETLOGON and SYSVOL shares no longer exist.

Exercise 2
Creating an Active Directory Forest Root Domain

In this exercise, you will work with a partner to create your own Active Directory forest. One of you will create the forest root domain and the other will create a child domain.

Scenario

You are creating a new Active Directory forest that will eventually be merged into a comprehensive administrative environment. As one of the regional locations for Northwind Traders, you must coordinate your efforts with a sister location in your country. One of the locations will establish the forest root domain and the other will create a child domain in the newly created forest. The forest root domain must be created before the child domain can join the forest. You must coordinate your effort with your sister location to ensure that the appropriate steps are taken at the correct time.

Your instructor will assign you one of the domain names from the following list.

Computer name	Forest root domain	Child domain
Vancouver	Nwtraders1.msft	
Denver		Corp1.Nwtraders1.msft
Perth	Nwtraders2.msft	
Brisbane		Corp2.Nwtraders2.msft
Lisbon	Nwtraders3.msft	
Bonn		Corp3.Nwtraders3.msft
Lima	Nwtraders4.msft	
Santiago		Corp4.Nwtraders4.msft
Bangalore	Nwtraders5.msft	
Singapore		Corp5.Nwtraders5.msft
Casablanca	Nwtraders6.msft	
Tunis		Corp6.Nwtraders6.msft
Acapulco	Nwtraders7.msft	
Miami		Corp7.Nwtraders7.msft
Auckland	Nwtraders8.msft	
Suva		Corp8.Nwtraders8.msft
Stockholm	Nwtraders9.msft	
Moscow		Corp9.Nwtraders9.msft
Caracas	Nwtraders10.msft	
Montevideo		Corp10.Ntraders10.msft.
Manila	Nwtraders11.msft	
Tokyo		Corp11. Nwtraders11.msft
Khartoum	Nwtraders12.msft	
Nairobi		Corp12. Nwtraders12.msft

Tasks	Specific instructions
1. Create a new forest root domain.	a. Refer to the table for your domain assignments. b. Log on to your server as **Administrator** with a password of **P@ssw0rd** if you are not already logged on. *You must install DNS by using the Active Directory Installation Wizard. The root domain controller's DNS resolver must be pointed to London.*
2. Create two user accounts for logon purposes.	▪ Create *ComputerName***User** for each computer in the forest.
3. Verify the creation of the new forest.	

Exercise 3
Creating an Active Directory Child Domain

In this exercise, you will finish creating the Active Directory forest by creating a child domain within the forest root.

Scenario

As the sister location to the newly created forest root, you will complete the forest by creating the first child domain. Do not complete this step until you have verified with your partner that the forest root domain has been configured and is running.

Tasks	Specific instructions
1. Create a new child domain.	▪ Log on to your local computer as **Administrator** with a password of **P@ssw0rd** *The child domain controller must have its DNS resolver pointed to the partner's forest root domain controller.*
2. Verify the installation of the new child domain.	

Exercise 4
Raising Domain and Forest Functional Level

In this exercise, you will raise the domain and forest functional levels to Windows Server 2003.

Scenario

Northwind Traders is preparing its environment for cross-forest trusts, which the IT team will implement at a later stage. Before implementing cross-forest trusts, domains and forests must have their functional level raised to support the forest trust feature.

Tasks	Specific instructions
1. Raise the domain functional level.	▪ Log on as **Nwtraders***x**ComputerName***User** (where *x* is the number for your domain assigned by your instructor) with a password of **P@ssw0rd**
2. Raise the forest functional level.	▪ You must raise the level by using only one member of the forest.

Exercise 5
Creating a Forest Trust

In this exercise, you will create a two-way forest trust with the nwtraders.msft forests.

Scenario

The Northwind Traders conglomerate is growing quickly. You must support the increase in connectivity requirements between the various organizations. To help meet these requirements, you will create the required trust to enable communications with and resource access between your forest and the corporate forest.

Tasks	Specific instructions
1. Configure DNS forwarding.	▪ Perform this task on the forest root domain controller.
2. Create a trust between the classroom forest and your forest, and then verify that the trust has been created.	▪ Perform this task on the child domain controller.

Microsoft®
Training &
Certification

Module 3: Implementing an Organizational Unit Structure

Contents

Overview

- Creating and Managing Organizational Units
- Delegating Administrative Control for Organizational Units
- Planning an Organizational Unit Strategy

Introduction

This module discusses how to create and manage organizational units, delegate common administrative tasks, and plan the implementation of an organizational unit structure.

Objectives

After completing this module, you will be able to:

- Create and manage organizational units.
- Delegate control of an organizational unit.
- Plan an organizational unit strategy.

Lesson: Creating and Managing Organizational Units

- Introduction to Managing Organizational Units
- Methods for Creating and Managing Organizational Units
- How to Create and Manage Organizational Units Using Directory Service Tools
- How to Create and Manage Organizational Units Using the Ldifde Tool
- How to Create Organizational Units Using Windows Script Host

Introduction

This lesson introduces the Microsoft Management Console (MMC) snap-ins and command-line tools for creating and managing organizational units, and provides the skills for creating, modifying, and deleting organizational units.

Lesson objectives

After completing this lesson, you will be able to:

- Describe the life cycle of organizational units.
- Describe the methods for creating organizational units.
- Manage organizational units by using directory services command-line tools.
- Manage organizational units by using the Ldifde command-line tool.
- Create organizational units by using Windows Script Host.

Introduction to Managing Organizational Units

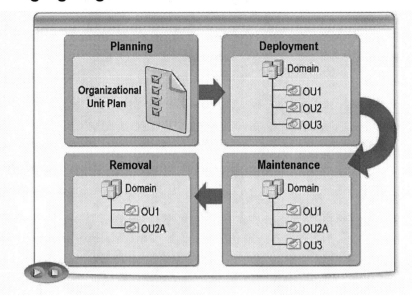

Introduction

Organizational units are the Active Directory® directory service containers that you use to place users, groups, computers, and other organizational units. By using organizational units, you can create containers in a domain that represents the hierarchical and logical structures in your organization. You can then manage the configuration and the use of accounts and resources based on your organizational model. For example, you can use the organizational units to automatically apply group policies that define default settings for user and computer accounts in Active Directory.

Life cycle of organizational units

The life cycle of organizational units includes four phases:

- *Planning*. In this phase, you plan the organizational unit structure. You determine which organizational units you will create, and how you will delegate administrative control of these organizational units.

- *Deployment*. In this phase, you create the organizational unit structure based on the organizational unit plan.

- *Maintenance*. After the organizational unit structure is created in Active Directory, you can rename, move, or modify organizational units as required to meet the ongoing requirements of the organization.

- *Removal*. All objects in Active Directory, including organizational units, occupy space on the domain controller that hosts Active Directory. When organizational units are no longer required, you must delete them.

Note For more information about organizational units, see Module 7, "Managing Access to Objects in Organizational Units," in Course 2274, *Managing a Microsoft Windows Server 2003 Environment*.

Methods for Creating and Managing Organizational Units

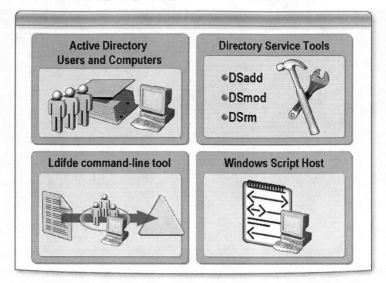

Active Directory Users and Computers	**Directory Service Tools** • DSadd • DSmod • DSrm
Ldifde command-line tool	**Windows Script Host**

Introduction

Microsoft® Windows® Server 2003 provides a number of snap-ins and command-line tools that you can use to create organizational units and manage the configuration and the use of accounts and resources in your organizational model. You can also use Windows Script Host, a scripting host for Microsoft Windows platforms, to manage organizational units.

Methods for creating and managing organizational units

The following list describes some of the snap-ins and command-line tools that you can use to create and manage organizational units:

- *Active Directory Users and Computers.* An MMC snap-in for creating, modifying, and deleting organizational units. Use this snap-in when you have only a few organizational units to manage, or when you want to manage organizational units interactively.

- *Directory service tools.* A suite of command-line tools that you can use to manage objects and perform queries for information in Active Directory. The command-line tools include Dsadd, Dsmod, and Dsrm. By using these tools with the ou parameter, you can add, modify, and delete organizational units from Active Directory. You can also use scripts and batch files with these tools to manage directory services.

- *Lightweight Directory Access Protocol Data Interchange Format Directory Exchange (Ldifde).* A command-line tool to create organizational units and other Active Directory objects in a batch operation. Ldifde uses an input file that contains information about the objects to add, modify, or delete. The information is stored as a series of records that are separated by a blank line in an input file.

- *Windows Script Host.* You can create organizational units by using Windows applications, or by using Windows scripts with the components that Active Directory Service Interfaces (ADSI) provides. By using scripts, you can create organizational units as part of application setup, if required.

How to Create and Manage Organizational Units Using Directory Service Tools

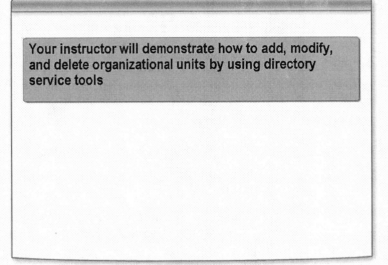

Your instructor will demonstrate how to add, modify, and delete organizational units by using directory service tools

Introduction

You can use directory service command-line tools Dsadd, Dsmod, and Dsrm to create and manage organizational units from the command prompt. You can also use these commands in scripts and batch files.

Procedure for creating an organizational unit

To create an organizational unit, run the following **Dsadd** command from the command prompt:

```
dsadd ou OrganizationalUnitDN -desc Description -d Domain -u
UserName -p Password
```

Where:

- *OrganizationalUnitDN* specifies the distinguished name of the organizational unit that you want to add. For example, to add an organizational unit named helpdesk to the nwtraders.msft domain, the distinguished name would be *ou=helpdesk,dc=nwtraders,dc=msft*.

- *Description* specifies the description of the organizational unit that you want to add.

- *Domain* specifies the domain to connect to. By default, the computer is connected to the domain controller in the logon domain.

- *UserName* specifies the user name to use to log on to a remote server. By default, the logged-on user name is used. You can specify a user name by using one of the following formats:

  - user name (for example, Linda)

  - domain\user name (for example, widgets\Linda)

  - user principal name (UPN) (for example, Linda@widgets.microsoft.com)

- *Password* is the password to use to log on to a remote server. If you type *, you are prompted for a password.

Procedure for modifying an organizational unit

To modify the description of an organizational unit, run the following command:

```
dsmod ou OrganizationalUnitDN -desc Description -d Domain -u
UserName -p Password
```

The parameters that are passed to the **dsmod** command are the same as those of the **dsadd** command. The new description must be passed as the *desc* parameter.

Procedure for removing an organizational unit

You must remove organizational units from Active Directory that are no longer in use. To remove an organizational unit, run the following command:

```
dsrm OrganizationalUnitDN -d Domain -u UserName -p Password
```

The parameters that are passed to the **dsrm** command are the same as those of the **dsadd** command. You can use the following additional parameters with **dsrm**:

- *subtree*. Specifies to delete the object and all objects that are contained in the subtree under that object.

- *Exclude*. Specifies not to delete the base object provided by *OrganizationalUnitDN* when you delete the subtree under it. By default, only the base object specified is deleted. The Exclude parameter can only be specified with the subtree parameter.

Note   For more information about using Dsadd, Dsmod, and Dsrm command-line tools, see Windows Server 2003 Help and Support Center. For additional examples of using these directory service command-line tools, see "How to Manage Organizational Units Using Directory Service Command-line Tools" in Module 3 on the Appendices page on the Student Materials compact disc.

How to Create and Manage Organizational Units Using the Ldifde Tool

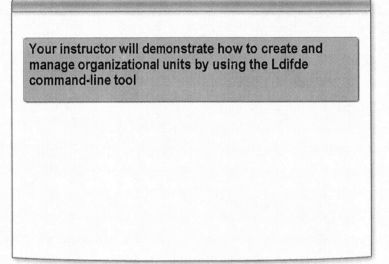

Your instructor will demonstrate how to create and manage organizational units by using the Ldifde command-line tool

Introduction

You can use the Ldifde command-line tool to create organizational units in a batch operation and to set up organizational unit hierarchies. You can also use Ldifde to modify and delete organizational units.

Procedure

The first step in using this tool is to create the input file to use with Ldifde. After creating this file, you will run the **Ldifde** command.

To create organizational units by using the Ldifde command-line tool, perform the following steps:

1. Create an input file. The following example shows the format of the file:

```
dn: OU=SampleOU,DC=nwtraders,DC=msft
changetype: add
objectClass: organizationalUnit
```

Changetype determines the type of operation that is performed on the Active Directory object. **ObjectClass** specifies the class of the Active Directory object. In the previous example, Ldifde adds an organizational unit object named *SampleOU* to the nwtraders.msft domain. You can add multiple organizational units by adding more entries like the one above. There must be a blank line before each dn entry, except for the first one.

2. Run Ldifde to create, modify, or delete organizational units by entering the
   following command:

```
C:\>ldifde -i -k -f OUList.ldf -b UserName Domain Password
```

Where:

- *-i* specifies the import mode. If not specified the default mode is export.

- *-k* ignores errors during an import operation and continues processing.

- *-f* specifies the import or export filename.

- OUList.ldf is the input file.

- *-b* specifies the username, domain name and password for the user
  account that will be used to perform the import or export operation.

Note   For more information about Ldifde, see Windows Server 2003 Help and
Support.

How to Create Organizational Units Using Windows Script Host

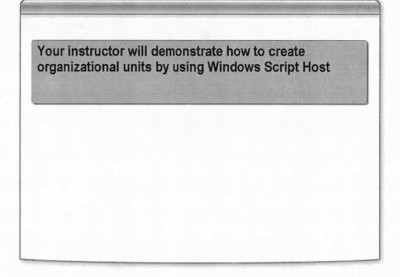

Introduction

ADSI is an application programming interface (API) that you can use from a Windows Script Host script to automate Active Directory administration. ADSI uses the Lightweight Directory Access Protocol (LDAP) to communicate with Active Directory. All ADSI operations that you perform on Active Directory follow the same procedure. First, you must connect to Active Directory. Then you can perform tasks, such as retrieving information about objects and adding, modifying, or deleting objects. If you make changes to Active Directory, you must save the changes to the Active Directory database to make them permanent.

Procedure

To create an organizational unit by using Windows Script Host, perform the following steps:

1. Use Notepad to create a text file with a .vbs extension. Place the following commands listed under steps a, b, and c in the file, and then save the file.

   a. First, connect to the domain in which you want to create the organizational unit, as shown in the following example:

   ```
   Set objDom = GetObject("LDAP://dc=nwtraders,dc=msft")
   ```

   Important   In the above example, LDAP must be in all uppercase letters, or the command will fail.

   In this example, nwtraders.msft is the domain in which you create the organizational unit.

b. Then, create the organizational unit by specifying OrganizationalUnit as the type of Active Directory object to create and the name of the organizational unit, as shown in the following example:

```
Set objOU = objDom.Create("OrganizationalUnit",
"ou=NewOU")
```

In this example, NewOU is the name of the organizational unit that you are creating.

c. Finally, save the information to the Active Directory database, as shown in the following example:

```
objOU.SetInfo
```

2. To run the commands in the .vbs file, at the command prompt, type the following:

```
wscript script_file_name.vbs
```

Note For more information about creating administrative scripts by using Windows Script Host, see the Microsoft Technet Script Center at: http://www.microsoft.com/technet/treeview/default.asp?url=/technet/ scriptcenter/default.asp
Also see Course 2433, *Microsoft Visual Basic Scripting Edition and Microsoft Windows Script Host Essentials*.

Practice: Creating Organizational Units

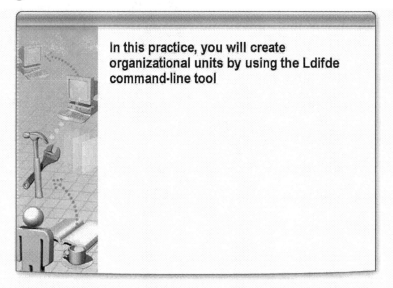

Objective

In this practice, you will create organizational units in the domain hosted by your student computer, by using the Ldifde command-line tool.

Scenario

Northwind Traders has several branch offices. At your location, there are three departments: Information Technology, Sales, and Human Resources. As the administrator of your office network, you must create organizational units for these departments.

Practice

▶ **To create organizational units by using the Ldifde command-line tool**

1. Log on as **Nwtraders**x*ComputerName***User** with a password of **P@ssw0rd**

2. Use Notepad to create an input file for the organizational units shown in the following illustration.

3. Create the new organizational units by using the Ldifde command-line tool.

Lesson: Delegating Administrative Control of Organizational Units

- **What Is Delegation of Administrative Privileges?**
- **Organizational Unit Administrative Tasks**
- **How to Delegate Administrative Control**
- **How to Customize Delegated Administrative Control**
- **How to Verify Delegation of Administrative Control**

Introduction

This lesson explains the purpose of delegating administrative privileges, the administrative tasks that you may delegate, how to delegate these tasks, and how to verify that you have delegated the required privileges to perform these tasks.

Lesson objective

After completing this lesson, students will be able to:

- Describe the conditions under which administrative control to an organizational unit can be delegated.

- Describe common organizational unit administrative tasks.

- Delegate administrative control of an organizational unit by using the Delegation of Control Wizard.

- Customize delegated administrative control by creating a custom task to be delegated.

- Verify the administrative privileges that have been delegated.

What Is Delegation of Administrative Privileges?

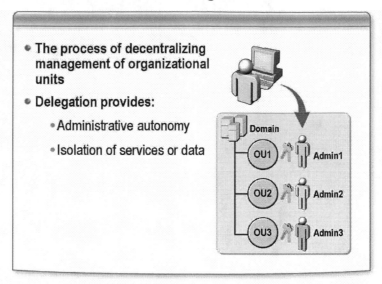

Introduction	The primary reason to create organizational units is to distribute administrative tasks across the organization by delegating administrative control to other administrators. Delegation is especially important when you develop a decentralized administrative model.
What is delegation of administration?	Delegation of administration is the process of decentralizing the responsibility for managing organizational units from a central administrator to other administrators. The ability to establish access to individual organizational units is an important security feature in Active Directory—you can control access to the lowest level of an organization without the necessity of creating many Active Directory domains.
	Authority delegated at the site level will likely span domains or, conversely, may not include targets in the domain. Authority delegated at the domain level will affect all objects in the domain. Authority delegated at the organizational unit level can affect that object and all of its child objects, or just the object itself.
Why delegate administration?	You delegate administrative control to provide administrative autonomy of services and data to organizations or to isolate services or data in an organization. You can eliminate the need for multiple administrative accounts that have broad authority, such as for an entire domain—yet still use the predefined Domain Admins group to manage the entire domain.

Autonomy is the ability of administrators in an organization to independently manage:

- All or part of service management (called *service autonomy*).

- All or part of the data in the Active Directory database or on member computers that are joined to the directory (called *data autonomy*).

Administrative autonomy:

- Minimizes the number of administrators who must have high levels of access.

- Limits the impact of an administrative mistake to a smaller area of administration.

Isolation is the ability of the administrators of an organization to prevent other administrators from:

- Controlling or interfering with service management (called *service isolation*).

- Controlling or viewing a subset of data in the directory or on member computers that are joined to the directory (called *data isolation*).

Windows Server 2003 contains specific permissions and user rights that you can use to delegate administrative control. By using a combination of organizational units, groups, and permissions, you can designate administrative rights to a particular user so that the user has an appropriate level of administration over an entire domain, all organizational units in a domain, or a single organizational unit.

Administrative Tasks for Organizational Units

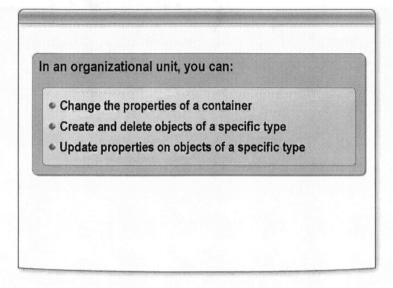

In an organizational unit, you can:

- Change the properties of a container
- Create and delete objects of a specific type
- Update properties on objects of a specific type

Introduction

Use organizational units to group Active Directory objects by type, such as users, groups, and computers, so that you can manage them effectively.

Common administrative tasks

Administrators routinely perform the following tasks in Active Directory:

- *Change properties on a particular container.* For example, when a new software package is available, administrators may create a group policy that controls the distribution of the software.

- *Create and delete objects of a specific type.* In an organizational unit, specific types may include users, groups, and printers. When a new employee joins the organization, for example, you create a user account for the employee and then add the employee to the appropriate organizational unit or group.

- *Update specific properties on objects of a specific type* in an organizational unit. Perhaps the most common administrative task that you perform, updating properties, includes tasks such as resetting passwords and changing an employee's personal information, such as her home address and phone number, when she moves.

How to Delegate Administrative Control

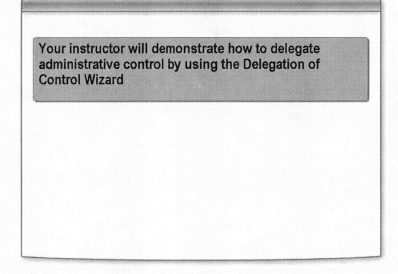

Your instructor will demonstrate how to delegate administrative control by using the Delegation of Control Wizard

Introduction

You can use the Delegation of Control Wizard to delegate administrative control of Active Directory objects, such as organizational units. By using the wizard, you can delegate common administrative tasks, such as creating, deleting, and managing user accounts.

Procedure

To delegate common administrative tasks for an organizational unit, perform the following steps:

1. Start the Delegation of Control Wizard by performing the following steps:

   a. Open Active Directory Users and Computers.

   b. In the console tree, double-click the domain node.

   c. In the details pane, right-click the organizational unit, click **Delegate control**, and then click **Next**.

2. Select the users or groups to which you want to delegate common administrative tasks. To do so, perform the following steps:

   a. On the **Users or Groups** page, click **Add**.

   b. In the **Select Users**, **Computers or Groups** dialog box, type the names of the users and groups to which you want to delegate control of the organizational unit, click **OK**, and then click **Next**.

3. Assign common tasks to delegate. To do so, perform the following steps:

   a. On the **Tasks to Delegate** page, click **Delegate the following common tasks**.

   b. On the **Tasks to Delegate** page, select the tasks you want to delegate, and then click **Next**.

4. Click **Finish**.

When you delegate control to a user or a group to create objects in Active Directory, these second parties can create an unlimited number of objects. In Windows Server 2003 you can limit the number of objects that a security principal can own in a directory partition, by implementing a quota for that security principal.

Note   For information about using quotas, see "How to Delegate Administrative Control" in Module 3 on the Appendices page on the Student Materials compact disc.

How to Customize Delegated Administrative Control

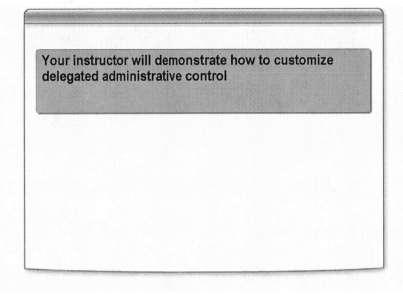

Your instructor will demonstrate how to customize delegated administrative control

Introduction

In addition to using the Delegation of Control Wizard to delegate a custom set of administrative tasks, such as the creation, deletion, and management of user accounts, you can use the wizard to select a set of custom tasks and delegate control of only those tasks.

For example, you can delegate control of all existing objects in an organizational unit and any new objects that are added, or you can select the objects in the organizational unit that you want to delegate administrative control of, such as only user objects in an organizational unit. You can also specify that you want to delegate only the creation of the selected object, or the deletion of the object, or both.

Procedure

To delegate custom administrative tasks for an organizational unit, perform the following steps:

1. Start the Delegation of Control Wizard.

2. Select the users or groups to which you want to delegate administrative tasks.

3. Assign the custom tasks to delegate. To do so, perform the following steps:

   a. On the **Tasks to Delegate** page, click **Create a custom task to delegate**, and then click **Next**.

   b. On the **Active Directory Object Type** page, do one of the following:

      i. Click **This folder, existing objects in this folder and creation of new objects in this folder**, and then click next.

      ii. Click **Only the following objects in the folder**, select the Active Directory object type that you want to delegate control of, and then click **Next**.

   c. Select the permissions that you want to delegate, and then click **Next**.

Note To obtain a list of permissions that you can delegate for the objects selected, or to delegate the creation and deletion of child objects in the objects selected, select the **Property-specific** check box.

---

4. Click **Finish**.

How to Verify Delegation of Administrative Control

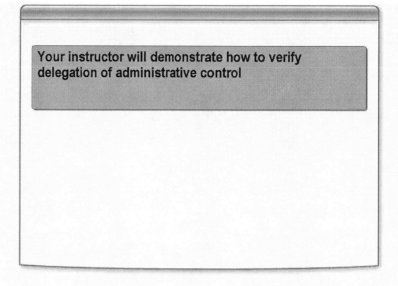

Introduction   Use Active Directory Users and Computers to verify that the Delegation of Control Wizard has correctly delegated the authority to perform the tasks.

Procedure   To verify delegation of control, perform the following steps:

1. In Active Directory Users and Computers, on the **View** menu, click **Advanced Features**.

2. In the console tree, double-click the domain node.

3. In the details pane, right-click the organizational unit, and then click **Properties**.

4. On the **Security** tab, click **Advanced**.

5. On the **Permissions** tab, under **Permission entries**, view the assigned permissions.

Practice: Delegating Administrative Tasks for an Organizational Unit

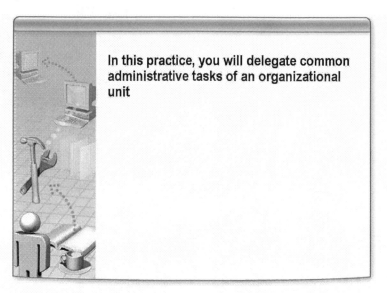

Objective

In this practice, you will delegate common administrative tasks of organizational units in the domain that is hosted by your student computer.

Scenario

You are the network administrator for Northwind Traders. Because of the size of your company, you do not have time to perform routine administrative tasks for each organizational unit. You want to delegate control of the organizational units to Help Desk personnel and managers in individual departments.

Practice

▶ **Delegate common administrative tasks for organizational units in the domain hosted by your student computer**

1. Log on as **Nwtraders*x**ComputerName*User** with a password of **P@ssw0rd**

2. Click **Start**, point to **Administrative Tools**, right-click **Active Directory Users and Computers**, and then click **Run as**.

3. In the **Run As** dialog box, click **The following user**, type *yourdomain***Administrator** as the user name with a password of **P@ssw0rd** and then click **OK**.

4. Create a domain local security group named **DL** *ComputerName***Admins** in the *ComputerName* organizational unit in your domain (where *ComputerName* is the name of the computer you are working on).

5. Add the Nwtraders\\G *ComputerName*Admins global group as a member of the DL *ComputerName*Admins domain local group.

6. Delegate the ability to create, delete, and manage user accounts in the *ComputerName* organizational unit to the DL *ComputerName*Admins group.

7. Verify that control has been delegated for these tasks by viewing the permissions assigned to the domain local group for the *ComputerName* organizational unit.

Lesson 3: Planning an Organizational Unit Strategy

- The Organizational Unit Planning Process
- Organizational Factors that Affect an Organizational Unit Structure
- Guidelines for Planning an Organizational Unit Structure
- Guidelines for Delegating Administrative Control

Introduction

Organizational units are containers in each Active Directory domain that represent the hierarchical structures in an organization. To create an organizational unit structure that best represents the organization's structure, you must understand the factors in your organization that affect the creation of organizational units. This lesson provides you with the knowledge and skills required to plan an organizational unit strategy.

Lesson Objectives

After completing this lesson, you will be able to:

- Describe the organizational unit planning process.

- Describe the organizational factors that affect organizational unit planning.

- Explain guidelines for determining the structure of an organizational unit.

- Explain guidelines for determining how to delegate administrative control to an organizational unit.

The Organizational Unit Planning Process

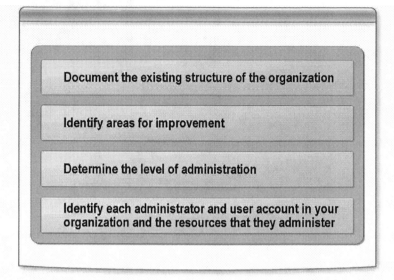

Document the existing structure of the organization

Identify areas for improvement

Determine the level of administration

Identify each administrator and user account in your organization and the resources that they administer

Introduction

The structure of organizational units in Active Directory is based on the administrative structure of the organization. The first step in planning an organizational unit structure is to document the structure of the organization.

Organizational unit planning process

To plan the organizational unit strategy for you organization, perform the following tasks:

- *Document the existing structure of the organization.* When documenting the existing structure of the organization, one strategy is to divide the administrative tasks into categories and then document the administrators who are responsible for each category.

- *Identify areas for improvement.* Work with the planning team to identify areas for improvement. For example, it may be more cost-effective to combine several IT teams from different divisions. You may identify non-IT employees who can assist in the administrative process and reduce the IT staff workload. This way, administrators can focus on the areas where their expertise is required.

Next, use the following as guidelines for your delegation plan:

- *Determine the level of administration.* Decide what each group will control and at which level you will delegate administration in the administrative hierarchy. When you create the plan, identify which groups will be:

  - Granted full control over objects of a particular class. These groups can create and delete objects in a specified class and modify any attribute on objects in the specified class.

  - Allowed to create objects of a particular class. By default, users have full control over objects that they create.

  - Allowed to only modify specific attributes of existing objects of a particular class.

- *Identify each administrator and user account in your organization and the resources that they administer.* This information will help you determine the ownership and the permissions assigned to the organizational units you create to support the delegation plan.

Organizational Factors that Affect an Organizational Unit Structure

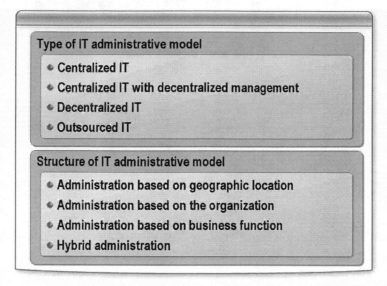

Introduction

The factors that affect an organizational unit structure are the type and structure of the IT administrative model. Understanding these factors will help you create an organizational unit structure that best suits your organization's requirements.

Types of IT administrative models

The most common IT organizations are:

- *Centralized IT.* In this model, the IT organization reports to one individual and is usually the group responsible for all network and information services, although some routine tasks may be delegated to certain groups or departments.

- *Centralized IT with decentralized management.* In this model, a centrally located core IT team is responsible for the core infrastructure services, but it delegates most day-to-day operations to IT groups in branch offices, which provide local administrative support to their users.

- *Decentralized IT.* This type of organization allows various business units to select an appropriate IT model to serve their requirements. Such an organization may have multiple IT groups with varying requirements and goals. Whenever there are organization-wide technology initiatives, such as an upgrade to a messaging application, the IT groups must work together to implement changes.

- *Outsourced IT.* Some organizations hire a third party to manage all or part of their IT organization. When only parts of the IT organization are outsourced, it becomes imperative to implement a proper delegation model. That way, the internal IT group maintains control of the organization without compromising the service level agreements that the third party has committed to provide.

IT administrative model structure

The administrative model structure reflects how an organization manages its IT resources, such as users, computers, groups, printers, and shared files.

Different ways that administrative models are structured include:

- *Administration based on geographic location.* The IT organization is centralized, such as at headquarters, but network administration is geographically distributed—for example, each branch has its own administrative group that manages resources at its location.

- *Administration based on the organization.* In this structure, the IT organization is divided into departments or business units, each of which has its own IT group.

- *Administration based on business function.* A decentralized IT organization often bases its administrative model on business functions in the organization.

- *Hybrid administration.* This structure combines strengths from several models to meet the administrative needs of the organization.

Guidelines for Planning an Organizational Unit Structure

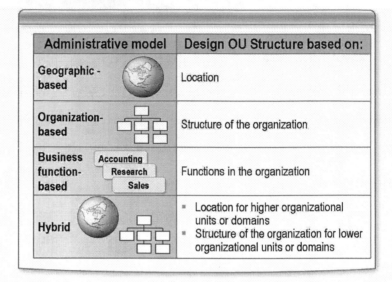

Administrative model	Design OU Structure based on:
Geographic - based	Location
Organization- based	Structure of the organization
Business function- based	Functions in the organization
Hybrid	• Location for higher organizational units or domains • Structure of the organization for lower organizational units or domains

Introduction

The design of organizational units is based on the IT administrative model of an organization.

Guidelines

Use the following guidelines to help you plan the organizational unit structure of an organization. The structure can be based on the:

- *Geographic location.* If the administrative model is geographically distributed and if administrators are present at each location, organize the Active Directory structure by location.

- *Organization.* If IT administration is department-based or division-based, design Active Directory based on the structure of the organization. Be sure to follow the administrative structure, rather than the organizational chart, when designing an organization-based Active Directory. The organizational chart may not map to the administrative needs of an organization.

- *Business functions.* If the IT administration is decentralized, design the Active Directory structure based on the functions in the organization. Choose this approach only if the IT function is not based on location or organization. This structure is ideal—in fact, it is the only appropriate one—for small organizations that have job functions that span several departments.

- *Hybrid model.* If it is a highly distributed organization with a centralized IT function and strong departmental or divisional separation, design the higher organizational units or domains by location, and the lower organizational unit or domain levels, by organization. Because the highest levels are based on location, this model is less likely to change, and therefore less likely to require a major effort during a reorganization.

Use the following flow chart as a decision tree for determining the appropriate organizational unit structure for an organization.

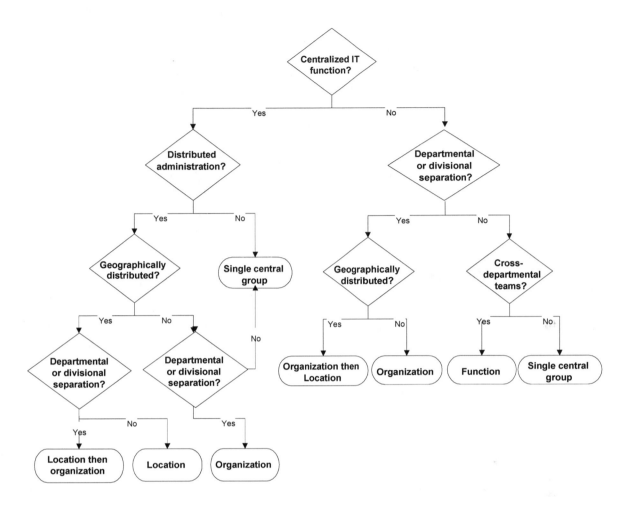

Guidelines for Delegating Administrative Control

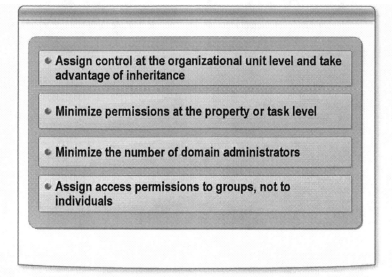

Introduction

Whenever possible, you delegate the ability to grant permissions in order to conserve administrative effort and cost, which reduces the total cost of ownership. Before assigning permissions to users in an organization, you must decide who can and cannot access an object and its contents, and the type of access that a person may or may not have.

Guidelines

Consider the following guidelines when you plan the delegation of administrative control in your organization:

- *Assign control at the highest organizational unit level possible and use inheritance.* You can then manage permissions more efficiently. It creates a simpler audit trail, and there is less chance for disaster if an administrator makes a mistake while logged on by using an administrative account.

Note Members of the Domain Admins group can always take ownership of an object in the domain and then change the permissions—one reason to limit the number of users in the Domain Admins group. When a member of the Administrators group creates or takes ownership of an object, the Administrators group becomes the object's owner. For tracking purposes, Windows Server 2003 lists the name of that member.

- *Avoid assigning permissions at the property or task level to simplify administration.* Consider placing objects in separate organizational units based on how they will be managed, rather than managing properties by using separate discretionary access control lists (DACLs) for objects in a single organizational unit.

  When assigning permissions:

  - Delegate the ability to assign access control permissions for objects to users or groups of users. In other words, delegate the ability to delegate.

  - Assign common or special permissions on objects.

  - Use inheritance to allow access control permissions to flow to child objects. At times, however, you must block inheritance to prevent a child object from inheriting permissions set on the parent object. Blocking inheritance makes it difficult to document and troubleshoot permissions on an object. Therefore, avoid it.

- *Assign access permissions to groups, rather than to individuals.* Group permissions make it easier to keep DACLs current on networks that have many users and objects. Also, assigning permissions to groups is powerful because you can nest groups, which reduces the total number of objects to manage.

Important   Delegate administrative control to domain local groups when you assign permissions to objects in a domain. Delegate administrative control to global or universal groups when you assign permissions to objects in the configuration partition or for attributes that are published in the global catalog.

- *Minimize the number of domain administrators.* The Domain Admins group has special abilities in a domain, such as the ability to take ownership of any object and define security policies for the entire domain. When you want to tightly control domain administrator privileges, grant administrative rights to users for the various organizational units and limit membership in the Domain Admins group.

Note   For more information about delegating control, see The Windows Server 2003 Deployment Planning Guide at http://www.microsoft.com/reskit. Also see the Active Directory Service Interfaces Overview at http://www.microsoft.com/windows2000/techinfo/howitworks/activedirectory/adsilinks.asp.

Practice: Planning an Organizational Unit Structure

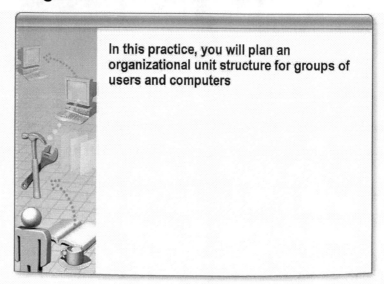

In this practice, you will plan an organizational unit structure for groups of users and computers

Objective

In this practice, you will work with your partner to plan an organizational unit structure for Northwind Traders.

Scenario

Northwind Traders is preparing to install Windows Server 2003 in its Sacramento, California and Portland, Oregon locations. The Active Directory design team will use an empty root domain, nwtraders$x$.msft, and a subdomain, corp$x$.nwtraders$x$.msft, where x is a number that your instructor will assign to you.

All computer and user accounts are in the corp$x$ domain. Northwind Traders has 1,500 users in six departments in these two locations.

Portland has 600 users in the following departments:

- Accounting
- IT
- Purchasing
- Shipping

Sacramento has 900 users in the following departments:

- Accounting
- Human Resources (HR)
- IT
- Purchasing
- Sales

In each department, a local administrator manages user accounts and group policy settings. The IT department wants to delegate the ability to manage all users in a specific department, or to manage all users in a department in a specific location.

Procedure

Work with your partner to plan an organizational unit structure. Use the following chart to document your plan for the organizational unit structure.

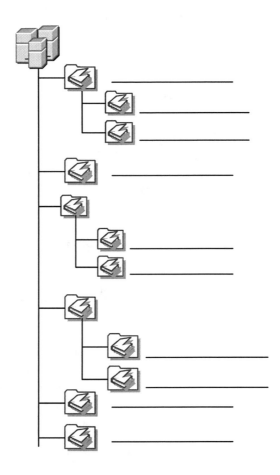

Lab A: Implementing an Organizational Unit Structure

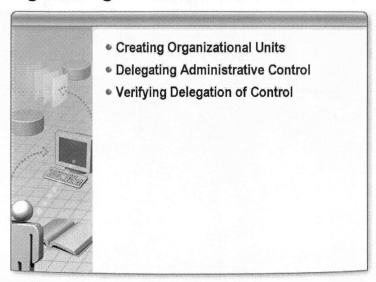

Objectives

After completing this lab, you will be able to:

- Create an organizational unit.
- Delegate control of an organizational unit.

Prerequisites

Before working on this lab, you must have:

- Knowledge of how to create a group by using Active Directory Users and Computers.
- Knowledge of and skills in creating organizational units.

Scenario

Northwind Traders is adding accounting and research personnel in all of its locations. New organizational units must be created for these departments at each location. Each department has a local administrator who manages user accounts.

You must create an Accounting organizational unit and a Research organizational unit in the *ComputerName* organizational unit in your domain. Additionally, you must create a DL AccountingAdmins and a DL ResearchAdmins domain local group, and then delegate permissions to each group in order to manage the appropriate organizational unit. You will create the new domain local groups in the *ComputerName*\IT organizational unit in your domain.

Note   Whenever corp*x* or nwtraders*x* appears in the lab, replace *x* with the number assigned to your domain.

Estimated time to complete this lab: 45 minutes

Exercise 1
Creating Organizational Units

In this exercise, you will use the Dsadd command-line tool to create the organizational units in your domain.

Tasks	Specific instructions
1. Use the Dsadd command-line tool to create the Accounting and Research organizational units in the *ComputerName* organizational unit in your domain.	▪ Log on as **Nwtraders***x**ComputerName***User** with a password of **P@ssw0rd**

Exercise 2
Delegating Administrative Control

In this exercise, you will use Active Directory Users and Computers to create groups, add global groups from the nwtraders.msft domain to the groups that you create, and then delegate control of each organizational unit to the appropriate group. Finally, you will verify delegation of control.

Tasks	Specific instructions
1. Create the following domain local groups in the *ComputerName*\IT organizational unit: • DL AccountingAdmins • DL ResearchAdmins	a. Log on as **Nwtraders***x**ComputerName***User** with a password of **P@ssw0rd** b. Use **Run as** to start Active Directory Users and Computers as *YourDomain***Administrator** with a password of **P@ssw0rd**
2. Add the G ComputerNameAdmins global group from the Nwtraders.msft domain to the DL AccountingAdmins and DL ResearchAdmins domain local groups in your domain.	
3. Use the Delegation of Control Wizard to delegate the ability to create, delete, and manage user accounts in the Accounting and Research organizational units to the appropriate domain local groups that you created.	

Exercise 3
Verifying Delegation of Control

In this exercise, you will verify the permissions assigned to the DL AccountingAdmins and DL ResearchAdmins groups in the Accounting and Research organizational units.

Tasks	Specific instructions
1. Enable the **Advanced Features** view in Active Directory Users and Computers.	a. Log on as **Nwtraders***x\ComputerName***User** with a password of **P@ssw0rd** b. Use **Run as** to start Active Directory Users and Computers as *YourDomain***Administrator** with a password of **P@ssw0rd**
2. View the permissions assigned to the DL AccountingAdmins and DL ResearchAdmins domain local groups in your domain for the Accounting and Research organizational units.	

❷ Which permissions are assigned to the DL AccountingAdmins group? What objects do the permissions apply to?

_____

_____

❷ Which permissions are assigned to the DL ResearchAdmins group? What objects do the permissions apply to?

_____

_____

Microsoft®
Training &
Certification

Module 4: Implementing User, Group, and Computer Accounts

Contents

Overview

- **Introduction to Accounts**
- **Creating and Managing Multiple Accounts**
- **Implementing User Principal Name Suffixes**
- **Moving Objects in Active Directory**
- **Planning a User, Group, and Computer Account Strategy**
- **Planning an Active Directory Audit Strategy**

Introduction

In this module, you will learn about planning and implementing user, group, and computer accounts in the Active Directory® directory service. You will also learn how to create multiple user and computer accounts and how to implement User Principle Name (UPN) suffixes.

Lesson objectives

After completing this module, you will be able to:

- Describe the types of Active Directory accounts and groups.
- Create multiple user and computer accounts.
- Implement UPN suffixes.
- Move objects within a domain and across domains in a forest.
- Plan a strategy for user, computer, and group accounts.
- Plan an Active Directory audit strategy.

Lesson: Introduction to Accounts

- Types of Accounts
- Types of Groups
- What Are Domain Local Groups?
- What Are Global Groups?
- What Are Universal Groups?

Introduction

This lesson describes the types of accounts and groups that you can create in Microsoft® Windows® Server 2003. The lesson also describes the behavior of global, domain local, and universal groups.

Enabling objectives

After completing this lesson, you will be able to:

- Describe the types of accounts that you can create in Window Server 2003.
- Describe the types of groups that you can create in Windows Server™ 2003.
- Describe the behavior of domain local groups.
- Describe the behavior of global groups.
- Describe the behavior of universal groups.

Types of Accounts

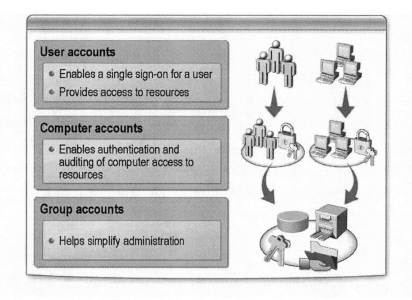

Introduction

You can create three types of accounts in Active Directory: user, group, and computer accounts. Active Directory user and computer accounts represent a physical entity, such as a computer or person. You can also use user accounts as dedicated service accounts for some applications.

User accounts

A *user account* is an object stored in Active Directory that enables *single sign-on*, that is, a user enters her name and password only once when logging on to a workstation to gain authenticated access to network resources.

There are three types of user accounts, each of which has a specific function:

- A *local user account* enables a user to log on to a specific computer to access resources on that computer.

- A *domain user account* enables a user to log on to the domain to access network resources or to log on to an individual computer to access resources on that computer.

- A *built-in user account* enables a user to perform administrative tasks or gain temporary access to network resources.

Computer accounts

Every computer running Microsoft Windows NT®, Windows 2000, or Windows XP, or a server running Windows Server 2003 that joins a domain, has a *computer account*. Like user accounts, computer accounts provide a way to authenticate and audit computer access to the network and to domain resources. Each computer account must be unique.

Group accounts

A *group account* is a collection of users, computers, or other groups. You can use groups to efficiently manage access to domain resources, which helps simplify administration. When you use groups, you assign permissions for shared resources, such as folders and printers, only once—rather than multiple times—to individual users.

Types of Groups

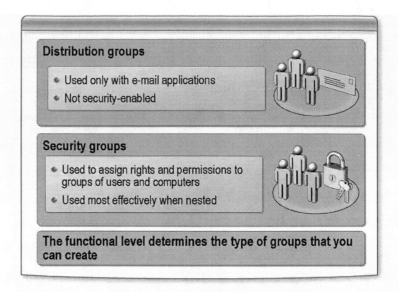

Distribution groups
- Used only with e-mail applications
- Not security-enabled

Security groups
- Used to assign rights and permissions to groups of users and computers
- Used most effectively when nested

The functional level determines the type of groups that you can create

---

Introduction

There are two types of groups in Active Directory, distribution groups and security groups. Both have a scope attribute, which determines who can be a member of the group and where you can use that group in a network. You can convert a group from a security group to a distribution group and vice versa at any time, but only if the domain functional level is set to Windows 2000 native or higher.

Distribution groups

You can use distribution groups only with e-mail applications, such as Microsoft Exchange, to send messages to collections of users. Distribution groups are not *security-enabled*, that is, they cannot be listed in discretionary access control lists (DACLs). To control access to shared resources, create a security group.

Security groups

You use security groups to assign rights and permissions to groups of users and computers. Rights determine which functions members of a security group can perform in a domain or forest. Permissions determine which resources a member of a group can access on the network.

One way to use security groups effectively is to use *nesting*, that is, to add a group to another group. The nested group inherits the permissions of the group that it is a member of, which simplifies the assigning of permissions to several groups at once and reduces the traffic that replication of group membership changes causes. In a mixed-domain mode, you cannot nest groups that have the same group scope.

Both distribution and security groups support one of the three group scopes: domain local, global, or universal. The domain functional level determines the type of group that you can create. In Windows 2000 mixcd mode, you cannot create universal security groups.

What Are Domain Local Groups?

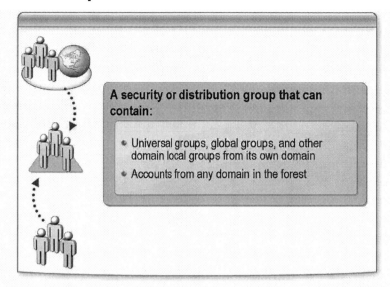

Introduction

A domain local group is a security or distribution group that can contain universal groups, global groups, other domain local groups from its own domain, and accounts from any domain in the forest. In domain local security groups, you can grant rights and permissions on resources that reside only in the same domain where the domain local group is located.

For example, you could create a domain local security group named Setup and grant the group permissions to a share named Setup on one of the member servers in the domain. You could add global and universal groups as members of the setup domain local group. The members would then have permissions to access the setup shared folder.

Domain local group membership, scope and permissions

The following rules apply to domain local group membership, scope, and permissions:

- *Membership.* In Windows 2000 mixed mode, domain local groups can contain user accounts and global groups from any domain. In Windows 2000 native mode, domain local groups can contain user accounts, global groups, universal groups from any trusted domain, and domain local groups from the same domain.

- *Can be a member of.* In Windows 2000 mixed mode, a domain local group cannot be a member of any group. In Windows 2000 native mode, a domain local group can be a member of domain local groups from the same domain.

- *Scope.* A domain local group is visible only in its own domain.

- *Permission for.* You can assign permission that applies to the domain in which the domain local group exists.

When to use domain local groups

Use a domain local group when you want to assign access permissions to resources that are located in the same domain in which you create the domain local group. You can add all global groups that must share the same resources to the appropriate domain local group.

What Are Global Groups?

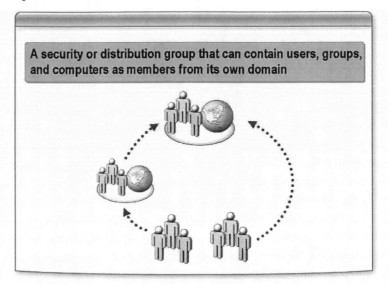

Introduction

A global group is a security or distribution group that can contain users, groups, and computers as members from its own domain. You can grant rights and permissions to global security groups for resources in any domain in the forest.

Use a global group to organize users who share the same job tasks and have similar network access requirements, such as all accountants in an organization's accounting department.

Global group membership, scope, and permissions

The following rules apply to global group membership, scope, and permissions:

- *Membership.* In Windows 2000 mixed mode, a global group can contain user accounts from the same domain. In Windows 2000 native mode and in Windows Server 2003 mode, global groups can contain user accounts and global groups from the same domain.

- *Can be a member of.* In Windows 2000 mixed mode, a global group can be a member of domain local groups in any trusted domain. In Windows 2000 native mode and in Windows Server 2003 mode, a global group can be a member of universal and domain local groups in any domain and can also be a member of global groups in the same domain.

- *Scope.* A global group is visible in its domain and all trusted domains, which include all of the domains in the forest.

- *Permissions.* You can assign permission to a global group that applies to all trusted domains.

When to use global groups

Because global groups are visible throughout the forest, do not create them for the purpose of allowing users access to domain-specific resources. Use global groups to organize users or groups of users. A domain local group is more appropriate to control user access to resources within a single domain.

What Are Universal Groups?

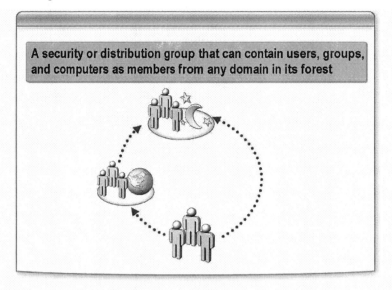

A security or distribution group that can contain users, groups, and computers as members from any domain in its forest

Introduction

A universal group is a security or distribution group that can contain users, groups, and computers as members from any domain in its forest. Universal security groups can be granted rights and permissions on resources in any domain in the forest.

Universal group membership, scope, and permissions

The following rules apply to universal group membership, scope, and permissions:

- *Membership.* You cannot create universal security groups in Windows 2000 mixed mode. In both Windows 2000 native mode and Windows Server 2003 mode, universal groups can contain user accounts, global groups, and other universal groups from any domain in the forest.

- *Can be a member of.* The universal group is not applicable in Windows 2000 mixed mode. In Windows 2000 native mode, the universal group can be a member of domain local and universal groups from any domain.

- *Scope.* Universal groups are visible in all domains in the forest.

- *Permissions.* You can assign permission to a universal group that applies to all domains in the forest.

When to use universal groups

Use universal groups when you want to nest global groups. This way, you can assign permissions to related resources in multiple domains. A Windows Server 2003 domain must be in Windows 2000 native mode or Windows Server 2003 mode to use universal security groups. You can use universal distribution groups in a Windows Server 2003 domain that is in Windows 2000 mixed mode or higher.

Lesson: Creating and Managing Multiple Accounts

- Tools for Creating and Managing Multiple Accounts
- How to Create Accounts Using the Csvde Tool
- How to Create and Manage Accounts Using the Ldifde Tool
- How to Create and Manage Accounts Using Windows Script Host

Introduction

This lesson describes the various command-line tools that you can use to create and manage multiple user accounts.

Lesson objectives

After completing this lesson, you will be able to:

- Describe the tools for creating and managing multiple accounts.
- Use the Csvde command-line tool to create accounts.
- Use the Ldifde command-line tool to create and manage accounts.
- Create and manage accounts by using Windows Script Host.

Tools for Creating and Managing Multiple Accounts

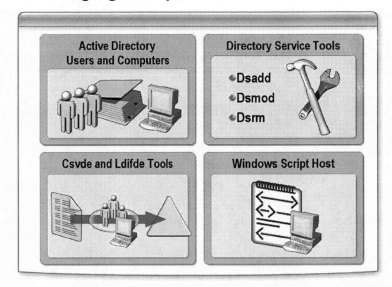

Introduction

Windows Server 2003 provides a number of Microsoft Management Console (MMC) snap-ins and tools to create multiple user accounts automatically in Active Directory. Some of these tools require that you use a text file that contains information about the user accounts that you want to create. You can also create scripts to add objects or make changes to objects in Active Directory.

Active Directory Users and Computers

Active Directory Users and Computers is an MMC snap-in that you can use to manage user, computer, and group accounts. Use this snap-in when the number of accounts you are managing is small.

Directory Service tools

You can also use the command-line tools Dsadd, Dsmod, and Dsrm to manage user, computer, and group accounts in Active Directory. You must specify the type of object that you want to create, modify, or delete. For example, use the **dsadd user** command to create a user account. Use the **dsrm group** command to delete a group account. Although you can use Directory Service tools to create only one Active Directory object at a time, you can use the tools in batch files and scripts.

The Csvde tool

The Csvde command-line tool uses a *comma-delimited* text file, also known as a *comma-separated value* format (Csvde format) as input to create multiple accounts in Active Directory.

You use the Csvde format to add user objects and other types of objects to Active Directory. You cannot use the Csvde format to delete or modify objects in Active Directory. Before importing a Csvde file, ensure that the file is properly formatted. The input file:

- Must include the path to the user account in Active Directory, the object type, which is the user account, and the user logon name (for Microsoft Windows NT® 4.0 and earlier).

- Should include the user principal name (UPN) and whether the user account is disabled or enabled. If you do not specify a value, the account is disabled.

- Can include personal information—for example, telephone numbers or home addresses. Include as much user account information as possible so that users can search in Active Directory successfully.

- Cannot include passwords. Bulk import leaves the password blank for user accounts. Because a blank password allows an unauthorized person to access the network by knowing only the user logon name, disable the user accounts until users start logging on.

To edit and format the input text file, use an application that has good editing capabilities, such as Microsoft Excel or Microsoft Word. Next, save the file as a comma-delimited text file. You can export data from Active Directory to an Excel spreadsheet or import data from a spreadsheet into Active Directory.

The Ldifde tool

The Ldifde command-line tool uses a *line-separated value* format to create, modify, and delete objects in Active Directory. An Ldifde input file consists of a series of records that are separated by a blank line. A *record* describes a single directory object or a set of modifications to the attributes of an existing object and consists of one or more lines in the file. Most database applications can create text files that you can import in one of these formats. The requirements for the input file are similar to those of the Csvde command-line tool.

Windows Script Host

You can create Windows Script Host scripts that use Active Directory Service Interfaces (ADSI) to create, modify, and delete Active Directory objects. Use scripts when you want to change the values of attributes for multiple Active Directory objects, or when the selection criteria for these objects are complex.

How to Create Accounts Using the Csvde Tool

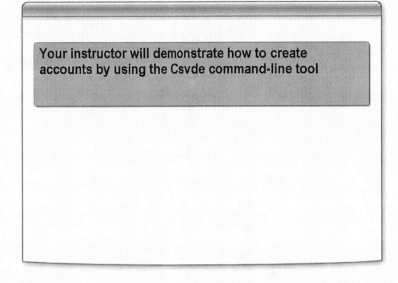

Introduction

You can use the Csvde command-line tool to create multiple accounts in Active Directory. You can only use the Csvde tool to create accounts, not to change them.

Procedure

To create accounts by using the Csvde command-line tool, perform the following steps:

1. Create the Csvde file for importing. Format the file so that it contains the following information:

   - *The attribute line.* This is the first line of the file. It specifies the name of each attribute that you want to define for the new user accounts. You can put the attributes in any order, but you must separate the attributes with commas. The following sample code is an example of an attribute line:

   ```
   DN,objectClass,sAMAccountName,userPrincipalName,
   displayName,userAccountControl
   ```

   - *The user account line.* For each user account that you create, the import file contains a line that specifies the value for each attribute in the attribute line. The following rules apply to the values in a user account line:

     - The attribute values must follow the sequence of the attribute line.

     - If a value is missing for an attribute, leave it blank, but include all of the commas.

     - If a value contains commas, include the value in quotation marks.

The following sample code is an example of a user account line:

```
"cn=Suzan Fine,ou=Human Resources,dc=asia,dc=contoso,
dc=msft",user,suzanf,suzanf@contoso.msft,Suzan Fine,514
```

This table provides the attributes and values from the previous example.

Attribute	Value
DN (distinguished name)	cn=Suzan Fine,ou=Human Resources, dc=asia,dc=contoso,dc=msft (This specifies the path to the organizational unit that contains the user account.)
objectClass	user
sAMAccountName	suzanf
userPrincipalName	suzanf@contoso.msft
displayName	Suzan Fine
userAccountControl	514 (The value 514 disables the user account, and the value 512 enables the user account.)

The attributes in this table are the required minimum attributes for running **csvde**.

Important   You cannot use Csvde to create enabled user accounts if the domain password policy requires a minimum password length or requires complex passwords. In this case, use a userAccountControl value of 514, which disables the user account, and then enable the account using Windows Script Host or Active Directory Users and Computers.

---

2. Run the **csvde** command by typing the following command at the command prompt:

```
csvde -i -f filename -b UserName Domain Password
```

Where:

-i indicates that you are importing a file into Active Directory

-f indicates that the next parameter is the name of the file that you are importing

–b sets the command to run as *username*, *domain*, and *password*.

The **csvde** command provides status information about the success or the failure of the process. It also lists the name of the file to view for detailed error information. Even if the status information indicates that the process was successful, use Active Directory Users and Computers to verify some of the user accounts that you created to ensure that they contain all of the information that you provided.

Note   For information about the common options used with the Csvde command-line tool, see "How to Create Accounts Using the Csvde Tool" in Module 4 on the Appendices page on the Student Materials compact disc. Also see Windows Server 2003 Help and Support.

How to Create and Manage Accounts Using the Ldifde Tool

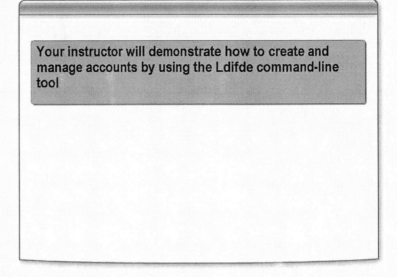

Your instructor will demonstrate how to create and manage accounts by using the Ldifde command-line tool

Introduction

You can use the Ldifde command-line tool to create and make changes to multiple accounts.

Procedure

To create accounts by using the Ldifde command-line tool, perform the following steps:

1. Prepare the Ldifde file for importing.

   Format the Ldifde file so that it contains a record that consists of a sequence of lines that describe either an entry for a user account or a set of changes to a user account in Active Directory. The user account entry specifies the name of each attribute that you want to define for the new user account. The Active Directory schema defines the attribute names. For each user account that you create, the file contains a line that specifies the value for each attribute in the attribute line. The following rules apply to the values for each attribute:

   - Any line that begins with a pound-sign (#) is a comment line and is ignored when you run the Ldifde file.

   - If a value is missing for an attribute, it must be represented as *AttributeDescription* ":" FILL SEP.

   The following sample code is an example of an entry in an Ldifde import file:

   ```
   # Create Suzan Fine
   dn: cn=Suzan Fine,ou=Human
   Resources,dc=asia,dc=contoso,dc=msft
   Changetype: Add
   objectClass: user
   sAMAccountName: suzanf
   userPrincipalName: suzanf@contoso.msft
   displayName: Suzan Fine
   userAccountControl: 514
   ```

The following table provides the attributes and values from the previous example.

Attribute	Attribute value
#	Create Suzan Fine (The # character indicates that this line is a comment.)
DN	cn=Suzan Fine, ou=Human Resources, dc=asia,dc=contoso,dc=msft (This value specifies the path to the object's container.)
Changetype	Add
objectClass	user
sAMAccountName	suzanf
userPrincipalName	suzanf@contoso.msft
displayName	Suzan Fine
userAccountControl	512

2. Run the **ldifde** command to import the file and create multiple user accounts in Active Directory.

   Type the following command at the command prompt:

   ```
   ldifde -i -k -f filename  -b UserName Domain Password
   ```

   Where:

   -i specifies the import mode. If not specified, the default mode is export.

   -k ignores errors during an import operation and continues processing.

   -f specifies the import or export filename.

   -b specifies the user name, the domain name, and the password for the user account that will be used to perform the import or export operation.

How to Create and Manage Accounts Using Windows Script Host

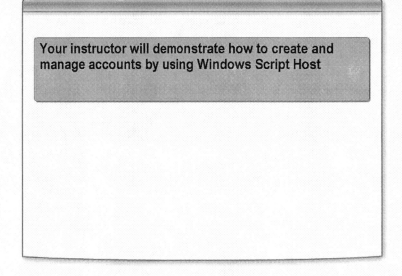

Your instructor will demonstrate how to create and manage accounts by using Windows Script Host

Introduction

You can create Active Directory objects from Windows Script Host scripts by using ADSI. Creating an Active Directory object is a four-step process, as shown in the following procedure.

Procedure for creating an Active Directory object

To create an Active Directory object, such as a user account in a domain, perform the following steps:

1. Use Notepad to create a text file with a .vbs extension. Place the following commands in the file, and then save the file.

   a. Connect to the container in which you want to create the Active Directory object by specifying the Lightweight Directory Access Protocol (LDAP) query.

   ```
   Set objOU =
   GetObject("LDAP://ou=management,dc=fabrikam,dc=com")
   ```

   Important In the above example, LDAP must be in all uppercase letters, or the command will fail.

   ---

   b. Create the Active Directory object and specify the object class and the object name.

   ```
   Set objUser = objOU.Create("User", "cn=MyerKen")
   ```

   c. Set the properties of the Active Directory object.

   ```
   objUser.Put "sAMAccountName", "myerken"
   ```

d. Write the information to the Active Directory database.

```
objUser.SetInfo
```

The properties of certain Active Directory objects cannot be set when you create them. For example, when you create a user account, you cannot enable the account or set its password. You can only set these properties after you create the object, as shown in the following sample code:

```
objUser.AccountDisabled = FALSE
objUser.ChangePassword "", "jl3R86df"
objUser.SetInfo
```

e. Save the file with the extension .vbs.

2. Run the script by typing the following command at a command prompt:

```
Wscript.exe filename
```

where *filename* is the name of the script file that you created in the previous step.

Note For a sample script to create a user account, see "How to Create and Manage Accounts Using the Windows Script Host" in Module 4 on the Appendices page on the Student Materials compact disc.

Procedure for changing the value of a property

To change the value of a property of an Active Directory object, such as the telephone number of a user, open Notepad to create a text file, add the following commands to the file, and then execute the script file by starting it from a command prompt:

1. Connect to the object that the property will be changed to.

```
Set objUser = GetObject _
    ("LDAP://cn=myerken,ou=TestOU,dc=nwtraders,dc=msft")
```

2. Set the new value of the property—for example, the room number of an employee who has moved to a new office.

```
objUser.Put "physicalDeliveryOfficeName", "Room 4358"
```

3. Write the change to Active Directory.

```
objUser.SetInfo
```

4. Save the file with the extension .vbs.

5. Execute the script by typing the following command at a command prompt:

```
wscript.exe filename
```

where *filename* is the name of the script file that you created in the previous step.

Note For more information about creating administrative scripts by using Windows Script Host, see the Microsoft TechNet Script Center at www.microsoft.com/technet/treeview/default.asp?url=/technet/scriptcenter/default.asp.

Also see Course 2433, *Microsoft Visual Basic Scripting Edition and Microsoft Windows Script Host Essentials*.

Practice: Creating User Accounts

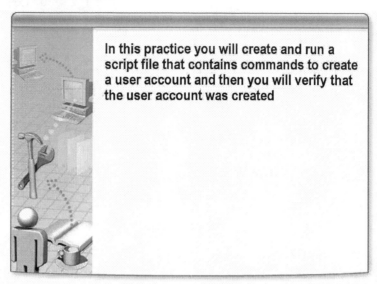

Objectives

In this practice, you will create and run a script file that contains commands to create a user account, and then you will verify that the user account was created.

Scenario

Northwind Traders has hired a new sales person, Brenda Diaz. You must create the user logon name for her. The current standard at Northwind Traders is to use the user's first name and the first three letters of the user's last name. You will use Windows Script Host to create this user account in the *YourComputerName*\Sales organizational unit.

Practice

To create the user account, perform the following steps:

1. Log on as **Nwtraders***x**ComputerName***User** with a password of **P@ssw0rd**

2. Use Notepad to create a script file that contains commands to create the new user account.

   a. Open Notepad.

   b. Type the script to create the user account.

   c. On the **File** menu, click **Save As**.

   d. In the **File name** box, type **createusers.vbs**

   e. In the **Save as type** box, select **All Files**.

   f. Click **Save**.

3. Run the script file.

    a. Click **Start**, right-click **Command Prompt**, and then click **Run as**.

    b. In the **Run As** dialog box, click **The following user**, type *YourDomain***Administrator** as the user name with a password of **P@ssw0rd** and then click **OK**.

    c. Change directory to the folder in which you saved the createusers.vbs file.

    d. At the command prompt, type **wscript.exe createusers.vbs**

4. Use Active Directory Users and Computers to verify that the user was created.

    a. Open Active Directory Users and Computers.

    b. In the console tree, click **Sales**.

    c. In the details pane, view the user accounts that are listed.

Lesson: Implementing User Principal Name Suffixes

- What Is a User Principal Name?
- Multimedia: How Name Suffix Routing Works
- How Name Suffix Conflicts Are Detected and Resolved
- How to Create and Remove a UPN Suffix
- How to Enable and Disable Name Suffix Routing in Forest Trusts

Introduction

This lesson describes the purpose of User Principle Names (UPN). It explains how a UPN suffix is routed in a trust environment and how to create, remove, enable, disable, and exclude name suffix routing in cross-forest trusts.

Lesson objectives

After completing this lesson, you will be able to:

- Describe the purpose of a UPN.

- Explain how a UPN suffix is routed in a trust environment.

- Describe how name suffix conflicts are detected and resolved.

- Create and remove a UPN suffix.

- Enable, disable, and exclude name suffix routing in cross-forest trusts.

What Is a User Principal Name?

- A logon name that is used only for logging on to a Windows Server 2003 network

  suzanf@contoso.msft

- Advantages
  - Unique in Active Directory
  - Can be the same as a user's e-mail address

Introduction

In a Windows Server 2003 network, a user can log on by using either a user principal name or a user logon name (Windows NT 4.0 and earlier). Domain controllers can use either the user principal name or the user logon name to authenticate the logon request.

What is a user principal name?

A *user principal name* is a logon name that is used only to log on to a Windows Server 2003 network. This name is also known as a user logon name.

There are two parts to a user principal name, which are separated by the @ sign—for example, suzanf@contoso.msft:

- The *user principal name prefix*, which in this example is suzanf.

- The *user principal name suffix*, which in this example is contoso.msft. By default, the suffix is the name of the domain in which the user account was created. You can use the other domains in the network, or additional suffixes that you created, to configure other suffixes for users. For example, you may want to configure a suffix to create user logon names that match users' e-mail addresses.

Advantages of using user principal names

Using user principle names has the following advantages:

- They do not change when you move a user account to a different domain because the name is unique in the Active Directory forest.

- They can be the same name as a user's e-mail address name because they have the same format as a standard e-mail address.

Uniqueness rules for user logon names

User logon names for domain user accounts must comply with the following uniqueness rules in Active Directory:

- The full name must be unique in the container in which you create the user account. The full name is used as the relative distinguished name.

- The user principal name must be unique in the forest.

Multimedia: How Name Suffix Routing Works

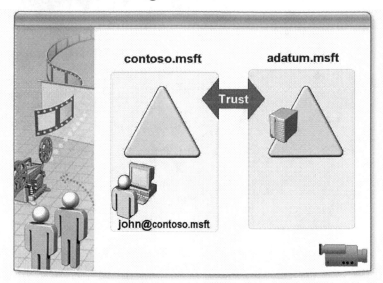

File location

To view the presentation, *How Name Suffix Routing Works*, open the Web page on the Student Materials compact disc, click **Multimedia**, and then click the title of the presentation. Do not open this presentation unless the instructor tells you to.

Objectives

At the end of this presentation, you will be able to explain how name suffix routing works in Active Directory.

Key points

Name suffix routing is a mechanism that provides name resolution across forests. Forests can contain multiple name suffixes.

When two Windows Server 2003 forests are connected by a forest trust, domain name suffixes that exist in both forests route authentication requests. Therefore, any authentication request made from Forest A to a suffix that resides in Forest B is routed successfully to its target resource.

Name suffixes that do not exist in one forest can be routed to a second forest. When a new child domain (for example, child.contoso.com) is added to a second-level domain name suffix (for example, contoso.com), the child domain inherits the routing configuration of the second-level domain that it belongs to.

Any new second-level name suffixes that you create after a forest trust has been established are visible in the **Properties** dialog box for that forest trust. However, the routing of suffixes for the domain trees that you create after the trust is established are disabled by default. You must manually enable routing for these suffixes. When Active Directory detects a duplicate name suffix, the routing for the newest name suffix is disabled by default. You can use the **Properties** dialog box to manually enable or disable routing for individual name suffixes.

How Name Suffix Conflicts Are Detected and Resolved

* **Name suffix conflicts occur when**

    * A DNS name is already in use

    * A NetBIOS name is already in use

    * A domain SID conflicts with another name suffix SID

* **Name suffix conflicts in a domain cause access to that domain from outside the forest to be denied**

Introduction

When two Windows Server 2003 forests are linked by a forest trust, a second-level domain name suffix or a UPN suffix that exists in one forest may collide with a similar name suffix in the second forest. By detecting collisions, the New Trust Wizard guarantees that only one forest is authoritative for a given name suffix.

Collision detection

The New Trust Wizard detects name suffix conflicts when any of the following situations occur:

* The same Domain Name System (DNS) name is already in use.

* The same NetBIOS name is already in use.

* A domain security ID (SID) conflicts with another name suffix SID.

For example, assume that you want to establish a two-way forest trust between the contoso.com forest and the fabrikam.com forest. Both contoso.com and fabrikam.com have the same UPN suffix: nwtraders.msft. When you create the two-way forest trust, the New Trust Wizard detects and displays the conflict between the two UPN name suffixes.

How conflicts are resolved

The New Trust Wizard automatically disables a second-level domain name suffix if the same name suffix exists in a second forest. For example, a conflict occurs if one forest is named fabrikam.com and the second forest is named sales.fabrikam.com.

When the New Trust Wizard detects a name suffix conflict, it denies access to that domain from outside the forest. However, access to the domain from within the forest functions normally.

For example, if the domain fabrikam.com exists in both the contoso.com and nwtraders.msft forests, users in the contoso.com forest can access resources in the fabrikam.com domain that resides in the contoso.com forest. However, users in the contoso.com forest are denied access to resources in the fabrikam.com domain that is located in the nwtraders.msft forest.

When the New Trust Wizard detects a name suffix conflict, it prompts you to save a log file of the conflicts. It then lists conflicts in the *Forest Trust Name* **Properties** dialog box on the **Name Suffix Routing** tab in the **Routing** column.

How to Create and Remove a UPN Suffix

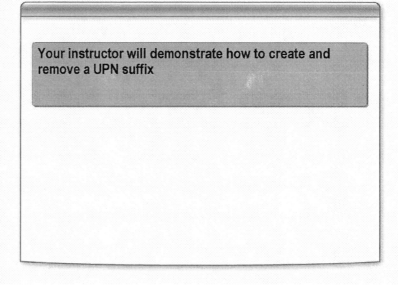

Your instructor will demonstrate how to create and remove a UPN suffix

Introduction

When you use a user principal name suffix, you simplify administration and user logon processes by providing one user principal name suffix for all users. When you create a user account, you can select a UPN suffix. If the suffix does not exist, you can add it by using Active Directory Domains and Trusts, provided that you are a member of the Enterprise Admins predefined group.

Procedure for adding a UPN suffix

To add a UPN suffix, perform the following steps:

1. Open Active Directory Domains and Trusts.

2. In the console tree, right-click **Active Directory Domains and Trusts**, and then click **Properties**.

3. On the **UPN Suffixes** tab, type an alternative UPN suffix, and then click **Add**.

Note If you create a user account by using Windows Script Host or something other than Active Directory Users and Computers, you are not limited by the user principal name suffixes that are stored in Active Directory. You can assign a suffix when you create the account. However, suffixes that you create this way are not automatically routed over forest trusts.

Procedure for removing a UPN suffix

To remove a UPN suffix, perform the following steps:

1. In Active Directory Domains and Trusts, in the console tree, right-click **Active Directory Domains and Trusts**, and then click **Properties**.

2. On the **UPN Suffixes** tab, select the UPN suffix name that you want to remove, and then click **Remove**.

How to Enable and Disable Name Suffix Routing in Forest Trusts

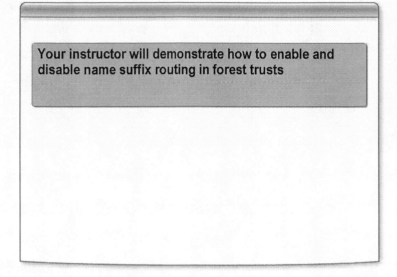

Your instructor will demonstrate how to enable and disable name suffix routing in forest trusts

Introduction

You use Active Directory Domains and Trusts to enable and disable routing for a name suffix.

Procedure

To change enable or disable routing for a second-level name suffix, perform the following steps:

1. In the console tree, right-click the domain node for the domain that you want to administer, and then click **Properties**.

2. On the **Trusts** tab, under either **Domains trusted by this domain (outgoing trusts)** or **Domains that trust this domain (incoming trusts)**, click the forest trust that you want to administer, and then click **Properties**.

3. On the **Name Suffix Routing** tab, under **Name suffixes in the** <*forest name*> **forest**, click the suffix that you want to enable or disable routing for, and then click **Enable** or **Disable**.

Important   When you disable routing for a second-level domain suffix, you also disable routing of suffixes for all of its child domain suffixes.

To change the routing status of a third-level or higher name suffix, perform the following steps:

1. In the console tree, right-click the domain node for the domain that you want to administer, and then click **Properties**.

2. On the **Trusts** tab, under either **Domains trusted by this domain (outgoing trusts)** or **Domains that trust this domain (incoming trusts)**, click the forest trust that you want to administer, and then click **Properties**.

3. On the **Name Suffix Routing** tab, under **Name suffixes in the** *<forest name>* **forest**, click the suffix that is the parent suffix of the suffix that you want to modify the routing status for, and then click **Edit**.

4. Under **Existing name suffixes in** *<forest name>*, click the suffix that you want to modify, and then click **Enable** or **Disable**.

Practice: Creating UPN Suffixes

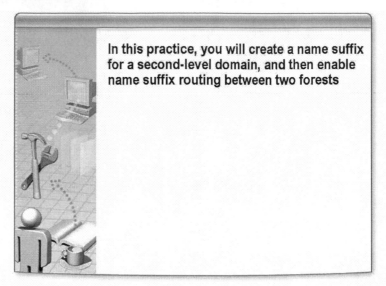

In this practice, you will create a name suffix for a second-level domain, and then enable name suffix routing between two forests

Objectives

In this practice, you will create a name suffix for a second-level domain, and then you will enable name suffix routing between two forests.

Scenario

Northwind Traders has a multiple domain forest. The company has chosen a new domain name, which it will use as the company's Web site name and e-mail address. You must add the new suffix and then enable routing for it.

Practice

▶ **Create a name suffix and enable routing of the name suffix**

1. Create a new name suffix for a second-level domain named *YourFirstName*.msft.

   a. Log on as **Nwtraders***x**ComputerName***User** with a password of **P@ssw0rd**

   b. Use **Run as** to start Active Directory Domains and Trusts as *YourDomain***Administrator** with a password of **P@ssw0rd**

   c. In the console tree, right-click **Active Directory Domains and Trusts**, and then click **Properties**.

   d. On the **UPN Suffixes** tab, type a UPN suffix of *YourFirstName*.msft, click **Add**, and then click **OK**.

2. Enable routing of the new name suffixes that you just created to the nwtraders.msft forest.

    a. In the console tree, right-click **Active Directory Domains and Trusts**, and then click **Connect to Domain Controller**.

    b. In the **Connect to Domain Controller** dialog box, in the **Domain** box, type **nwtraders.msft**

    c. Click **OK** and then click **Yes**.

    d. In the console tree, right-click **nwtraders.msft**, and then click **Properties**.

    e. On the **Trusts** tab, under **Domains that trust this domain (incoming trusts)**, click **nwtraders*x*.msft**, click **Properties**, and then click the **Name Suffix Routing** tab.

    f. In the **Active Directory** dialog box, type a user name of **Administrator** and a password of **P@ssw0rd** and then click **OK**.

    g. On the **Name Suffix Routing** tab, under **Name suffixes in the nwtraders*x* forest**, click *YourFirstName*.**msft**, click **Enable** and then click **OK** twice.

Lesson: Moving Objects in Active Directory

- What Is SID History?
- Implications of Moving Objects
- How to Move Objects Within a Domain
- How to Move Objects Between Domains
- How to Use LDP to View Properties of Moved Objects

Introduction

This lesson discusses SID history and the implications of moving Active Directory objects. It also explains how to move an Active Directory object between containers in the same domain, and between domains in the same forest.

Lesson objectives

After completing this lesson, you will be able to:

- Describe the purpose of SID history.
- Explain the implications of moving objects in Active Directory.
- Move objects in a domain.
- Move objects between domains.
- View the properties of moved objects.

What Is SID History?

SID History

* Is a list of all SIDs that were assigned to a user account
* Provides a migrated user account with continuity of access to resources

Introduction

When you move an Active Directory object, such as a user account, the security principals that are associated with the object also move. Active Directory keeps track of these security principles in a list called the SID history.

The purpose of SID History

SID history provides a migrated user with continuity of access to resources. When you migrate a user account to another domain, Active Directory assigns it a new SID. SID history holds the previous SID of the migrated user account. When you migrate a user account multiple times, SID history stores a list of all SIDs that the user was assigned. It then updates the necessary groups and ACLs with the new account SID. Group memberships based on the old account SID no longer exist.

Implications of Moving Objects

- **Within a domain**
  - No change to SID or GUID
- **Within a forest**
  - New SID
  - SID history
  - Same GUID
- **Across forests**
  - New SID
  - SID history
  - New GUID

Introduction

For SID history to be enabled, the domain functional level must be set to Windows 2000 native or Windows Server 2003. Sid history is disabled if the functional level is set to Windows 2000 mixed. When an object moves within a domain, no change occurs to its SID or to its Globally Unique Identifier (GUID). When you move an object across domains in the same forest, Active Directory assigns the object a new SID but retains its GUID.

Security implications of SID history

SID history allows migrated users continued access resources in their old domains. However, it also allows users to spoof access to other domains—that is, to make a transmission appear to come from an authorized user—by placing SIDs of other domains in the SID history of their user accounts. You can safeguard against such spoofing by applying SID filtering to trust relationships.

Caution   SID filtering is designed to be used on trusts between forests or on external trusts. Using SID filtering between domains in the same forest is a misapplication of SID filtering. If you quarantine a domain within the same forest, SID filtering will remove SIDs that are required for Active Directory replication. Sid filtering can also cause authentication to fail for users from domains that are trusted transitively through the quarantined domain.

To prevent a user account that has been moved between domains from accessing resources with permissions that are associated with the account's SID history attribute, remove the SID history information from the user account.

Note   For more information about removing SID history, see the article 295798, "How to Use Visual Basic Script to Clear SidHistory" in the Microsoft Knowledge Base at http://support.microsoft.com/default.aspx?scid=kb%3Ben-us%3B295758.

Other implications of moving objects

Consider the following additional implications of moving objects in Active Directory:

- User accounts that have administrative privileges for the organizational unit that a user account is moved to can manage the properties of the moved user account.

- The group policy restrictions of the organizational unit, domain, or site that the user account was moved from no longer apply to the user account.

  The Group Policy settings in the new location apply to the user account.

How to Move Objects Within a Domain

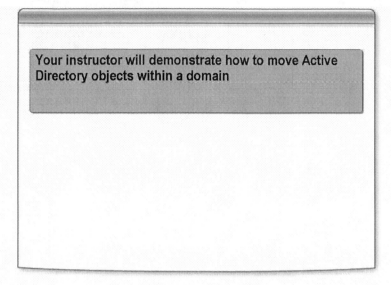

Your instructor will demonstrate how to move Active Directory objects within a domain

Introduction

You use Active Directory Users and Computers to move objects in a domain.

Procedure

To move an object in a domain, perform the following steps:

- In Active Directory Users and Computers, in the details pane, drag the object to the new container.

How to Move Objects Between Domains

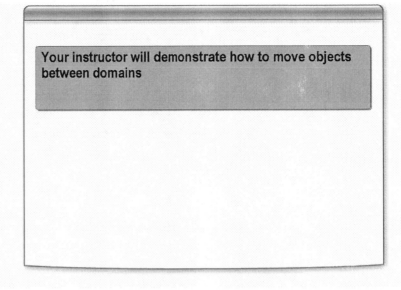

Your instructor will demonstrate how to move objects between domains

Introduction

Use the Active Directory Migration Tool in Windows Server 2003 to move objects from one domain to another or from a domain in one forest to a domain in another forest.

Procedure

To migrate users or groups from one domain to another, perform the following steps:

1. Run the Active Directory Migration Tool.

   Note The Active Directory Migration Tool is not installed by default. You can install it from the \i386\ADMT folder on the Windows Server 2003 compact disc.

2. Right-click **Active Directory Migration Tool**, and then select the wizard for the object that you want to migrate.

   For example, to move a user account, click **User Account Migration Wizard**.

3. On the **Welcome** page, click **Next**.

4. Perform a test migration by performing these steps:

   a. On the **Test or Make Changes** page, click **Test the migration settings and migrate later**, and then click **Next**.

   b. On the **Domain Selection** page, select the source domain and the target domain, and then click **Next**.

   c. On the **User Selection** page, click **Add**, type the object name, click **OK**, and then click **Next**.

   d. On the **Organizational Unit Selection** page, click **Browse**, select the target container, click **OK**, and then click **Next**.

    e. On the **User Options** page, set the user options, and then click **Next**.

        These options determine whether the group membership, profiles, and security settings will be migrated.

    f. If a **Warning** dialog box appears, click **OK**.

    g. On the **Naming Conflicts** page, select the appropriate options to specify what will be done when a naming conflict arises, and then click **Next**.

    h. On the **Completing the User Account Migration Wizard** page, click **Finish**.

    i. In the **Migration Progress** dialog box, click **View Log** to view the error log.

5. Perform an actual migration by repeating steps 2 through 4.l. In step 4.a, select **Migrate now** instead of **Test the migration settings and migrate later**.

How to Use LDP to View Properties of Moved Objects

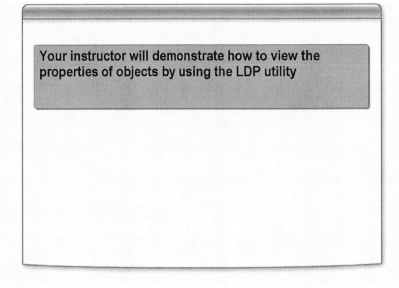

Your instructor will demonstrate how to view the properties of objects by using the LDP utility

Introduction

After you move a user, group, or other object, verify that the object's properties have been updated correctly. For example, check the SID and SID History properties of the object. To view this information, use Ldp.exe. You must install the Windows Support Tools from the \Support\Tools folder on the Windows Server 2003 compact disc before you can use Ldp.exe.

Procedure

To view the properties of a moved object, perform the following steps:

1. Click **Start**, click **Run**, type **ldp** and then click **OK**.

2. In the **Ldp** dialog box, on the **Connection** menu, click **Connect**.

3. In the **Connect** dialog box, in the **Server** box, type the name of your server, and then click **OK**.

4. In the **Ldp** dialog box, on the **Connection** menu, click **Bind**.

5. In the **Bind** dialog box, type a user name of **Administrator**, the Administrator's password, and the name of the domain that you want to examine, and then click **OK**.

6. On the **View** menu, click **Tree**.

7. In the **Tree View** dialog box, in the **BaseDN** list, select the appropriate domain name from the list, and then click **OK**.

8. In the console tree, double-click the object that you want to view the properties for.

9. In the details pane, view the properties of the object.

Practice: Moving Objects

In this practice, you will use Ldp.exe to:

• Examine the SID, SIDHistory, and GUID of a user object.

• Move a user object to another organizational unit in the same domain.

• View any changes to the SID, SIDHistory, and GUID of the user object.

Objectives

In this practice, you will perform the following tasks:

- Use Ldp.exe to examine the SID, SID history, and GUID of a user object.

- Move a user object to another organizational unit in the same domain.

- Use Ldp.exe to view any changes to the SID, SID history, and GUID of the user object.

Scenario

Your organization has 2,000 users. Brenda Diaz, a user in your domain, has taken a new position in the company. You must move her user account object to correspond to her new job role.

Practice

▶ **Move a user account and view the changes that move made to the account**

1. Log on as **Nwtraders**x*ComputerName***User** with a password of **P@ssw0rd**

2. Use Ldp.exe to examine the SID, SIDHistory, and GUID of Brenda Diaz's user object in the *YourComputerName*\\Sales organizational unit in the domain that is hosted by your student computer.

   a. Click **Start**, click **Command Prompt**, type **ldp** and then press ENTER.

   b. In the **Ldp** dialog box, on the **Connection** menu, click **Connect**.

   c. In the **Connect** dialog box, in the **Server** text box, type the name of your server, and then click **OK**.

   d. In the **Ldp** dialog box, on the **Connection** menu, click **Bind**.

   e. In the **Bind** dialog box, type a user name of **Administrator**, a password of **P@ssw0rd**, and the name of the domain hosted by your server, and then click **OK**.

   f. On the **View** menu, click **Tree**.

   g. In the **Tree View** dialog box, in the **BaseDN** list, select your domain name, and then click **OK**.

h. In the console tree, expand your domain, double-click *YourComputerName*, double-click the object for the Sales organizational unit, and then double-click the user object for Brenda Diaz.

i. In the details pane, view the properties of the object.

     i. What is the objectGUID of this account?

     _____

     ii. What is the objectSid of this account?

     _____

     iii. Is there a sIDHistory entry for this user account? If yes, what SIDs are listed?

     _____

3. Move the user object for Brenda Diaz to the *YourComputerName*\HR organizational unit in your domain.

a. Use **Run as** to start Active Directory Users and Computers as *YourDomain***Administrator** with a password of **P@ssw0rd**

b. In the details pane, drag the **BrendaDia** user object from the *YourComputerName*\Sales organizational unit to the *YourComputerName*\HR organizational unit.

4. Use Ldp.exe to see if any changes occurred to the SID, SIDHistory, or GUID of the user object for Brenda Diaz.

    a. In the console tree, double-click **HR**, and then double-click the user object for Brenda Diaz.

    b. In the details pane, view the properties of the object.

    Were there any changes to the SID, SIDHistory, or GUID of this account? If so, which ones changed?

    _____

    _____

Lesson: Planning a User, Group, and Computer Account Strategy

- Guidelines for Naming Accounts
- Guidelines for Setting a Password Policy
- Guidelines for Authenticating, Authorizing, and Administering Accounts
- Guidelines for Planning a Group Strategy

Introduction

This lesson describes guidelines for planning a user and computer account strategy. A well-planned account strategy helps prevent a security breech in your network.

Lesson objectives

After completing this lesson, you will be able to:

- Explain guidelines for defining an account naming convention.
- Explain guidelines for setting a password policy.
- Explain guidelines for authenticating, authorizing, and administering user accounts.
- Explain guidelines for planning a group account strategy.

Guidelines for Naming Accounts

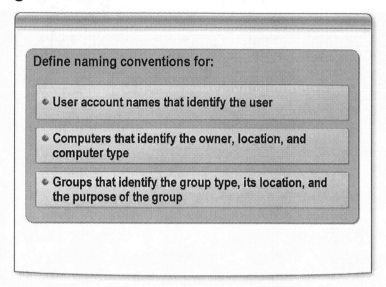

Introduction

When you create an account strategy for the forests and domains in your organization's network, you must set up conventions for naming accounts.

Guidelines

The following guidelines apply to naming user, computer, and group accounts in a Windows Server 2003 network.

- Define a user account naming convention for your organization that makes the user names easy for other users to identify and enables you to manage user name conflicts for users who have very similar names. The naming convention should include:

  - The user's first name, the first three characters of it, or the first initial of the user. For example, use Brenda for the user Brenda Diaz.

  - The first initial, the first few letters of the user's last name, or the complete last name of the user. For example, use BrendaDiaz for the user Brenda Diaz.

  - Additional characters from the first or last name, or the user's middle initial, to resolve naming conflicts.

Consider using:

- Prefixes or suffixes to identify special user account types, such as contractors, part-time personnel, and service accounts.

- An alternative domain name for the UPN suffix to increase logon security and simplify logon names.

  For example, if your organization has a deep domain tree that is organized by department and region, domain names can get quite long. The default UPN suffix for a user in that domain could be sales.example.nwtraders.msft. The logon name for a user named Brenda Diaz in that domain could be BDiaz@sales.example.nwtraders.msft. However, if you create the suffix nwtraders or nwtraders.msft, a user can log on by using the much simpler logon name of BDiaz@nwtraders or BDiaz@nwtraders.msft. It is not necessary for these alternative UPN suffix to be a valid DNS name.

- Define a computer account naming convention that identifies the computer's owner, location, and computer type. Include the following information in the naming convention.

Naming convention	Example
Owner's user name	BrendaD1
Location or an abbreviation	RED or Redmond
Type of computer or an abbreviation	SVR or server

- Define a group naming convention that identifies the group type, its location, and the purpose of the group. Include the following information in the naming convention.

Naming convention	Example
Group type	G for global group, UN for universal group, DL for domain local group
Location of the group	Red for Redmond
Purpose of the group	Admins for administrators

Guidelines for Setting a Password Policy

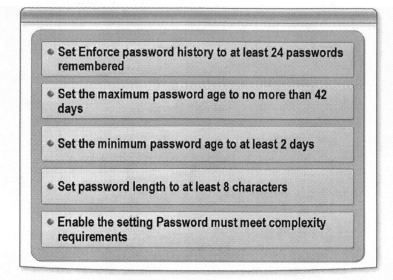

- Set Enforce password history to at least 24 passwords remembered
- Set the maximum password age to no more than 42 days
- Set the minimum password age to at least 2 days
- Set password length to at least 8 characters
- Enable the setting Password must meet complexity requirements

Introduction

The role that passwords play in securing an organization's network is often underestimated and overlooked. Passwords provide the first line of defense against unauthorized access to your organization.

The Windows Server 2003 family includes a new feature that checks the complexity of the password for the Administrator account. If the password is blank or does not meet complexity requirements, the **Windows Setup** dialog box appears, warning you about the dangers of not using a strong password for the Administrator account. If you leave the password blank, you cannot access the account over the network.

Guidelines

A password policy ensures that every user is following the password guidelines that you determine are appropriate for your organization. Define the following elements of a password policy:

- Define the **Enforce password history** policy setting to remember at least 24 previous passwords. This way, users cannot use the same password when their password expires.

- Define the **Maximum password age** policy setting so that passwords expire as often as necessary for your environment and the access level of users. This policy setting prevents an attacker who cracks a password from accessing the network until the password expires. For users who have domain administrator access, set the maximum password age lower than that for normal users.

- Define the **Minimum password age** policy setting so that users cannot change their passwords until after a certain number of days. When you define a minimum password age, users cannot repeatedly change their passwords to avoid the **Enforce password history** policy setting and then use their original password.

- Define a **Minimum password length** policy setting so that passwords must consist of a minimum number of characters. Long passwords—at least eight characters—are usually stronger than short ones. This policy setting also prevents users from using blank passwords.

- Enable the **Password must meet complexity requirements** policy setting. This setting checks all new passwords to ensure that they meet basic strong password requirements.

A strong password has the following characteristics:

- Is at least eight characters long.

- Does not contain a user name, real name, or company name.

- Does not contain a complete dictionary word.

- Is significantly different from previous passwords. Passwords that are incremental (*Password1*, *Password2*, *Password3*...) are weak.

- Contains uppercase and lowercase characters, numerals, and symbols.

- Contains extended ASCII characters. These characters include accent marks, and special symbols used for creating pictures.

Examples of strong passwords are *H!elZl2o* and *J*p2leO4>©F*.

Caution Any potential attacker can find extended ASCII characters in the Character Map. Do not use an extended character if a keystroke is not defined for it in the lower-right corner of the Character Map. Before you use extended ASCII characters in your password, test them thoroughly to make sure that passwords that contain extended ASCII characters are compatible with the applications that your organization uses. Be especially cautious about using extended ASCII characters in passwords if your organization uses several operating systems.

The following table shows recommended minimum password policy settings for secure network environments.

Setting	Value
Enforce password history	24 passwords remembered
Maximum password age	42 days
Minimum password age	2 days
Minimum password length	8 characters
Password must meet complexity requirements	Enabled
Store password using reversible encryption	Disabled

Tip If you create a root domain in your forest for the purpose of placing administrative accounts, consider requiring more stringent password policy settings on this domain than on your account domain. For example, consider requiring a maximum password age of 30 days, a minimum password age of seven days, and a minimum password length of 14 characters.

Guidelines for Authenticating, Authorizing, and Administering Accounts

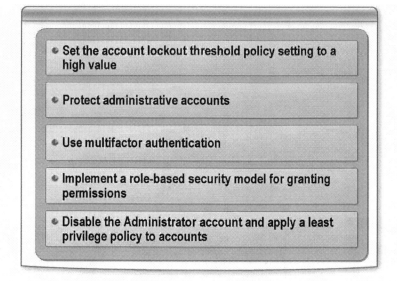

Introduction

Planning an account authentication, authorization, and administration strategy will help protect your organization's network. For example, implement an account lockout policy to help prevent an attack on your organization. However, use care when you create an account lockout policy to avoid unintentionally locking out authorized users.

Guidelines

Use the following guidelines to authenticate, authorize, and administer accounts in your organization:

- *Set the Account lockout threshold policy setting to a high value.* This way, authorized users are not locked out of their user accounts if they mistype a password.

  Windows can lock out authorized users if they change their passwords on one computer but not on another. The computer that uses the old password continuously attempts to authenticate the user with the wrong password. Eventually, the computer locks out the user account until the account is restored. This issue does not exist for organizations that use only domain controllers that are members of the Windows Server 2003 family.

- *Avoid using administrative accounts to perform routine computing needs.* Also, minimize the number of administrators and avoid giving users administrative access. Require administrators to log on by using a regular user account and to use the **runas** command to perform all administrative tasks.

- *Use multifactor authentication.* For example, require smart cards for administrative accounts and remote access to help validate that the user is who he claims to be.

- *Use security groups based on the A-G-U-DL-P strategy.* This strategy provides the most flexibility while also reducing the complexity of assigning access permissions to the network. Also, implement a role-based security model for granting permissions. In the A-G-U-DL-P strategy domain:

  - User accounts (A) are added into global groups (G).

  - Global groups are added into universal groups (U).

  - Universal groups are added into domain local groups (DL).

  - Resource permissions (P) are assigned to the domain local groups.

- *Disable the Administrator account and assign users and administrators the least privilege they require to perform their job tasks.*

  You can never delete or remove the Administrator account from the Administrators built-in group. However, it is a good practice to disable the account. Even when an Administrator account is disabled, an attacker or an unauthorized user can use safe mode to gain access to a domain controller. The only way to prevent this is to ensure that servers are physically secure.

Guidelines for Planning a Group Strategy

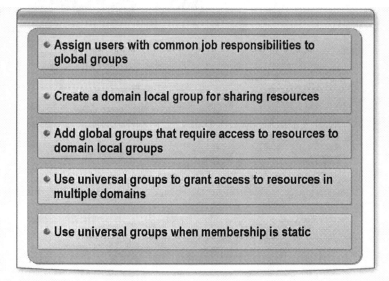

* Assign users with common job responsibilities to global groups

* Create a domain local group for sharing resources

* Add global groups that require access to resources to domain local groups

* Use universal groups to grant access to resources in multiple domains

* Use universal groups when membership is static

Introduction

Planning a group strategy involves planning for how you will use global groups, domain local groups, and universal groups to simplify administrative tasks.

Guidelines

Use the following guidelines to plan a group strategy:

- *Assign users with common job responsibilities to global groups*. Identify groups based on the tasks that the members perform. Create global groups for these users, and add users who have common responsibilities to these groups.

- *Create a domain local group for sharing resources*. Identify shared resources, such as printers, files, and folders. Next, create a domain local group for each of the resources and add users who require access to these resources.

- *Add global groups that require access to resources to domain local groups*. When you want to share a resource on a domain across several global groups, add these global groups to the domain local group that grants access to the shared resource.

- *Use universal groups to grant access to resources in multiple domains*. If user accounts require access to file shares that are located in a different domain from the user accounts, create a universal group for these users and grant access to the universal group for the file shares.

- *Use universal groups when membership is static*. Universal groups work best when you add users who are unlikely to be removed frequently from the universal group. Active Directory replicates any changes in membership across a universal group, which increases network traffic.

Note If the forest functional level is set to Windows 2000 native and a change occurs to the membership of a universal group, Active Directory replicates the entire membership list to all other global catalog servers. If the forest functional level is set to Windows Server 2003, only the changes are replicated to the other Global Catalog servers. In other words, more frequent changes to universal group membership have less effect on the network than in a Windows 2000 forest functional level.

Planning group accounts

Use the following table to plan group accounts. It contains sample information for a universal group named U RedAccts, which is created in the Redmond domain. Its members include global groups from the London, Vancouver, and Denver domains.

Group	Description	Location	Type	Members
U RedAccts	Accountants	Redmond domain	Universal group	G LonAccts
				G VanAccts
				G DenAccts

Practice: Planning an Account Strategy

In this practice, you will determine:

- An account naming strategy
- A password policy
- An authentication, authorization, and administration strategy
- A group strategy for your forest

Objectives

In this practice, you will:

- Determine the account naming strategy.
- Determine the password policy.
- Determine the authentication, authorization, and administration strategy.
- Determine the group strategy for your forest.

Scenario

Your company is in a highly competitive corporate environment. Maintaining the security of your company's business information and trade secrets is critical. Your organization has 1,000 users in an Active Directory forest. The forest consists of an empty root domain named nwtraders.msft, a child domain named corp.nwtraders.msft that contains all of your user and group accounts. All domain controllers in your forest run Windows Server 2003. The root domain contains only administrative accounts, which you use to perform forest-wide administrative tasks.

Practice

▶ **Plan and Account Strategy**

1. What account naming policy will you use for users in the corp domain?

    _____

    _____

2. What password policy settings will you use for the corp domain?

    _____

    _____

    _____

    _____

3. What password policy settings will you use for your root domain?

    _____

    _____

    _____

    _____

4. What will your authentication, authorization, and administration strategy include?

_____

_____

_____

_____

5. What will your group strategy include?

_____

_____

_____

_____

Lesson: Planning an Active Directory Audit Strategy

- Why Audit Access to Active Directory?
- Guidelines for Monitoring Changes to Active Directory

Introduction

After completing this lesson, you will understand why it is important to audit user access to Active Directory and be able to plan an Active Directory audit strategy.

Lesson objectives

After completing this lesson, you will be able to:

- Explain the need for auditing access to Active Directory.

- Explain guidelines for monitoring modifications to Active Directory.

Why Audit Access to Active Directory?

- To record all successful changes to Active Directory
- To track access to a resource or by a specific account
- To detect and log failed access attempts

Introduction

You use auditing to track security-related activities on a system. Because Active Directory stores information about all objects that exist on a Windows Server 2003 network, you must track changes to these objects and their attributes. For example, you may want to audit changes to group membership or changes to the Active Directory infrastructure components, such as site objects or the Active Directory schema.

Purpose of auditing Active Directory

When you audit Active Directory, you record successful changes to Active Directory and failed attempts to make changes to Active Directory in order to:

- *Record all successful changes to Active Directory.* Recording all successful changes helps ensure that authorized personnel are not performing unauthorized changes to Active Directory objects. It is also useful to fix incorrect changes to Active Directory. For example, if permissions were applied to the wrong group, thereby giving the wrong set of people access to resources, you can use the audit trail to identify when the change was made and who made it.

- *Track access to a resource or by a specific account.* Tracking access helps you understand events that occur on your network. For example, if an application uses a service account to access resources, and the application malfunctions, the audit trail can help identify what went wrong.

- *Detect and log failed access attempts.* Recording failed attempts to access resources or to make changes to Active Directory helps identify external as well as internal security threats.

To audit successful or failed changes to Active Directory objects or attributes, you must enable auditing of directory services on all domain controllers and configure the system access control list (SACL) for each object or attribute that you want to audit.

Guidelines for Monitoring Changes to Active Directory

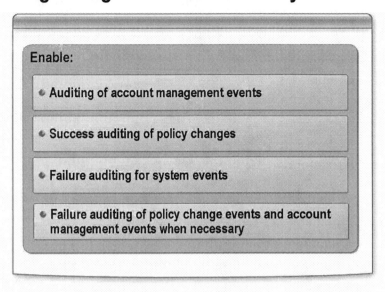

Enable:

- Auditing of account management events
- Success auditing of policy changes
- Failure auditing for system events
- Failure auditing of policy change events and account management events when necessary

Introduction

Successful audits generate an audit entry when any account management event succeeds. Although successful account management events are usually innocuous, they provide an invaluable record of activities that may compromise the security of a network.

Guidelines

Use the following guidelines when you create an audit strategy:

- *Enable auditing of account management events*. Audit the following successful changes:

  - The creation, modification, or deletion of user or group accounts

  - The enabling, disabling, or renaming of user accounts

  - The changing of passwords or the computer's security policy

- *Enable success auditing of policy changes*. If auditing of these changes and account management policy changes are not enabled, an attacker can potentially subvert the security of a network without an audit trail.

  For example, if an administrator made the user account Sally a member of the Backup Operators group, auditing would record an account management event. However, if the same administrator granted Sally's account the **Backup files and folder** advanced user right, auditing would not record an account management event.

- *Enable failure auditing of system events.* This security setting generates an event when a user unsuccessfully attempts to restart or shut down a computer or unsuccessfully attempts to modify the system security or the security log. Enable this audit policy setting for the entire domain.

  Failure events in the system event category can detect unusual activity, such as an intruder who is trying to gain access to your computer or network. The number of audits that are generated when this setting is enabled tends to be relatively low, and the quality of information that is gained from the events tends to be relatively high.

- *Enable failure auditing of policy change events and account management events only when necessary.* The number of audits that are generated when these settings are enabled can be very high, so enable this setting only when necessary.

Caution   Enabling failure audits for these events can pose a risk to your organization. If users attempt to access a resource for which they are not authorized, they can create so many failure audits that the security log becomes full, and the computer cannot collect more audits. If the **Audit: Shut down system immediately if unable to log security audits** policy setting is enabled, servers will shut down when the log becomes full. Intruders can initiate a denial-of-service attack by using your audit policy if this is the case.

Note   For information about how to enable auditing, see Module 10, "Auditing Accounts and Resources," in Course 2274: *Administering Microsoft Windows Server 2003 Accounts and Resources*.

Practice: Planning an Audit Strategy

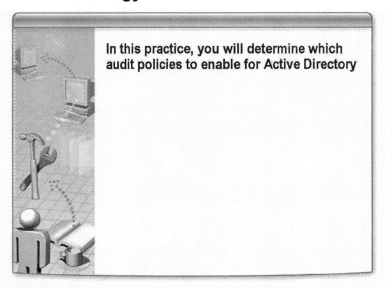

In this practice, you will determine which audit policies to enable for Active Directory

Objectives

In this practice, you will determine which audit policies to enable for Active Directory.

Scenario

You must plan an audit policy for Northwind Traders, which has 1,000 users in an Active Directory forest. Your forest consists of an empty root domain named nwtraders.msft and a child domain named corp.nwtraders.msft. The child domain contains all of your user and group accounts.

Practice

▶ **Plan an audit strategy**

- Which events will you enable auditing for?

_____

_____

Lab A: Implementing an Account and Audit Strategy

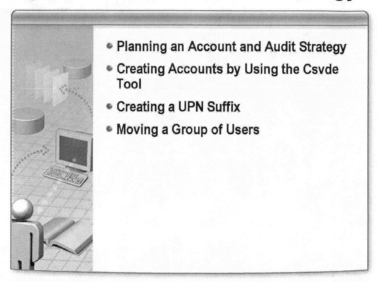

- Planning an Account and Audit Strategy
- Creating Accounts by Using the Csvde Tool
- Creating a UPN Suffix
- Moving a Group of Users

Objectives

After completing this lab, you will be able to:

- Plan a strategy for user, group, and computer accounts.
- Plan an Active Directory audit strategy.
- Create multiple user and computer accounts.
- Implement UPN suffixes.
- Move objects within a domain and across domains in a forest.

Prerequisites

Before working on this lab, you must:

- Know the guidelines for planning an account strategy.
- Know the guidelines for planning an audit strategy.

Scenario

Northwind Traders is implementing Windows Server 2003 on its network. It plans to use a forest with two domains—an empty root domain and a corporate domain. The corporate domain will contain the user, group, and computer accounts.

Estimated time to complete this lab: 60 minutes

Exercise 1
Planning an Account and Audit Strategy

In this exercise, you will plan an account naming strategy for the new forest at Northwind Traders. Use the guidelines that the Engineering and Design team gave you.

Scenario

The new forest will consist of an empty root domain named nwtraders.msft and a child domain named corp.nwtraders.msft, which will contain all of the user accounts. Northwind traders has offices in seven cities.

Your account and audit strategy should take into account the following requirements:

- The strategy for naming user accounts must make it easy for employees who know only the first and last name of another user to determine the user's e-mail address.

- The strategy for naming computer accounts must make it easy for employees to identify a computer's location and purpose.

- All employees must have an e-mail address of *UserName*@nwtraders.msft.

- The audit strategy must be able to detect attempted, unauthorized modifications to Active Directory.

Tasks
1. Plan a user account naming strategy for the nwtraders.msft forest.
❓ What will user account names consist of?
❓ What strategy will you use to resolve user account naming conflicts?
❓ What will you use for a UPN suffix for user accounts?
2. Plan a computer account naming strategy for the nwtraders.msft forest.
❓ What naming convention will you use for server computers?

(continued)

Tasks
?   What naming convention will you use for client computers?   _____   _____
3.   Plan a password policy for the nwtraders.msft forest.
?   What password policy settings will you apply to the nwtraders.msft domain?   _____   _____
?   What password policy settings will you apply to the corp.nwtraders.msft domain?   _____   _____
4.   Plan an audit strategy for the nwtraders.msft forest.
?   Which success audit settings will you include in your plan?   _____   _____
?   Which failure audit settings will you include in your plan?   _____   _____

Exercise 2
Creating Accounts Using the Csvde Tool

In this exercise, you will use the Csvde command-line tool to import multiple accounts into Active Directory from a .csv import file, which has been created for you by using Microsoft Excel.

Scenario

As one of the administrators at Northwind Traders, you receive requests daily for new user accounts. A team member enters the requests in a spreadsheet, which is saved in a comma separated value (.csv) format. At the beginning of each business day, you are responsible for importing this file into Active Directory to create the user accounts.

Tasks	Specific instructions
1. Use the Csvde command-line tool to import the .csv file into Active Directory.	▪ The name of the .csv file is the same as the domain that is hosted by your computer. You find this file in the *<install folder>*MOC\2279\Labfiles\Lab4 folder on your computer.
2. Use Active Directory Users and Computers to determine which new organizational units, users, and groups were created.	

❓ Which new organizational units were created?

_____

_____

❓ Which of the new organizational units contain user and group accounts?

_____

_____

Exercise 3
Creating a UPN Suffix

In this exercise, you will create a UPN suffix and then troubleshoot a UPN suffix routing conflict between two forests.

Scenario

Users in your domain have requested the ability to log on to their domain by using a UPN suffix that consists only of the name of the city in which they are located. You will create the UPN suffix in your forest for your city.

Tasks	Specific instructions
1. Create a new UPN suffix in your forest named *YourCityName*.	a. Log on as **Nwtraders***x**ComputerName***User** with a password of **P@ssw0rd** b. Use **Run as** to start Active Directory Domains and Trusts as *YourDomain***Administrator** with a password of **P@ssw0rd**
2. Enable routing of the new UPN suffix to the nwtraders.msft forest.	
❷ What is the status of the *YourCityName* UPN suffix after you enable it?	
❷ What can you do to resolve this UPN suffix routing conflict?	

Exercise 4
Moving a Group of Users

In this exercise, you will grant global group permissions to a shared folder on your server. You will then move the group and its members to an organizational unit in the other domain in your forest. Finally, you will verify that the moved group still has permissions to the shared folder on your server.

Scenario

As a result of a recent reorganization at Northwind Traders, a group of users must move to a new location. This move also affects Active Directory because the group and its user accounts must be moved to another location in the forest. It will be several months before the servers that contain the user's data can be moved. You must ensure that users can still access their files after their accounts have been moved.

Tasks	Specific instructions
1. Create and share a folder on your server named ITAdmin, and then grant the G IT Admins global group full control NTFS permissions to the folder and full control permissions to the share.	a. Log on as **Nwtraders*x****ComputerName*User** with a password of **P@ssw0rd** b. Use **Run as** to start Computer Management as *YourDomain***Administrator** with a password of **P@ssw0rd**
2. Use Ldp.exe to examine the SID, SID history, and GUID of the G IT Admins global group object in the IT Admin\IT Groups organizational unit in the domain that is hosted by your student computer.	
❓ What is listed for the objectGUID, objectSID, and sIDHistory entries for the G IT Admins global group?	
_____ _____	
3. Install the Active Directory Migration Tool on your computer.	a. Use **Run as** to start a command prompt as *YourDomain***Administrator** with a password of **P@ssw0rd** b. At the command prompt, start the installation by typing **\\London\OS\ADMT\ADMIGRATION.MSI** and then press ENTER to start the installation.

(continued)

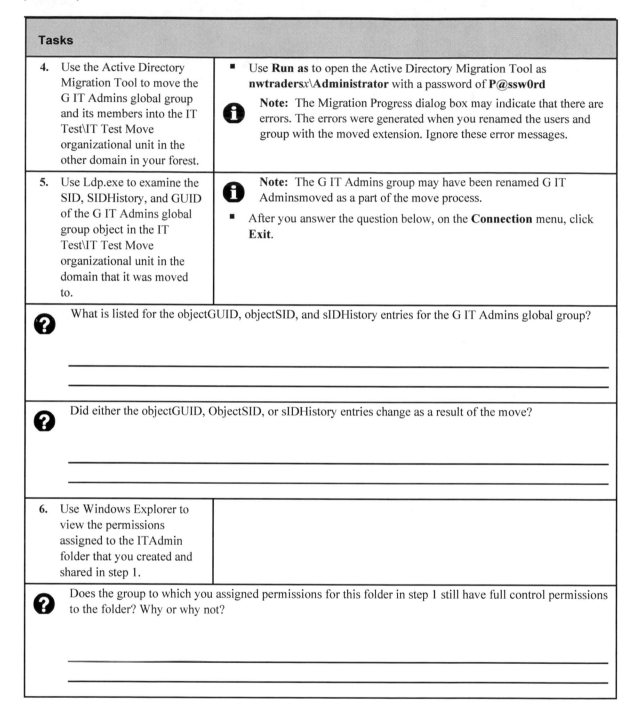

Tasks	
4. Use the Active Directory Migration Tool to move the G IT Admins global group and its members into the IT Test\IT Test Move organizational unit in the other domain in your forest.	▪ Use **Run as** to open the Active Directory Migration Tool as **nwtradersx\Administrator** with a password of **P@ssw0rd** ⓘ **Note:** The Migration Progress dialog box may indicate that there are errors. The errors were generated when you renamed the users and group with the moved extension. Ignore these error messages.
5. Use Ldp.exe to examine the SID, SIDHistory, and GUID of the G IT Admins global group object in the IT Test\IT Test Move organizational unit in the domain that it was moved to.	ⓘ **Note:** The G IT Admins group may have been renamed G IT Adminsmoved as a part of the move process. ▪ After you answer the question below, on the **Connection** menu, click **Exit**.

❓ What is listed for the objectGUID, objectSID, and sIDHistory entries for the G IT Admins global group?

_____

_____

❓ Did either the objectGUID, ObjectSID, or sIDHistory entries change as a result of the move?

_____

_____

| 6. Use Windows Explorer to view the permissions assigned to the ITAdmin folder that you created and shared in step 1. | |

❓ Does the group to which you assigned permissions for this folder in step 1 still have full control permissions to the folder? Why or why not?

_____

_____

Microsoft®
Training &
Certification

Module 5: Implementing Group Policy

Contents

Overview

- Creating and Configuring GPOs
- Configuring Group Policy Refresh Rates and Group Policy Settings
- Managing GPOs
- Verifying and Troubleshooting Group Policy
- Delegating Administrative Control of Group Policy
- Planning a Group Policy Strategy for the Enterprise

Introduction

You use Group Policy in the Active Directory® directory service to centrally manage users and computers in an enterprise. You can centralize policies by setting Group Policy for an entire organization at the site domain or at an organizational unit level. Or, you can decentralize Group Policy settings by setting Group Policy for each department at an organizational unit level.

You can ensure that users have the user environments that they require to perform their jobs and enforce an organization's policies, including business rules, goals, and security requirements. Additionally, you can lower the total cost of ownership by controlling user and computer environments, thereby reducing the level of technical support that users require and the lost user productivity due to user error.

Objectives

After completing this module, you will be able to:

- Create and configure Group Policy objects (GPOs).
- Configure Group Policy refresh rates and Group Policy settings.
- Manage GPOs.
- Verify and troubleshoot Group Policy.
- Delegate administrative control of Group Policy.
- Plan a Group Policy strategy for the enterprise.

Lesson: Creating and Configuring GPOs

* Multimedia: Review of Group Policy
* GPO Components
* Why Specify a Domain Controller for Managing GPOs?
* How to Specify a Domain Controller for Managing GPOs
* What Are WMI Filters?
* How to Filter Group Policy Settings Using WMI Filters
* What Is Loopback Processing?
* How to Configure the User Group Policy Loopback Processing Mode

Introduction

Group Policy gives you administrative control over users and computers in your network. By using Group Policy, you can define the state of a user's work environment once, and then rely on Microsoft® Windows® Server 2003 to continually enforce the Group Policy settings that you defined. You can apply Group Policy settings across an entire organization or to specific groups of users and computers.

Lesson objectives

After completing this lesson, you will be able to:

- Explain the purpose of Group Policy and how it is processed in Active Directory.
- Describe GPO components.
- Explain the purpose of specifying a domain controller for GPO management.
- Specify a domain controller for managing GPOs.
- Explain the purpose of Windows Management Instrumentation (WMI) filters.
- Filter Group Policy settings by using WMI filters.
- Explain the purpose of loopback processing.
- Configure the User Group Policy loopback processing mode.

Multimedia: Review of Group Policy

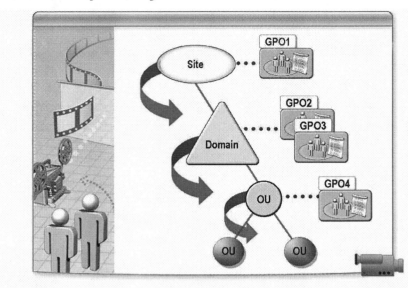

File location

To view the *Review of Group Policy* presentation, open the Web page on the Student Materials compact disc, click **Multimedia**, and then click the title of the presentation. Do not open this presentation unless the instructor tells you to.

Objectives

After completing this lesson, you will be able to:

- Describe the types of settings that you can define in Group Policy.

- Describe how Windows Server 2003 applies Group Policy objects.

Types of settings

You can configure Group Policy settings to define the policies that affect users and computers. The following table presents the types of settings that you can configure.

Type of setting	Description
Administrative templates	Registry-based settings for configuring application settings and user workstation environments
Scripts	Settings for specifying when Windows Server 2003 runs specific scripts
Remote installation services	Settings that control the options available to users when they run the Client Installation Wizard used by Remote Installation Services (RIS)
Internet Explorer maintenance	Settings for administering and customizing Microsoft Internet Explorer on computers running Windows Server 2003
Folder redirection	Settings for storing specific user profile folders on a network server
Security	Settings for configuring local computer, domain, and network security
Software installation	Settings for centralizing the management of software installations, updates, and removals

Flow of inheritance

GPOs are linked to sites, domains, and organizational units. You can set centralized policies that affect the entire organization and decentralized policies that affect a particular department. There is no hierarchy of domains like there is for organizational units, such as parent and child organizational units.

Order in which GPOs are processed

The order in which Windows Server 2003 applies GPOs is based on the Active Directory container that the GPOs are linked to. Windows Server 2003 applies the GPOs first to the site, then to domains, and then to organizational units within the domains.

Multivalued GPO settings

Some GPO settings are multivalued. These settings are treated like single valued settings. That is, if the setting is defined in multiple GPOs, only the settings in one of the GPOs that adheres to the inheritance rules apply.

Block Inheritance

You can prevent a child container from inheriting all GPOs from parent containers by enabling Block Inheritance on the child container. Block Inheritance is useful when an Active Directory container requires unique Group Policy settings.

Enforced option

The **Enforced** (named **No Override** if the Group Policy Management console is not installed) option is an attribute of the link, not of the GPO. If the same GPO is linked elsewhere, the **Enforced** option does not apply to that link unless you modify that link as well. If you have a GPO that is linked to multiple containers, you can configure the **Enforced** option individually for each container. When more than one link is set to **Enforced**, the linked GPOs apply to a common container. If they contain conflicting settings, the GPO that is highest in the Active Directory hierarchy takes precedence.

Filter GPOs

You may need to link GPOs that are associated with other directory objects. By setting the appropriate permissions for security groups, you can filter Group Policy to apply only to the computers and users you specify.

The Group Policy Management console

The Group Policy Management console is a set of programmable interfaces for managing Group Policy and a Microsoft Management Console (MMC) snap-in that is built on those programmable interfaces. Together, the components of Group Policy Management unify the management of Group Policy across the enterprise.

Note   For more information about creating and linking GPOs and Group Policy inheritance, see Module 8, "Implementing Group Policy," in Course 2274, *Managing a Microsoft Windows Server 2003 Environment.*

GPO Components

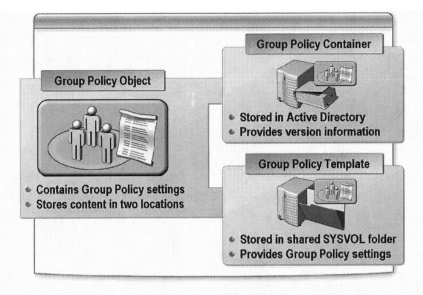

Introduction	Windows Server 2003 applies the Group Policy settings that are contained in the GPO to the user and computer objects in the site, domain, or organizational unit that the GPO is associated with. The content of a GPO is stored in two locations: the Group Policy container (GPC) and the Group Policy template (GPT).
The Group Policy container	The GPC is an Active Directory object that contains GPO status, version information, WMI filter information, and a list of components that have settings in the GPO. Computers can access the GPC to locate Group Policy templates, and domain controllers can access the GPC to obtain version information. If the domain controller does not have the most recent version of the GPO, replication occurs to obtain the latest version of the GPO.
The Group Policy template	The GPT is a folder hierarchy in the shared SYSVOL folder on a domain controller. When you create a GPO, Windows Server 2003 creates the corresponding GPT, which contains all Group Policy settings and information, including administrative templates, security, software installation, scripts, and folder redirection settings. Computers connect to the SYSVOL folder to obtain the settings.

The name of the GPT folder is the globally unique identifier (GUID) of the GPO that you created. It is identical to the GUID that Active Directory uses to identify the GPO in the GPC. The path to the GPT on a domain controller is *systemroot*\SYSVOL\sysvol.

Note For more information about GPC, see "GPO Components" in Module 5 on the Appendices page on the Student Materials compact disc.

Why Specify a Domain Controller for Managing GPOs?

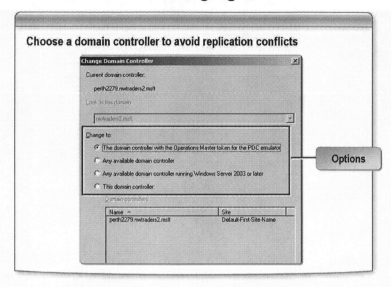

Introduction

Group Policy Management uses the primary domain controller (PDC) emulator in each domain as the default domain controller.

Why select a specific domain controller?

To avoid replication conflicts, consider the selection of domain controller, especially because the GPO data resides in both Active Directory and the SYSVOL folder. Active Directory uses two independent replication mechanisms to replicate GPO data to the various domain controllers in the domain. If two administrators simultaneously edit the same GPO on different domain controllers, one administrator's changes can overwrite those made by the other administrator, depending on replication latency.

The PDC emulator

By default, the Group Policy Management console uses the PDC emulator in each domain to ensure that all administrators use the same domain controller. However, you may not always want to use the PDC emulator. For example, if you reside in a remote location, or if the majority of the users or computers targeted by the GPO are in a remote location, you may want to target a domain controller there.

Important   If multiple administrators manage a common GPO, it is recommended that all administrators use the same domain controller when editing a particular GPO to avoid collisions in File Replication Services (FRS).

Options for selecting a domain controller

You can specify a domain controller to manage GPOs by selecting any of the following options:

- **The domain controller with the Operations Master token for the PDC emulator**. This is the default and the preferred option.

- **Any available domain controller**. When you use this option, you are likely selecting a domain controller in the local site.

- **Any available domain controller running Windows 2003 or later**. This option is unavailable in environments that contain both Windows Server 2003 and Windows 2000 servers.

- **This domain controller**. When you use this option, you are selecting the current domain controller.

How to Specify a Domain Controller for Managing GPOs

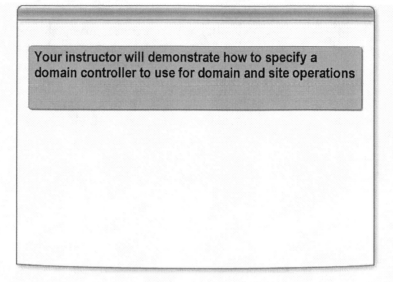

Your instructor will demonstrate how to specify a domain controller to use for domain and site operations

Introduction

You use the Group Policy Management console to specify a domain controller for domains or sites.

Procedure

To specify a domain controller, perform the following steps:

1. Open Group Policy Management, expand the forest, expand **Domains**, and then use one of the following methods:

   - To specify a domain controller to use for domain operations, right-click the required domain, and then click **Change Domain Controller**.

   - To specify a domain controller to use for operations on sites, right-click **Sites**, and then click **Change Domain Controller**.

2. In the **Change Domain Controller** dialog box, under **Change to**, click **This domain controller**, and then click **OK**.

What Are WMI Filters?

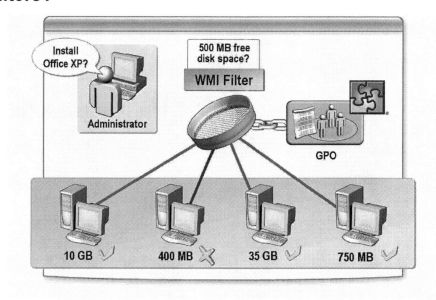

Introduction

You use Windows Management Instrumentation (WMI) filters to dynamically determine the scope of GPOs based on attributes of the user or computer. In this way, you can extend the filtering capabilities for GPOs beyond the security group filtering mechanisms that were previously available.

How does a WMI filter work?

A WMI filter is linked to a GPO. When you apply a GPO to the destination computer, Active Directory evaluates the filter on the destination computer. A WMI filter consists of one or more queries that Active Directory evaluates against the WMI repository of the destination computer. If the total set of queries is false, Active Directory does not apply the GPO. If all queries are true, Active Directory applies the GPO. You write the query by using the WMI Query Language (WQL), which is a language similar to SQL for querying the WMI repository.

Each GPO can have only one WMI filter. However, you can link the same WMI filter to multiple GPOs. Like GPOs, WMI filters apply to only one domain object at a time.

Uses of WMI filters

You can use WMI filters to target policies based on various objects in the network. The following list includes some sample uses of WMI filters.

- *Services*. Computers where DHCP is installed and running.

- *Hardware inventory*. Computers that have a Pentium III processor and at least 128 megabytes (MB) of RAM.

- *Software configuration*. Computers with multicasting turned on.

For client computers running Windows 2000, Active Directory ignores WMI filters and always applies the GPO.

Note For more information about WMI filters, see "What Are WMI Filters?" in Module 5 on the Appendices page on the Student Materials compact disc.

How to Filter Group Policy Settings Using WMI Filters

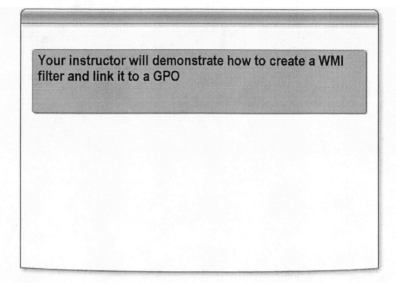

Your instructor will demonstrate how to create a WMI filter and link it to a GPO

Introduction

You can create new WMI filters from the WMI Filters container in the Group Policy Management console. You can also import a filter that was previously exported.

Procedure

To create a WMI filter and link it to a GPO, perform the following steps:

1. Open Group Policy Management, expand the forest that contains the GPO that you want to add a WMI filter to, expand **Domains**, expand the domain that contains the GPO, expand **WMI Filters**, right-click **WMI Filters**, and then click **New**.

2. In the **New WMI Filter** dialog box, in the **Name** box, type a name of the query.

3. In the **Description** box, type a description of the query.

4. Click **Add**.

5. In the **WMI Query** dialog box, in the **Namespace** box, type the namespace path of the query, or click **Browse** to see a list of available namespaces.

   For each query, you must specify the WMI namespace where the query is to be executed. The default namespace is root\CIMv2, which should be appropriate for most scenarios.

6. In the **Query** box, type a valid WQL query statement, and then click **OK**.

7. In the **New WMI Filter** dialog box, click **Save**.

8. Expand **Group Policy Objects**, and then drag the WMI filter to a GPO.

Example WQL query

For example, to target computers that have more than 10 MB of available space on the C, D, or E drive, the partitions must be located on one or more hard disks and they must be running NTFS file system. Type the following WMI query:

```
Select * FROM Win32LogicalDisk WHERE (Name = "C:" OR Name =
"D:" OR Name
= "E:") AND DriveType = 3 AND FreeSpace > 10485760 AND
FileSystem = "NTFS"
```

In the example, DriveType value = 3 is a hard disk. The FreeSpace units are in bytes (10 MB = 10,485,760 bytes).

Note For more examples of WMI filters, see "How to Filter Group Policy Settings by Using WMI Filters" in Module 5 on the Appendices page on the Student Materials compact disc.

What Is Loopback Processing?

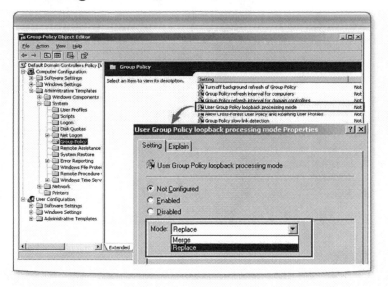

Introduction

By default, a user's GPOs determine which user settings apply when a user logs on to a computer. In contrast, loopback processing applies the set of GPOs for the computer to any user who logs on to the computer who is affected by this setting. Loopback processing is intended for special-use computers, such as computers in public places, laboratories, and classrooms, where you must modify the user setting based on the computer that is being used.

Example

For example, the user whose user object is located in the Sales organizational unit logs on to a computer. The computer object is located in the Servers organizational unit. The Group Policy settings that are applied to the user are based on any GPOs that are linked to the Sales organizational unit or to any parent containers. The settings that are applied to the computer are based on any GPOs that are linked to the Servers organizational unit or to any parent containers.

This default behavior, however, may not be appropriate for certain servers or computers that are dedicated to a certain task. For example, applications that are assigned to a user should not be automatically available on a server.

Loopback processing modes

Loopback processing has two modes:

- *Replace mode*. This mode replaces the user settings that are defined in the computer's GPOs with the user settings that are normally applied to the user.

- *Merge mode*. This mode combines the user settings that are defined in the computer's GPOs and the user settings that are normally applied to the user. If the settings conflict, the user settings in the computer's GPOs take precedence over the user's normal settings.

How to Configure the User Group Policy Loopback Processing Mode

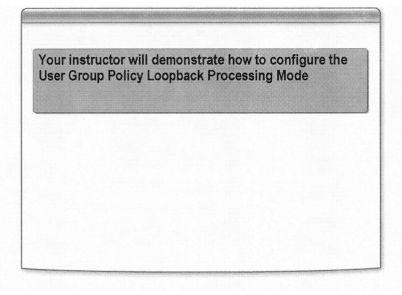

Your instructor will demonstrate how to configure the User Group Policy Loopback Processing Mode

Introduction

To enable loopback processing, you select the User Group Policy Loopback Processing mode option in Group Policy Management.

Procedure

To configure the User Group Policy Loopback Processing mode, perform the following steps:

1. Open Group Policy Management, expand the forest, expand **Domains**, expand your domain, and then click **Group Policy Objects**.

2. In the details pane, right-click the Group Policy object, and then click **Edit**.

3. In Group Policy Object Editor, expand **Computer Configuration**, expand **Administrative Templates**, expand **System**, and then click **Group Policy**.

4. Double-click **User Group Policy loopback processing mode**, if it is not already selected, click **Enabled**.

5. Under **Mode**, click **Replace** or **Merge**, and then click **OK**.

Practice: Creating and Configuring GPOs

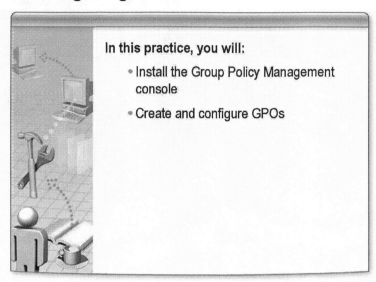

Objectives

In this practice, you will install the Group Policy Management console and create and configure GPOs for your domain.

Scenario

As the systems engineer for Northwind Traders, you are responsible for implementing Group Policy for the organization. You will install Group Policy Management and create GPOs to help enforce the desktop environment. You will remove the **Run** menu option for all users and then remove the shut down command from the menu. You also want to apply this policy only to computers in which the C drive contains at least 10 MB of free disk space and that are configured with the NTFS file system.

Practice: Installing the Group Policy Management console

▶ **Install the Group Policy Management console**

1. Log on to your domain as *ComputerName***User** (where *ComputerName* is the name of the computer you are working on) with a password of **P@ssw0rd**

2. Click **Start**, right-click **Command Prompt**, and then click **Run as**.

3. In the **Run As** dialog box, click **The following user**, type a user name of **Nwtraders*x*\Administrator** with a password of **P@ssw0rd** and then click **OK**.

4. At the command prompt, type **\\LONDON\SETUP\GPMC.MSI** and then press ENTER.

5. In the **File Download** dialog box, click **Open**.

6. On the **Welcome to the Microsoft Group Policy Management Console Setup Wizard** page, click **Next**.

7. On the **License Agreement** page, click **I Agree**, and then click **Next**.

8. On the **Completing the Microsoft Group Policy Management Console Setup Wizard** page, click **Finish**.

9. Close the command prompt.

Practice: Creating and Configuring GPOs

▶ **Create and configure GPOs**

1. Click **Start**, point to **Administrative Tools**, right-click **Group Policy Management**, and then click **Run as**.

2. In the **Run As** dialog box, click **The following user**, type a user name of *YourDomain***Administrator** with a password of **P@ssw0rd** and then click **OK**.

3. Expand **Forest**, expand **Domains**, expand your domain, expand **Group Policy Objects**, right-click **Group Policy Objects**, and then click **New**.

4. Type **PracticeGPO** as the name for your GPO, and then click **OK**.

5. Right-click your domain name, click **Link an Existing GPO**, click **PracticeGPO**, and then click **OK**.

6. Right-click **PracticeGPO**, and then click **Edit**.

7. In Group Policy Object Editor, under **User Configuration**, expand **Administrative Templates**, and then click **Start Menu and Taskbar**.

8. In the details pane, double-click **Remove Run menu from Start Menu**, click **Enabled**, and then click **OK**.

9. In the details pane, double-click **Remove and prevent access to the Shut Down command**, click **Enabled**, and then click **OK**.

10. Close Group Policy Object Editor.

11. In Group Policy Management, expand and right-click **WMI Filters**, and then click **New**.

12. Type **PracticeFilter** as the name for the WMI filter, click **Add**, type an appropriate query to retrieve the required information, click **OK**, and then click **Save**.

13. In the console tree, in the list under **Group Policy Objects**, click **PracticeGPO**.

14. In the details pane, select **PracticeFilter** in the **This GPO is linked to the following WMI filter** box.

15. In the **Group Policy Management** dialog box, click **Yes**.

16. Close Group Policy Management.

Lesson: Configuring Group Policy Refresh Rates and Group Policy Settings

- When Is Group Policy Applied?
- How to Assign Group Policy Script Settings
- How to Configure Refresh Rates for Group Policy Components
- How to Configure Refresh Rates for Domain Controllers and Computers
- How to Refresh the Group Policy Settings on a User's Computer Using Gpupdate.exe

Introduction

Windows Server 2003 executes computer and user settings and policies in a specific order. By understanding Group Policy processing and their order, you can create appropriate scripts and configure refresh rates.

Lesson objectives

After completing this lesson, you will be able to:

- Explain the process of applying Group Policy.
- Assign Group Policy Script settings.
- Configure refresh rates for Group Policy components.
- Configure refresh rates for domain controllers and computers.
- Refresh the Group Policy settings on a user's computer by using Gpupdate.exe.

When Is Group Policy Applied?

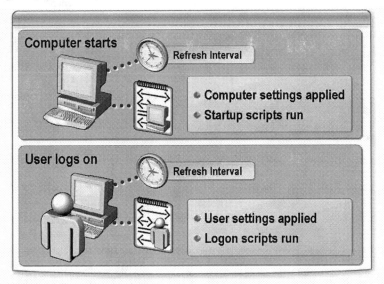

Introduction

When a user starts a computer and logs on, Windows Server 2003 processes computer settings first and then user settings.

Order in which Group Policy is applied

When a user starts a computer and logs on, the following things occur:

1. The network starts. Remote Procedure Call System Service (RPCSS) and Multiple Universal Naming Convention Provider (MUP) start.

2. Windows Server 2003 obtains an ordered list of GPOs for the computer. The list depends on the following factors:

   - Whether the computer is part of a domain and therefore subject to Group Policy through Active Directory.

   - The location of the computer in Active Directory.

   - Whether the list of GPOs has changed.

3. Windows Server 2003 applies the computer policy. These are the settings under Computer Configuration from the gathered list of GPOs. This list is synchronous by default and in the following order: local, site, domain, organizational unit, and child organizational unit. No user interface appears while computer policies are processed.

4. The startup scripts run. The scripts are hidden and synchronous by default. Each script must be completed or time out before the next one starts. The default time-out is 600 seconds. You can use Group Policy settings to modify the default time-out.

Note   You can adjust the time-out value by configuring the wait time in "Maximum wait time for Group Policy scripts" under Computer Configuration\Administrative Templates\System\Logon\. This setting affects all scripts that run.

5. The user presses CTRL-ALT-DEL to log on.

6. After Windows Server 2003 validates the user, it loads the user profile, which is controlled by the Group Policy settings that are in effect.

7. Windows Server 2003 obtains an ordered list of GPOs for the user. The list depends on the following factors:

   - Whether the user is part of a domain and therefore subject to Group Policy through Active Directory.

   - Whether loopback processing is enabled, and the state of the loopback policy setting.

   - The location of the user in Active Directory.

   - Whether the list of GPOs has changed.

8. Windows Server 2003 applies the user policy, which includes the settings under User Configuration from the gathered list. The settings are synchronous by default and in the following order: local, site, domain, organizational unit, and child organizational unit. No user interface appears while user policies are processed.

9. Logon scripts run. Logon scripts that are based on Group Policy are hidden and asynchronous by default.

10. The operating system user interface that Group Policy prescribes appears.

User or computer refresh interval

Computers running Windows Server 2003 refresh or reapply Group Policy settings at established intervals. Refreshing settings ensures that Group Policy settings are applied to computers and users even if users never restart their computers or log off.

Note For more information about when Group Policy is applied and a sample logon script, see "When Is Group Policy Applied?" in Module 5 on the Appendices page on the Student Materials compact disc.

How to Assign Group Policy Script Settings

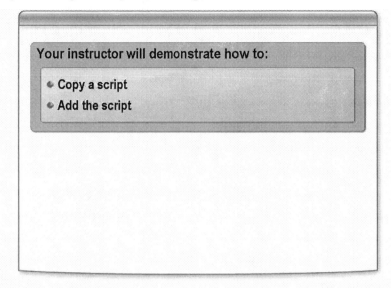

Your instructor will demonstrate how to:

- Copy a script
- Add the script

Introduction

When you implement a script, you use Group Policy to add the script to the appropriate setting in the GPT so that it runs during startup, shutdown, logon, or logoff.

Procedure for copying a script

To copy a script to the appropriate GPT, perform the following steps:

1. Locate the script on your hard disk by using Windows Explorer.

2. Edit the appropriate GPO in Group Policy Management, expand either **Computer Configuration** (for startup and shutdown scripts) or **User Configuration** (for logon and logoff scripts), expand **Windows Settings**, and then click **Scripts**.

3. Double-click the appropriate script type (**Startup**, **Shutdown**, **Logon**, or **Logoff**), and then click **Show Files**.

4. Copy the script file from Windows Explorer to the window that appears, and then close the window.

Important   You cannot perform this task using Run as; you must be logged on as Administrator in order to perform this task.

Procedure for adding the script

To add a script to a GPO, perform the following steps:

1. In the **Properties** dialog box for the script type, click **Add**.

2. Click **Browse**, select a script, and then click **Open**.

3. Add any necessary script parameters, and then click **OK**.

Note   For more information about creating a script in the Microsoft Visual Basic®, Scripting Edition (VBScript) language, see Course 2433, *Microsoft Visual Basic Scripting Edition and Microsoft Windows Script Host Essentials*, and Course 2439, *WMI Scripting.*

How to Configure Refresh Rates for Group Policy Components

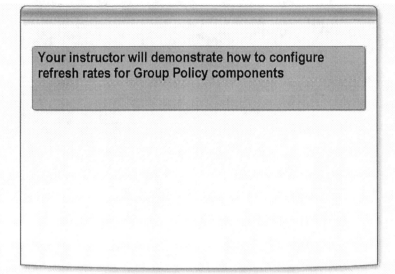

Your instructor will demonstrate how to configure refresh rates for Group Policy components

Introduction

If Group Policy detects a slow link, it sets a flag to indicate the slow link to the client-side extensions. The client-side extensions can then determine whether to process applicable Group Policy settings.

Group Policy and slow links

Group Policy compares the connection speed of the link with 500 kilobytes per second (KBps)—the speed that it considers slow—or with a threshold of your choice. Group Policy uses an algorithm to determine whether a link is considered slow.

Default settings

The following table shows the default settings for slow link processing.

Client-side extension	Slow-link processing	Refreshed	Can it be changed?
Registry policy processing	On	On	No
Internet Explorer Maintenance policy processing	Off	On	Yes
Software Installation policy processing	Off	N/A	Yes
Folder Redirection policy processing	Off	N/A	Yes
Scripts policy processing	Off	On	Yes
Security policy processing	On	On	No
IP Security policy processing	Off	On	Yes
Wireless policy processing	Off	On	Yes
EFS recovery policy processing	On	On	Yes
Disk Quota policy processing	Off	On	Yes

Procedure

To configure which Group Policy components are refreshed and can be modified, perform the following steps:

1. Open the appropriate GPO in Group Policy, expand **Computer Configuration**, expand **Administrative Templates**, expand **System**, click **Group Policy**, and then double-click each item in the preceding table.

2. Click **Enabled**.

3. Click **Do not apply during periodic background processing**.

4. If available, click **Allow processing across a slow network connection**, and then click **OK**.

Note For more information about the algorithm that Group Policy uses to detect slow links, see "How to Configure Which Group Policy Components Are Refreshed" in Module 5 on the Appendices page on the Student Materials compact disc.

How to Configure Refresh Rates for Domain Controllers and Computers

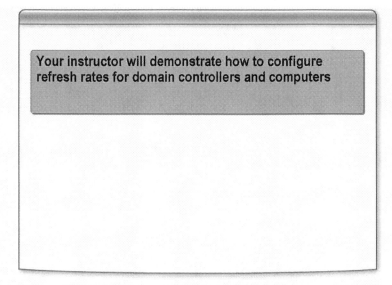

Your instructor will demonstrate how to configure refresh rates for domain controllers and computers

Introduction

You can change the default refresh rates by modifying the administrative template settings for a user or computer configuration.

Default refresh intervals

The following table lists the default intervals for refreshing Group Policy.

Type of computer	Refresh interval
Computers running Windows XP Professional and domain member servers running Windows Server 2003	Every 90 minutes. It also refreshes on a random time offset every 30 minutes, which helps load balance application processing of Group Policy and ensures that multiple computers do not contact a domain controller at the same time.
Domain controllers	Every five minutes. This way, critical new Group Policy settings, such as security settings, are applied at least every five minutes unless you change the default setting.

Procedure

To configure refresh rates, perform the following steps:

1. Open the appropriate GPO in Group Policy, expand **User Configuration** or **Computer Configuration** (depending on which GPO you want to edit), expand **Administrative Templates**, expand **System**, click **Group Policy**, and then double-click one of the following settings:

   - **Group Policy refresh interval for users**
   - **Group Policy refresh interval for computers**
   - **Group Policy refresh interval for domain controllers**

2. Select **Enabled**.

3. Set the refresh interval in minutes.

4. Set the random time offset, and then click **OK**.

Note If you disable these settings, Group Policy is updated by default every 90 minutes. To specify that Group Policy should never be updated when the computer is in use, select the **Turn off background refresh of Group Policy** option.

How to Refresh the Group Policy Settings on a User's Computer Using Gpupdate.exe

> Your instructor will demonstrate how to refresh the Group Policy settings on a user's computer by using Gpupdate.exe

Introduction

You can refresh a Group Policy object by using the **gpupdate** command.

Procedure

To refresh the Group Policy settings on a user's computer by using the **gpupdate** command, perform the following steps:

1. In the **Run** dialog box, type **cmd** and then press ENTER.

2. Type

```
gpupdate [/target:{computer|user}] [/force] [/wait:value]
[/logoff] [/boot]
```

The following table describes each parameter of the gpupdate syntax.

Parameter	Description
/target:{computer|user}	Processes either the computer settings or the current user settings, depending on what destination you specify. If you do not specify this parameter, the computer and the user settings are processed by default.
/force	Reapplies all settings and ignores processing optimizations.
/wait:value	Specifies the number of seconds that policy processing waits to finish, which by default, is 600 seconds. A value of 0 means no wait; -1 means wait indefinitely.
/logoff	Logs off after the policy refresh is completed. This parameter is required for Group Policy client-side extensions that do not process Group Policy settings on a background refresh cycle but do process them when the user logs on. This option has no effect if there are no extensions called that require the user to log off.
/boot	Restarts the computer after the policy refresh is completed. Restarting the computer is required for those Group Policy client-side extensions that do not process Group Policy settings on a background refresh cycle but do process them when the computer starts up. This option has no effect if there are no extensions called that require the computer to be restarted.

Practice: Configuring Group Policy Refresh Rates and Group Policy Settings

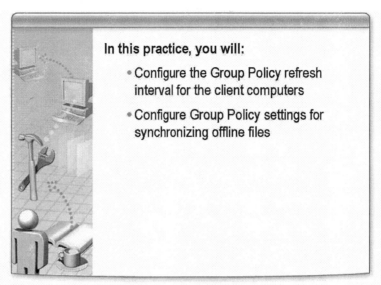

In this practice, you will:

- Configure the Group Policy refresh interval for the client computers
- Configure Group Policy settings for synchronizing offline files

Objectives

In this practice, you will configure the Group Policy refresh interval for client computers and then configure Group Policy settings for synchronizing offline files.

Scenario

Northwind Traders relies heavily on Group Policy to manage client computers and to keep the organization agile. Because of the large number of GPOs you must modify daily, you want to reduce network traffic by decreasing the refresh interval for client computers to 180 minutes and by using a random time offset of 60 minutes.

People in your organization often travel and use slow dial-up connections. They also frequently visit remote sales offices that have high-speed connections to the corporate network. They need access to files that normally are accessible only by using a network connection to a file server. These files must be up to date as soon as the user logs on to the corporate network. You must configure the availability and synchronization of offline files in Group Policy for the users who require this capability.

Practice

▶ **Configure Group Policy settings**

1. Open Group Policy Management as *YourDomain***Administrator** by using **Run as**.

2. Expand **Forest**, expand **Domains**, expand your domain, expand **Group Policy Objects**, click **Group Policy Objects**, right-click **PracticeGPO**, and then click **Edit**.

3. In Group Policy Object Editor, under **Computer Configuration**, expand **Administrative Templates**, expand **System**, and then click **Group Policy**.

4. Double-click **Group Policy Refresh Interval for computers**, click **Enabled**, type the appropriate time intervals, and then click **OK**.

5. In Group Policy Object Editor, under **User Configuration**, expand **Administrative Templates**, expand **Network**, and then click **Offline Files**.

6. Double-click **Synchronize all offline files when logging on**, click **Enabled**, and then click **OK**.

7. Close Group Policy Object Editor, and then close Group Policy Management.

Lesson: Managing GPOs

- What Is a Copy Operation?
- How to Copy a GPO
- What Is a Backup Operation?
- How to Back Up a GPO
- What Is a Restore Operation?
- How to Restore a GPO
- What Is an Import Operation?
- How to Import Settings into a GPO

Introduction

You use the Group Policy Management console to manage GPOs, which includes copying a GPO to another location, backing up a GPO, restoring a GPO from the backup, and importing settings from one GPO to another.

Lesson objectives

After completing this lesson, you will be able to:

- Explain the purpose of copying a GPO.
- Copy a GPO by using Group Policy Management.
- Explain the purpose of backing up a GPO.
- Back up a GPO by using Group Policy Management.
- Explain the purpose of restoring a GPO.
- Restore a GPO by using Group Policy Management.
- Explain the purpose of importing settings into a GPO.
- Import settings into a GPO by using Group Policy Management.

What Is a Copy Operation?

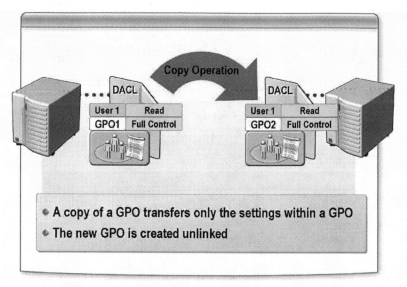

- A copy of a GPO transfers only the settings within a GPO
- The new GPO is created unlinked

Introduction

A copy of a GPO transfers only the settings in the GPO. The newly created GPO has a new GUID and the default discretional access control list (DACL) for the GPO. The new GPO is created unlinked because links are a property of the object that defined the GPO, rather than a property of the GPO.

Mapping behavior for a copy operation

When you copy a GPO from one domain to another, you must specify the mapping behavior of the security principals for the copy operation. Group Policy Management provides two basic mapping techniques for copying GPOs:

- Copy them identically from the source
- Use a migration table to map them to new values in the new GPO

To use either approach, references to security principals and Universal Naming Convention (UNC) paths must exist in the source GPO.

What is security principal mapping?

When you copy GPOs across domains or forests, Group Policy Management can perform *security principal mapping*. That is, it can modify settings that refer to security principals by translating the destination security principals to new values in the new GPO.

What is a migration table?

If you require additional customization, you can use scripting to implement a *migration table*, which is an Extensible Markup Language (XML) text file that specifies custom mapping of security principals from the source domain to the destination domain. The migration table contains a security principal mapping section and a path mapping section. You use these sections to set specific mapping rules.

How to Copy a GPO

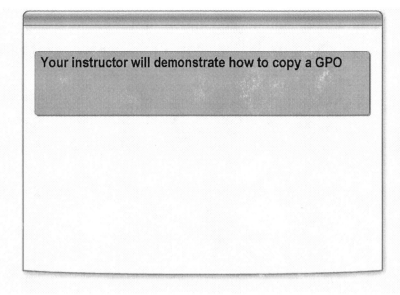

Your instructor will demonstrate how to copy a GPO

Introduction

To copy a GPO, you must have permission to create GPOs in the destination domain.

Procedure

To copy a GPO, perform the following steps:

1. Open Group Policy Management, expand **Group Policy Objects** in the forest and domain that contains the GPO that you want to copy, right-click the GPO, and then click **Copy**.

2. Do one of the following:

   - To place the copy of the GPO in the same domain as the source GPO, right-click **Group Policy Objects**, and then click **Paste**.

     i.   On the **Copy GPO** page, select either **Use the default permissions for New GPOs** or **Preserve the existing permissions,** and then click **OK**.

     ii. When copy progress has completed, click **OK**.

   - To place the copy of the GPO in a different domain, whether in the same forest or a different forest, expand the destination domain, right-click **Group Policy Objects**, and then click **Paste**.

     i.   On the **Welcome to the Cross-Domain Copying Wizard** page, click **Next**.

     ii. On the **Specifying permissions** page, select either **Use the default permissions for new GPOS** or **Preserve or migrate the permissions from the original GPOs**, and then click **Next**.

     iii. On the **Scanning Original GPO** page, click **Next**.

         If the source GPO contains references to security principals and UNC paths, you will see the window mentioned in the next step. Otherwise, continue to step v.

iv. On the **Migrating References** page, select either **Copying them identically from the source** or **Using this migration table to map them to new values in the new GPOs**, select the migration table from the list, and then click **Next**.

v. On the **Completing the Cross-Domain Copying Wizard** page, click **Finish**.

vi. After the copy operation is completed, click **OK**.

Note   Some of these steps may not appear if you are copying a GPO to the same domain.

What Is a Backup Operation?

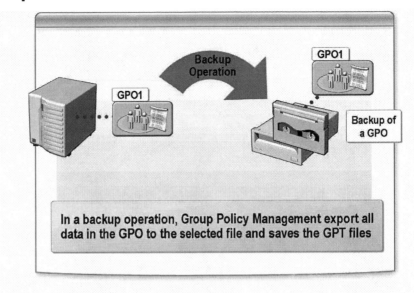

In a backup operation, Group Policy Management export all data in the GPO to the selected file and saves the GPT files

Introduction

When Group Policy Management backs up a GPO, it exports the data to a file that you choose and saves all Group Policy template (GPT) files. You can send the backed-up GPO to a folder by using a restore or import operation. You can only restore a backed-up GPO to another domain by using an import operation.

How to store a backup?

You can store multiple backed-up GPOs, including versions of the same GPO, in one file folder. Regardless of how many GPOs you store in a folder, you can identify each backed-up GPO by one of the following criteria:

- GPO display name
- GPO GUID
- Description of the backup
- Date and time stamp of the backup
- Domain name.

You can back up one or more GPOs to a previously specified backup location, or you can specify a new backup location.

Note Be sure that the backup directory is in a secure location in the file system.

How to Back Up a GPO

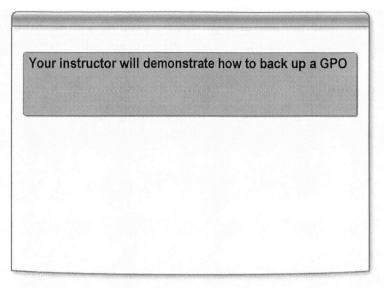

Your instructor will demonstrate how to back up a GPO

Introduction

To back up a GPO, you must have Read permission to the GPO and Write permission to the file system location where you want to store the backed-up GPO.

Procedure

To back up a GPO, perform the following steps:

1. Open Group Policy Management, expand the forest that contains the GPO that you want to back up, expand **Domains**, expand the domain that contains the GPO, expand **Group Policy Objects**, and then do one of the following:

   - To back up a single GPO, right-click the GPO, and then click **Back Up**.

   - To back up all GPOs, right-click **Group Policy Objects**, and then click **Back Up All**.

2. In the **Backup Group Policy Object** dialog box, type the path to the location where you want to store the backed-up GPO.

3. Type a description for the GPO that you want to back up, and then click **Backup**.

4. After the backup operation is completed, click **OK**.

What Is a Restore Operation?

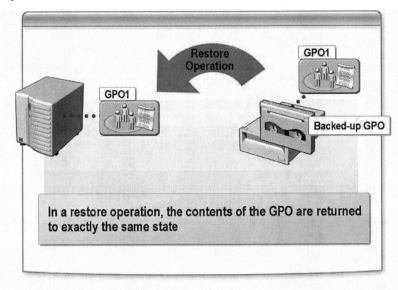

In a restore operation, the contents of the GPO are returned to exactly the same state

Introduction

The restore operation returns the contents of the GPO to the same state it was in when the backup was performed. This operation is only valid in the domain where the GPO was created.

Which GPOs can be restored?

You can restore an existing GPO or a deleted GPO that was backed up. The permissions that are required to restore a GPO depend on whether the GPO exists in Active Directory when you restore it.

How to Restore a GPO

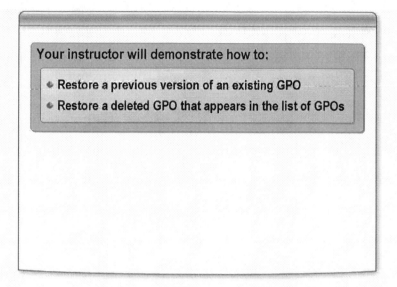

Your instructor will demonstrate how to:

- Restore a previous version of an existing GPO
- Restore a deleted GPO that appears in the list of GPOs

Introduction

To restore an existing GPO by using Group Policy Management, you must have Edit, Delete, and Modify Security permissions for the GPO. You must also have Read permission to the folder that contains the backed-up GPO.

To restore a deleted GPO that was backed up, you must have the permission to create GPOs in the domain and also Read permission to the file system location of the backed-up GPO.

Procedure for restoring a previous version of a GPO

To restore a previous version of an existing GPO, perform the following steps:

1. Open Group Policy Management, expand the forest that contains the GPO that you want to restore, expand **Domains**, expand the domain that contains the GPO, right-click **Group Policy Objects**, and then click **Manage Backups**.

2. In the **Manage Backups** dialog box, select the backed-up GPO that you want to restore, and then click **Restore**.

3. When you are prompted to restore the selected backup, click **OK**.

4. In the **Restore Progress** dialog box, click **OK** after the restore is completed.

5. In the **Manage Backups** dialog box, either select another GPO to restore or click **Close** to complete the restore operation.

Procedure for restoring a deleted GPO

To restore a deleted GPO that appears in the list of **Group Policy Objects**, perform the following steps:

1. Open Group Policy Management, expand the forest that contains the GPO that you want to restore, expand **Domains**, and then expand the domain that contains the GPO.

2. Right-click **Group Policy Objects**, and then click **Manage Backups**.

3. In the **Manage Backups** dialog box, click **Browse**, locate the file system that contains the deleted GPO, select the GPO, click **Restore**, and then click **OK** to confirm the restore operation.

What Is an Import Operation?

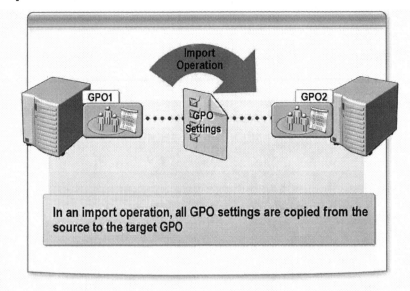

In an import operation, all GPO settings are copied from the source to the target GPO

Introduction

An import operation copies all of the GPO settings from the source GPO to the destination GPO.

Why specify a migration table?

You specify a migration table to ensure that the UNC path in the source GPO maps correctly to the UNC path of the destination GPO. You provide the path to the appropriate migration table when you import GPO settings from one domain to another. If you specify a migration table, you must specify the UNC path mapping behavior.

If you do not select the **Use migration table exclusively** check box, you must specify the mapping behavior for security principals that are not contained in the migration table.

If you do not specify a migration table, all security principals are mapped according to the behavior that you specify.

How to Import Settings into a GPO

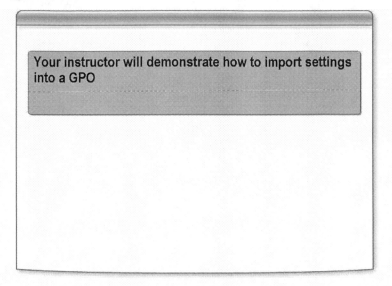

Your instructor will demonstrate how to import settings into a GPO

Introduction   To import settings into a GPO, you must have Edit permissions on the GPO.

Procedure   To import settings into a GPO, perform the following steps:

1. Open Group Policy Management, expand the forest that contains the GPO that you want to import settings into, expand **Domains**, expand the domain that contains the GPO, expand **Group Policy Objects**, right-click the GPO, and then click **Import Settings**.

2. On the **Welcome to the Import Settings Wizard** page, click **Next**.

3. On the **Backup GPO** page, click **Backup**.

4. In the **Backup Group Policy Object** dialog box, type a location and description for the GPO backup, and then click **Backup**.

5. When the backup operation is complete, click **OK**, and then click **Next**.

6. On the **Backup location** page, click **Browse** to locate the backup folder that you want to import settings from, and then click **Next**.

7. On the **Source GPO** page, select the GPO that you want to import settings from, and then click **Next**.

    If the source GPO contains references to security principals and UNC paths, the **Migrating References** dialog box appears. Choose how to migrate security principals and UNC paths by selecting either **Copying them identically from the source** or **Using this migration table to map them in the destination GPO**, and then select a migration table.

8. Click **Next**.

9. On the **Completing the Import Settings Wizard** page, click **Finish**.

10. When the import operation is completed, click **OK**.

Practice: Managing GPOs

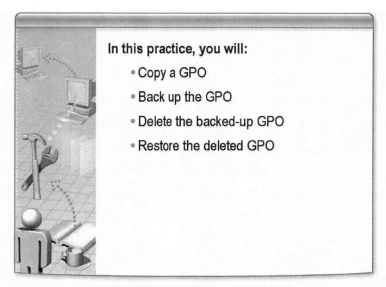

In this practice, you will:

* Copy a GPO
* Back up the GPO
* Delete the backed-up GPO
* Restore the deleted GPO

Objectives

In this practice, you will copy a GPO, create a backup of it, delete the backed-up copy, and then restore it.

Scenario

You are responsible for implementing the corporate desktop standards by using Group Policy for your domain. Although most groups in the domain can use the same standard corporate desktop configuration, some departments require a slightly different configuration. You will create a base GPO, copy it to the various applications, and then modify the settings.

Because you are concerned that backing up and restoring GPOs may not work correctly, you want to test recovery capabilities and simulate your implementation plan in your test environment.

Practice: Copying a GPO

▶ **Copy a GPO**

1. Open Group Policy Management as *YourDomain***Administrator** by using **Run as**.

2. In your domain, expand **Group Policy Objects**, right-click **PracticeGPO**, click **Copy**, right-click **Group Policy Objects**, and then click **Paste**.

3. In the **Copy GPO** dialog box, click **OK**.

4. After the copy progress is completed, click **OK**.

Practice: Backing up a GPO

▶ **Back up a GPO**

1. In Group Policy Management, right-click **Copy of PracticeGPO**, and then click **Back Up**.

2. In the **Back Up Group Policy Object** dialog box, type **C:** in the **Location** box, and then click **Backup**.

3. After the operation is completed, click **OK**.

Practice: Restoring a GPO

▶ **Delete and restore a GPO**

1. In Group Policy Management, right-click **Copy of PracticeGPO**, click **Delete**, and then click **OK**.

2. Right-click **Group Policy Objects**, and then click **Manage Backups**.

3. In the **Manage Backups** dialog box, select **Copy of PracticeGPO**, and then click **Restore**.

4. When prompted to restore the backup, click **OK**.

5. In the **Restore Progress** dialog box, click **OK** after the backed-up copy is restored.

6. In the **Manage Backups** dialog box, click **Close**.

7. Verify that the GPO has been restored.

8. Close Group Policy Management.

Lesson: Verifying and Troubleshooting Group Policy

- Common Problems with Implementing Group Policy
- How to Verify Group Policy Settings Using Group Policy Modeling Wizard
- How to Verify Group Policy Settings Using Group Policy Results

Introduction

You may encounter problems when you implement Group Policy. When you troubleshoot Group Policy problems, be sure to consider dependencies between components. For example, Group Policy relies on Active Directory, which relies on proper configuration of network services.

Windows Server 2003 has two new Group Policy management features that help you determine the effect of Group Policy settings for a particular user or computer. These features are Group Policy Modeling Wizard and Group Policy Results.

Lesson objectives

After completing this lesson, you will be able to:

- Identify the common problems with implementing Group Policy.
- Verify Group Policy settings by using Group Policy Modeling Wizard.
- Verify Group Policy settings by using Group Policy Results.

Common Problems with Implementing Group Policy

Symptom	Cause
Cannot open a GPO	Read and Write permissions for the GPO are not assigned
Cannot edit a GPO	A networking problem
Cannot apply Group Policy on a security group	GPOs are not applied to security groups
No effect of Group Policy on a site, domain, or organizational unit	Group Policy settings are not configured correctly
No effect of Group Policy in an Active Directory container	GPOs cannot be linked to Active Directory containers
No effect of Group Policy on a client computer	A non-local GPO can overwrite local policies

Introduction

The first step in troubleshooting Group Policy is to identify the symptoms and possible causes.

How to verify if the correct Group Policy settings are applied

In most cases, a Group Policy setting is not being applied as expected because another GPO contains a conflicting value for the same setting. The GPO is taking precedence because of Block Inheritance, Enforced, filtering, or the order of application. Use the Group Policy Modeling Wizard or the Group Policy Results Wizard to determine which GPO is being used for the setting.

Symptoms, cause, and resolution

The following table lists some common symptoms and their possible resolution methods.

Symptom	Resolution
You cannot open a GPO, even with Read permission	Be a member of a security group with Read and Write permission for the GPO.
When you try to edit a GPO, the message Failed To Open The Group Policy Object appears	Make sure DNS is working properly.
Group Policy is not applied to users and computers in a security group that contains them, even though a GPO is linked to an organizational unit that contains the security group	Link GPOs to sites, domains, and organizational units only.
Group Policy is not affecting users and computers in an Active Directory container	Link a GPO to an organizational unit that is a parent to the Active Directory container. Those settings are then applied by default to the users and computers in the container through inheritance.
Group Policy is not taking effect on the client computer	Determine which GPOs are being applied through Active Directory and if those GPOs have settings that are in conflict with the local settings.

How to Verify Group Policy Settings Using Group Policy Modeling Wizard

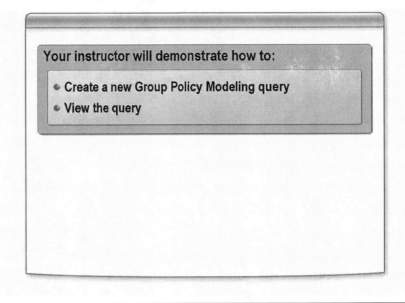

Your instructor will demonstrate how to:

- Create a new Group Policy Modeling query
- View the query

Introduction

You can simulate a policy deployment for users and computers before actually applying the policies. This feature in Group Policy Management is known as Resultant Set of Policies (RSoP) – Planning Mode. It requires a domain controller running Windows Server 2003 in the forest. To verify Group Policy settings by using Group Policy Modeling Wizard, you first create a Group Policy Modeling query and then view that query.

Procedure for creating a Group Policy Modeling query

To create a new Group Policy Modeling query, perform the following steps:

1. Open Group Policy Management, browse to the forest in which you want to create a Group Policy Modeling query, right-click **Group Policy Modeling**, and then click **Group Policy Modeling Wizard**.

2. On the **Welcome to the Group Policy Modeling Wizard** page, click **Next**, type the appropriate information in the wizard pages, and then click **Finish**.

Procedure for viewing the Group Policy Modeling query

To view the Group Policy Modeling query, perform the following steps:

1. Open Group Policy Management.

2. Browse to the forest that contains the Group Policy Modeling query that you want to view, expand **Group Policy Modeling**, right-click the query, and then click **Advanced View**.

Note   For information about verifying Group Policy settings by using Gpresult.exe, see "How to Verify Group Policy Settings by Using Group Policy Results" in Module 5 on the Appendices page on the Student Materials compact disc.

How to Verify Group Policy Settings Using Group Policy Results

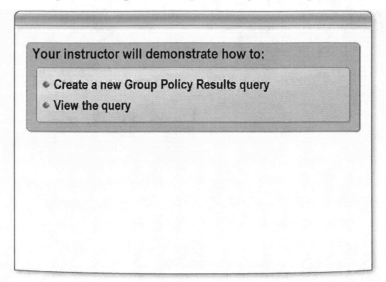

Your instructor will demonstrate how to:

- Create a new Group Policy Results query
- View the query

Introduction

You use Group Policy Results to determine the policy settings that are applied to a computer and the user who logged on to that computer. Although this data is similar to Group Policy Modeling data, it is obtained from the client computer, rather than simulated on the domain controller. To obtain data by using Group Policy Results, the client computer must be running Windows XP or Windows Server 2003.

Procedure for creating a Group Policy Results query

To create a Group Policy Results query, perform the following steps:

1. In Group Policy Management, browse to **Group Policy Results**, right-click **Group Policy Results**, and then click **Group Policy Results Wizard**.

2. On the **Welcome to the Group Policy Results Wizard** page, click **Next**.

3. On the **Computer Selection** page, select the current computer or click **Browse** to select another computer, and then click **Next**.

4. On the **User Selection** page, select the current user or specify a user, and then click **Next**.

5. On the **Summary of Selections** page, verify your selections, and then click **Next**.

6. On the **Completing the Group Policy Results Wizard** page, click **Finish**.

Procedure for viewing the Group Policy Results query

To view the Group Policy Results query, perform the following steps.

1. Open Group Policy Management.

2. Browse to the forest that contains the Group Policy Modeling query that you want to view, expand **Group Policy Results**, right-click the query, and then click **Advanced View**.

Note   You can monitor Group Policy by enabling diagnostic logging and verbose logging. For information about enabling Group Policy logging, see "How to Troubleshoot Conflicts in Group Policy Settings" in Module 5 on the Appendices page on the Student Materials compact disc.

Practice: Verifying and Troubleshooting Group Policy

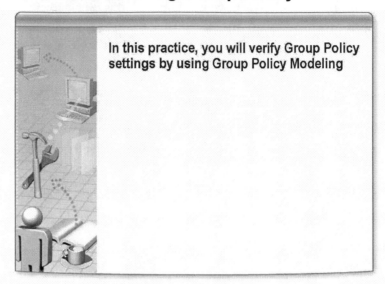

In this practice, you will verify Group Policy settings by using Group Policy Modeling

Objectives

In this practice, you will verify Group Policy settings by using the Group Policy Modeling Wizard.

Scenario

You want to verify that the GPO settings that you plan to deploy—including user and computer settings for your domain—take effect and are accurate at Northwind Traders. You decide to use the Group Policy Management console to verify the settings.

Practice

▶ **Verify user and computer settings for your domain**

1. Open Group Policy Management as *YourDomain***Administrator** by using **Run as**.

2. Right-click **Group Policy Modeling**, and then click **Group Policy Modeling Wizard**.

3. On the **Welcome to the Group Policy Modeling Wizard** page, click **Next**.

4. On the **Domain Controller Selection** page, click **Next**.

5. On the **User and Computer Selection** page, in the **User Information** and **Computer Information** sections, click **Browse**, select your domain for each section, and then click **Next**.

6. On each of the following wizard pages, click **Next** to accept the default settings.

7. On the **Completing the Group Policy Modeling Wizard** page, click **Finish**.

8. If an **Internet Explorer** dialog box appears, click **Add**, in the **Trusted Sites** dialog box, click **Add**, and then click **Close**.

9. View the report in the details pane, and then close Group Policy Management.

Lesson: Delegating Administrative Control of Group Policy

- Delegation of GPOs
- Delegation of Group Policy for a Site, Domain, or Organizational Unit
- Delegation of WMI Filters
- How to Delegate Administrative Control for Managing Group Policy Links
- How to Delegate Administrative Control for Creating and Editing GPOs

Introduction

You can use Group Policy to delegate certain Group Policy tasks to other administrators. For example, the creation, linking, and editing of GPOs are independent permissions that you can delegate separately. Group Policy Management simplifies the management of permissions by combining the low-level permissions on an object and managing them as a single unit. You use Group Policy Management to delegate administrative control of GPOs, Group Policy for a site, domain, and organizational unit, and WMI filters.

Lesson objectives

After completing this lesson, you will be able to:

- Explain the delegation of GPOs.
- Explain the delegation of Group Policy for a site, domain, or an organizational unit.
- Explain the delegation of WMI filters.
- Delegate administrative control for managing Group Policy links.
- Delegate administrative control for creating and editing Group Policy objects.

Delegation of GPOs

Methods to assign permission to create GPOs	Allows users to only create GPOs in the domain	Allows users to edit or delete GPOs or link GPO
Add the group or user to the Group Policy Creator Owners group	✓	✗
Explicitly assign the group or user permission to create GPOs	✓	✗

Introduction

You can delegate the ability to create GPOs in a domain and assign permissions on an individual GPO by using Group Policy Management.

Delegate the ability to create GPOs

By default, the Group Policy Creator Owners group is assigned the ability to create GPOs. However, you can delegate that ability to any group or user by using one of the following two ways:

- *Add the group or user to the Group Policy Creator Owners group.* This was the only method available prior to Group Policy Management.

- *Explicitly assign the group or user permission to create GPOs.* This method is available only by using Group Policy Management.

When to use the Group Policy Creator Owners group

For users and groups within the domain, use the Group Policy Creator Owners group to assign permissions for creating a GPO. Because the Group Policy Creator Owners group is a domain global group, it cannot contain members from outside the domain. If users outside the domain need the ability to create GPOs, do the following:

1. Create a new domain local group in the domain.

2. Assign that group permission for GPO creation in the domain.

3. Add external domain users to that group.

Comparison of the two methods of delegation

The permissions are identical, whether you add a user to the Group Policy Creator Owners group or assign the user permissions for GPO creation directly by using Group Policy Management. Users can create GPOs in the domain and enjoy full control of them, but they do not have permissions on GPOs that other users create.

Granting a user the ability to create GPOs in the domain does not enable him to link the GPO to a site, domain, or organizational unit.

Delegate permissions on an individual GPO

You can also manage permissions on the GPO at the task level. The following five categories are Allowed Permissions on a GPO.

- Read
- Edit settings
- Edit, Delete, Modify Security
- Read (from Security Filtering)
- Custom

Note For more information about delegating administrative control of Group Policy, see "Group Policy Tasks that Can Be Delegated" in Module 5 on the Appendices page on the Student Materials compact disc.

Delegation of Group Policy for a Site, Domain, or Organizational Unit

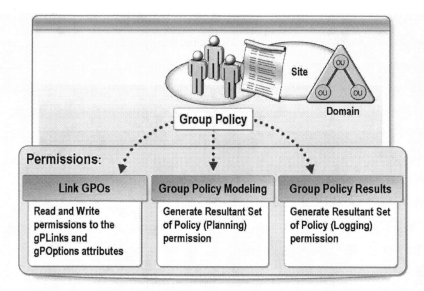

Link GPOs	**Group Policy Modeling**	**Group Policy Results**
Read and Write permissions to the gPLinks and gPOptions attributes	Generate Resultant Set of Policy (Planning) permission	Generate Resultant Set of Policy (Logging) permission

Introduction

Delegation of Group Policy for site, domain, and organizational unit includes delegating the ability to link GPOs, and delegate permissions for Group Policy Modeling and Group Policy Results.

Delegate the ability to link GPOs

Group Policy Management uses a single permission named Link GPOs to manage the gPLink and gPOptions attributes. You apply the settings in a GPO to users and computers by linking the GPO—either as a direct child or indirectly through inheritance—to a site, domain, or organizational unit that contains the user or computer objects.

The Link GPOs permission is specific to that site, domain, or an organizational unit. The permission equates to having the Read and Write permissions to the gPLink and gPOptions attributes on the site, domain, or organizational.

Delegate permissions for Group Policy Modeling

You can use Group Policy Modeling to simulate the set of policies for objects in a domain or organizational unit—or you can delegate it to other users or groups. This delegation assigns the user or group the Generate Resultant Set of Policy (Planning) permission, which is available in any forest that has the Windows Server 2003 schema.

Group Policy Management simplifies the management of this permission by listing it on the **Delegation** tab for any domain or organizational unit. The administrator can select **Perform Group Policy Modeling Analyses**, and then select the **Name**, **Applies To**, **Setting**, and **Inherited** properties for the delegations.

Delegate permissions for Group Policy Results

You can use Group Policy Results to read RSoP logging data for objects in the domain or organizational unit. Like Group Policy Management, you can delegate this permission to other users or groups. You delegate permissions on either a domain or an organizational unit. Users who have this permission can read Group Policy Results data for any object in that container. This delegation also assigns the user or group the Generate Resultant Set of Policy (Logging) permission, which is available in any forest that has the Windows Server 2003 schema.

Group Policy Management simplifies the management of this permission by listing it on the **Delegation** tab for the domain or organizational unit. The administrator can select **Read Group Policy Results Data**, and then select the users and groups that have this permission.

Delegation of WMI Filters

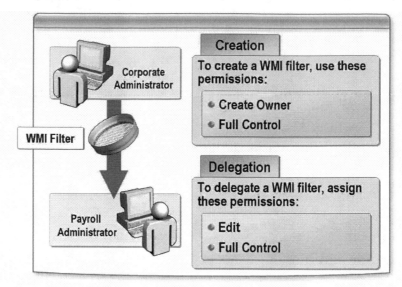

Introduction

You can delegate the ability to create WMI filters in a domain and assign permissions on them.

Delegate the ability to create WMI filters

You create WMI filters in the WMI Filters container in Group Policy Management. When you create a new WMI filter, Active Directory stores it in the WMIPolicy container in the domain's System container. The permissions on the WMIPolicy container determine the permissions that a user has to create, edit, and delete WMI filters.

There are two permissions for creating WMI filters:

- *Creator Owner*. Allows the user to create new WMI filters in the domain. It does not assign the user permissions on WMI filters that other users create.

- *Full Control*. Allows the user to create WMI filters and assign Full Control on all WMI filters in the domain, including new filters that the user creates after she is granted this permission.

Delegate permissions on a WMI filter

You can use Group Policy Management to delegate permissions on a particular WMI filter. There are two permissions that you can assign to a user or group:

- *Edit*. Allows the user or group to edit the WMI filter.

- *Full Control*. Allows the user or group to edit, delete, and modify security on the WMI filter.

How to Delegate Administrative Control for Managing Group Policy Links

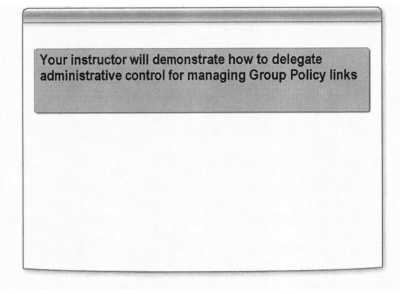

Introduction

You can delegate the ability to manage Group Policy links by selecting **Manage Group Policy links** n the **Delegation of Control Wizard** to enable a user to link and unlink GPOs.

Procedure

To delegate administrative control for managing Group Policy links, perform the following steps:

1. Open Group Policy Management.

2. Browse to the forest and the domain in which you want to delegate administrative control for managing Group Policy links, and then click the link.

3. In the details pane, on the **Delegation** tab, click **Add**.

4. In the **Select User, Computer, or Group** dialog box, in the **Enter the object name to select (examples)** box, type the security principal, click **Check Names**, and then click **OK**.

5. In the **Add Group or User** dialog box, in the **Permissions** box, select the appropriate permission, and then click **OK**.

Note If you prefer the flexibility of the **Properties** dialog box, it is still available in Group Policy Management by clicking **Advanced** on the **Delegation** tab.

How to Delegate Administrative Control for Creating and Editing GPOs

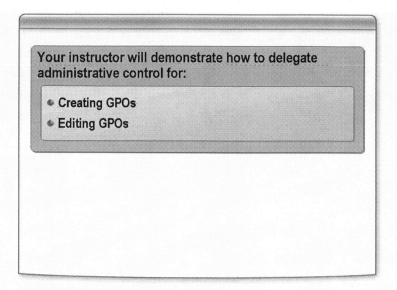

Introduction

You use the Delegation of Control Wizard to delegate administrative control to create and edit GPOs.

Procedure for delegating administrative control for creating GPOs

To delegate administrative control for creating GPOs, perform the following steps:

1. Open Group Policy Management.
2. Browse to the forest and the domain in which you want to delegate administrative control for creating GPOs, and then click **Group Policy Objects**.
3. In the details pane, on the **Delegation** tab, click **Add**.
4. In the **Select User, Computer, or Group** dialog box, in the **Enter the object name to select (examples)** box, type the security principal, click **Check Names**, and then click **OK**.

Procedure for delegating administrative control for editing GPOs

To delegate administrative control for editing GPOs, perform the following steps:

1. Open Group Policy Management.
2. Browse to the forest and the domain in which you want to delegate administrative control for editing GPOs, and then click the link.
3. In the details pane, on the **Delegation** tab, click **Add**.
4. In the **Select User, Computer, or Group** dialog box, in the **Enter the object name to select (examples)** box, type the security principal, click **Check Names**, and then click **OK**.
5. In the **Add Group or User** dialog box, in the **Permissions** box, select the appropriate permission, and then click **OK**.

Practice: Delegating Administrative Control of Group Policy

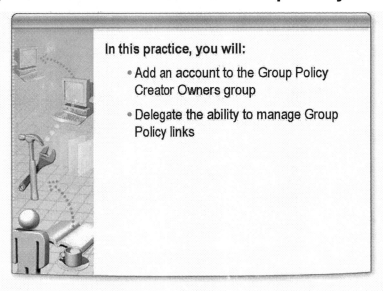

Objectives

In this practice, you will add the junior administrator's account to the Group Policy Creator Owners group and then delegate the ability for her to manage Group Policy links.

Scenario

You have decided to delegate Group Policy administration for the Accounting, Accounts Payable, and Accounts Receivable organizational units to a junior administrator. She will be responsible for linking and unlinking GPOs, creating new GPOs, and modifying the existing GPOs. She will also manage any other objects in the organizational units.

Practice

▶ **Delegate administrative control of Group Policy to a user**

1. Open Group Policy Management as *YourDomain***Administrator** by using **Run as**.

2. Expand **Forest**, expand **Domains**, expand *YourDomain,* expand **Group Policy Objects**, and then click **PracticeGPO**.

3. On the **Delegation** tab, add **Nwtraders***x\ComputerName***User** to the list with **Edit settings, delete, and modify security** permissions, and then click **OK**.

4. In Group Policy Management, click *YourDomain*, and then in the details pane, click the link to **PracticeGPO**.

5. In the details pane, on the **Delegation** tab, click **Add**.

6. In the **Select User, Computer, or Group** dialog box, in the **Enter the object name to select** box, type **Nwtraders***x\ComputerName***User**, click **Check Names**, and then click **OK**.

7. In the **Add Group or User** dialog box, in the **Permissions** box, select the appropriate permission, and then click **OK**.

8. Close Group Policy Management.

Lesson: Planning a Group Policy Strategy for the Enterprise

- Guidelines for Planning GPOs
- Guidelines for Determining GPO Inheritance
- Guidelines for Determining a Group Policy Strategy for Sites
- Guidelines for Planning the Administration of GPOs
- Guidelines for Deploying GPOs

Introduction

When you plan an Active Directory structure, create a plan for GPO inheritance, administration, and deployment that provides the most efficient Group Policy management for your organization.

Also consider how you will implement Group Policy for the organization. Be sure to consider the delegation of authority, separation of administrative duties, central versus decentralized administration, and design flexibility so that your plan will provide for ease of use as well as administration.

Lesson objectives

After completing this lesson, you will be able to:

- Explain guidelines for planning GPOs.
- Explain guidelines for determining GPO inheritance.
- Explain guidelines for determining a Group Policy strategy for sites.
- Explain guidelines for planning the administration of GPOs.
- Explain guidelines for deploying GPOs.

Guidelines for Planning GPOs

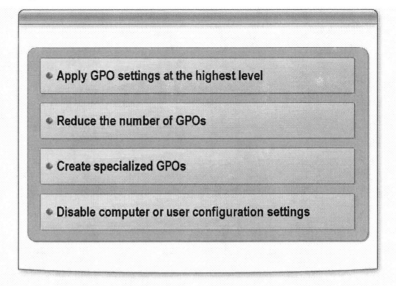

Introduction

Create GPOs in a way that provides for the simplest and most manageable design—one in which you can use inheritance and multiple links.

Guidelines

Apply the following guidelines for planning GPOs:

- *Apply GPO settings at the highest level.* This way, you take advantage of Group Policy inheritance. Determine what are the common GPO settings for the largest container, starting with the domain, and then link the GPO to this container.

- *Reduce the number of GPOs.* You reduce the number by using multiple links instead of creating multiple identical GPOs. Try to link a GPO to the broadest container possible to avoid creating multiple links of the same GPO at a deeper level.

- *Create specialized GPOs.* Use these GPOs to apply unique settings when necessary. GPOs at a higher level will not apply the settings in these specialized GPOs.

- *Disable computer or user configuration settings.* When you create a GPO to contain settings for only one of the two levels—user or computer—disable the other area. It improves the performance of a GPO application during user logon and prevents accidental GPO settings from being applied to the other area.

Guidelines for Determining GPO Inheritance

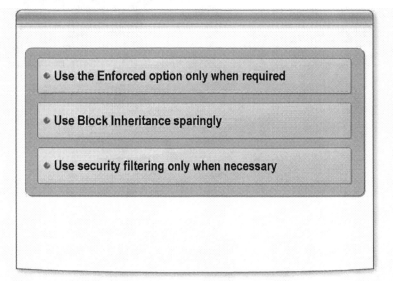

- Use the Enforced option only when required

- Use Block Inheritance sparingly

- Use security filtering only when necessary

Introduction

GPO inheritance plays an important part in implementing Group Policy in an enterprise. Therefore, you must decide beforehand whether to apply Group Policy to all or to specific users and computers.

Guidelines

Apply the following guidelines for determining GPO inheritance:

- *Use the Enforced (No Override) option only when required.* Use this option only for GPOs that you want to absolutely enforce, such as corporate-mandated security settings. Ensure that you design these GPOs to contain only these important settings.

- *Use Block Inheritance sparingly.* These settings make the troubleshooting and administration of GPOs more difficult.

- *Use security filtering only when necessary.* Use security filtering when settings apply only to a specific security group in a container. Limit the amount of security filtering by creating and linking GPOs at the appropriate level.

Guidelines for Determining a Group Policy Strategy for Sites

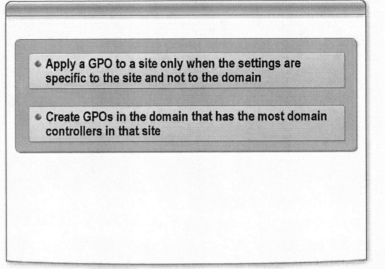

Introduction

You can link GPOs to a site, which enforces settings on all computers and users that are physically located at that site. When Group Policy is set at the site level, it does not affect mobile users on that site if they access the network from another site.

Guidelines

Apply the following guidelines for determining a Group Policy strategy for sites:

- *Apply a GPO to a site only when the settings are specific to the site and not to the domain.* Troubleshooting GPO settings that are linked to the site can be difficult.

- *Create GPOs in the domain that has the most domain controllers in that site.* A domain controller from the domain that contains the site-linked GPO is contacted before the GPO is applied, regardless of what domain the user or computer is a member of.

Guidelines for Planning the Administration of GPOs

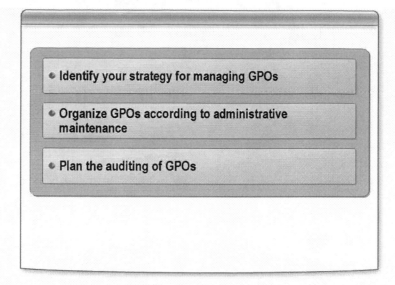

* Identify your strategy for managing GPOs

* Organize GPOs according to administrative maintenance

* Plan the auditing of GPOs

Introduction

Be sure to document the following information about your strategy for managing GPOs in your organization.

Guidelines

Apply the following guidelines for planning the administration of GPOs:

- *Identify your administrative strategy for managing GPOs.* Determine who will create and link GPOs in your organization, and who will link GPOs but not create them. Also, determine who manages GPOs.

- *Organize GPOs according to administrative maintenance.* This way, you can delegate control of GPOs to the appropriate group and also reduce the potential for one administrator to overwrite changes that were made by another administrator on a given GPO. For example, you can organize Group Policy into the following categories of administration:

  - User configuration management

  - Data management

  - Software distribution

- *Plan for the auditing of GPOs.* Your organization may require you to log changes to GPOs and their use so that you can verify that Active Directory applied the settings correctly.

Guidelines for Deploying GPOs

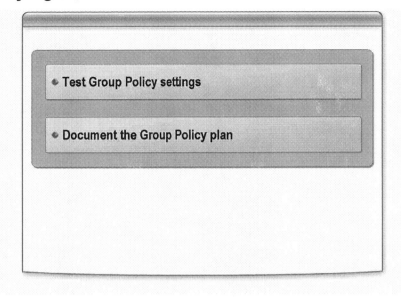

Introduction

When planning to implement Group Policy, be sure to test and document your Group Policy strategy.

Guidelines

Apply the following guidelines for deploying GPOs:

- *Test Group Policy settings.* Test the results of GPOs in many situations. Many medium- and large-sized organizations create a miniature version of the production environment to use as a test bed. In small organizations that lack the resources to create a test bed, implement Group Policy in the production environment at off-peak times, and have a regression strategy in place to rectify any problems. Testing strategies include:

  - Log on as representative users at representative workstations to verify that the expected Group Policy settings have been applied and that inheritance conflicts do not occur. You can use the Group Policy Modeling Wizard and the Group Policy Results Wizard to determine which Group Policy settings from which GPOs have been applied.

  - Log on in all possible conditions to ensure that Group Policy settings are applied consistently.

  - Test portable computers by connecting them to the network from various sites where users are likely to log on.

- *Document the Group Policy plan.* Always keep a detailed list of all GPOs so that you can easily troubleshoot and manage Group Policy. Consider including the following information in your list:

  - The name and purpose of each GPO.

  - Group Policy settings in each GPO.

  - GPO links to a site, domain, or organizational unit.

  - Any special settings that are applied to the GPO, such as Enforce, partial disable, and full disable.

Practice: Planning a Group Policy Strategy for the Enterprise

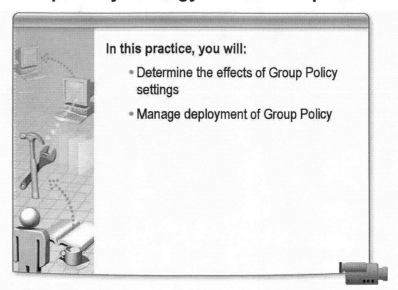

File Location

To view the *Planning a Group Policy Strategy for the Enterprise* activity, open the Web page on the Student Materials compact disc, click **Multimedia**, and then click the title of the presentation. Do not open this presentation unless the instructor tells you to.

Objective

In this practice, you will determine the effect of applying some Group Policy settings and GPO inheritance.

Instructions

The *Planning a Group Policy Strategy for the Enterprise* activity includes multiple choice and drag-and-drop exercises that test your knowledge. Read the instructions, and then begin the activity on the **Effects of Group Policy Settings** tab.

Lab A: Implementing Group Policy

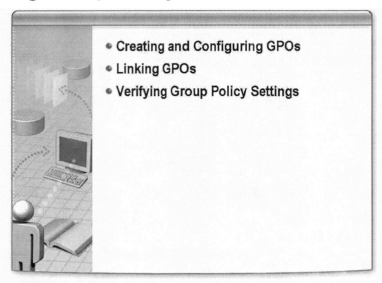

Objectives

After completing this lab, you will be able to:

- Create and configure GPOs.
- Link GPOs.
- Verify the Group Policy settings.

Prerequisites

Before working on this lab, you must have:

- Experience using Group Policy Management.
- Experience using the Group Policy Object Editor and the Group Policy Modeling Wizard.

Estimated time to complete this lab: 75 minutes

Exercise 1
Creating and Configuring GPOs

In this exercise, you will create an organizational unit for the Accounting department and separate organizational units for the Accounts Receivable and Accounts Payable groups in the Accounting department. Next, you will create and configure GPOs for the Accounts Receivable and Accounts Payable groups. You will perform these tasks on your domain in the forest.

Scenario

Northwind Traders wants strict control over policies that the Accounting department uses. You must ensure that the department uses certain global settings from the corporate GPO. You will create an Accounting standard GPO to remove the **Run** command from the **Start** menu and to remove the **Shut Down** command from users and computers. The corporate standard requires that passwords be reset every 30 days and have a minimum password length of eight characters. Each password must meet complexity requirements. Northwind Traders also wants to implement password history so that employees cannot reuse the past ten passwords.

The Accounting department wants a standard workstation for all users in each part of the organization. The Accounts Receivable group has a requirement to disable the **Add or Remove Programs** feature from Control Panel. The Accounts Payable group has an open computing environment that requires that users sometimes log on to different computers. For this reason, Northwind Traders wants to disable the computer locking feature.

Tasks	Specific instructions
1. Create the three organizational units.	a. Log on as **Nwtraders***x******ComputerName***User** (where *ComputerName* is the name of the computer you are working on) with a password of **P@ssw0rd** if you are not already logged on. b. Use **Run as** to open Active Directory Users and Computers. Use *YourDomain***\\Administrator** as the user name with a password of **P@ssw0rd** and then create the following organizational units: • Accounting • Accounts Receivable • Accounts Payable
2. Create the Accounting GPO and ensure that key settings are propagated to all users in Accounting.	a. Create a new GPO. b. Link the GPO to the Accounting OU. c. Configure the following Group Policy settings: • **Remove Run menu from Start Menu** • **Remove and prevent access to the Shut Down command** • **Enforced**

(continued)

Tasks	Specific instructions
3. Copy the Accounting GPO and rename it Accounts Receivable.	a. Copy the Accounting GPO. b. Rename the copy Accounts Receivable.
4. Configure the Accounts Receivable GPO.	■ Edit the Accounts Receivable GPO to set the policies to enable the following value: • **Remove Add or Remove Programs**
5. Copy the Accounting GPO and rename it Accounts Payable.	a. Copy the Accounting GPO. b. Rename the copy Accounts Payable.
6. Configure the Accounts Payable GPO.	■ Edit the Accounts Payable GPO to set the policies to the following value: • **Disable Computer locking** – the path to this option is User Configuration\Administrative Templates\System\Ctrl+Alt+Del Options.

Exercise 2
Linking GPOs

In this exercise, you will link GPOs to the appropriate organizational unit. After you link the GPOs, you can begin to enforce policies at the computer or user level.

Tasks	Specific instructions
▪ Link the Accounts Receivable and Accounts Payable GPOs to the appropriate organizational unit.	▪ In Group Policy Management, link the following organizational units to the appropriate GPO: ● Accounts Receivable ● Accounts Payable

Exercise 3
Verifying Group Policy Settings

In this exercise, you will use the Group Policy Modeling Wizard to verify the GPO settings that you configured in the previous exercises.

Tasks	Specific instructions
1. Use the Group Policy Modeling Wizard to verify the Accounting GPOs.	a. In Group Policy Management, open Group Policy Modeling Wizard. b. Accept default values for each Accounting organizational unit.
2. Review the Group Policy Modeling Wizard results to verify the GPO settings.	a. View the three modeling results that you created in the previous step. b. Review the settings for accuracy.

Microsoft® Training & Certification

Module 6: Deploying and Managing Software by Using Group Policy

Contents

Overview

- Introduction to Managing Software Deployment
- Deploying Software
- Configuring Software Deployment
- Maintaining Deployed Software
- Troubleshooting Software Deployment
- Planning a Software Deployment Strategy

Introduction

Microsoft® Windows® Server 2003 includes a feature called Software Installation and Maintenance that uses the Active Directory® directory service, Group Policy, and Microsoft Windows Installer to install, maintain, and remove software on computers in your organization. By using a policy-based method to manage software deployment, you can ensure that the applications that users require to perform their jobs are available whenever and wherever they are needed.

Objectives

After completing this module, you will be able to:

- Explain the basic concepts of software deployment by using Group Policy.
- Deploy software by using Group Policy.
- Configure software deployment by using Group Policy.
- Maintain deployed software by using Group Policy.
- Troubleshoot some common problems with software deployment.
- Plan a software deployment strategy.

Lesson: Introduction to Managing Software Deployment

- The Software Installation and Maintenance Process
- What Is Windows Installer?

Introduction

When you manage software by using the Software Installation extension of Group Policy, users have immediate access to the software that they require to perform their jobs, and they have an easy and consistent experience when working with software through its life cycle. The software life cycle consists of four phases: preparation, deployment, maintenance, and removal. Group Policy Software Installation uses Microsoft Windows® Installer technology to manage the installation process.

Lesson objectives

After completing this lesson, you will be able to:

- Describe each phase in the software installation and maintenance process of software deployment.

- Explain how you use Windows Installer to install and maintain software.

The Software Installation and Maintenance Process

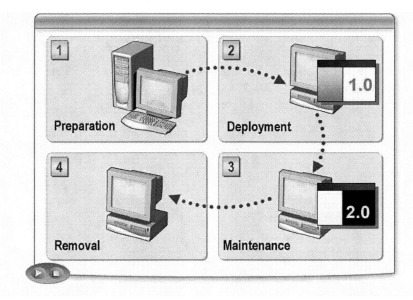

Introduction

In Windows Server 2003, you can use Group Policy to manage the software deployment process centrally or from one location. You can apply Group Policy settings to users or computers in a site, domain, or an organizational unit to automatically install, upgrade, or remove software. By applying Group Policy settings to software, you can manage the various phases of software deployment without deploying software on each computer individually.

Process

The following list describes each phase in the software installation and maintenance process:

1. *Preparation.* You must first determine if you can deploy the software by using the current Group Policy object (GPO) structure. You also must identify risks in using the current infrastructure that may prevent software installation. You prepare the files that enable an application to be deployed with Group Policy by copying the Windows Installer package files for an application to a software distribution point, which can be a shared folder on a server. You can acquire a Windows Installer package file from the application's vendor, or you can create a package file by using a third-party utility.

2. *Deployment.* You create a GPO that installs the software on the computer and links the GPO to an appropriate Active Directory container. The software is installed when the computer starts or when a user starts the application.

3. *Maintenance.* You upgrade software with a new version or redeploy software with a service pack or software update. The software is then automatically upgraded or redeployed when the computer starts or when a user starts the application.

4. *Removal.* To eliminate software that is no longer required, you remove the software package setting from the GPO that originally deployed the software. The software is then automatically removed when the computer starts or when a user logs on.

What Is Windows Installer?

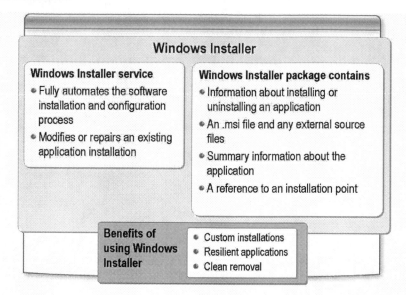

Introduction

To enable Group Policy to deploy and manage software, Windows Server 2003 uses Windows Installer. This component automates the installation and removal of applications by applying a set of centrally defined setup rules during the installation process.

Windows Installer components

Windows Installer contains two components:

- *Windows Installer service.* This client-side service fully automates the software installation and configuration process. The Windows Installer service can also modify or repair an existing installed application. It installs an application either directly from the CD-ROM or by using Group Policy. To install an application, the Windows Installer service requires a Windows Installer package.

- *Windows Installer package.* This package file contains all of the information that the Windows Installer service requires to install or uninstall software. A package file contains:

  - A Windows Installer file with an .msi extension.

  - Any external source files that are required to install or uninstall the software.

  - Standard summary information about the software and the package.

  - The product files or a reference to an installation point where the product files reside.

Benefits

The benefits of using the Windows Installer technology include:

- *Custom installations*. Optional features in an application, such as clip art or a thesaurus, can be visible in a program without the feature being installed. Although the menu commands are accessible, the feature is not installed until the user accesses the command on the menu. This method of installation helps reduce both the complexity of the application and the amount of hard disk space that the application uses.

- *Resilient applications*. If a critical file is deleted or becomes corrupt, the application automatically acquires a new copy of the file from the installation source, without requiring user intervention.

- *Clean removal*. Windows Installer uninstalls applications without leaving orphaned files or inadvertently breaking another application—for example, when a user deletes a shared file that another application requires. Also, Windows Installer removes all of the application-related registry settings and stores installation transactions in a database and subsequent log files.

Note When it is not feasible to use repackaging software to repackage an application, or when a Windows Installer package file is unavailable, you use .zap files (non-Windows Installer packages) to publish applications. For information about non-Windows Installer packages, see Appendix B, "Publishing Non-Windows Installer Packages," on the Student Materials compact disc. Also, see the white paper, *The Windows Installer Service*, under **Additional Reading** on the Web page on the Student Materials compact disc.

Lesson: Deploying Software

- Overview of the Software Deployment Process
- Assigning Software vs. Publishing Software
- How to Create a Software Distribution Point
- How to Use a GPO to Deploy Software
- Default Options for Software Installation
- How to Change the Options for Software Installation

Introduction

Deploying software ensures that required applications are available from any computer that a user logs on to. From the user's point of view, software is always available and functional. Administrators can either install software for users in advance or give users the option to install the software that they require, when they require it.

Lesson objectives

After completing this lesson, you will be able to:

- Explain the process of deploying software by using Group Policy.
- Explain the purpose of assigning software and publishing software.
- Create a software distribution point to deploy software.
- Create a GPO to assign or publish software.
- Describe the default options for installing software.
- Change options for installing software.

Overview of the Software Deployment Process

Introduction   When you deploy software, you are specifying how applications are installed and maintained in your organization.

Process   You perform the following tasks to use Group Policy to deploy new software:

1. *Create a software distribution point.* This shared folder on your server contains the package and software files for deploying software. When software is installed on a local computer, the Windows Installer copies files from to the computer. Keeping the files together for each application simplifies administration.

2. *Use a GPO to deploy software.* You must create or make necessary changes to a GPO for the container that you want to deploy the application to. You can configure the GPO to deploy software for a user or computer account. This task also includes selecting the type of deployment that you require.

3. *Change the software deployment properties.* Depending on your requirements, you can change the properties that were set during the initial deployment of software.

Assigning Software vs. Publishing Software

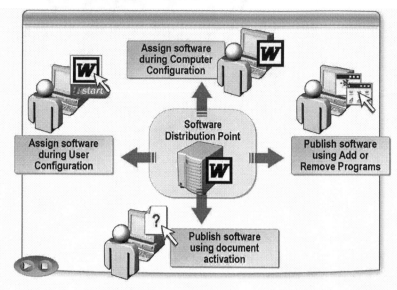

Introduction	The two deployment types are assigning software and publishing software.
Why assign software?	By assigning software, you ensure that the software is always available to the user. **Start** menu shortcuts and desktop icons for the application appear when the user logs on. For example, if the user opens a file that uses Microsoft Excel on a computer that does not have Excel, but Excel has been assigned to the user, Windows Installer installs Excel on that computer when the user opens the file.
	In addition, assigning software makes the software resilient. If for any reason the user deletes the software, Windows Installer reinstalls it the next time the user logs on and starts the application.
Why publish software?	By publishing software, you ensure that the software becomes available for users to install on their computers. Windows Installer adds no shortcuts to the user's desktop or **Start** menu, and no local registry entries are made. Because users must install the published software, you can publish software only to users, not to computers.

Methods for assigning and publishing software

You can assign and publish software by using one of the methods in the following table.

Deployment method	Method 1	Method 2
Assign	*During user configuration.* When you assign software to a user, the software is advertised on the user's desktop when the user logs on. Installation does not begin until the user double-clicks the application's icon or a file that is associated with the application, which is a method called document activation. If the user does not activate the application, the software is not installed, thus saving hard disk space and time.	*During computer configuration.* When you assign software to a computer, no advertising occurs. Instead, the software is installed automatically when the computer starts. Assigning software to a computer ensures that certain applications are always available on that computer, regardless of who uses it. You cannot assign software to a computer that is a domain controller.
Publish	*Using Add or Remove Programs.* A user can open Control Panel and double-click **Add or Remove Programs** to display the available applications. The user can select an application and then click **Add**.	*Using document activation.* When you publish an application in Active Directory, the file name extensions of the documents that it supports are registered in Active Directory. If a user double-clicks an unknown file type, the computer sends a query to Active Directory to determine whether any applications are associated with the extension. If Active Directory contains such an application, the computer installs it.

How to Create a Software Distribution Point

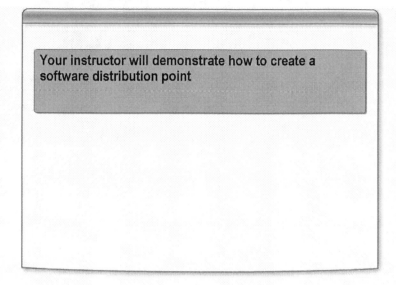

Your instructor will demonstrate how to create a software distribution point

Introduction

To deploy software for users or to make software available for users to install when required, create one or more software distribution points, and then copy the software to the software distribution points.

Procedure

To create a software distribution point, perform the following tasks:

1. Create a shared folder.

2. Create the appropriate application folders in the shared folder.

3. Set the appropriate permission for the shared folder. Assign users the Read NTFS file system permission so that they can access the software installation files on the software distribution point.

4. Copy the Windows Installer packages and the related files to the appropriate folders.

How to Use a GPO to Deploy Software

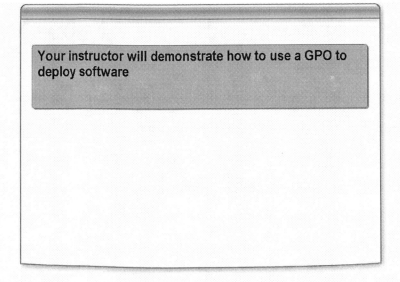

Introduction

After you create a software distribution point, you create a GPO that deploys those applications, and then link the GPO to the container that contains the users or computers that you want to deploy software to.

Important Do not assign or publish a Windows Installer package more than once in the same GPO. For example, if you assign Microsoft Office XP to the computers that are affected by a GPO, do not assign or publish it to users affected by the same GPO.

Procedure

To use a GPO to deploy software, perform the following steps:

1. Create or edit a GPO.

2. Under either **User Configuration** or **Computer Configuration** (depending on whether you are assigning the software to users or computers or publishing it to users), expand **Software Settings**, right-click **Software Installation**, point to **New**, and then click **Package**.

3. In the **File Open** dialog box, browse to the software distribution point by using the Universal Naming Convention (UNC) name—for example, *ServerName\\ShareName*, select the package file, and then click **Open**.

4. In the **Deploy Software** dialog box, select a deployment method, and then click **OK**.

Default Options for Software Installation

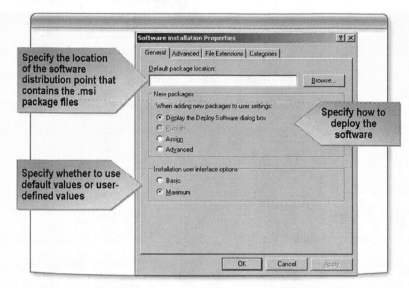

Introduction

You can configure the default options for software installation for the current GPO when you want to add several applications to a GPO at one time or want to use the same options for all of them by default.

Options

The following table lists the software installation default options.

Option	Description
Default package location	The location of the software distribution point that contains the .msi package files. You can specify any location that contains the software package, but make sure that the distribution point is a UNC path and not a local drive.
When adding new packages to user settings	Use the **Display the Deploy Software dialog box** option to display a dialog box for each package file that you add to the GPO. This dialog box prompts you to either publish or assign the new package file.
	Use the **Publish** option to automatically publish by default a new installation package file under **User Configuration** (this option does not appear under **Computer Configuration**). Use this option if you plan to add several applications to this GPO that must be published.
	Use the **Assign** option to automatically assign a new package file. Use this option if you plan to add several applications to this GPO that must be assigned.
	Use the **Advanced** option to achieve finer control on a per-package basis—for example, when you use transforms.

(continued)

Option	Description
Installation user interface options	Windows Installer packages often come with two setup interfaces. The **Basic** interface installs the software by using default values. The **Maximum** interface prompts the user to enter values. You can choose which interface to display to users during setup.

Note For more information about options for deployed software, see "Default Software Installation Options" in Module 6 on the Appendices page on the Student Materials compact disc.

How to Change the Options for Software Installation

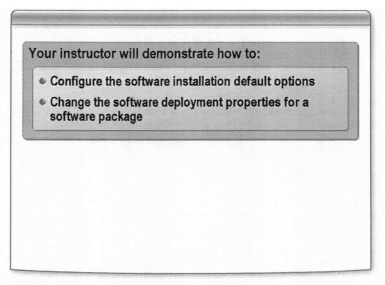

Your instructor will demonstrate how to:

- Configure the software installation default options
- Change the software deployment properties for a software package

Introduction

A GPO can contain several settings that affect how an application is installed, managed, and removed. You can define the default settings globally for the new packages in the GPO. You can change some of these settings later by editing the package properties in the Software Installation extension.

After you deploy a software package, you can change the deployment properties that were set during the initial deployment of software. For example, you can prevent users from installing a software package by using document activation.

Procedure for configuring software installation defaults

To configure the default options for software installation, perform the following steps:

1. Create or edit a GPO.

2. Under either **User Configuration** or **Computer Configuration** (depending on whether you are assigning the software to users or computers or publishing it to users), expand **Software Settings**, right-click **Software Installation**, and then click **Properties**.

3. On the **General** tab, configure the following software installation options:

   - **Default package location**

   - **When adding new packages to user settings**

   - **Installation user interface options**

4. On the **Advanced** tab, select the **Uninstall the application when they fall out of the scope of management** option.

Procedure for changing options for deployed software packages

To change the software deployment properties for a software package, perform the following steps:

1. In Software Installation, right-click the deployed package, and then click **Properties**.

2. In the **Properties** dialog box of the application, on the **Deployment** tab, change the following deployed software package options:

   - **Deployment type**

   - **Deployment options**

   - **Installation user interface options**

Practice: Deploying Software

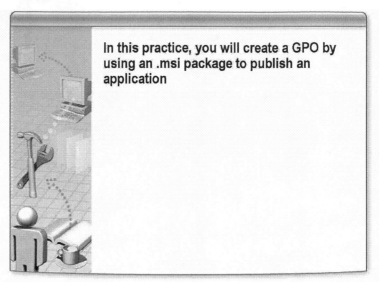

In this practice, you will create a GPO by using an .msi package to publish an application

Objectives

In this practice, you will create a GPO by using an .msi package to publish an application.

Scenario

Northwind Traders wants to ensure that all of the IT staff can manage the deployment of software throughout the organization. Before the IT team deploys software to the entire organization, you must ensure a safe environment. You will use the Windows Support Tools package as the test application. You must deploy this application successfully in the test environment before you release it to the production environment.

Practice

▶ **Deploy software**

1. Log on as **Nwtraders**x*ComputerName***User** (where *ComputerName* is the name of the computer you are working on).

2. Click **Start**, point to **Administrative Tools**, right-click **Group Policy Management**, and then click **Run as**.

3. In the **Run As** dialog box, click **The following user**, type *YourDomain***Administrator** as the user name with a password of **P@ssw0rd** and then click **OK**.

4. In Group Policy Management, expand **Forest**, expand **Domains**, expand *YourDomain*, and expand and then click **Group Policy Objects**.

5. Right-click **Group Policy Objects**, click **New**, type **Practice Software Deployment** and then click **OK**.

6. Right-click **Practice Software Deployment**, and then click **Edit**.

7. In Group Policy Object Editor, under **User Configuration**, expand **Software Settings**, and then click **Software Installation**.

8. Right-click **Software Installation**, point to **New**, and then click **Package**.

9. In the **Open** dialog box, browse to \\\\London\\Labfiles\\Lab6\\COSMO1, click **COSMO1.MSI**, and then click **Open**.

10. In the **Deploy Software** dialog box, click **OK**.

11. Close Group Policy Object Editor.

12. In Group Policy Management, expand the *ComputerName* organizational unit, right-click the **Research** organizational unit, click **Link an Existing GPO**, click **Practice Software Deployment**, and then click **OK**.

13. Close Group Policy Management.

Lesson: Configuring Software Deployment

- What Are Software Categories?
- How to Create Software Categories
- What Is Software Association?
- How to Associate File Name Extensions with Applications
- What Is Software Modification?
- How to Add Modifications to a Software Package

Introduction

Software Installation in Group Policy includes options for configuring deployed software. You can deploy several different configurations of one application and control how that application is assigned or published whenever a user's job duties change. You can also simplify the task of deploying software by categorizing programs that are listed in **Add or Remove Programs**, associating file name extensions with applications, and adding modifications to the deployed software.

Lesson objectives

After completing this lesson, you will be able to:

- Explain the purpose of software categories.

- Create software categories to classify applications in **Add or Remove Programs**.

- Explain the purpose of associating file name extensions with software packages.

- Associate file name extensions with applications by using Software Installation.

- Explain the purpose of adding software modifications.

- Add modifications to a software package to enable different groups in an organization to use a software package in different ways.

What Are Software Categories?

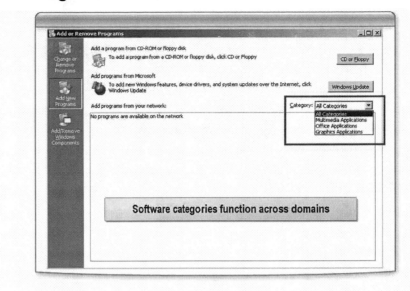

Software categories function across domains

Introduction

You use software categories to organize assigned and published software into logical groups so that users can easily locate applications in **Add or Remove Programs** in Control Panel. Windows Server 2003 does not ship with any predefined software categories.

Why create software categories?

You can create software categories to arrange different applications under a specific heading. Instead of relying on a single alphabetical list of applications that is available by default, you can organize software into categories, such as Graphics, Microsoft Office, and Accounting categories. Users can then choose which applications from the categories to install in **Add or Remove Programs**.

Scope and requirements

Software categories function across domains. You define them once for an entire forest. You can use the same list of software categories in all policies in the forest.

Categorizing applications requires you to first create a category, and then assign the applications to the category. You can list packages under more than one category.

How to Create Software Categories

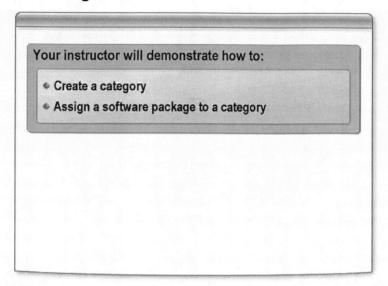

Introduction

To categorize software, you first create a software category, and then assign software to the category.

Procedure for creating a category

To create a category, perform the following steps:

1. Create or edit a GPO.

2. Under either **User Configuration** or **Computer Configuration** (depending on whether you are assigning the software to users or computers or publishing it to users), expand **Software Settings**, right-click **Software Installation**, and then click **Properties**.

3. On the **Categories** tab, click **Add** to enter a new category.

4. In the **Category** box, type the category name, and then click **OK** twice.

Procedure for assigning a software package to a category

To assign a software package to a category, perform the following steps:

1. Create or edit a GPO that contains the software package to categorize.

2. In the console tree, expand **Software Settings**, and then click **Software installation**.

3. In the details pane, right-click the software package, and then click **Properties**.

4. On the **Categories** tab, assign one or more categories to the package by clicking the category in the **Available categories** list, clicking **Select**, and then click **OK**.

What Is Software Association?

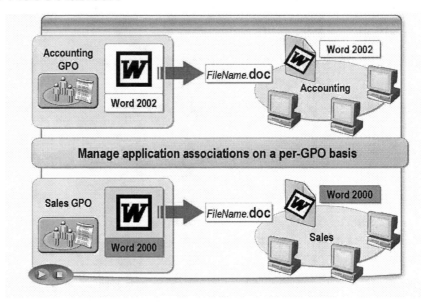

Introduction	To determine which software users install when they select a file, you can choose a file name extension and configure a priority for installing applications that are associated with the extension.
Why associate extensions with applications?	A client computer maintains a list of extensions and registered applications that use those extensions. When a user double-clicks an unknown file type, Windows Installer uses this list to install an application. Administrators cannot dictate the contents of this list, but they can determine the priority for installing or starting applications upon document activation.
Example	For example, your organization may require the use of both Microsoft Word 2000 and Word 2002. Each word processor may be preferred in a different department, but both of these applications use the .doc file extension. You must adjust the extension priorities for each department so that the preferred word processor is installed when the user activates a document.
Scope	You manage application associations on a per-GPO basis. Changing the priority order in a GPO affects only those users to whom the GPO applies. So, if you set Word 2002 as the default application for a GPO, it is the default application for only the users in that GPO.

How to Associate File Name Extensions with Applications

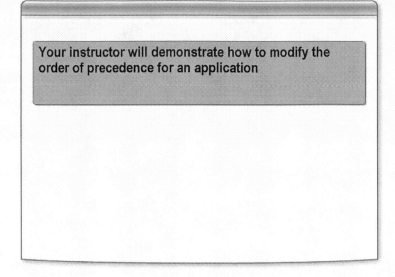

Your instructor will demonstrate how to modify the order of precedence for an application

Introduction

When you deploy software by using Group Policy, Active Directory creates a list of file name extensions that are associated with the application. When you set application precedence for extensions, Windows Installer queries Active Directory for this association.

Important   You cannot create new file name associations in Software Installation. Based on the built-in associations of the deployed applications, you can set a precedence order for only those applications that have multiple extensions associated with them.

Procedure

To modify the order of precedence for an application, perform the following steps:

1. Open the GPO that you used to deploy the application.

2. Expand **User Configuration**, expand **Software Settings**, right-click **Software Installation**, and then click **Properties**.

3. In the **Software installation Properties** dialog box, on the **File Extensions** tab, select an extension from the drop-down list box.

4. Under **Application Precedence**, click **Up** or **Down** to set the priority order for the extension that you selected.

   The first application listed in Windows Installer is the first one that Windows Installer installs if a document with the selected extension is invoked before the application has been installed.

Note   You may associate document types only with applications that you have deployed by using Group Policy. For example, you cannot associate the .doc extension with Word 2002 unless you have deployed Word 2002 by using Group Policy.

What Is Software Modification?

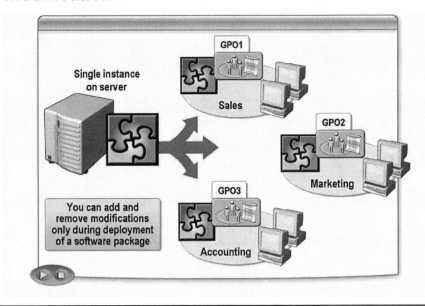

Introduction

Modifications are associated with the Windows Installer package at deployment time rather than when the Windows Installer uses the package to install or modify the application.

Why add modifications?

Deploying several configurations of one application enables different groups in your organization to use a software package in different ways. You can use software modifications, or *.mst files* (also called *transform files*), to deploy several configurations of one application. An .mst file is a custom software package that modifies how Windows Installer installs the associated *.msi* package.

Windows Installer applies modifications to packages in the order that you specify. To save modifications to an .mst file, you run the custom installation wizard, and then choose the .msi file on which to base transforms. You must determine the order in which to apply transform files before assigning or publishing the application.

Example

A large organization, for example, may want to deploy Microsoft Office XP, but department requirements for the Office suite vary widely in the organization. Rather than manually configure each department's installation, you can use different GPOs and .mst files in combination with the default .msi files for each department to deploy several configurations of Office XP. In this example, you would run the Office XP custom installation wizard from the Office Resource Kit to create the transform file.

How to Add Modifications to a Software Package

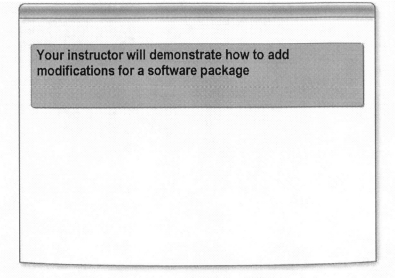

Your instructor will demonstrate how to add modifications for a software package

Introduction

You can add and remove modifications only when you initially deploy a software package. The transform file must exist before you attempt to add a modification to a package that you are deploying.

Procedure

To add modifications for a software package, perform the following steps:

1. Open the **Properties** dialog box for the application package.

2. On the **Modifications** tab, click **Add**.

3. In the **Open** dialog box, select the path and file name of the modification (.mst) file, click **Open**, and then click **OK**.

Important   Do not click **OK** until you have finished configuring the modifications. When you click **OK**, you assign or publish the package immediately. If you do not properly configure the modifications, you must uninstall the package or upgrade the package with a correctly configured version.

You can also add multiple modifications. Windows Installer applies the modifications according to the order that you specify in the **Modifications** list. To arrange the list, click a modification in the list, and then click **Move Up** or **Move Down**.

Practice: Configuring Software Deployment

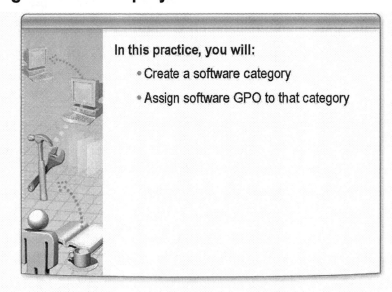

Objectives

In this practice, you will create a software category, and then assign software GPO to that category.

Scenario

Northwind Traders is deploying a large number of applications that are specific to the Accounting group. You have decided to create an Accounting software category so that accounting staff can quickly find the applications that they require. Not all accounting personnel require all of the accounting applications, so you decided to publish rather than assign the applications.

Practice

▶ **Configure software deployment**

1. Log as **Nwtraders*x**ComputerName*User**.

2. Open **Group Policy Management** as *YourDomain***Administrator** by using **Run as**.

3. In Group Policy Management, edit the **Practice Software Deployment** GPO to create a software category called Accounting.

4. Select the Accounting category for the COSMO1 software that you published in the **Practice Software Deployment** GPO.

Lesson: Maintaining Deployed Software

* Types of Software Upgrades
* How to Upgrade Deployed Software
* How Software Redeployment Works
* How to Redeploy Software
* Methods for Removing Deployed Software
* How to Remove Deployed Software

Introduction

After you deploy software, it may be necessary to modify it in order to maintain or upgrade users' software so that they have the most current version. Windows Server 2003 provides three options for maintaining software: upgrading software versions, redeploying software, and removing software.

Lesson objectives

After completing this lesson, you will be able to:

- Describe the options for upgrading deployed software.
- Upgrade deployed software by using Group Policy.
- Describe the options for redeploying software.
- Redeploy software by using Group Policy.
- Describe the options for removing deployed software.
- Remove deployed software by using Group Policy.

Types of Software Upgrades

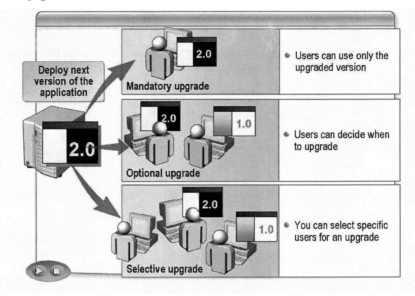

Introduction

The tasks in an organization are dynamic and varied. You can use Group Policy to deploy and manage software upgrades that meet departmental requirements in your organization. Upgrades typically involve major changes to software and have new version numbers. Usually, a substantial number of files change for an upgrade.

Why upgrade?

Several events in an application's lifecycle can trigger the need for an upgrade, including the following:

- A new version of the software is released that contains new and improved features.

- Patches and security or functional enhancements have been made to the software since the last release.

- An organization decides to use a different vendor's software.

Upgrade methods

There are three types of upgrades:

- *Mandatory upgrades*. These upgrades automatically replace an old version of software with an upgraded version. For example, if users currently use software version 1.0, this version is removed, and software version 2.0 is installed the next time that the computer starts or the user logs on.

- *Optional upgrades*. These upgrades allow users to decide when to upgrade to the new version. For example, users can determine if they want to upgrade to version 2.0 of the software or continue using version 1.0.

- *Selective upgrades*. If some users require an upgrade but not others, you can create multiple GPOs that apply to the users who require the upgrade and create the appropriate software packages in them.

How to Upgrade Deployed Software

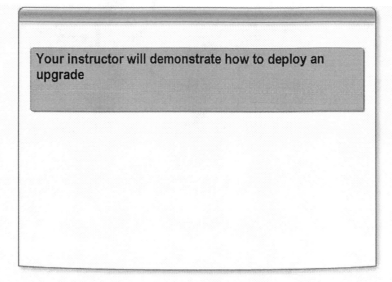

Introduction

You use Software Installation to establish the procedure to upgrade an existing software to the current release.

Procedure

To deploy an upgrade, perform the following tasks:

1. Deploy the next version of the software.

2. Open Software Installation, right-click the new version, and then click **Properties**.

3. In the **Properties** dialog box, on the **Upgrades** tab, in the **Packages that this package will upgrade** section, click **Add**, and then select the previous (current) version of the application.

   You can upgrade an application by using the current GPO or by selecting a specific GPO. If both software versions are native Windows Installer packages, this step is performed automatically.

4. Click either **Package can upgrade over existing package** or **Uninstall the existing package, then install the upgrade package**, and then click **OK**.

5. Select the type of upgrade:

   • To perform a mandatory upgrade, select the **Required upgrade for existing packages** check box, and then click **OK**.

   • To perform an optional upgrade, clear the **Required upgrade for existing packages** check box, and then click **OK**.

How Software Redeployment Works

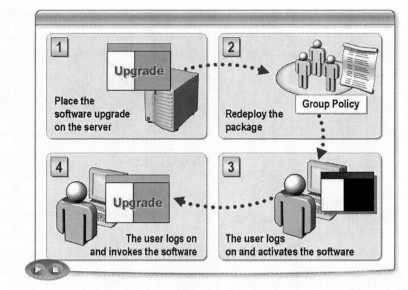

Introduction

Redeployment is the application of service packs and software upgrades to deployed software. You can redeploy a deployed package to force a reinstallation of the software. Redeployment may be necessary if the software package that was previously deployed is updated but remains the same version, or if there are interoperability issues or viruses that a reinstallation of the software will fix.

Redeployment methods

When you mark a package file for redeployment, the software is advertised to everyone who has been granted access to the application, either through assigning or publishing. Then, depending on how the original package was deployed, one of the three scenarios occurs:

- When you assign software to a user, the **Start** menu, desktop shortcuts, and registry settings that are relevant to the software are updated the next time the user logs on. The next time the user starts the software, the service pack or software update is automatically applied.

- When you assign software to a computer, the service pack or software upgrade is automatically applied the next time the computer starts.

- When you publish and install software, the **Start** menu, desktop shortcuts, and registry settings that are relevant to the software are updated the next time the user logs on. The next time the user starts the software, the service pack or software upgrade is automatically applied.

How to Redeploy Software

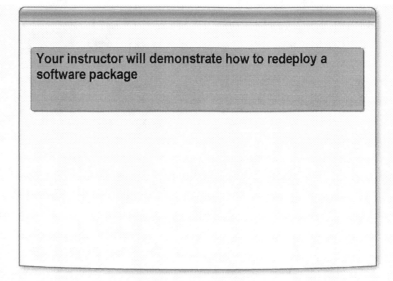

Your instructor will demonstrate how to redeploy a software package

Introduction

You use Software Installation to establish the procedure to redeploy a software package. Before redeployment, ensure that the service includes a new Windows Installer package file (.msi file). If it does not, you cannot redeploy the software, because only the new package file contains instructions for deploying the new files that the service pack or software upgrade contains.

Procedure

To redeploy a software package, perform the following tasks:

1. Obtain the service pack or software upgrade from the application vendor and place the files in the appropriate installation folders.

2. Edit the GPO that originally deployed the software.

3. Open Software Installation, right-click the package file name, point to **All Tasks**, and then click **Redeploy Application**.

4. In the dialog box, click **Yes**.

Note   For information about how to upgrade software that is stored on network servers, see the article, "Q226936: Patch a Software Installation Stored on a Network Server That Is Deployed Using Microsoft Software Installer" under **Additional Reading** on the Web page on the Student Materials compact disc.

Methods for Removing Deployed Software

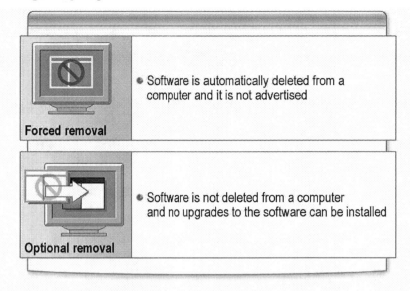

Forced removal	● Software is automatically deleted from a computer and it is not advertised
Optional removal	● Software is not deleted from a computer and no upgrades to the software can be installed

Introduction

It may be necessary to remove software if a version is no longer supported or if users no longer require the software. You can either force the removal of software or give the users the option of using the old software.

Removal methods

There are two removal methods:

- *Forced removal.* You can force the removal of the software, which automatically deletes it from a computer the next time the computer starts or the next time a user logs on—which occurs in the case of a user Group Policy setting. Removal takes place before the desktop appears.

- *Optional removal.* You can remove the software from Software Installation without forcing the physical removal of the software. Software is not actually removed from computers. The software no longer appears in **Add or Remove Programs**, but users can still use it. If users manually delete the software, they cannot reinstall it.

How to Remove Deployed Software

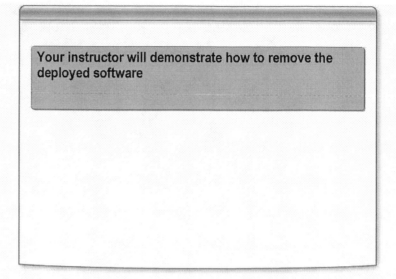

Your instructor will demonstrate how to remove the deployed software

Introduction

When you use Group Policy to deploy software, you can configure a GPO to remove software that is outdated or is no longer required by your organization. You can also remove old software by configuring the GPO to allow users to optionally upgrade to a new software package.

Procedure

To remove the deployed software, perform the following steps:

1. Open the GPO that was originally used to deploy the software.

2. In Software Installation, right-click the name of the package, point to **All Tasks**, and then click **Remove**.

3. In the **Remove Software** dialog box, click one of the following, and then click **OK**.

   - **Immediately uninstall the software from users and computers**.

   - **Allow users to continue to use the software, but prevent new installations**.

Note   You must ensure that users restart their computers if the change affects the computer or to log on again if the change affects the user.

Practice: Maintaining Deployed Software

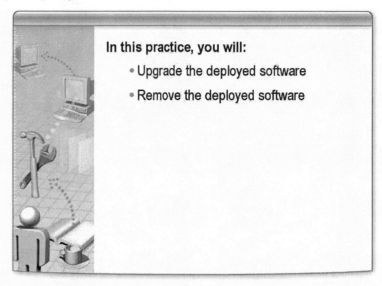

In this practice, you will:

• Upgrade the deployed software

• Remove the deployed software

Objectives

In this practice, you will upgrade the deployed software and remove the deployed software.

Scenario

You are testing software maintenance for previously deployed software. You must determine the steps necessary to deploy an application upgrade.

Practice

▶ **Maintain deployed software**

1. Log on as *YourDomain***Administrator**.

2. Open Group Policy Management as *YourDomain***Administrator** by using **Run as**.

3. In Group Policy Management, edit the **Practice Software Deploy** GPO to create a new software installation package for **\\\\London\\Labfiles\\Lab6\\COSMO2\\COSMO2.MSI**.

4. Set the properties of the Cosmo2 package to upgrade the Cosmo1 package.

5. Remove deployed software Cosmo 1 because the evaluation time has expired.

Lesson: Troubleshooting Software Deployment

- Common Problems When Using Group Policy to Deploy Software
- How to Determine the Cause of the Problem
- How to Resolve Software Installation Problems When Using Group Policy

---

Introduction

You may encounter problems when you use Group Policy to deploy software. Some methods exist to help you identify and fix these problems.

An important part of troubleshooting Group Policy problems is to consider dependencies between components. For example, software deployment relies on Group Policy, and Group Policy relies on Active Directory. Active Directory relies on the proper configuration of network services. When you try to fix problems in one component, check whether the components, the services, and the resources that it relies on are working correctly. Event logs can help you find problems that this type of hierarchical dependency can cause.

Lesson objectives

After completing this lesson, you will be able to:

- Explain some common problems that may occur when using Group Policy to deploy software.
- Determine the root cause of a problem by performing some tests.
- Resolve software installation problems when using Group Policy.

Common Problems When Using Group Policy to Deploy Software

Symptom	Possible cause
Applications do not appear in Add or Remove Programs	• Application is assigned instead of published • GPO was not applied
Applications do not appear in the Start menu	• Application is published instead of assigned • GPO was not applied
Applications appear but cannot be installed	• Software distribution point is not accessible • Previously installed applications prevent new installations

Introduction

Some common problems may occur when you use Group Policy to deploy software. Identifying the symptoms and possible causes is the first step in resolving these problems.

Symptoms and their possible causes

The following table lists the symptoms and their possible causes.

Symptom	Possible causes
Applications do not appear in **Add or Remove Programs**	• The application was assigned instead of published; it was never deployed or it was deployed in the wrong organizational unit; or Group Policy conflicts may prevent it from being deployed. It is possible to assign a user an application at one level of Active Directory (for example, at the domain level), and then deny the user access to that application at a lower level (for example, at the organizational unit level). • The application was assigned to computers, and computer policy in most cases overrides user policy. For example, if a user was assigned Word, but Word has been marked for mandatory removal from a computer, the user cannot open Word when she logs on to the computer. • The GPO was not applied. Possible reasons include: GPO did not apply to the user or the computer because of GPO conflict and precedence, security group filtering, WMI filtering, the Enforced and Block Inheritance options are Enabled, the GPO is linked to an incorrect container, or the GPO is partially or fully disabled. For example, the user is a member of a security group that is being filtered out from the effects of this GPO.
Applications do not appear in the **Start** menu	• The application was published instead of assigned, never deployed, or it was deployed in the wrong organizational unit. • The GPO was not applied.

(continued)

Symptom	Possible causes
Applications appear in the **Start** menu or in **Add or Remove Programs** but cannot be installed	• The software distribution point may not be accessible. It is likely that either the software distribution point is unavailable on the host server or affected users do not have proper permissions. Verify that users have at least Read NTFS permission for the software distribution point. • Previously installed applications may prevent new applications from being installed.

How to Determine the Cause of the Problem

Cause	Testing method
Application is published instead of assigned	• Use RSoP to determine which GPO is being applied
Application is assigned instead of published	
GPO was not applied	
Software distribution point is not accessible	• Manually install the Windows Installer package
Previously installed applications prevent new installations	• Create the Windows Installer log file

Introduction

After you identify the possible cause of a problem, the next step is to determine the root cause. To do this, determine whether the software distribution point is available, manually install the .msi package, determine the GPO that is applied by using Resultant Set of Policies (RSoP), and create the Windows Installer log file.

Procedure for verifying the availability of the software distribution point

Before you use this diagnostic procedure, verify that the software distribution point is available by performing the following tasks:

1. Connect to the server by using the UNC path to the software distribution point. For example, **net use** * *ServerName\ShareName*

   A mapped drive to the software distribution point on the destination server appears or a message appears that the software distribution point is not available.

2. Perform one of the following tasks:

   • If the network path is not available, ensure that the software distribution point is accessible from the server hosting the shared folder and attempt the installation again.

   • If the software distribution point is available, you can test a manual installation to ensure that the installation package file is working as expected.

Procedure for manually installing the Windows Installer package

To manually install the Windows Installer package, perform the following tasks:

1. At the command prompt, type **msiexec /I** *drive:\Package*.**msi**

   Where *drive* refers to the drive that the installation package resides on, *package.msi* refers to the MSI installation package file for the application that you are installing, and /I refers to the option to install a package based on the path following the /I switch.

2. Perform one of the following tasks:

   - If the manual installation is successful, check the GPO software installation setting to ensure that the user can install this application and that no other policies conflict with this one.

   - If the manual installation fails, verify permission settings for the software distribution point. The user who is trying to install the software requires at least Read permissions to install the application.

   Be sure to remove the manually installed application because it is not a managed application.

Procedure for determining whether the GPO is applied

You can use Group Policy Results to determine whether a GPO has been applied and its location. To determine the resultant set of policies, perform the following tasks:

1. Create RSoP by using the Group Policy Results Wizard, and then under **User Configuration**, click **Software Installation**.

   The origin of all applications appears in relation to the GPO that the application was deployed from.

2. Using this information, determine whether the settings in the GPO inheritance chain are causing application installation problems.

Procedure for enabling logging and creating the Windows Installer log file

When you enable Windows Installer logging, Windows Installer creates entries in the Windows event log by default. The events that you must monitor appear under the headings Software Installation, MsiInstaller, and Application Management. These entries provide useful information about the problem you are encountering in a software deployment.

To enable logging in Windows Installer, perform the following tasks:

1. Open Group Policy Management, right-click the GPO, and then click **Edit**.

2. In Group Policy Editor, under **Computer Configuration**, expand **Administrative Templates**, expand **Windows Components**, and then click **Windows Installer**.

3. Right-click **Logging**, and then click **Properties**.

While performing a manual installation, you can set various log levels to help you determine any problems that affect software installation.

Note   In this window, you can set the logging options for Windows Installer, configure user installations, and enable or disable System Restore checkpoints. You can use the checkpoints to roll back user systems to a previous state in the event of a problem with the installer.

To create a log file, perform the following task:

- At the command line, type **msiexec /I** *<path_to_package>* **/I***[x]*
  <path_to_logfile> and press ENTER.

  Where *x* is the logging level.

Note For more information about available options for the **msiexcec**
command, see Help and Support Center. Also see the article "Q223300: How to
Enable Windows Installer Logging" under **Additional Reading** on the Web
page on the Student Materials compact disc.

Warning Return logging to the normal state after diagnosis because logging
will severely affect the performance of the client computer.

The log file is created in the %windir% folder unless otherwise specified in the
command line. You can then view the log file with any text viewer, such as
Notepad.

How to Resolve Software Installation Problems When Using Group Policy

Cause	Resolution method
Application is published instead of assigned	Modify the GPO
Application is assigned instead of published	
GPO was not applied	
Software distribution point is not accessible	Change the permissions
Previously installed applications prevent new installations	Remove the registry components

Introduction

After you identify the root cause of a problem, the final step is to fix the problem or, if possible, provide an alternative method.

Resolution methods

To fix a software installation problem when using Group Policy:

- Modify the GPO to assign instead of publish and vice versa if an application was deployed incorrectly.

- Fix whatever prevented the GPO from being applied. If the GPO was applied to an incorrect set of users, altering this may cause the application to be uninstalled on the previous user's computers. Send a communication to them. You can use RSoP to determine why the GPO was not applied.

- Change the permissions on either the shared folder or NTFS files to allow Read access to the users or computers installing the application.

- Use MSIZap.exe to remove the registry components of the previously installed applications that prevent new applications from being installed.

Practice: Troubleshooting Software Deployment

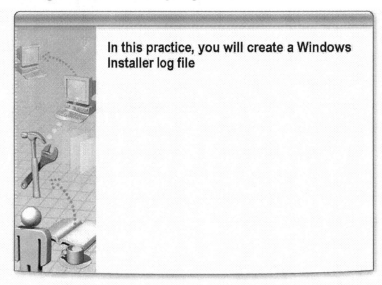

In this practice, you will create a Windows Installer log file

Objectives

In this practice, you will create a Windows Installer log file.

Scenario

Northwind Traders is having problems with a mission-critical application that was deployed by using Group Policy. Your manager has asked you to determine what has caused the problems.

Practice

▶ **Create a Windows Installer log file**

1. Log on as **Nwtraders***x**ComputerName***User**.

2. Open Group Policy Management as *YourDomain***Administrator** by using **Run as**.

3. In Group Policy Management, edit the **Practice Software Deploy** GPO to create a Windows Installer log file for this GPO.

Lesson: Planning a Software Deployment Strategy

- Guidelines for Planning Software Distribution Points
- Guidelines for Planning Software Deployment Using Group Policy
- Guidelines for Planning Software Maintenance

Introduction

When you plan software deployment, review the organization's software requirements for the overall Active Directory structure and the existing GPOs. Determine what methods you will use to deploy software. Be sure to have a plan for software deployment before you begin deploying software.

Lesson objectives

After completing this lesson, you will be able to:

- Explain guidelines for planning software distribution points.
- Explain guidelines for planning software deployment by using Group Policy.
- Explain guidelines for planning software maintenance.

Guidelines for Planning Software Distribution Points

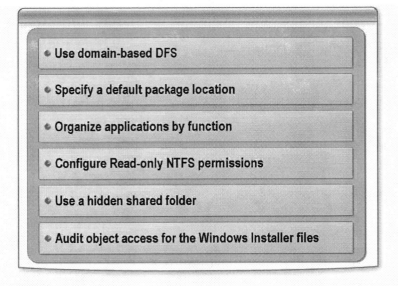

- Use domain-based DFS
- Specify a default package location
- Organize applications by function
- Configure Read-only NTFS permissions
- Use a hidden shared folder
- Audit object access for the Windows Installer files

Introduction

Before you create software distribution points for users to install software from, you must decide whether your organization will use a centralized approach to software deployment. By implementing a combination of the following guidelines, you will minimize the number of problems and troubleshooting paths when deployment issues arise.

Guidelines

Apply the following guidelines when you plan to create software distribution points:

- *Use domain-based Distributed File System (DFS) for the software distribution points.* DFS provides a single software distribution point for all published and assigned applications. Take advantage of DFS redundancy and load-balancing features. Create a DFS replica for the software distribution point in each site, from which many users will install the applications. Client computers then attempt to install deployed software from a DFS replica in their own site, which reduces network traffic across slow wide area network (WAN) links.

- *Specify a default package location.* Use it to point to the single software distribution point where package files are located. A default package location enables you to deploy new packages to one software distribution point. And by maintaining one software repository source, you can track problems more easily.

- *Organize applications by function.* Functional organization makes it easier to locate applications when you create software policies. For example, create a folder named Graphic Tools in the Software Distribution shared folder. Under the Graphic Tools folder, create a folder for each graphics application that you plan to deploy. Try to use folder names that are consistent with the software categories for the applications.

- *Configure NTFS permissions.* Use Read-only permission for users and Full Control to the administrators of these files.

- *Use a hidden shared folder.* For example, use *packages$* if you want to reduce the likelihood that users will manually install the package by using the shared folder.

- *Audit object access for Windows Installer files.* You can verify user or group permissions for accessing files.

Note   For more information about DFS, see Appendix C, Using DFS, on Student Materials compact disc.

Guidelines for Planning Software Deployment Using Group Policy

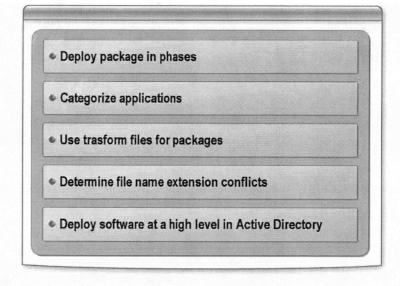

Introduction

When you plan your software deployment using Group Policy, consider the following guidelines.

Guidelines

Apply the following guidelines:

- *Deploy package files in phases.* Before you make package files available to all users, deploy them in phases or to a pilot group of users. Gradual deployment and testing helps you identify and resolve package problems before you deploy an application widely in an organization. It also helps reduce the network traffic and load on the software distribution point servers by staggering the installation requests by users. Be sure to gather feedback from the pilot users so that you can streamline and improve your deployment process.

- *Categorize applications for your organization.* Use categories that make it easy for users to find an application in **Add or Remove Programs**. For example, create categories such as Sales applications and Accounting applications. You can place an application in more than one category, as appropriate.

- *Use transform files for packages where possible.* Determine whether you require these software modification files. Before you deploy the generic package across the organization, establish common installation default options for specific groups of users and use software modification to provide the custom installation for these groups. Creating common installation default options in advance reduces the risk of users installing the generic package before the transform is created.

- *Determine potential conflicts in file name extensions.* These conflicts arise when more than one application tries to register the same extension. Determine conflicts among the applications that you installed by using Group Policy and applications you installed on workstations by using other methods. Configure the precedence of the extensions accordingly. This decision is best made at a level in the organization that can ensure that the plan meets all organizational requirements. After a decision is made, be sure that you document it so that you can quickly resolve extension conflicts in the future.

- *Deploy software at a high level in the Active Directory hierarchy.* Determine the highest level container that encompasses the users and computers that you plan to deploy the application to. Create and link the GPO that deploys this software package to this container. Because Group Policy settings apply by default to child Active Directory containers, it is efficient to assign or publish software by linking a GPO to a parent organizational unit or domain.

Guidelines for Planning Software Maintenance

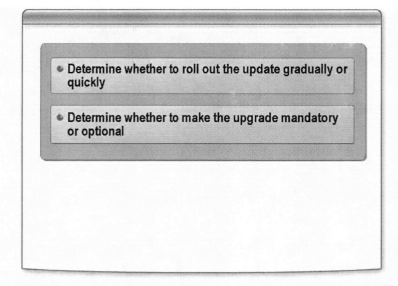

Introduction

When planning software maintenance by using Group Policy, consider the following guidelines.

Guidelines

Apply the following guideline:

- *Determine whether to roll out the update gradually or quickly to all users and computers.* Consider performing a gradual rollout when the update is not critical and the application is large and applies to many users or computers. It not only reduces the load on the software distribution point servers and the network; it also provides an early warning system if a problem occurs during the upgrade, when only a subset of the users or computers are affected. If the application is small, apply it to a small number of users or computers. If it is a critical update, apply it to all users and computers at once.

- *Determine whether to make the upgrade mandatory or optional.* If the upgrade is critical, make it mandatory. If it is not, make it optional, which users prefer. If you do not want to support multiple versions of an application, determine an appropriate transition period when both versions are available to. During this time, use the optional upgrade and then change it to mandatory at the end of the transition period. This way, a gradual upgrade occurs on a volunteer basis.

Practice: Planning a Software Deployment Strategy

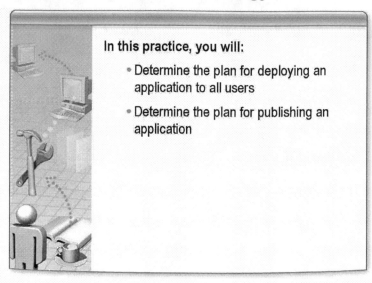

In this practice, you will:

- Determine the plan for deploying an application to all users
- Determine the plan for publishing an application

Objectives

In this practice, you will determine a plan for deploying an application to all users and a plan for publishing an application.

Scenario

Your organization recently expanded its market into the graphics field. It has purchased several graphics applications and a site license for Application 1. You must plan a software deployment strategy to deploy the applications to all users.

Practice

▶ **Plan a software deployment strategy**

1. What will you include in your plan?

   _____

   _____

2. Another graphics company named Fabrikam, Inc., has given you evaluation copies of its graphics suite for your organization to evaluate, in the hope that you will purchase a site license. To avoid being intrusive to your users, how do you plan to publish the application?

_____

_____

Lab A: Deploying and Managing Software Using Group Policy

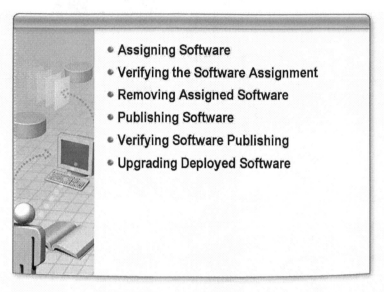

Objectives

After completing this lab, you will be able to:

- Assign software to users by using Group Policy.
- Publish software to users by using Group Policy.
- Remove deployed software by using Group Policy.
- Upgrade deployed software by using Group Policy.

Prerequisites

Before working on this lab, you must have:

- Knowledge and skills to create GPOs.
- Familiarity with using command-line tools.
- Knowledge of the software installation process.

Estimated time to complete this lab: 60 minutes

Exercise 1
Assigning Software

In this exercise, you will prepare your domain controller to host software that you will install by using Group Policy. You will work on your assigned domain controller to create the GPOs necessary to support software installation.

Scenario

Northwind Traders has decided to use Software Installation to deploy its recently purchased Cosmo 1 application. Your task is to research the two available methods to install the application: assigning software and publishing software.

Tasks	Specific instructions
1. Create a GPO to assign the Cosmo1 software installation package to the Sales organizational unit in your domain.	a. Logon as **Nwtraders***x******ComputerName***User** with the password of **P@ssw0rd** b. Use **Run As** to start Group Policy Management as *YourDomain***/Administrator** with a password of **P@ssw0rd** c. Create the **Lab Software Deploy** GPO and link it to the Sales organizational unit under the *ComputerName* organizational unit in *YourDomain*. d. Use the Cosmo1.msi package located on \\LONDON\Labfiles\Lab6\COSMO1.
2. Grant brendadia the right to log on locally.	a. Use **Run As** to start Domain Controller Security Policy as *YourDomain*/**Administrator** with a password of **P@ssw0rd** b. Grant brendadia the right to log on locally. c. Run **gpupdate** as *YourDomain***Administrator**.

Exercise 2
Verifying the Software Assignment

In this exercise, you must verify that the software assignment worked as expected. You will log on as a test user and verify whether the software assigned in the previous exercise is installed.

Tasks	Specific instructions
1. Log off and then log on as brendadia from your domain.	■ Log off and then log on as brendadia from your domain using a password of **P@ssw0rd**
❷ Does Cosmo 1 appear on the **All Programs** menu? Why or why not?	
2. Open the software package from the All Programs menu item that you created for it.	
❷ What happens when you try to open the software package?	

Exercise 3
Removing Assigned Software

In this exercise, you will remove the package that you assigned in the previous exercise. Now that you successfully deployed software by assigning a package to users, you are ready to evaluate the publishing option by using the same package. You must remove the package before you can create a package to publish the application.

Tasks	Specific instructions
■ Remove the Cosmo 1 application.	a. Log on as **Nwtraders***x**ComputerName***User** with a password of **P@ssw0rd**
	b. Use **Run as** to start Group Policy Management as *YourDomain***Administrator** with a password of **P@ssw0rd**
	c. Log off and then log on as brendadia from your domain with a password of **P@ssw0rd**
	d. Verify that the application was removed immediately for users and computers.

Exercise 4
Publishing Software

In this exercise, you will edit Group Policy to publish an application. You will publish software to better understand the differences between publishing and assigning software.

Tasks	Specific instructions
1. Open Group Policy Management.	a. Use Run as. b. When prompted, log on with the password of **P@ssw0rd**
2. Browse to your software deployment policy and edit the policy.	
3. Create a software installation package to publish the Cosmo1 package.	▪ On the instructor's software distribution point where the package is located, click **Cosmo1.msi**.

Exercise 5
Verifying Software Publishing

In this exercise, you will verify that the software that you published in the previous exercise is installed and working as expected. You will log on as a test user and verify the software publishing settings in Exercise 4.

Tasks	Specific instructions
1. Log on as brendadia from your domain.	▪ Use a password of **P@ssw0rd**
2. Install the published software.	▪ In Control Panel, use **Add or Remove Programs**.
3. Verify that the published software was installed.	▪ On the **All Programs** menu, verify the installation of Cosmo 1.
4. Log on as *YourDomain\ ComputerNameUser*.	

? Is the application installed for this user? Why or why not?

_____

_____

? Is Cosmo 1 listed in **Add or Remove Programs**? Why or why not?

_____

_____

Exercise 6
Upgrading Deployed Software

In this exercise, you will upgrade the software that you deployed by editing Group Policy. Northwind Traders has purchased an upgrade to the Cosmo application. All computers must be upgraded to the new release of this software. You are responsible for ensuring that Group Policy can meet the corporate requirements. By using Group Policy, you will find that it is not necessary to upgrade each user or computer manually. Management would like you to pilot the software upgrade to ensure that you can fix any bugs that you find in the process before you deploy the software to the entire organization.

Tasks	Specific instructions
1. Upgrade Cosmo 1.	a. Use **Run as** to open Group Policy Management. b. Edit the software deployment policy to create an upgrade package.
2. Verify the upgrade of Cosmo 1.	a. Verify that the existing application is removed before you install the new application. b. Verify that Cosmo 2 replaced Cosmo 1.

Microsoft®
Training &
Certification

Module 7: Implementing Sites to Manage Active Directory Replication

Contents

Overview

- ● Introduction to Active Directory Replication
- ● Creating and Configuring Sites
- ● Managing Site Topology
- ● Troubleshooting Replication Failures
- ● Planning a Site

Introduction

Replication in a Microsoft® Windows® Server 2003 Active Directory® directory service involves the transfer and maintenance of Active Directory data between domain controllers on a network. Active Directory uses a *multimaster replication model*. Multimaster means that there are multiple domain controllers, also called masters, which have the authority to modify or control the same information. In this replication model, any change to data on one domain controller must be replicated to all domain controllers. By understanding the Active Directory replication model, you can manage replication network traffic and ensure the consistency of Active Directory data across your network.

Objectives

After completing this module, you will be able to:

- ■ Explain the components of replication and the replication process.
- ■ Create and configure sites.
- ■ Manage an Active Directory site topology.
- ■ Monitor and troubleshoot Active Directory replication failures.
- ■ Plan a site strategy.

Lesson: Introduction to Active Directory Replication

- Multimedia: Replication Within Sites
- Replication of Linked Multivalued Attributes
- What Are Directory Partitions?
- What Is Replication Topology?
- Automatic Generation of Replication Topology
- Global Catalog and Replication of Partitions

Introduction

When a user or an administrator performs an action that initiates an update to Active Directory, an appropriate domain controller is automatically chosen to perform the update. This change is made transparently on one of the domain controllers. Active Directory uses multimaster replication with loose consistency to ensure that all domain controllers are updated. By understanding the replication process and replication topology, you can efficiently manage replication in Active Directory.

Replication is the process of updating information in Active Directory from one domain controller to other domain controllers on a network. The replication process synchronizes the movement of updated information between domain controllers. Synchronization ensures that all information in Active Directory is available to all domain controllers and client computers across the network.

Lesson objectives

After completing this lesson, you will be able to:

- Explain how Active Directory replication works.
- Explain the purpose of linked multivalued attributes replication.
- Explain how the directory partitions enable replication among the domain controllers during replication.
- Explain the purpose of replication topology.
- Explain how KCC enables automatic generation of replication topology.
- Explain how Active Directory modifies the replication topology when you add a new global catalog sever to the forest.

Multimedia: Replication Within Sites

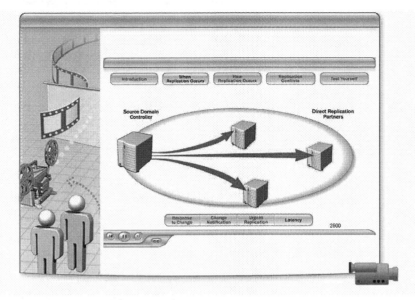

File location

To view the *Replication Within Sites* presentation, open the Web page on the Student Materials compact disc, click **Multimedia**, and then click the title of the presentation. Do not open this presentation unless the instructor tells you to.

Objectives

At the end of this presentation, you will be able to:

- Define replication and predict when it will occur.

- Describe how replication occurs.

- Describe replication conflicts and how to resolve them.

Key points

The key points of Active Directory replication within a site are:

- *When does replication occur?* When there is:

  - An addition of an object to Active Directory.

  - A modification of an object's attribute values.

  - A name change of an object's container.

  - A deletion of an object from the directory.

- *Change notification.* When a change occurs on a domain controller, the domain controller notifies its replication partners within the same site. This process is called change notification.

- *Replication latency.* The delay between the time that a change occurs and the time that the update reaches all of the domain controllers in a site. The default replication latency is 15 seconds.

- *Urgent replication.* Rather than wait the default 15 seconds, security-sensitive attribute updates trigger an immediate change notification.

- *Convergence.* Each update in Active Directory eventually propagates to every domain controller in the site that hosts the partition on which the update was made. This complete propagation is called convergence.

- *Propagation dampening.* The process of preventing unnecessary replication. Each domain controller assigns every changed attribute and object an Update Sequence Number (USN) to prevent unnecessary replication.

- *Conflicts.* When concurrent updates that originate on two separate master replicas are inconsistent, conflicts may arise. Active Directory resolves three types of conflicts: attribute, deleted container, and Relative Distinguished Name (RDN) conflicts.

- *Globally unique stamp.* Active Directory maintains a stamp that contains the version number, timestamp, and server globally unique identifier (GUID) that Active Directory created during the originating update.

Note   For more information about USNs, see "Replication Within Sites" in Module 7 on the Appendices page on the Student Materials compact disc.

Replication of Linked Multivalued Attributes

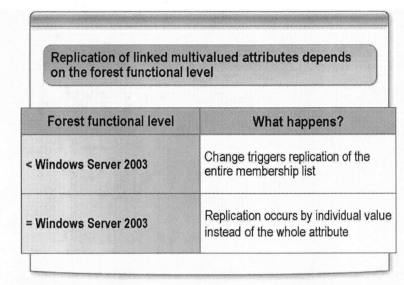

Replication of linked multivalued attributes depends on the forest functional level

Forest functional level	What happens?
< Windows Server 2003	Change triggers replication of the entire membership list
= Windows Server 2003	Replication occurs by individual value instead of the whole attribute

Introduction

The process of replication of linked multivalued attributes is different than the normal replication that occurs in Active Directory.

Linked multivalued attributes and forest functional levels

The process by which linked multivalued attributes are replicated varies, depending on the functional level of the forest:

- When the functional level of the forest is below Windows Server 2003, any change that was made to a group membership triggers replication of the entire membership list. The multivalued **member** attribute is considered a single attribute for the purpose of replication in this case. This replication increases the probability of overwriting a membership change that another administrator performed on another domain controller before the first change was replicated.

- When the functional level of the forest is set to Windows Server 2003, an individual value replicates changes to linked multivalued attributes. This improved functionality replicates only changes to group membership and not to the entire membership list.

Note For more information about adjusting replication and configuring entries in Active Directory, see "Replication of Linked Multivalued Attributes" in Module 7 on the Appendices page on the Student Materials compact disc.

What Are Directory Partitions?

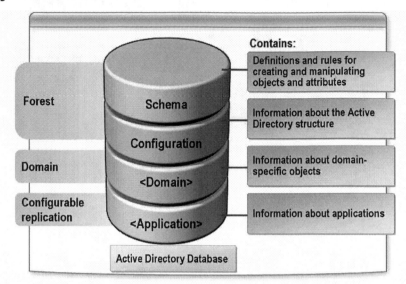

Introduction

The Active Directory database is logically separated into directory partitions, a schema partition, a configuration partition, domain partitions, and application partitions. Each partition is a unit of replication, and each partition has its own replication topology. Replication is performed between directory partition replicas. All domain controllers in the same forest have at least two directory partitions in common: the schema and configuration partitions. All domain controllers in the same domain, in addition, share a common domain partition.

What is a schema partition?

Only one schema partition exists per forest. The schema partition is stored on all domain controllers in a forest. The schema partition contains definitions of all objects and attributes that you can create in the directory, and the rules for creating and manipulating them. Schema information is replicated to all domain controllers in the forest. Therefore, all objects must comply with the schema object and attribute definitions.

What is a configuration partition?

There is only one configuration partition per forest. Stored on all domain controllers in a forest, the configuration partition contains information about the forest-wide Active Directory structure, including what domains and sites exist, which domain controllers exist in each forest, and which services are available. Configuration information is replicated to all domain controllers in a forest.

What is a domain partition?

Many domain partitions can exist per forest. Domain partitions are stored on each domain controller in a given domain. A domain partition contains information about all domain-specific objects that were created in that domain, including users, groups, computers, and organizational units. The domain partition is replicated to all domain controllers of that domain. All objects in every domain partition in a forest are stored in the global catalog with only a subset of their attribute values.

What is an application partition?

Application partitions store information about applications in Active Directory. Each application determines how it stores, categorizes, and uses application-specific information. To prevent unnecessary replication of specific application partitions, you can designate which domain controllers in a forest host specific application partitions. Unlike a domain partition, an application partition cannot store security principal objects, such as user accounts. In addition, the data in an application partition is not stored in the global catalog.

As an example of application partition, if you use a Domain Name System (DNS) that is integrated with Active Directory, you have two application partitions for DNS zones: ForestDNSZones and DomainDNSZones.

- ForestDNSZones is part of a forest. All domain controllers and DNS servers in a forest receive a replica of this partition. A forest-wide application partition stores the forest zone data.

- DomainDNSZones is unique for each domain. All domain controllers that are DNS servers in that domain receive a replica of this partition. The application partitions stores the domain DNS zone in the DomainDNSZones *<domain name>*.

Each domain has a DomainDNSZones partition, but there is only one ForestDNSZones partition. No DNS data is replicated to the global catalog server.

What Is Replication Topology?

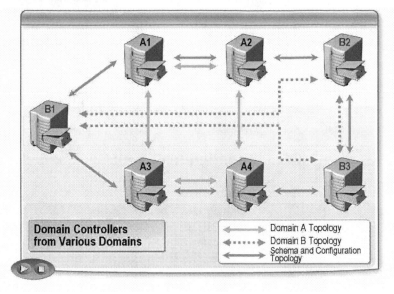

Introduction

Replication topology is the route by which replication data travels throughout a network. Replication occurs between two domain controllers at a time. Over time, replication synchronizes information in Active Directory for an entire forest of domain controllers. To create a replication topology, Active Directory must determine which domain controllers replicate data with other domain controllers.

Replication of partitions

Active Directory creates a replication topology based on the information that is stored in Active Directory. A replication topology can differ for schema, configuration, domain, and application partitions.

Because all domain controllers within a forest share schema and configuration partitions, Active Directory replicates schema and configuration partitions to all domain controllers. Domain controllers in the same domain also replicate the domain partition. In addition, domain controllers that host an application partition replicate the application partition.

To optimize replication traffic, a domain controller may have several replication partners for different partitions. Active Directory replicates updates to the directory across domain controllers that contain the updated partition in the forest.

Connection objects

Domain controllers that are linked by connection objects are called *replication partners*. The links that connect replication partners are called *connection objects*. Connection objects are created on each domain controller and point to another domain controller for a source of replication information. They are a one-way replication path between two server objects.

The default replication topology in a site is a bidirectional ring, which consists of two complementary unidirectional connection objects between adjacent domain controllers. This topology improves fault tolerance when one of the domain controllers is offline.

Active Directory creates additional connection objects as necessary to ensure statistically that the maximum number of hops that it takes to replicate an originating update to all replicas of a given partition in a ring is not more than three.

Automatic Generation of Replication Topology

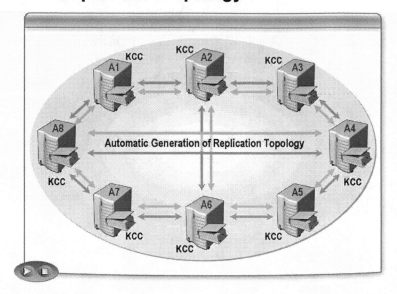

Introduction	When you add domain controllers to a site, Active Directory uses the Knowledge Consistency Checker (KCC) to establish a replication path between domain controllers.
What is Knowledge Consistency Checker?	The KCC is a built-in process that runs on each domain controller and generates the replication topology for all directory partitions that are contained on that domain controller. The KCC runs at specified intervals—every 15 minutes by default—and designates replication routes between domain controllers that are the most favorable connections that are available at the time.
How does KCC work?	To generate a replication topology automatically, the KCC evaluates information in the configuration partition on sites, the cost of sending data between these sites (cost refers to the relative value of the replication paths), any existing connection objects, and the replication protocols that the KCC can use between the sites. Next, the KCC calculates the best connections for a domain controller's directory partitions to other domain controllers. If replication within a site becomes impossible or has a single point of failure, the KCC automatically establishes new connection objects between domain controllers to maintain Active Directory replication.
How are additional connection objects created?	You can create connection objects automatically or manually. When you run the KCC on the destination domain controller, you automatically create connection objects. You can create connection objects manually by using Active Directory Sites and Services.

KCC and connection objects

The KCC algorithm is designed to match domain controllers with common directory partitions, which results in complimentary connection objects between replication partners and makes two domain controllers sources for each other whenever possible. Replication from any partition uses one connection object.

For example, to fully replicate directory information between domain controller A and domain controller B requires two connection objects:

- One connection object enables replication from domain controller A to domain controller B. This connection object exists in the NTDS Settings object of domain controller B.

- A second connection object enables replication from domain controller B to domain controller A. This connection object exists in the NTDS Settings object of domain controller A.

Global Catalog and Replication of Partitions

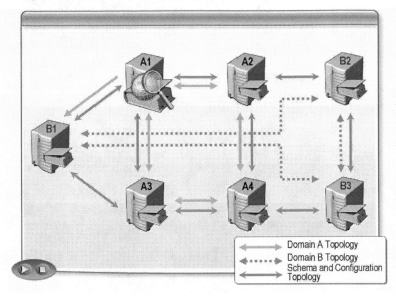

Domain A Topology
Domain B Topology
Schema and Configuration
Topology

Introduction

A *global catalog server* is a domain controller that stores two forest-wide partitions—the schema and configuration partitions—plus a read/write copy of the partition from its own domain and a partial replica of all other domain partitions in the forest. These partial replicas contain a read-only subset of the information in each domain partition.

How does replication affect the global catalog server?

When you add a new domain to a forest, the configuration partition stores information about the new domain. Active Directory replicates the configuration partition to all domain controllers, including global catalog servers, through normal forest-wide replication. Each global catalog server becomes a partial replica of the new domain by contacting a domain controller for that domain and obtaining the partial replica information. The configuration partition also provides the domain controllers a list of all global catalog servers in the forest.

Global catalog servers register special DNS records in the DNS zone that corresponds to the forest root domain. These records, which are registered only in the Forest Root DNS zone, help clients and servers locate global catalog servers throughout the forest.

Practice: Introduction to Active Directory Replication

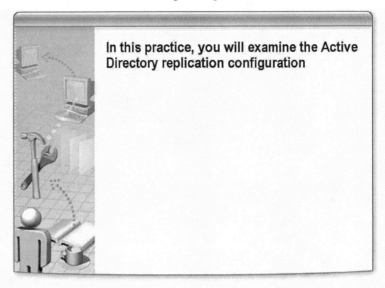

In this practice, you will examine the Active Directory replication configuration

Objectives

In this practice, you will examine the Active Directory replication configuration.

Instructions

You will work with your partner.

Scenario

Northwind Traders is experiencing problems with replication conflicts. You must understand how replication conflicts occur and how to resolve them.

Practice

▶ **Examine Active Directory replication**

1. Log on as **Nwtraders***x**ComputerName***User** (where *ComputerName* is the name of the computer you are working on) with a password of **P@ssw0rd**

2. Click **Start**, point to **Administrative Tools**, right-click **Active Directory Sites and Services**, and then click **Run as**.

3. In the **Run As** dialog box, click **The following user**, type a user name of *YourDomain***Administrator** with a password of **P@ssw0rd** and then click **OK**.

4. Expand **Sites**, expand **Default-First-Site-Name**, expand **Servers**, expand *ComputerName*, click **NTDS Settings**, right-click **NTDS Settings**, and then click **Properties**.

5. In the **NTDS Settings Properties** dialog box, on the **Connections** tab, note the replication partners for your computer, and then click **Cancel**.

6. In the details pane, right-click the connection object listed, and then click **Properties**.

7. In the **automatically generated Properties** dialog box, click **Transport**, note the transports that are available, and then click **RPC**.

8. Click **Change Schedule**, note the replication schedule, and then click **Cancel** twice.

Lesson: Creating and Configuring Sites

- What Are Sites and Subnet Objects?
- What Are Site Links?
- Replication Within Sites vs. Replication Between Sites
- How to Create and Configure Sites and Subnets
- How to Create and Configure Site Links
- Why Disable Default Bridging of All Site Links?
- How to Create a Site Link Bridge

Introduction

Replication ensures that all information in Active Directory is current on all domain controllers and workstations throughout your network. Many networks consist of a number of smaller networks, and the network links between these networks may operate at varying speeds.

You use sites in Active Directory to control replication and other types of Active Directory traffic across various network links. When you configure replication between sites, you can use subnet objects, site links, and site link bridges to help control replication topology. An efficient, reliable replication topology depends on the configuration of site links and site link bridges.

Lesson objectives

After completing this lesson, you will be able to:

- Explain the purpose of sites and subnet objects.
- Explain the purpose of site links and site link attributes.
- Describe the differences between replication within sites and replication between sites.
- Create and configure sites and subnets.
- Create and configure site links.
- Explain the purpose of disabling default bridging of all site links.
- Create a site link bridge.

What Are Sites and Subnet Objects?

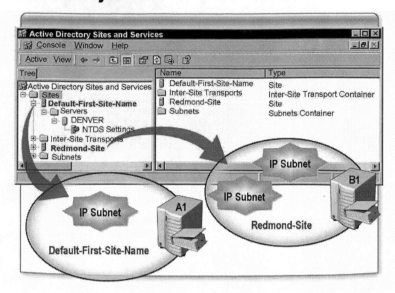

Introduction	You use sites to control replication traffic, logon traffic, and client computer requests to the global catalog server.
What are sites?	In Active Directory, sites help define the physical structure of a network. A set of TCP/IP subnet address ranges defines a site, which in turn defines a group of domain controllers that have similar speed and cost. Sites consist of server objects, which contain connection objects that enable replication.
What are subnet objects?	Subnet objects identify the network addresses that are used to map computers to sites. A subnet is a segment of a TCP/IP network to which a set of logical IP addresses are assigned. Because the subnet objects map to the physical network, so do the sites. For example, if three subnets are located at three campuses in a city, and these campuses are connected by high-speed, highly available connections, you could associate each of those subnets with one site.
	A site can consist of one or more subnets. For example, on a network that has three subnets in Redmond and two in Paris, you can create a site in Redmond, a site in Paris, and then add the subnets to the respective sites.
Default first site	Active Directory creates a default site when you install the first domain controller in a forest. By default, this site is called *Default-First-Site-Name*. You can rename this site to a more descriptive name of your choice. When you create your first domain in a forest, Active Directory automatically places it in the default site.

What Are Site Links?

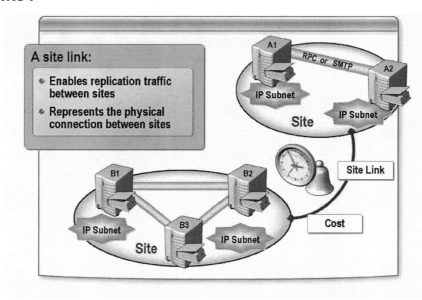

Introduction	For two sites to exchange replication data, they must be connected by a *site link*, which is a logical path that the KCC uses to establish replication between sites.
Why create a site link?	When you create additional sites, you must select at least one site link for each site. Unless a site link is in place, connections cannot be made between computers at different sites, nor can replication occur between sites. Additional site links are not created automatically; you must use Active Directory Sites and Services to create them.
Default site link	When you create the first domain in a forest, Active Directory creates a default site link named DEFAULTIPSITELINK. It includes the first site and is located in the IP container in Active Directory. You can rename the site link.
Site link attributes	When you create a site link, you must select the transport protocol that it will use, give it a name, and add two or more sites to it. The characteristics of the site link are determined by its attributes, which you can configure on the link, so all sites that are connected by a single site link use the same replication path and transport.

Configuring site link attributes is one part of configuring replication between sites. Site link attributes determine the characteristics of the connection, such as the cost, frequency of replication traffic, and the protocols that the connection uses.

Site link cost

Site link cost is a dimensionless number that includes the relative speed, reliability, and preference of the underlying network. The lower the site link cost, the higher the priority for that link, thus making that link a preferred path. For example, your organization has a site in Colorado and a site in Chile with two connections between them: a high-speed connection and a dial-up connection in case the high-speed connection fails. You would configure two site links—one for each connection. Because the high-speed connection is preferable to a dial-up connection, you would configure that site link with a lower cost than the site link for the dial-up connection. Because the site link with the high-speed connection has a lower cost, it has a higher priority. Therefore, that site link is always used if possible.

By setting the site link cost, you can determine the relative priority for each site link. The default cost value is 100, with possible values from one to 99999.

Site link replication schedule

Replication schedule is another site link attribute that you can configure. When you configure a link's replication schedule, you specify the times when the link is available for replication. Often, replication availability is configured for times when there is little other network traffic—for example, from 2:00 A.M. to 5:00 A.M.

The fewer hours that a link is available for replication, the greater the latency between sites that are connected by that link. Therefore, balance the requirement to replicate a link during off-peak hours with the requirement to have up-to-date information at each site that is connected by the link.

Site link replication frequency

When you configure the frequency of replication, you specify how many minutes Active Directory should wait before it uses the link to check for updates. The default value for replication frequency is 180 minutes. You must choose a value between 15 minutes and one week. Replication frequency only applies to the times when the link is scheduled to be available.

Longer intervals between replication cycles reduce network traffic and increase the latency between sites. Shorter intervals increase network traffic and decrease latency. Therefore, you must balance the requirement to reduce network traffic with the requirement for up-to-date information at each site that is connected by the link.

Site link transport protocols

A *transport protocol* is a common language that computers share in order to communicate during replication. Active Directory uses only one protocol for replication within a site. When you create a site link, you must choose to use one of the following transport protocols:

- *Remote procedure call (RPC) over IP*. RPC is the default protocol. An industry standard protocol for client/server communications, RPC over IP provides reliable, high-speed connectivity within sites. Between sites, RPC over IP enables replication of all Active Directory partitions. RPC over IP is the best transport protocol for replication between sites.

- *Simple mail transfer protocol (SMTP)*. SMTP supports replication of the schema, configuration, and global catalog between sites and between domains. You cannot use this protocol for replication of the domain partition, because some domain operations—for example, Group Policy—require the support of the File Replication service (FRS), which does not support an asynchronous transport for replication. If you use SMTP, you must install and configure a certificate authority to sign the SMTP messages and ensure the authenticity of directory updates. Additionally, SMTP does not provide the same level of data compression as RPC over IP.

Replication Within Sites vs. Replication Between Sites

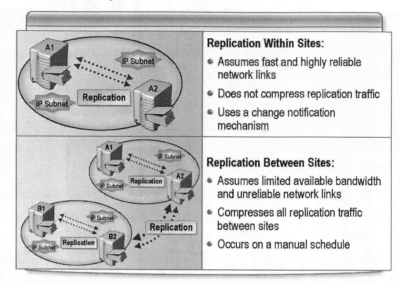

Replication within sites

The main characteristics or assumptions of replication within sites are:

- The network connections within a site are both reliable and have sufficient available bandwidth.

- Replication traffic within a site is not compressed because a site assumes fast, highly reliable network links. Not compressing replication traffic helps reduce the processing load on the domain controllers. However, uncompressed traffic may increase the network bandwidth that replication messages require.

- A change notification process initiates replication within a site.

Replication between sites

The main characteristics or assumptions of replication between sites are:

- The network links between sites have limited available bandwidth and may not be reliable.

- Replication traffic between sites is designed to optimize bandwidth by compressing all replication traffic between sites. Replication traffic is compressed to 10 to 15 percent of its original size before it is transmitted. Although compression optimizes network bandwidth, it imposes an additional processing load on domain controllers—both when it compresses and decompresses replication data.

- Replication between sites happens automatically after you define configurable values, such as a schedule or a replication interval. You can schedule replication for inexpensive or off-peak hours. By default, changes are replicated between sites according to a schedule that you define manually—not according to when changes occur. The schedule determines when replication can to occur. The interval specifies how often domain controllers check for changes during the time that replication can occur.

How to Create and Configure Sites and Subnets

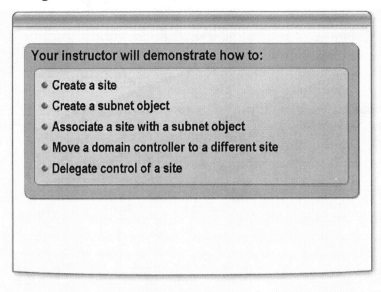

Your instructor will demonstrate how to:

- Create a site
- Create a subnet object
- Associate a site with a subnet object
- Move a domain controller to a different site
- Delegate control of a site

Introduction

To use sites to manage replication between sites, you create additional sites and subnets and delegate control of sites. Creating a site involves providing a name for the new site and associating the site with a site link. To create sites, you must log on as a member of the Enterprise Admins group or the Domain Admins group in the forest root domain.

Procedure for creating a site

To create a site, perform the following steps:

1. Open Active Directory Sites and Services from the **Administrative Tools** menu.
2. In the console tree, right-click **Sites**, and then click **New Site**.
3. In the **Name** box, type the name of the new site.
4. Click a site link object, and then click **OK** twice.

Procedure for creating a subnet object

After you create sites, you create subnets and then associate them with sites.

To create a subnet object, perform the following steps:

1. In Active Directory Sites and Services, in the console tree, double-click **Sites**, right-click **Subnets**, and then click **New Subnet**.
2. In the **Address** box, type the subnet IP address.
3. In the **Mask** box, type the subnet mask that describes the range of addresses for the subnet.
4. Select a site to associate the subnet with, and then click **OK**.

Procedure for changing the association of a site with a subnet

To associate a site with a subnet object, perform the following steps:

1. In Active Directory Sites and Services, expand **Sites**, expand **Subnets**, and then in the console tree, right-click the subnet that you want to associate the site with, and then click **Properties**.

2. On the **General** tab, in the **Site** box, click the site that you want to associate with this subnet, and then click **OK**.

Procedure for moving a domain controller to a different site

To move a domain controller to a different site, perform the following steps:

1. In Active Directory Sites and Services, expand **Sites**, expand the site that the domain controller is in, expand **Servers**, and then in the console tree, right-click the domain controller, and then click **Move**.

2. In the **Move Server** dialog box, in the **Site Name** list, select the site that you want to move the domain controller to, and then click **OK**.

Note   It may be necessary to change the IP address on the domain controller to an address that maps to the site that you want to move it to.

Procedure for delegating control of sites

You can use the Delegation of Control Wizard in Active Directory Sites and Services to delegate control of a site to other groups. To delegate control, perform the following steps:

1. Open Active Directory Sites and Services.

2. Do one of the following:

   - To delegate control for all sites, site links, site link bridges, and subnet object, right-click **Sites**, and then click **Delegate Control**.

   - To delegate control for a specific site, expand **Sites**, right-click the site, and then click **Delegate Control**.

3. Use the Delegation of Control Wizard to perform the delegation.

How to Create and Configure Site Links

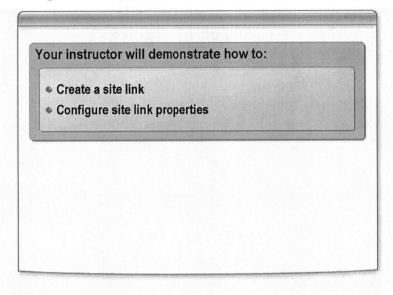

Introduction

You create site links in Active Directory to map connections between two or more sites. When you configure site links, you can define the site link properties, which include the cost, replication interval, schedule, and sites that the link is associated with.

Procedure for creating site links

To create a site link, perform the following steps:

1. In Active Directory Sites and Services, expand **Sites**, expand **Inter-Site Transports**, right-click **IP** or **SMTP**, depending on which protocol the site link you will use, and then click **New Site Link**.

2. In the **Name** box, type a name for the link.

3. Click two or more sites to connect, click **Add**, and then click **OK**.

Procedure for configuring site links

To configure site links, perform the following steps:

1. Open Active Directory Sites and Services, expand **Sites**, expand **Inter-Site Transports**, and then click **IP** or **SMTP**, depending on which protocol the site link is configured to use.

2. Right-click the site link, and then click **Properties**.

3. On the **General** tab of the **Properties** dialog box, change the values for site associations, cost, replication interval, and schedule as required, and then click **OK**.

4. Perform one of the following as appropriate:

   - In the **Sites not in this site link** box, click the site you want to add, and then click **Add**.

   - In the **Sites in this site link** box, click the site you want removed and then click **Remove**.

   - In the **Cost** box, enter a value for the cost of replication.

   - Click **Change Schedule**, select the block of time you want to schedule, and then click either **Replication Not Available** or **Replication Available**, and then click **OK**.

Why Disable Default Bridging of All Site Links?

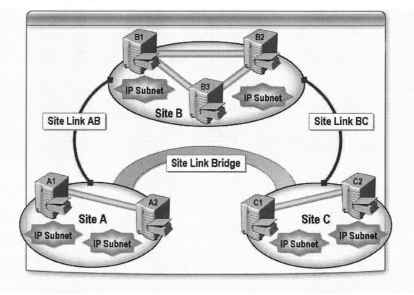

Introduction

A site link bridge creates a chain of site links that domain controllers from different sites in the site links can use to communicate directly. Bridging is useful to constrain the KCC to particular paths in the site-link topology. By default, site link bridging is enabled and all site links are considered *transitive*. That is, all site links for a given transport implicitly belong to a single site link bridge for that transport. So, in a fully routed IP network, it is not necessary to configure any site link bridges. If your IP network is not fully routed, you can disable site link bridging to turn off the transitive site link feature for the IP transport, and then configure site link bridges to model the actual routing behavior of your network.

Example

A site link bridge enables site links that share a common intermediate site to route data through that site and produce a transitive path that is the sum of the individual site links. For example, when site link bridging is disabled, and there is a bridge from site A to site B and from site B to site C, the KCC can deduce a routed, transitive path from site A to site C with a cost that is the sum of the site link costs. In this example, the intermediate site B is considered by the KCC only for IP routing between A and C. It does not matter to the KCC if site B has a copy of the given domain whose topology it is trying to calculate. Bridging can be useful to constrain the KCC to particular paths through the site-link topology.

How to Create a Site Link Bridge

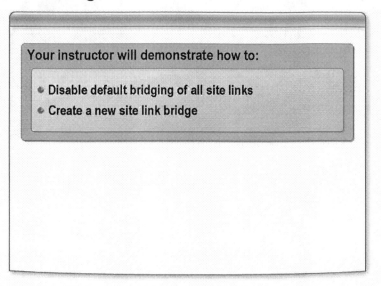

Your instructor will demonstrate how to:

- Disable default bridging of all site links
- Create a new site link bridge

Introduction

Before you can create new site link bridges, you must first disable default bridging of all site links to permit the creation of new site link bridges.

Procedure for disabling default bridging of all site links

To disable default bridging of all site links, perform the following steps:

1. Open Active Directory Sites and Services, expand **Sites**, expand **Inter-Site Transports**, right-click either **IP** or **SMTP**, depending on the protocol for which you want to disable bridging of all site links, and then click **Properties**.

2. In the **Properties** dialog box, clear the **Bridge all site links** check box, and then click **OK**.

Procedure for creating a site link bridge

To create a site link bridge, perform the following steps:

1. Open Active Directory Sites and Services, expand **Sites**, expand **Inter-Site Transports**, right-click either **IP** or **SMTP**, depending on the protocol that you want to create a site link bridge for, and then click **New Site Link Bridge**.

2. In the **Name** box, type a name for the site link bridge.

3. Click two or more site links to be bridged, click **Add**, and then click **OK**.

Practice: Creating and Configuring Sites

In this practice, you will:

- Create IP subnet and site objects
- Associate subnet objects with sites
- Move server objects into the site
- Create IP site links between sites
- Configure the replication cost, schedule, and interval of the links

Objectives

In this practice, you will create IP subnet and site objects in Active Directory and associate subnets with sites. Next, you will move server objects into the site you created, create IP site links between sites, and configure the replication cost, schedule, and interval of the links.

Instructions

You will work in pairs that are organized by domain to complete this exercise. Your domain configuration has two domain controllers in the *Default-First-Name-Site*.

Scenario

Northwind Traders is geographically distributed with many wide area network (WAN) links that connect these regions. Network bandwidth on these WAN links is scarce. To optimize replication and minimize the use of network bandwidth across WAN links, you must configure Active Directory to permit topology creation based on local area network (LAN) and WAN connections.

Active Directory IP subnet and site objects are configured based on the physical network of Northwind Traders. The sites on the corporate network have already been configured.

Practice: Creating a site and subnet object

▶ **Create a site and a subnet object**

1. Log on as **Nwtraders***x******ComputerName***User** with a password of **P@ssw0rd**

2. Click **Start**, point to **Administrative Tools**, right-click **Active Directory Sites and Services**, and then click **Run as**.

3. In the **Run As** dialog box, click **The following user**, type a user name of **Nwtraders***x***\\Administrator** with a password of **P@ssw0rd** and then click **OK**.

4. Expand **Sites**, and then create a site object.

   a. Create a new site with the name *ComputerName***Site** (where *ComputerName* is the host name of your computer).

   b. Link it to DEFAULTIPSITELINK.

5. Create an IP subnet object, and then associate the subnet with a site.

    a. Create a new subnet object with the network ID of 10.10.*n*.0 (where *n* is your assigned student number) and a subnet mask of 255.255.255.0.

    b. Associate the subnet object with your site *ComputerName***Site**.

6. Refresh Active Directory Sites and Services, and verify that replication occurred and that you can see the subnet that your student partner created.

Practice: Creating and configuring site links

▶ **Create IP site links between your site and your partner's site**

1. Create a new IP site link called *YourComputerName-PartnerComputerName*.

2. Add the sites *YourComputerName***Site** and partner-*partnerComputerName***Site** to the new site link.

3. Configure the properties of the *YourComputerName-PartnerComputerName*site link by setting replication cost to 50, a frequency of 15 minutes, and a daily schedule that excludes replication from 6:00 A.M. to 8:00 A.M.

4. Move *YourComputerName* into the site that you created.

Note   The replication interval between sites is set to 15 minutes, but you can manually trigger replication so that updates occur when they are required.

Lesson: Managing Site Topology

- What Is a Bridgehead Server?
- What Is the Intersite Topology Generator?
- How to Create a Preferred Bridgehead Server
- How to Refresh the Replication Topology
- How to Force Replication over a Connection

Introduction

To meet the replication requirements of an organization, you may be required to perform some tasks manually to manage the site topology. These tasks include identifying preferred bridgehead servers, refreshing replication topology, and forcing replication.

Lesson objectives

After completing this lesson, you will be able to:

- Explain the purpose of a bridgehead server.

- Explain the purpose of the intersite topology generator.

- Create a preferred bridgehead server.

- Refresh the replication topology by:

  - Determining the domain controller that holds the role of the intersite topology generator in a site.

  - Updating the bridgehead server list.

- Force replication over a connection.

What Is a Bridgehead Server?

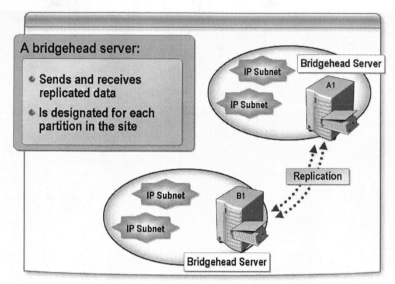

A bridgehead server:

- Sends and receives replicated data
- Is designated for each partition in the site

Introduction

The *bridgehead server* is a domain controller that you designate to send and receive replicated data at each site. The bridgehead server from the originating site collects all of the replication changes and then sends them to the receiving site's bridgehead server, which replicates the changes to all domain controllers in the site.

Bridgehead server required per partition

You must designate a bridgehead server for each partition in the site. For example, a domain controller can be the bridgehead server for the forest-wide schema and configuration partitions, as well as the domain partition for the domain that it represents. If there are other domains in the site, you must assign a bridgehead server for each domain.

The bridgehead server at each site is automatically selected, or you can specify a list of preferred bridgehead servers. To ensure efficient updates to the directory, a preferred bridgehead server must have the processing power and bandwidth to efficiently compress, send, receive, and decompress replication data. Active Directory uses only one bridgehead server at any time. If the first preferred server becomes unavailable, another one on the preferred list is used.

If your deployment uses a firewall to protect a site, you must designate the firewall proxy server as the preferred bridgehead server, which makes it the contact point for exchanging information with other sites. If you do not do this step, Active Directory may not replicate the directory information successfully.

What Is the Intersite Topology Generator?

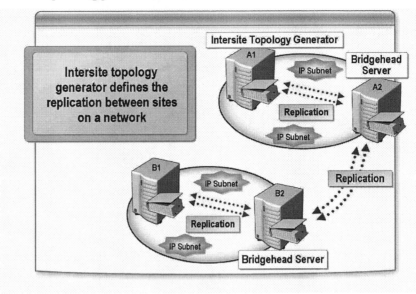

Introduction

The *intersite topology generator* is an Active Directory process that defines the replication between sites on a network. A single domain controller in each site is automatically designated to be the intersite topology generator. Because this action is performed by the intersite topology generator, you are not required to take any action to determine the replication topology and bridgehead server roles.

Functions

The domain controller that holds the intersite topology generator role performs two functions:

- It automatically selects one or more domain controllers to become bridgehead servers. This way, if a bridgehead server becomes unavailable, it automatically selects another bridgehead server, if possible.

- It runs the KCC to determine the replication topology and resultant connection objects that the bridgehead servers can use to communicate with bridgehead servers of other sites.

How to Create a Preferred Bridgehead Server

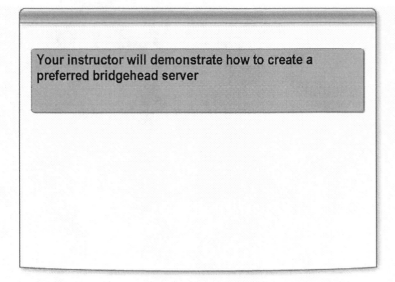

Your instructor will demonstrate how to create a preferred bridgehead server

Introduction

You use Active Directory Sites and Services to designate a domain controller as a bridgehead server to specify which domain controller Active Directory prefers as the recipient for the replication between sites.

Procedure

To create a preferred bridgehead server, perform the following steps:

1. Open Active Directory Sites and Services, expand **Sites**, expand the site that contains the server that you want to configure, expand **Servers**, and then in the console tree, right-click the domain controller that you want to make a preferred bridgehead server, and then click **Properties**.

2. Choose the inter-site transport or transports to designate the computer a preferred bridgehead server, click **Add**, and then click **OK**.

How to Refresh the Replication Topology

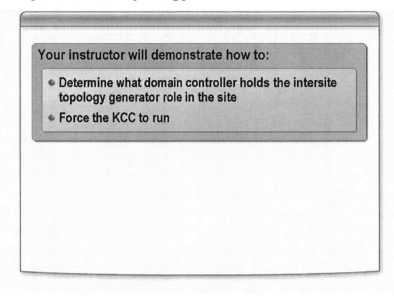

Introduction

To refresh replication topology, first determine whether you want to refresh the replication topology between sites or the replication topology within a site.

- To regenerate it between sites, run the KCC on the domain controller that holds the intersite topology generator role.

- To regenerate it within a site, run the KCC on any domain controller that is not the intersite topology generator.

Procedure for determining what domain controller holds the intersite topology generator role

To determine the domain controller that holds the role of the intersite topology generator in the site, perform the following steps:

1. In Active Directory Sites and Services, expand **Sites**, and then select the site.

2. In the details pane, right-click **NTDS Site Settings**, and then click **Properties**.

   The site and server that holds the intersite topology generator role appears on the properties page under Inter-Site Topology Generator.

Procedure for forcing the KCC to run

To force the KCC to run, perform the following steps:

1. In Active Directory Sites and Services, in the console tree, expand **Sites**, expand the site that contains the server on which you want to run the KCC, expand **Servers**, and then select the server object for the domain controller that you want to run the KCC on.

2. In the details pane, right-click **NTDS Settings**, click **All Tasks**, and then click **Check Replication Topology**.

How to Force Replication over a Connection

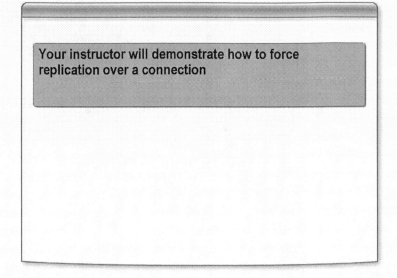

Your instructor will demonstrate how to force replication over a connection

Introduction

You use the Active Directory Sites and Services to force replication over a connection. You may be required to force replication if the event log displays replication inconsistencies or if you receive a message on the domain controller console alerting you to replication problems.

Procedure

To force replication over a connection, perform the following steps:

1. In Active Directory Sites and Services, expand the domain controller for the site that contains the connection that you use to replicate directory information.

2. In the console tree, click **NTDS Settings**.

3. In the details pane, right-click the connection that you use to replicate directory information, and then click **Replicate Now**.

Practice: Manually Initiating Replication

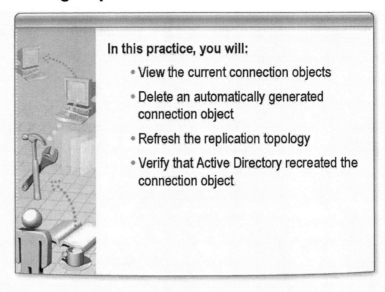

In this practice, you will:

* View the current connection objects

* Delete an automatically generated connection object

* Refresh the replication topology

* Verify that Active Directory recreated the connection object

Objectives

In this practice, you will view the current connection objects, delete an automatically generated connection object, and then refresh the replication topology. You will also verify that Active Directory re-created the connection object.

Instructions

You will work in pairs that are organized by domain to complete this exercise.

Scenario

The corporate testing group for Northwind Traders performs many verification tests in Active Directory. You must ensure that the replication topology is quickly regenerated if a connection object is deleted. To verify that a connection object can be regenerated, manually refresh the replication topology after you delete a connection object.

Practice: Manually initiate replication

▶ **Manually initiate replication**

1. Log on as **Nwtraders***x******ComputerName***User** with a password of **P@ssw0rd**

    a. Start Active Directory Sites and Services as **Nwtraders***x***\\Administrator** by using **Run as**.

    b. Connect to your *ComputerName* by right-clicking **Active Directory Sites and Services** in the console tree, and then clicking **Connect to domain controller**.

2. View the current connection objects.

3. Expand *ComputerName***Site**, browse to the NTDS settings for your server, and then examine the properties of the connection objects.

    Where will the connection objects replicate from and what replication transport will they use?

4. Delete an automatically generated connection object.

   a. Browse to the NTDS Settings for your computer.

   b. In the details pane, delete the connection object.

5. Refresh the replication topology.

   a. Expand *YourComputerName*Site, and then in the console tree, select your server.

   b. In the details pane, right-click **NTDS settings**, and then, on the **All Tasks** menu, click **Check Replication Topology**.

Practice: Verifying the recreation of the connection object

▶ **Verify that the connection object that you deleted was re-created**

1. In the console tree, right-click **Active Directory Sites and Services**, and then click **Refresh**.

2. Expand *ComputerName*Site, browse to the NTDS settings for your server, and then verify in the details pane that the connection object was automatically created.

Lesson: Troubleshooting Replication Failures

- ● Common Replication Problems
- ● What Is Replication Monitor?
- ● How to Configure Replication Monitor
- ● What Is the Repadmin Tool?
- ● What Is the Dcdiag Tool?
- ● How to Determine the Cause of a Problem
- ● How to Resolve Replication Problems

Introduction

You may encounter replication problems in Active Directory. Although you can resolve most common problems by using Active Directory Sites and Services, advanced utilities and command-line tools exist to analyze replication problems. Some of the common problems are new user accounts are not recognized, directory information is outdated, or domain controllers are unavailable.

To monitor, diagnose, and resolve replication problems, you can use the Replication Monitor utility and the Repadmin.exe and Dcdiag.exe command-line tools. The utility and tools are available in the Windows Server 2003 Support Tools, which are included on the Windows Server 2003 CD-ROM.

Lesson objectives

After completing this lesson, you will be able to:

- Explain the common replication problems that may occur.
- Explain the purpose of replication monitor.
- Configure Replication Monitor for viewing replication between domain controllers.
- Explain the purpose of the Repadmin.exe command-line tool.
- Explain the purpose of the Dcdiag.exe command-line tool.
- Determine the root cause of a problem by performing tests.
- Resolve replication problems.

Common Replication Problems

Symptom	Possible causes
Replication does not finish or occur	• Sites not connected by site links • No bridgehead server in the site
Replication is slow	• Inefficient site topology and schedule
Client computers receive a slow response	• No domain controller online in client site • Not enough domain controllers
Replication greatly increases network traffic	• Insufficient bandwidth • Incorrect site topology
The KCC cannot complete the topology	• Exception in the KCC

Introduction

When you encounter replication problems in Active Directory, your first step is to identify the symptoms and possible causes.

Symptoms and their possible causes

The following table lists common symptoms and their possible common causes.

Symptom	Possible causes
Replication does not finish or occur	• Sites that contain the workstations and domain controllers are not connected by site links to domain controllers in other sites in the network. • There is no bridgehead server in the site.
Replication is slow	• The topology and schedule of the site links cause the replication of information to go through many sites serially before replication updates all sites.
Client computers experience a slow response for authentication, directory information, or other services	• The client computers request authentication, information, and services from a domain controller through a low-bandwidth connection. • No domain controller is online in the client site. • There are not enough domain controllers to meet the demands of the workstations.
Replication increases network traffic	• The current bandwidth is insufficient to manage the amount of replication traffic. • The site topology is incorrect.
KCC cannot complete the topology for the distinguished name of the site	• There is an exception in the KCC.

What Is Replication Monitor?

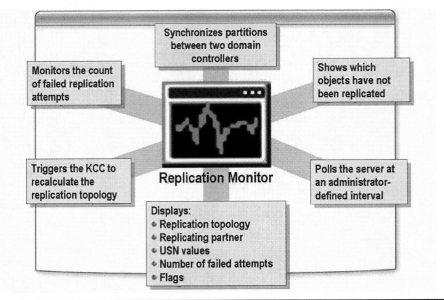

Introduction

To adjust replication traffic patterns, you must be able to view replication traffic across your network. You can view replication traffic by using Replication Monitor.

Definition

Replication Monitor graphically displays the replication topology of connections between servers on the same site. You can view low-level status and performance of replication between domain controllers. You can also use functions that are wrapped application programming interfaces (APIs), which make it easy to write a replication script with just a few lines of code.

Functions

Replication Monitor:

- Displays replicating information both directly and transitively.

- Displays each USN value, the number of and reason for failed replication attempts, and the flags that are used for direct replication partners. If the failure meets or exceeds an administrator-defined value, Replication Monitor can write to an event log and then send e-mail notification.

- Polls the server at an administrator-defined interval to obtain current statistics and replication state, and to save a log file's history.

- Shows which objects have not yet been replicated from a particular computer.

- Synchronizes Active Directory partitions between two domain controllers.

- Triggers the KCC to recalculate the replication topology.

You can run Replication Monitor on any domain controller, member server, or stand-alone computer that runs Windows Server 2003.

Note For more information about Replication monitoring in Active Directory, see the Windows Server 2003 Help and Support Center.

How to Configure Replication Monitor

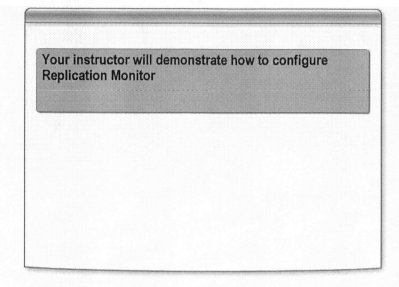

Introduction

You use Replication Monitor to view replication between domain controllers, member server and stand-alone computers in a domain.

Procedure

To configure Replication Monitor, perform the following steps:

1. To open Active Directory Replication Monitor, click **Start**, click **Run**, type **replmon** and then click **OK**.

2. On the **View** menu, click **Options**.

3. On the **Active Directory Replication Monitor Options** page, on the **Status Logging** tab, click **Display Changed Attributes when Replication Occurs**, and then click **OK**.

4. In the console pane, right-click **Monitored servers**, and then click **Add Monitored Server**.

5. In the **Add Server to Monitor** dialog box, click **Add the server explicitly by name**, and then click **Next**.

6. In the **Enter the name of the server to monitor explicitly** box, type the server name, and then click **Finish**.

What Is the Repadmin Tool?

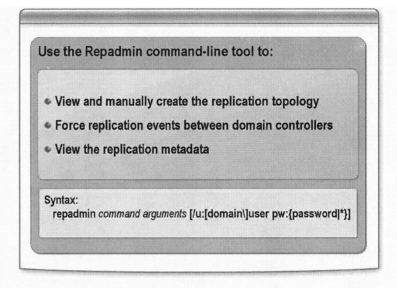

Use the Repadmin command-line tool to:

- View and manually create the replication topology
- Force replication events between domain controllers
- View the replication metadata

Syntax:
repadmin *command arguments* [/u:[domain\]user pw:{password|*}]

Introduction

You use the Repadmin.exe command-line tool to view the replication topology from the perspective of each domain controller. You can also use Repadmin.exe to manually create the replication topology, force replication events between domain controllers, and view the replication metadata, which is information about the data, and up-to-date state of vectors.

Repadmin syntax

To run the **repadmin** command, you use the following syntax:

```
repadmin command arguments [/u:[domain\]user /pw:{password|*}]
```

Examples of using the repadmin command

The following examples use some of the available command arguments for the **repadmin** command:

- To display the replication partners of the domain controller named domaincontroller1, use the syntax:

  repadmin /showreps domaincontroller1.contoso.msft

- To display the highest USN on the domain controller named domaincontroller2, use the syntax:

  repadmin /showvector dc=contoso,dc=msft domain controller2.contoso.msft

- To display the connection objects for the domain controller named domaincontroller1, use the syntax:

  repadmin /showconn domaincontroller1.microsoft.com

Note For more information about the arguments that you can use with the **repadmin** command, at a command prompt, run **repadmin /?** and then read the usage statement.

What Is the Dcdiag Tool?

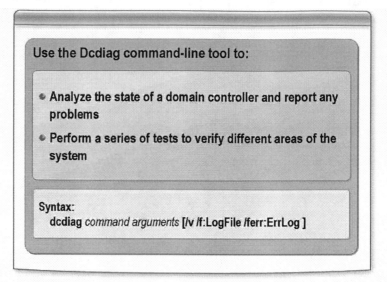

Introduction

You use the Dcdiag.exe command-line tool to analyze the state of a domain controller and report any problems. The Dcdiag.exe tool performs a series of tests to verify different aspects of the system. These tests include connectivity, replication, topology integrity, and intersite health.

Dcdiag syntax

At a command prompt, type:

```
dcdiag command arguments [/v /f:LogFile /ferr:ErrLog ]
```

The following table describes the three common switches that you can use with the **dcdiag** command.

Switch	Description
/v	Provides verbose results. When you use **/v**, the output from **dcdiag** provides a lot of information that can help you troubleshoot a problem.
/f:LogFile	Redirects output to a specified log file.
/ferr:ErrLog	Redirects fatal error output to a separate log file.

Note For more information about the arguments that you can use with the **dcdiag** command, at a command prompt, run **dcdiag /?** and then read the usage statement.

How to Determine the Cause of the Problem

Possible causes	Testing method
Sites are not connected by site links	• Dcdiag /test:Topology
No bridgehead server in the site	• Repadmin /bridgeheads
Inefficient site topology and schedule	• Repadmin /latency
No domain controller online in the site	• Dcdiag /test:Replication • Dcdiag /test:Connectivity
Not enough domain controllers	• System monitor NTDS counters
Incorrect site topology	• Active Directory Sites and Services • Repadmin /latency • Dcdiag /test:Intersite
Exception in the KCC	• Dcdiag /test:kccevent

Introduction

Perform tests by using the Repadmin.exe and Dcdiag.exe command-line tools to determine the root cause of the problem.

Testing methods

The following table lists the possible causes and one or more testing methods that you can use to determine the root cause of the problem.

Possible cause	Testing method
Sites are not connected by site links	• Check that the generated topology is fully connected for all domain controllers by using the syntax: **dcdiag /test:Topology /v**
No bridgehead server exists in the site	• Display the list of current bridgehead servers by using the syntax: **repadmin /bridgeheads domaincontroller1.contoso.msft / verbose**
The site topology and schedule are inefficient	• Display the connection objects for the domain controller called domaincontroller1 by using the syntax: **repadmin /latency domaincontroller1.contoso.msft / verbose**
No domain controller is online in the site	• Test whether the domain controllers are registered with DNS, can be pinged, and have LDAP/RPC connectivity by using the syntax: **dcdiag /test:Connectivity /v** • Also check for timely replication between domain controllers by using the syntax: **dcdiag /test:Replication /v**

(continued)

Possible cause	Testing method

Not enough domain controllers exist to meet the demand of client computers	• View the following system monitor NTDS counters:
	
	  • KDC AS Requests = The number of AS requests that the KDC services per second. Clients use AS requests to obtain a ticket granting ticket (TGT).
	
	  • KDC TGS Requests = The number of ticket granting service (TGS) requests that the KDC services per second. Clients use TGS requests to obtain a ticket to a resource.
	
	  • Kerberos Authentications = The number of times per second that clients use a ticket to a domain controller to authenticate to the domain controller.

The site topology is incorrect	• Check the site link schedule by using Active Directory Sites and Services.
	
	• Check for failures that prevent or delay intersite replication by using the syntaxes:
	
	  • repadmin /latency
	
	  • dcdiag /test:Intersite /v

An exception occurs in the KCC	• Check that the KCC is completing all tests without errors by using the syntax: **dcdiag /test:kccevent /v**

How to Resolve Replication Problems

Cause	Resolution method
Sites are not connected by site links	• Create and configure site links
No bridgehead server in the site	• Add or remove domain controllers from the preferred bridgehead server list
Inefficient site topology and schedule	• Modify the site topology and schedule
No domain controller online in the site	• Install or fix domain controllers
Not enough domain controllers	• Install additional domain controllers
Incorrect site topology	• Modify the site topology • Ensure site links match WAN links
Exception in the KCC	• Enable KCC logging • Run Repadmin /kcc

Introduction

After you identify the root cause of a problem, the final step is to fix the problem or, if possible, provide a resolution. You can resolve most problems by using Active Directory Sites and Services.

Resolution methods

The following table lists methods to resolve some common replication problems.

Cause	Resolution method
Sites are not connected by site links	• Create a site link from the current site to a site that is connected to the other sites in the network.
No bridgehead server exists in the site	• Add domain controller to the preferred bridgehead server list. • Remove all domain controllers from the preferred bridgehead server list.
Inefficient site topology and schedule	• Modify the site topology and schedule to increase replication frequency. • Schedule the replication to occur during off-peak hours when more network bandwidth is available for replication.
No domain controller online in the site	• Install or fix domain controllers. • Associate a subnet that is served well by a site with the client site. • Install a connection with more bandwidth.
Not enough domain controllers to meet the demand of the client computers	• Install additional domain controllers.

(continued)

Cause	Resolution method
Incorrect site topology	• Modify the site topology and ensure that site links match network WAN links.
Exception in the KCC	• Enable KCC logging. To log more information, increase the value of the **9 Internal Processing** registry entry and **1 Knowledge Consistency Checker** registry entry to three and wait 15 minutes. The registry entries are located at: **HKEY_LOCAL_MACHINE\SYSTEM\ CurrentControlSet\Services\NTDS\Diagnostics**
	• Run **repadmin /kcc**, and reset the value of the registry entry to 0. By default, the KCC logs only the most important events. You can increase the level of detail by resetting the value in the Replication Events entry in the Directory Services event log.

Practice: Troubleshooting Replication Failures

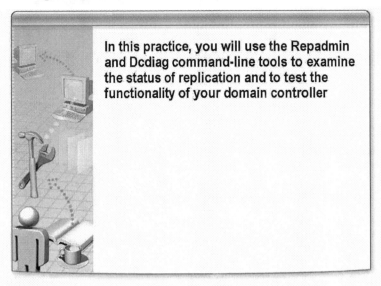

In this practice, you will use the Repadmin and Dcdiag command-line tools to examine the status of replication and to test the functionality of your domain controller

Objectives

In this practice, you will use the Repadmin and Dcdiag command-line tools to examine the status of replication in your site and to execute diagnostics to test the functionality of your domain controller.

Scenario

Use Repadmin.exe and Dcdiag.exe to trigger replication and then analyze the replication architecture. The tools provide detailed baseline information that can help you understand why slow or incomplete replication is occurring.

Practice: Using Repadmin.exe to troubleshoot

▶ **Troubleshoot Active Directory replication failures by using Repadmin.exe**

1. Start a command prompt as *YourDomain***Administrator** by using **Run As**.

2. At the command prompt, type **Repadmin /?** and then press ENTER.

3. Read the information on the help screen to familiarize yourself with the command.

4. Run **repadmin /replsummary** and examine the output. Notice the status of replication and the number of errors.

5. Run **repadmin /showconn** *YourComputerName* and examine the output. Notice the information about replication data that is inbound from your student partner site. Also notice the syntax of the distinguished names that are required for Repadmin.

6. Run the command again by specifying your *PartnerComputerName* and examine the output.

7. Run **repadmin /replicate** *YourComputerName PartnerComputerName* **CN=Configuration,DC=nwtraders***x***,DC=msft /force**

   Verify that the output shows successful replication of the configuration partition to your server from your partner's server.

8. Run **repadmin /showrepl /verbose** and examine the output. Notice that it specifies the USN numbers that are used during replication, the GUIDs for your server, the inbound neighbors, and the DNS name that is used to resolve your partner server.

Practice: Using Dcdiag.exe to troubleshoot replication failures

▶ **Troubleshoot Active Directory replication failures by using Dcdiag.exe**

1. Run **dcdiag /?** and examine the command structure to understand the available options.

2. Run **dcdiag** and examine the output. Notice that tests run on the local partitions to test their integrity.

3. Run **dcdiag /e**. Run this command as **dcdiag /e /v** so that the output is a verbose listing of all diagnostics run.

Note   Refer to the resource kit for additional information on diagnosis of the replication architecture.

Lesson: Planning a Site

- Overview of the Site Planning Process
- Guidelines for Determining Schedule, Interval, and Protocol of Site Links
- Guidelines for Determining the Need for Site Link Bridges
- Guidelines for Determining the Requirements for Bridgehead Servers
- Guidelines for Securing Active Directory Replication

Introduction

When you plan a site strategy, you determine site link schedules, intervals, and protocols; assess the need for site link bridges; designate bridgehead servers; and secure Active Directory replication.

In this lesson, it is assumed that you were given the site topology design by the systems architect. The design specifies the number and location of sites, site links to connect each site and their cost, availability requirements for sites to operate independently, the number of users, and site security policies.

Lesson objectives

After completing this lesson, you will be able to:

- Explain the site planning process.
- Explain guidelines for determining the schedule, interval, and protocol of site links.
- Explain guidelines for determining the need for site link bridges.
- Explain guidelines for determining bridgehead server requirements.
- Explain guidelines for securing Active Directory replication.

Overview of the Site Planning Process

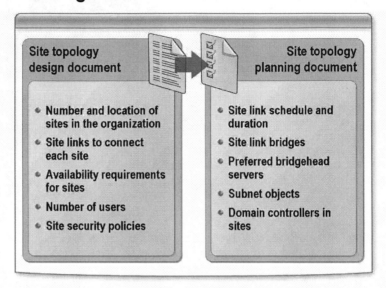

Introduction

The output of an Active Directory design contains the technical decisions that will meet the business requirements of the organization. The bridge between the design output and the actual implementation is called *planning*.

Site topology design components

As a systems engineer, you can expect to receive a site topology design document that includes the following components:

- The number and location of sites in the organization.

- Site links to connect each site, including the cost of the site links.

- Availability requirements for sites to operate independently in the event of a WAN failure.

- The number of users and a recommendation of whether logon services should be local in the site.

- Site security policies that Delegation of Control and other Active Directory features implement.

Note For more information about site topology design considerations, see Chapter 3, "Designing the Site Topology," in the Windows Server 2003 Resource Kit.

Site topology planning components

You must refine the design output before you implement it. The slide contains the site topology planning components in your planning document.

Guidelines for Determining the Schedule, Interval, and Protocol of Site Links

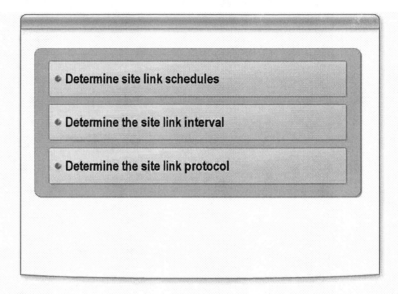

Introduction

When you plan for site links, you determine the replication schedule, interval, and protocol that your organization will use.

Guidelines

Apply the following guidelines:

- *Determine site link schedules.* Try to schedule replication between sites during times when bandwidth use is low to minimize replication traffic during peak hours. For example, schedule the link to be used once each day and only at night. Or, to offset the increase in latency that replication outside of regular business hours causes, schedule replication to occur once an hour each day.

- *Determine the site link interval.* To control the replication interval, set the number of minutes between replication attempts on site links. Typically, you set the global default replication frequency to 15 minutes and set a longer frequency on site links that correspond to slow connections to branch offices. The longer frequency uses the link more efficiently, but it increases replication latency.

- *Determine the site link protocol.* Use RPC. Use SMTP only as a back-up transport method or when a network link does not support RPC. Because SMTP can store messages and then forward them, use this transport method on an unreliable network. It supports replication of the schema, configuration, and global catalog directory partitions. You cannot use it, however, to replicate the domain partition between domain controllers that belong to that domain.

Note If you want to use multiple replication schedules for the same transport, create multiple site links that have different configurations.

Guidelines for Determining the Need for Site Link Bridges

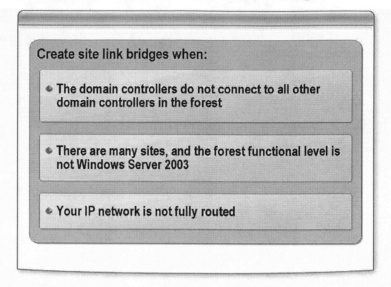

Create site link bridges when:

- The domain controllers do not connect to all other domain controllers in the forest

- There are many sites, and the forest functional level is not Windows Server 2003

- Your IP network is not fully routed

Introduction

A site plan should include a plan for site link bridges if you are using multiple site links.

Guidelines

Apply the following guidelines to determine whether you require site link bridges. Plan to create site link bridges when:

- *Domain controllers do not connect to every other domain controller in the forest.* Your network may prevent such connection when a firewall restricts domain controllers to replicate only with other domain controllers on specific subnets. Disable the default site link bridging and create the necessary site link bridges to indicate which domain controllers in a specific site can connect to other domain controllers in other sites.

- *There are many sites, and the forest functional level is not Windows Server 2003.* Consider disabling the default site link bridging and create the necessary site link bridges to ensure that replication can occur between all sites for all domains. Pay particular attention to sites without domain controllers for domains that have domain controllers in adjacent sites.

- *Your IP network is not fully routed.* Turn off the transitive site link feature for the IP transport, for example, if a firewall allows replication only from domain controllers in a specific location or subnet. When the default bridging of all sites is disabled, all IP site links are considered intransitive. Therefore, configure the site link bridges to model the actual routing behavior of the network. Specify two or more site links to create a site link bridge object for a specific intersite transport, which is typically RPC over TCP/IP.

Note For information about the algorithm used to calculate site paths, see "Guidelines for Determining the Need for Site Link Bridges" in Module 7 on the Appendices page on the Student Materials compact disc.

Guidelines for Determining the Requirements for Bridgehead Servers

* Use preferred bridgehead servers to exclude specific domain controllers from being bridgehead servers

* Create a list of preferred bridgehead servers based on which server you want the intersite topology generator to use

* Create multiple bridgehead servers for multiple directory partitions

Introduction

You may choose to use the bridgehead server that the intersite topology generator automatically designates from the available domain controllers or a smaller preferred list that you manually configure. In either case you still must plan for the requirements of bridgehead servers in your network.

Guidelines

Apply the following guidelines to determining the requirements for bridgehead servers:

- *Use preferred bridgehead servers if you want to exclude some domain controllers in the site from being bridgehead servers.* Some domain controllers may not be powerful enough to replicate reliably between sites. Otherwise, allow the intersite topology generator to automatically select bridgehead servers.

- *Create a list of preferred bridgehead servers.* Create this list according to which servers you want the intersite topology generator to use.

  If:

  • You manually configure a domain controller as a preferred bridgehead server for a site, the intersite topology generator uses only that server.

  • You configure multiple domain controllers in the same site as preferred bridgehead servers, the intersite topology generator arbitrarily selects one of the preferred servers.

  • The list of preferred bridgehead servers includes only one domain controller, which results in reduced fault tolerance when the domain controller becomes unavailable.

  • The preferred bridgehead server is unavailable, the intersite topology generator assigns another preferred bridgehead servers that is configured.

- *Create multiple bridgehead servers for multiple directory partitions.*
  Because a bridgehead server is designated for each directory partition, there
  may be multiple bridgehead servers in one site.

  For example, you have two sites, Redmond and Charlotte, and two domains,
  contoso.msft and nwtraders.msft. Each site has a domain controller from
  each domain. Replication of the two domain directory partitions can occur
  between Redmond and Charlotte because the domain controllers for
  nwtraders.msft and contoso.msft are selected as bridgehead servers in each
  site.

Guidelines for Securing Active Directory Replication

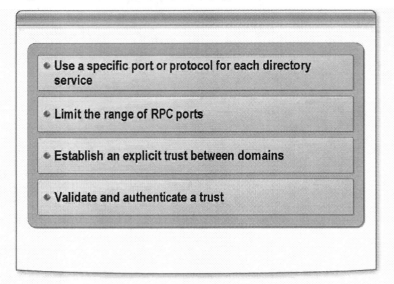

Introduction

When one or more firewalls separate domain controllers and domain members in Active Directory, you must configure the firewalls to enable computers to authenticate resources that reside on the other side of the firewall.

Guidelines

Apply the following guidelines to secure Active Directory replication:

- *Use a specific port or protocol for each instance of Active Directory.* Typically, the directory service and FRS use dynamically allocated ports that require firewalls to have a range of ports open. Although you cannot restrict FRS to a fixed port, you can restrict the directory service to communicate on a static port by using the following registry entry:

    [HKEY_LOCAL_MACHINE\SYSTEM\CurrentControlSet\Services\NTDS\ Parameters]
    "TCP/IP Port"=dword:0000c000

    After you change this registry key and restart the domain controller, the directory service uses the TCP port that is named in the registry entry. In this example, the port is 49152 (hex 0000c000).

- *Limit the range of RPC ports.* You can use the registry key to limit the range of the dynamic RPC ports that a particular computer assigns. To limit the range of dynamic RPC ports, set the following registry key:

    [HKEY_LOCAL_MACHINE\SOFTWARE\Microsoft\Rpc\Internet]
    "Ports"=REG_MULTI_SZ:5000-5020

    This setting starts the dynamic ports range at or above 5000 and consists of at least 20 ports. If additional applications that use dynamic RPC are installed on a computer, increase this range.

- *Establish an explicit trust between domains.* When you establish a trust between domain controllers in different domains, the domain controllers communicate with each other by using specific ports and protocols.

- *Validate and authenticate a trust.* You use specific ports and protocols to validate trust between two domain controllers in different domains uses.

Note For more information about the specific port numbers and protocols that are used for Active Directory replication, see "Guidelines for Securing Active Directory Replication" in Module 7 on the Appendices page on the Student Materials compact disc.

Note For more information about configuring and securing replication between sites that use firewalls, see the white paper, *Active Directory in Networks Segmented by Firewalls*, under **Additional Reading** on the Web page on the Student Materials compact disc.

Practice: Planning a Site

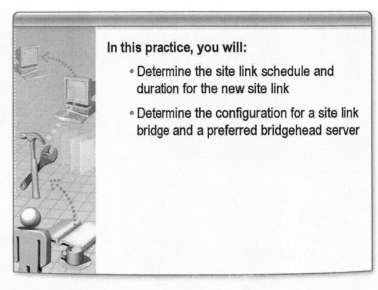

Objectives

In this practice, you will determine the site link schedule, the duration for the new site link, the site link bridge configuration, and the preferred bridgehead server configuration.

Scenario

Your organization made record profits last year. To continue this trend, it has decided to expand its market into New Delhi. Your organization has the following configuration:

- A 384 kilobits per second (Kbps) network link between your existing Hyderabad site and New Delhi. Past usage reports indicate that there may be intermittent connectivity problems over this link. In other words, it is an unreliable link.

- Adequate physical security exists in the new main office in New Delhi.

- About 3,000 users in New Delhi operate in two shifts from 6 A.M. to 10 P.M. local time, and the number of users is projected to triple in five years.

- There will be three domain controllers in the New Delhi site with the following hardware configurations:

  - DC1: 2 gigahertz (GHz) CPU with 1 gigabyte (GB) RAM

  - DC2: 1 GHz CPU with 512 megabyte (MB) RAM

  - DC3: 450 megahertz (Mhz) CPU with 512 MB RAM

- Requirements for new the configuration are:

  - Prohibit replication traffic during work hours in New Delhi because it reduces the available bandwidth for file and data transfers.

  - Minimize the potential impact of replication on the performance of the domain controllers in the New Delhi site.

Practice

▶ **Plan a site**

1. What will your plan contain for a replication schedule, replication frequency, and replication period to ensure that replication traffic does not negatively affect data transfers during work hours on the WAN link at the New Delhi site?

   _____

   _____

2. Would you configure a preferred bridgehead server, and if so, which of the New Delhi servers would you use?

   _____

   _____

3. What site link bridge configuration you would use for the New Delhi site?

   _____

   _____

Lab A: Implementing Sites to Manage Active Directory Replication

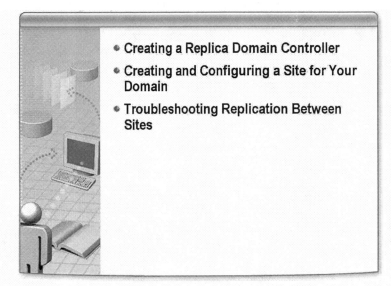

Objectives

After completing this lab, you will be able to:

- Create and configure a site, site links, and site link bridges.
- Configure replication schedules for domain controllers.
- Troubleshoot and verify replication between sites.

Prerequisites

Before working on this lab, you must have:

- Knowledge and skills to create user accounts.
- An understanding of TCP/IP subnets.

Scenario

You are a systems engineer for Northwind Traders. Your manager has asked you to pilot and test the replication architecture. For each forest in the enterprise, you must establish replication standards and test them. Because the organization wants to minimize the operating cost of replication connections, replication occurs only once each day, and the connections are maintained for a maximum of two hours.

You must create a pilot configuration so that the company's software design group can test the Active Directory replication and the application file transfers. To investigate the size and impact of the Active Directory replication, you will create multiple sites in a LAN environment and acquire baseline information about network data transfers from software tests that you will run on each site.

Where required, create a new subnet object with the network ID of 10.10.*n*.0 (where *n* is your assigned student number + 100 (for example, if your student number is 10, specify 110), and a subnet mask of 255.255.255.0).

Estimated time to complete this lab: 45 minutes

Lab Setup

This section lists the tasks that you must perform before you begin the lab. Complete the following table before you start the first exercise.

Item	Name
1. The name of the forest root domain controller	
2. The name of the child domain controller	
3. The name of your domain	
4. The fully qualified domain name for your domain	
5. The name of your site	

Exercise 1
Creating a Replica Domain Controller

In this exercise, you will remove Active Directory from the child domain's domain controller in preparation for creating sites for the Active Directory replication. You will then install this server as a replica domain controller in the nwtraders*x*.msft forest.

Tasks	Specific instructions
⚠ Important: Perform this exercise only on the child domain controller.	
1. Remove Active Directory from the child domain's domain controller.	▪ Log on as **Nwtraders***x**ComputerName***User** (where *ComputerName* is the name of the computer you are working on) with a password of **P@ssw0rd** ▪ Run **dcpromo** as **Nwtraders***x***Administrator** by using **Run As** with a password of **P@ssw0rd**
2. Add the domain controller from the previous task as a replica domain controller in the domain nwtraders*x*.msft.	▪ Log on as the local **Administrator** with a password of **P@ssw0rd**

Exercise 2
Creating and Configuring a Site for Your Domain

In this exercise, you will create and configure a site for your computer in the nwtraders*x*.msft forest.

Tasks	Specific instructions
1. Create a site object in Active Directory for the domain.	▪ Create a site named **LAB***ComputerName***Site**.
2. Configure the properties of the site link by setting the replication cost, interval, and schedule.	▪ Set the following properties: • Replication = 50 • Interval = 60 • Schedule to exclude 6:00 P.M. to 6:00 A.M., Monday through Friday, for the link.

Exercise 3
Troubleshooting Replication Between Sites

In this exercise, you will gather information about the replication and then diagnose replication status. Run **replmon**, **dcdiag**, and **repadmin** to view the status of the replication for your site.

Tasks	Specific instructions
1. Run **replmon**	▪ Use **Run as** to run **replmon** as **Nwtraders*x*\Administrator** with a password of **P@ssw0rd**
❓ What is the distinguished name for your domain controller?	
❓ What is the last updated USN used for the domain partition? In Active Directory Sites and Services, force a replication cycle and record any change in the USN. What changes occurred?	
2. Run **dcdiag** to view the status of the replication and then execute tests for your domain controller.	▪ Examine the diagnostic output to answer the following question.
❓ Are there any errors listed for your domain controller?	
3. Run **repadmin** to view the status of the replication for your domain controller.	▪ Examine the output to answer the following questions.
❓ Which servers are your replication partners? Are any errors listed?	

Microsoft®
Training &
Certification

Module 8: Implementing the Placement of Domain Controllers

Contents

Overview

- Implementing the Global Catalog in Active Directory
- Determining the Placement of Domain Controllers in Active Directory
- Planning the Placement of Domain Controllers

Introduction

A *domain controller* is a computer running Microsoft® Windows® Server 2003 that stores a replica of the domain directory. Having more than one domain controller in a domain provides fault tolerance. If one domain controller is offline, another domain controller can provide all of the required functions, such as recording changes to the Active Directory® directory service. Domain controllers manage all aspects of users' domain interaction, such as locating Active Directory objects and validating user logon attempts.

Because a domain may contain one or more domain controllers, and domain controllers perform various key functions, the placement of domain controllers is an important task in the implementation of Active Directory.

Objectives

After completing this module, you will be able to:

- Implement the global catalog in Active Directory.
- Determine the placement of domain controllers in Active Directory.
- Plan for the placement of domain controllers in Active Directory.

Lesson: Implementing the Global Catalog in Active Directory

> * Review of a Global Catalog Server
> * How to Enable a Global Catalog Server
> * When to Customize a Global Catalog Server
> * How to Customize a Global Catalog Server
> * What Is Universal Group Membership Caching?
> * Multimedia: The Role of Universal Groups in the Logon Process
> * How to Enable Universal Group Membership Caching for a Site

Introduction

The global catalog is the central repository of information about objects in a forest in Active Directory. Universal group membership caching in Windows Server 2003 reduces traffic and improves logon response across slow wide area network (WAN) links. You must understand global catalog servers and universal group membership caching to plan the placement of domain controllers successfully in your network.

Lesson objectives

After completing this lesson, you will be able to:

- Review the purpose of a global catalog server.
- Enable a global catalog server.
- Explain considerations for customizing a global catalog server.
- Customize a global catalog server.
- Explain the purpose of universal group membership caching.
- Explain the role of universal groups in the logon process.
- Enable universal group membership caching for a site.

Review of a Global Catalog Server

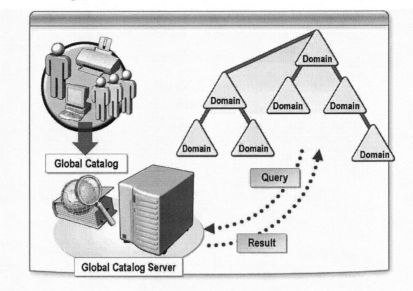

Introduction

Active Directory automatically creates a global catalog on the first domain controller in the forest and is known as a *global catalog server*. You can add global catalog functionality to other domain controllers or change the default location of the global catalog to another domain controller.

Key functions

A global catalog server performs the following key functions:

- It enables network logon by providing universal group membership information to a domain controller when a logon process is initiated.

- It finds directory information regardless of which domain in the forest actually contains the data.

Global catalog and user principal name authentication

A global catalog resolves user principal names when the authenticating domain controller does not know the account. For example, if a user account is located in example1.nwtraders.msft and the user decides to log on by using a user principal name of user1@example1.nwtraders.msft from a computer that is located in example2.nwtraders.msft, the domain controller in example2. nwtraders.msft cannot find the user account, and will then contact a global catalog server to complete the logon process.

Global catalog and universal group membership

A global catalog supplies information about universal group memberships in a multiple domain environment. Unlike global group memberships, which Active Directory stores in each domain, universal group memberships are stored only in a global catalog. For example, when a user who belongs to a universal group logs on to a domain that is set to Windows 2000 native or Windows Server 2003 domain functional level, the global catalog provides universal group membership information about the user account.

What happens when there is no global catalog?

If a global catalog is not available when a user logs on to a domain running in Windows 2000 native or Windows Server 2003 domain functional level, the domain controller that processes the user's logon request denies the request, and the user cannot log on.

If no domain controllers are available to process a user's logon request, the domain controller processes the logon request by using the user's cached credentials. This feature allows users to log on to portable computers when they are not connected to the corporate network.

The Administrator account in the domain can always log on, even when no global catalog server is available.

Important   Client computers must have access to a global catalog server to log on. Therefore, in most cases, you must have at least one global catalog server in every site to gain the benefits of minimizing network traffic that using sites provides.

Note   For more information about cached credentials, see "Review of a Global Catalog Server" in Module 8 on the Appendices page on the Student Materials compact disc.

How to Enable a Global Catalog Server

> Your instructor will demonstrate how to enable a global catalog server by using Active Directory Sites and Services

Introduction

To perform this procedure, you must be a member of the Domain Admins group or the Enterprise Admins group in Active Directory, or you must have been delegated the appropriate permissions.

Procedure

To enable a global catalog server, perform the following steps:

1. Open Active Directory Sites and Services.

2. In the console tree, browse to the domain controller that will host the global catalog.

3. In the details pane, right-click **NTDS Settings**, and then click **Properties**.

4. Select the **Global Catalog** check box, and then click **OK**.

Note Enabling a global catalog server can cause additional replication traffic while the server gets a complete initial copy of the entire global catalog. The domain controller does not advertise itself as a global catalog server until it has received the global catalog information through replication.

When to Customize a Global Catalog Server

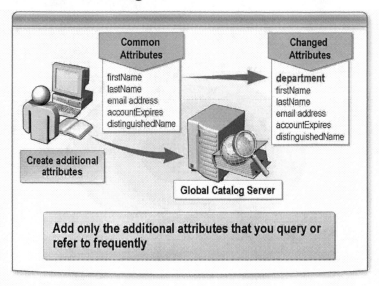

Introduction

Sometimes you may want to customize the global catalog server to include additional attributes. However, consider your options carefully because changes to attributes can affect network traffic.

By default, the global catalog server contains an object's most common attributes for every object in the entire forest. Applications and users can query these attributes. For example, you can find a user by first name, last name, e-mail address, or other common properties of a user account.

Considerations

To decide whether to add an attribute to a global catalog server, use these considerations:

- Add only attributes that users or applications in your organization frequently query or refer to.

- Determine how frequently an attribute is updated during replication. Active Directory replicates all attributes that are stored in the global catalog to every global catalog server in the forest. The smaller the attribute, the lower the impact on replication. If the attribute is large, but seldom changes, it has a smaller replication impact than a small attribute that changes often.

Note   For more information about attributes in a global catalog server, see "When to Customize the Global Catalog Server" in Module 8 on the Appendices page on the Student Materials compact disc.

How to Customize a Global Catalog Server

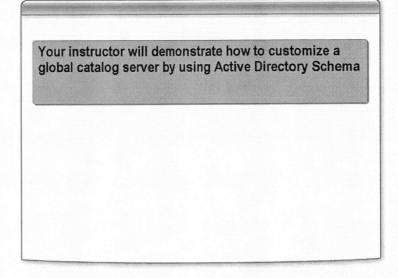

Your instructor will demonstrate how to customize a global catalog server by using Active Directory Schema

Introduction

To perform this procedure, you must be a member of the Schema Admins group in Active Directory, or you must have been delegated the appropriate permissions.

Procedure

To add an attribute to a global catalog server, perform the following steps:

1. Create a new custom MMC console:

    a. Click **Start**, click **Run**, type **regsvr32 schmmgmt.dll** and then click **OK**.

    b. Click **Start**, click **Run**, type **mmc** and then press ENTER.

    c. On the **File** menu, click **Add/Remove Snap-in**.

    d. In the **Add/Remove Snap-in** dialog box, click **Add**.

    e. In the **Add Standalone Snap-in** dialog box, double-click **Active Directory Schema**, and then click **Close**.

    f. In the **Add/Remove Snap-in** dialog box, click **OK**.

    g. On the **File** menu, click **Save As**.

    h. In the **File name** box, type **Active Directory Schema** and then click **Save**.

    i. Close the custom MMC console.

2. Click **Start**, click **All Programs**, click **Administrative Tools**, and then click **Active Directory Schema.msc**.

3. In the console tree, expand **Active Directory Schema**, and then click **Attributes**.

4. In the details pane, right-click the attribute that you want to add to the global catalog server, and then click **Properties**.

5. Click **Replicate this attribute to the Global Catalog**, and then click **OK**.

Warning   If the forest functional level is not set to Windows Server 2003, adding a new attribute to the global catalog server causes a full synchronization of the global catalog server.

What Is Universal Group Membership Caching?

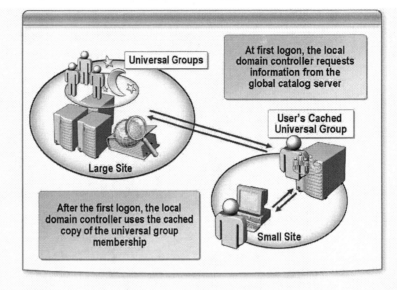

| Introduction | Network bandwidth and server hardware limitations may make it impractical for an organization to have a global catalog server in smaller branch office locations. For these sites, you can deploy domain controllers running Windows Server 2003, and then enable universal group membership caching for the site. |

Introduction

Network bandwidth and server hardware limitations may make it impractical for an organization to have a global catalog server in smaller branch office locations. For these sites, you can deploy domain controllers running Windows Server 2003, and then enable universal group membership caching for the site.

Why use universal group membership caching?

A domain controller in a site that has universal group membership caching enabled stores information locally after a user attempts to log on for the first time. The domain controller obtains the universal group membership information for the user from a global catalog server in another site. It then caches the information indefinitely and periodically refreshes it. The next time that the user tries to log on, the domain controller obtains the universal group membership information from its local cache without contacting a global catalog server.

Refresh interval for universal group membership caching

By default, the universal group membership information contained in the cache of each domain controller is refreshed every eight hours. To refresh the cache, domain controllers running Windows Server 2003 send a universal group membership confirmation request to a designated global catalog server. Windows Server 2003 updates up to 500 universal group memberships at once.

Multimedia: The Role of Universal Groups in the Logon Process

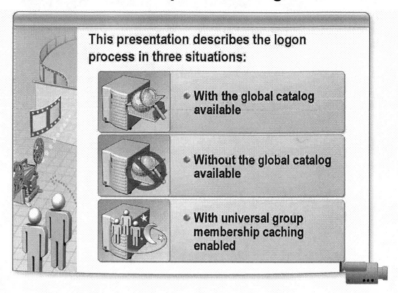

File Location

To view *The Role of Universal Groups in the Logon Process* presentation, open the Web page on the Student Materials compact disc, click **Multimedia**, and then click the title of the presentation. Do not open this presentation unless the instructor tells you to.

Objectives

After viewing this presentation, you will be able to:

- Discuss the role of group membership in authentication and authorization.

- Describe how universal group membership is stored in the global catalog.

- Discuss the role of the global catalog server during authentication and authorization.

- Determine when to place a global catalog server at a remote site.

- Determine when to enable universal group membership caching.

- Discuss the role of group membership in authentication and authorization.

Key points

The key points of this presentation are:

- Universal group membership is critical to a successful logon. If the domain controller cannot enumerate the user's universal group membership, the user is denied an interactive logon. To complete the logon process, the client computer on which the user is performing the interactive logon must have access to either a global catalog server or the cached information.

- When a user logs on, the domain controller that authenticates the user must be able to contact a global catalog server to enumerate the user's universal group memberships. If the domain controller accesses the global catalog server over a WAN, users cannot log on if the WAN link is down.

- If a WAN connection can bear the replication traffic, locate a global catalog server at the site. If replication traffic is a burden to the WAN link, enable universal group membership caching in the site.

How to Enable Universal Group Membership Caching for a Site

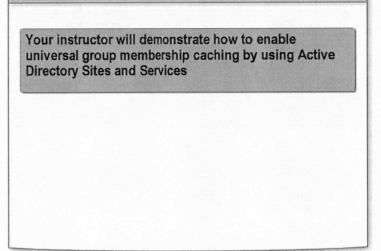

Your instructor will demonstrate how to enable universal group membership caching by using Active Directory Sites and Services

Introduction

To perform this procedure, you must be a member of the Domain Admins group in the forest root domain or the Enterprise Admins group in Active Directory, or you must have been delegated the appropriate permissions.

Procedure

To enable universal group membership caching for a site that does not have a global catalog server, perform the following steps:

1. In Active Directory Sites and Services, in the console tree, expand sites, and then click the site for which you want to enable universal group membership caching.

2. In the details pane, right-click **NTDS Site Settings**, and then click **Properties**.

3. Select the **Enable Universal Group Membership Caching** check box, select a site on which this site refreshes its cache, and then click **OK**.

Note By default, a domain controller refreshes the cache on the nearest site that has a global catalog server. You can select another site that has a global catalog server on which to refresh the cache.

Practice: Implementing the Global Catalog in Active Directory

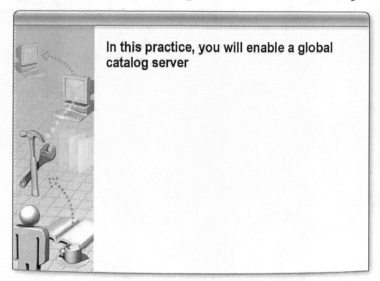

In this practice, you will enable a global catalog server

Objective

In this practice, you will enable a global catalog server.

Scenario

Your organization has 4,000 users in a multidomain forest. There is one domain controller in a branch office that has 200 users who are part of a domain that has 2000 user accounts. You want to enable users to log on to the domain, even if the WAN link is unavailable.

Practice

▶ **Enable a global catalog server**

1. Log on as **Nwtraders***x**ComputerName***User** (where *ComputerName* is the name of the computer you are working on) with a password of **P@ssw0rd**

2. Click **Start**, point to **Administrative Tools**, right-click **Active Directory Sites and Services**, and then click **Run as**.

3. In the **Run As** dialog box, click **The following user**, type *YourDomain***Administrator** as the user name with a password of **P@ssw0rd** and then click **OK**.

4. Use Active Directory Sites and Services to access NTDS properties for your domain controller.

5. Ensure that the **Global Catalog** check box is selected, and then click **OK**.

6. Close Active Directory Sites and Services.

Lesson: Determining the Placement of Domain Controllers in Active Directory

* What Is Active Directory Sizer?
* Parameters for Active Directory Sizer
* How to Use Active Directory Sizer

Introduction

Before you place domain controllers in sites, you must determine the number of domain controllers that your organization needs and their hardware requirements. Active Directory Sizer is an executable file that helps you perform these two tasks, so that you can minimize cost and maintain an effective service level for your users.

Lesson objectives

After completing this lesson, you will be able to:

■ Explain the purpose of Active Directory Sizer.

■ Describe the parameters of Active Directory Sizer.

■ Determine the placement of domain controllers by using Active Directory Sizer.

What Is Active Directory Sizer?

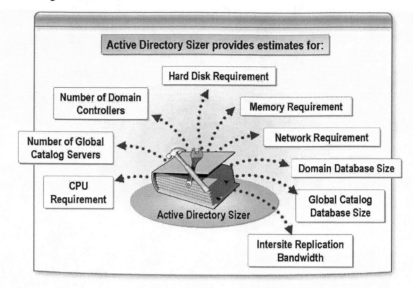

Introduction

Active Directory Sizer (ADSizer.exe) helps you estimate the hardware that is required to deploy Active Directory based on the organization's profile, domain information, and site topology.

What does Active Directory Sizer provide?

You use Active Directory Sizer to provide estimates of the number of:

- Domain controllers per domain per site.
- Global catalog servers per domain per site.
- CPUs per computer, and the type of CPU.
- Disks that are required to store Active Directory data.

Active Directory Sizer also provides approximate estimates for the following requirements or parameters:

- Amount of memory
- Network requirement
- Domain database size
- Global catalog database size
- Intersite replication bandwidth

Parameters for Active Directory Sizer

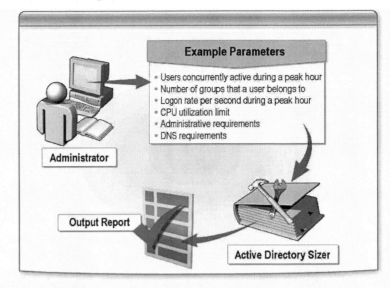

Introduction

When you run Active Directory Sizer gathers the following information on each domain so you can accurately place the domain controllers:

- Number of users
- Attributes per user
- Groups that a user belongs to
- Logon rate during peak hours
- Password expiration rate
- Number of computers
- CPU utilization limit
- Administration
- Information about the Domain Name System (DNS)

Considerations

When you enter critical information in some of the parameters in Active Directory Sizer, consider these factors:

- *Percent of users who are concurrently active during a peak hour*. If most users log on during a peak hour, specify a value of 100 percent. Typically, this parameter pertains to an Internet Service Provider (ISP), which may have a million users in a domain, but not all of them are active at the same time. Although it helps to know the total number of users to calculate the database size, Active Directory Sizer uses only the number of concurrent users to calculate the client logon traffic.

- *Average number of groups that a user belongs to*. This number can affect the time it takes a domain controller to process a logon request because user access depends on the access permissions for each group. During the logon process, the domain controller adds each group's security identifier (SID) to the security token of the user. This parameter pertains to all types of groups—local, global, and universal.

- *Average logon rate per second during a peak hour*. If you do not know the rate, use the following method to estimate it:

  a. Determine how many concurrent users in your organization are likely to log on to the system during a peak hour. For example, between 8 A.M. and 9 A.M.

  b. Divide this number by 3,600 seconds for the average logon rate per second.

  The estimate assumes that, for every interactive logon, Windows 2003 Server performs on average 15 network logons. If users log on to two or more computers, adjust the logon rate appropriately.

- *Required average CPU utilization limit for each domain controller*. This limit is only applicable for Active Directory. If you plan to use the domain controller to host services other than Active Directory, consider specifying a lower value to account for the average CPU utilization of those services.

  Specifying a lower value allows the domain controller to accommodate a sudden increase in workload. However, if you lower this value too much you may cause Active Directory Sizer to predict more domain controllers than may be required to manage a typical workload.

- *Administrative requirements*. Typically, you perform certain directory operations such as adding, deleting, or modifying objects on a daily, weekly, or annual basis. Before you stipulate your administrative requirements, consider whether your domain has more than one administrator, or more than one user has permissions to add, delete, and modify objects in the domain, and include that data in your estimate.

  If an application uses Active Directory, do not add that information here.

- *DNS requirements*. Specify values in these parameters only if you use an Active Directory integrated DNS.

  - *Aging and scavenging*. *Aging* is the process of identifying resource records that DNS created dynamically, and that the client computer that created the records has not updated in a timely manner. Records that are identified by this process are considered *stale*. Having many aging resource records can cause problems. For example, they take up space on the server, and DNS server performance can suffer because a server may use an aging resource record to answer a query. To solve these problems, the DNS server in Windows Server 2003 can scavenge aging records. *Scavenging* is the process of deleting stale resource records from the DNS server's zone databases.

  - *NoRefreshInterval*. This value is the interval between the last time a record was refreshed and the earliest time that it can be refreshed again. Note that the server still accepts updates during this interval.

Note For more information about aging and scavenging, see the DNS MMC console help.

How to Use Active Directory Sizer

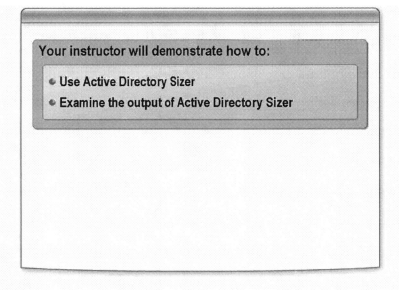

Your instructor will demonstrate how to:

- Use Active Directory Sizer
- Examine the output of Active Directory Sizer

Introduction

You use Active Directory Sizer to determine the placement of domain controllers.

Procedure

To use Active Directory Sizer, perform the following steps:

Important   Active Directory Sizer is not installed by default. You can download and install it from: http://download.microsoft.com/download/win2000platform/ASsizer/1.0/NT5/EN-US/setup.exe.

In this classroom, you can install Active Directory Sizer by running **\\london\setup\adsizer\setup.exe** and completing the setup wizard.

---

1. Click **Start**, point to **Programs**, click **Active Directory Sizer**, click **File**, and then click **New**.

2. In the Active Directory Wizard, specify a name for the domain, and then click **Next**.

3. On the **User Accounts** page, specify the total number of users and the number of users logged on during peak times, specify additional attributes, and then click **Next**.

4. On the next **User Accounts** page, specify the average number of groups that a user will belong to, specify the number of days for password expiration, specify a value for interactive, batch, and network in the average logon rate, and then click **Next**.

5. On the **Computers and Other Objects** page, specify the number of computers running Windows 2000, the number of other computers, and the number of other objects, and then click **Next**.

6. On the next **Computers and Other Objects** page, accept the default values for CPU utilization and preferred CPU type, and then click **Next**.

7. On the **Administration** page, specify values for the **Interval**, **Add**, **Delete**, and **Modify** boxes, and then click **Next**.

8. On the **Exchange 2000** page, specify whether you plan to use Exchange, specify the average messages per day and the number of recipients, the number of Exchange servers and routing groups, and then click **Next**.

9. On the **Services Using Active Directory** page, select whether you plan to use an Active Directory-enabled DNS, specify the dial-in connections, and use the default values for Dynamic Host Configuration Protocol (DHCP) lease and NoRefreshInterval, and then click **Next**.

10. On the next **Services Using Active Directory** page, select the values for the services under **Active Directory**, click **Next**, and then click **Finish**.

After completing the wizard, if you have a multiple domain or multiple site environments, you can use the console tree to create additional domains or sites, and then distribute the user to the appropriate domains or sites.

The Active Directory Sizer output

When the procedure is completed, the Active Directory Sizer report displays the following information:

- The number of objects and the number of domain controllers that this domain requires. Always have at least two domain controllers per domain to provide fault tolerance.

- The size of Active Directory and the global catalog.

- The number of global catalog servers and bridgehead servers in each domain. The Active Directory Sizer makes the following assumptions:

  - A bridgehead server is a global catalog server.

  - One bridgehead server per site even if the site has multiple domains.

- The intersite replication traffic. Clicking a site shows the total volume of inbound and outbound replication traffic for that site. All intersite replication is Remote procedure call (RPC)-based. Active Directory Sizer accounts for compression when it calculates the amount of replication traffic.

Note   The Active Directory Sizer makes hardware recommendations based on information that key vendors include with their current products. You can install a domain controller on a different hardware setup. Active Directory Sizer uses an algorithm that is based on scaling up rather than scaling out. Therefore, by using fewer computers that provide good hardware support for your domain workload, you can reduce replication latency in the system.

Because the algorithm is based on scaling up, its recommendations may not meet the fault tolerance requirements for a domain or a site.

Practice: Determining the Placement of Domain Controllers in Active Directory

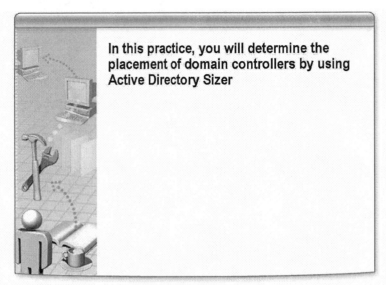

In this practice, you will determine the placement of domain controllers by using Active Directory Sizer

Objectives

In this practice, you will determine the placement of domain controllers by using Active Directory Sizer.

Scenario

Woodgrove Bank is a small local bank with five branches in Chicago. The bank has 375 employees: 300 employees at its corporate headquarters and 15 employees at each branch. Woodgrove Bank has chosen to use:

- A single-domain strategy.
- A domain name of corp.woodgrove.msft.
- A single-site strategy, with no servers at the branch offices.

Use the Active Directory Sizer to help you develop a placement plan for domain controllers for Woodgrove Bank.

Practice

▶ **Determine server placement**

1. Log on as **Nwtraders***x**ComputerName***User** with a password of **P@ssw0rd**

2. Click **Start**, point to **All Programs**, point to **Active Directory Sizer**, and then click **Active Directory Sizer**.

3. In the **Active Directory Sizer** dialog box, click **File**, and then click **New**.

4. When prompted, type the domain name, and then click **Next**.

5. On the **User Accounts** page, type the number of users, and then click **Finish**.

   In the console tree, under **Domain Configuration**, the domain corp.woodgrove.msft appears and under **Site Configuration**, a default site named Default-First-Site appears. In the details pane, view the number of servers that Active Directory Sizer recommends that you place in the site.

6. Close Active Directory Sizer.

Lesson: Planning the Placement of Domain Controllers

* Guidelines for Placing Domain Controllers
* Guidelines for Placing Global Catalog Servers
* Guidelines for Enabling Universal Group Membership Caching
* Guidelines for Placing Active Directory Integrated DNS Servers

Introduction

Planning the placement of domain controllers helps you determine your organization's hardware requirements and prevents you from underestimating hardware requirements. It also ensures that you do not overload domain controllers running Windows Server 2003.

Before you plan the placement of domain controllers, you must design and deploy an Active Directory site topology. For Windows Server 2003, the DNS service has been carefully integrated into the design and implementation of Active Directory. Therefore, when you deploy Active Directory and Windows Server 2003 together, you also must plan for the placement of Active Directory integrated DNS servers.

Lesson objectives

After completing this lesson, you will be able to:

■ Explain guidelines for placing domain controllers.

■ Explain guidelines for placing global catalog servers.

■ Explain guidelines for enabling universal group membership caching.

■ Explain guidelines for placing Active Directory integrated DNS servers.

Guidelines for Placing Domain Controllers

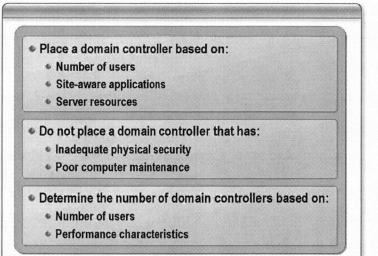

Introduction

By following guidelines for placing domain controllers, you can minimize the response time to user inquiries and provide fault tolerance.

Guidelines

Apply the following guidelines to place domain controllers:

- *Place a domain controller in a site if*:

  - *There are many users in the site.* When these users log on, they can contact a local domain controller for authentication, instead of contacting a remote domain controller over a WAN link.

  - *Site-aware applications will be used in the site.* These applications can then access a user account and other information from a local domain controller.

  - *The site contains server resources that users can access when the WAN link is unavailable.* If the WAN link is unavailable and no local domain controllers are available to process logon requests, users log on by using cached credentials They cannot access resources on any computers other than the one they are logged on to. If users must be able to access resources on other computers on the network, configure the domain controller as a global catalog server. Or, at a minimum, enable universal group membership caching for the site.

- *Do not place a domain controller in a site that has inadequate physical security or poor corporate maintenance.* If an intruder can physically access a server, it is much easier for him to bypass the security settings and access or modify critical corporate data. Without personnel to maintain local computers, a hardware or software failure on a domain controller may disrupt service for an unacceptable period of time.

- *Determine the number of domain controllers based on the number of users and the required performance.* Use Active Directory Sizer to determine specific CPU, memory, and network values. Also consider fault tolerance requirements. If Active Directory Sizer recommends only one domain controller for a site, but users must be able to log on and access local, server-based resources if a WAN link fails, consider placing a second domain controller in the site to meet your fault tolerance requirements.

Guidelines for Placing Global Catalog Servers

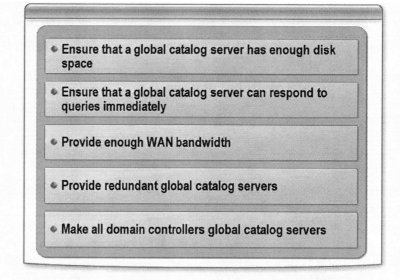

- ● Ensure that a global catalog server has enough disk space
- ● Ensure that a global catalog server can respond to queries immediately
- ● Provide enough WAN bandwidth
- ● Provide redundant global catalog servers
- ● Make all domain controllers global catalog servers

Introduction

In an ideal environment, there is a global catalog server at each site that can process Active Directory query requests. However, too many global catalog servers may increase network traffic significantly because of the partial replication of all objects from all domains. Therefore, base your plan for placing global catalog servers on the capability of your network.

Guidelines

Apply the following guidelines to place global catalog servers in sites:

- ■ *Ensure that a global catalog server has enough disk space.* The disk must be able to hold partial replicas of all objects from all other domains in Active Directory.

- ■ *Ensure that a global catalog server can respond to client queries and authentication requests immediately.* If there are many users in a site or if logon authentication is slow, consider placing more than one global catalog server in the site.

- ■ *Provide enough WAN bandwidth.* Bandwidth is required to support global catalog replication traffic.

- *Provide redundant global catalog servers.* If you have access to a second global catalog server on your network , it helps you protect against failure of a global catalog server. If the servers are remote, redundant global catalog servers will not protect your organization against WAN failures.

- *Make all domain controllers global catalog servers if you have only one domain in a forest.* Because there is only one domain, making each domain controller a global catalog server will not increase replication traffic. Also, it will allow each domain controller to resolve queries to the global catalog locally, instead of contacting a global catalog server over the network.

Note In a single-domain forest environment, domain controllers do not contact a global catalog server when authenticating users because all universal group information is guaranteed to be stored on the domain controller.

Note For more information about global catalog and sites, see "Guidelines for Placing Global Catalog Servers" in Module 8 on the Appendices page on the Student Materials compact disc.

Guidelines for Enabling Universal Group Membership Caching

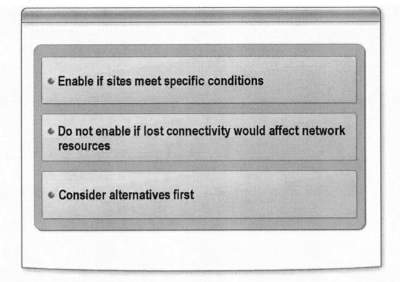

Introduction

When you consider which sites to enable universal group membership caching for, develop a plan based on the ability of your network structure to manage replication and query traffic.

Guidelines

Apply the following guidelines to determine whether to enable universal group membership caching for a site:

- *Enable universal group membership caching in sites that meet these conditions*:

  - Hardware or bandwidth limitations prevent you from placing global catalog servers in the site.

  - One or more local domain controllers are available.

  - Loss of connectivity to the global catalog server may be frequent or prolonged.

  - Network resource access cannot be interrupted.

  The presence of these conditions does not mean that you must enable universal group membership caching in a site; rather, it indicates that using this feature may provide required redundancy.

- *Do not enable universal group membership caching if lost connectivity would affect connectivity to other network resources.* For example, do not enable universal group membership caching in small satellite offices with no local servers.

■ *Consider alternatives before you enable universal group membership caching.* The following alternatives may indicate situations for which universal group membership caching is not appropriate.

- *Provide local global catalog servers.* It helps protect each site against WAN failures. It may not be possible if hardware limitations or bandwidth restrictions obstruct the conversion of local domain controllers to global catalog servers.

- *Provide redundant WAN connections.* Many local area networks (LANs) have redundant WAN connections in times of emergency. Typically, these connections have less available bandwidth than more permanent connections, but they are usually sufficient until network connectivity is restored.

- *Make all domain controllers global catalog servers.* If there is one single domain in the forest, a global catalog server is not contacted during authentication. However, a global catalog server is still used for global catalog searches.

Guidelines for Placing Active Directory Integrated DNS Servers

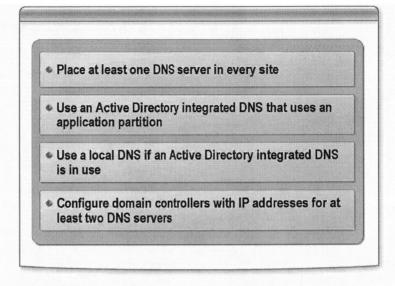

- Place at least one DNS server in every site

- Use an Active Directory integrated DNS that uses an application partition

- Use a local DNS if an Active Directory integrated DNS is in use

- Configure domain controllers with IP addresses for at least two DNS servers

Introduction

The availability of DNS directly affects the availability of Active Directory. Client computers use DNS to locate domain controllers, and domain controllers rely on DNS to locate other domain controllers. Even if DNS servers are deployed in the network, it may be necessary to adjust the number and placement of DNS servers to meet the requirements of the client computers and domain controllers.

Guidelines

Apply the following guidelines to determine the placement of DNS servers in sites:

- *Place at least one DNS server in every site.* The DNS servers in the site must be authoritative for the locator records of the domain controllers in the site so that all DNS queries for domain controllers in the site are resolved by the local DNS server. Also, domain controllers periodically verify that the entries on the primary master server are correct for each locator record.

- *Use an Active Directory integrated DNS that uses an application partition.* Use this approach for all DNS servers in the domain. Run the DNS service on one or more domain controllers for each site where those domain controllers appear.

- *Use a local DNS if an Active Directory integrated DNS is already in use.*
  Logging on often takes longer when the DNS server is not located locally
  because the client computer must contact the DNS server over the WAN
  link to locate a domain controller to authenticate the user. If Active
  Directory integrated DNS is already in use on your network, and if you have
  a local domain controller, consider making the local domain controller a
  DNS server. This will enable client computers to resolve all DNS queries
  locally, instead of over the WAN.

- *Configure domain controllers with IP addresses for at least two DNS
  servers.* The two DNS servers are a preferred local server and an alternate
  server. The alternate server can be in the local site, or it can be remote if you
  only have a single DNS server in the local site.

Note For more information about DNS, see Module 2, "Implementing an
Active Directory Forest and Domain Structure," in Course 2279, *Planning,
Implementing, and Maintaining a Microsoft Windows Server 2003 Active
Directory Infrastructure*.

Multimedia Practice: Placing Domain Controllers

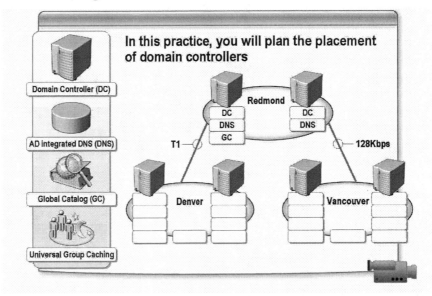

File location	To view the *Placing Domain Controllers* multimedia practice, open the Web page on the Student Materials compact disc, click **Multimedia**, and then click the title of the presentation. Do not open this presentation unless the instructor tells you to.
Objective	In this practice, you will plan the placement of Active Directory domain controllers in an organization.
Instructions	The *Placing Domain Controllers* activity includes multiple choice and drag-and-drop exercises that enable you to test your knowledge. Click **Multimedia**, and then click *Placing Domain Controllers*. Read the instructions, and then begin the practice.

Lab A: Implementing the Placement of Domain Controllers

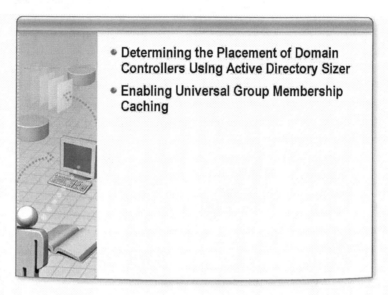

Objectives

After completing this lab, you will be able to:

- Determine the placement of domain controllers by using Active Directory Sizer.

- Enable universal group membership caching and specify which site domain controllers will contact to refresh the cache.

Prerequisites

Before working on this lab, you must have:

- Knowledge about how the logon process works.

- Knowledge about how sites, subnets, domain controllers, and global catalog servers affect the logon process.

Scenario

Northwind Traders is an investment trading bank with 200 branches in Illinois, Indiana, and Ohio. Each regional center has its own IT staff that reports to the corporate IT staff, which is based at the bank's headquarters in Chicago. Northwind Traders has chosen a single-domain strategy with the domain name of corp.nwtraders.msft. It will include three sites: Chicago, Indianapolis, and Columbus.

Estimated time to complete this lab: 30 minutes

Exercise 1
Determining the Placement of Domain Controllers Using Active Directory Sizer

In this exercise, you will input information from the scenario into Active Directory Sizer to determine how many domain controllers, global catalog servers, and preferred bridgehead servers to place at each site for Northwind Traders.

Scenario

Northwind Traders has chosen:

- A single-domain strategy.

- A domain name of corp.nwtraders.msft.

- Three sites: Chicago, Indianapolis, and Columbus.

Operations at the Chicago site are critical for Northwind Traders. Users in this site must be able to log on and access network resources 24 hours per day, 7 days per week.

Northwind Traders officials have provided you with the following information about the number of users at each regional center.

Site	Number of branches	Total number of users
Chicago	100	2,675
Indianapolis	60	1,350
Columbus	35	925
Total	195	4,950

You have consulted the IT staff at the regional centers about their network and workstations. They provided the following information.

Item	Information
Percent of users concurrently active	90
Average additional attributes	25
Average groups per user	30
Password expiration in days	45
Average interactive logon rate peak per second	5
Average batch logon rate peak per second	0
Average network logon rate peak per second	25
Windows 2000 computers	4,000
Other computers	1,000
Other objects to be published	2,030
Desired average CPU utilization	60%
Preferred domain controller CPU	Auto select
Number of processors in domain controllers	Auto select
Object additions per week	20
Object deletions per week	15
Object modifications per week	500
Microsoft Exchange 2000	Yes
Microsoft Exchange 2000 messages	75
Microsoft Exchange 2000 recipients per message	15
Exchange Servers	2
Exchange routing groups	1
Windows 2000 DNS	Yes
Dial-in connections	100
DHCP lease expiration in days	12
DNS NoRefreshInterval in days	7
Other Active Directory services	None

Tasks	Specific instructions
1. Open a new project in Active Directory Sizer, and then specify the required information.	a. Log on as **Nwtraders*x**ComputerName*User** (where *ComputerName* is the name of the computer you are working on) with a password of **P@ssw0rd** b. In the Active Directory Sizer Wizard, when prompted, use the information provided in the scenario to complete the wizard.
2. Create three sites in Active Directory Sizer.	▪ Create the following three sites: • Chicago • Indianapolis • Columbus
3. Distribute users to the sites that you just created.	a. Use Active Directory Sizer. b. Move all users from Default-First-Site-Name site.
4. View the site report in Active Directory Sizer.	▪ Note the recommended distribution of domain controllers, bridgehead servers, and global catalogs for each site.

How many domain controllers does Active Directory Sizer recommend for the Chicago site?

_____

_____

How many domain controllers will you recommend for the Chicago site?

_____

_____

Exercise 2
Enabling Universal Group Membership Caching

In this exercise, you will enable universal group membership caching for a site, and specify which site you will use to refresh the cache.

Scenario

One of the branch offices for Northwind Traders has grown so much that you have created a new site for it in Active Directory, and you have placed a domain controller that is not a global catalog server in the site. You must ensure that users can log on and access resources on local servers even if the WAN link fails. However, the WAN link to corporate headquarters is used heavily during the day to carry mainframe session traffic. You must minimize the amount of Active Directory replication traffic that is sent over this WAN link.

Tasks	Specific instructions
▪ Enable universal group membership caching for the LAB*ComputerName*Site site, and configure it to be refreshed from the Default-First-Site-Name site.	a. Log on as **Nwtraders***x******ComputerName***User** with a password of **P@ssw0rd** b. Use **Run as** to start Active Directory Sites and Services as **Nwtraders***x***\\Administrator** with a password of **P@ssw0rd**

Microsoft®
Training &
Certification

Module 9: Managing Operations Masters

Contents

Overview

- Introduction to Operations Master Roles
- Transferring and Seizing Operations Master Roles
- Planning the Placement of Operations Masters

Introduction

An *operations master* is a domain controller that performs a specific role in the Active Directory® directory service. Knowing the specific operations master roles of each domain controller in an Active Directory network can help you replicate data and use network bandwidth efficiently. This module describes the operations master roles, how to transfer and seize operations master roles, and how to plan for placing operations masters.

Objectives

After completing this module, you will be able to:

- Explain the purpose of the five operations master roles in Active Directory.
- Transfer and seize operations master roles in Active Directory.
- Plan for placing operations masters in Active Directory.

Lesson: Introduction to Operations Master Roles

- What Is the Schema Master?
- What Is the Domain Naming Master?
- What Is the PDC Emulator?
- What Is the RID Master?
- What Is the Infrastructure Master?

Introduction

Active Directory defines five operations master roles: the schema master, domain naming master, primary domain controller (PDC) emulator, relative identifier (RID) master, and the infrastructure master. This lesson explains the purpose of each operations master role.

Lesson objectives

After completing this lesson, you will be able to:

- Explain the purpose of a schema master.
- Explain the purpose of a domain naming master.
- Explain the purpose of a PDC emulator.
- Explain the purpose of a RID master.
- Explain the purpose of an infrastructure master.

What Is the Schema Master?

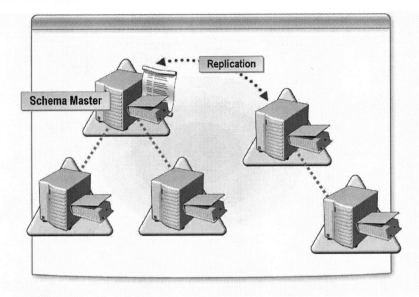

Introduction

An Active Directory s*chema* defines the kinds of objects—and the types of information about those objects—that you can store in Active Directory. Active Directory stores these definitions as objects. Active Directory manages the schema objects by using the object management operations that its uses to manage other objects in the directory.

Roles performed by the schema master

The *schema master* performs the following roles:

- Controls all originating updates to the schema

- Contains the master list of object classes and attributes that are used to create all Active Directory objects

- Replicates updates to the Active Directory schema to all domain controllers in the forest by using standard replication of the schema partition

- Allows only the members of the Schema Admins group to modify the schema

Each forest has only one schema master. This prevents any conflicts that would result if two or more domain controllers attempt to simultaneously update the schema. If the schema master is not available, you cannot modify the schema or install applications that modify the schema.

What Is the Domain Naming Master?

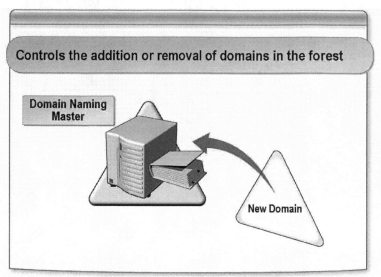

Controls the addition or removal of domains in the forest

Domain Naming Master

New Domain

Introduction

When you add or remove a domain from a forest, the change is recorded in Active Directory.

Roles performed by the domain naming master

The *domain naming master* controls the addition or removal of domains in the forest. There is only one domain naming master in each forest.

When you add a new domain to the forest, only the domain controller that holds the domain naming master role can add the new domain. The domain naming master prevents multiple domains with the same domain name from joining the forest. When you use the Active Directory Installation Wizard to create a child domain, it contacts the domain naming master and requests the addition or deletion. If the domain naming master is unavailable, you cannot add or remove domains.

What Is the PDC Emulator?

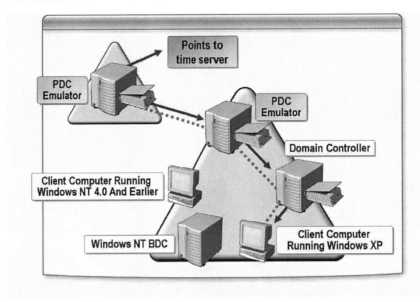

Introduction

The *PDC emulator* acts as a Microsoft® Windows NT® primary domain controller (PDC) to support any backup domain controllers (BDCs) running Windows NT in a mixed-mode domain. When you create a domain, Active Directory assigns the PDC emulator role to the first domain controller in the new domain.

Roles performed by the PDC emulator

The PDC emulator performs the following roles:

- *Acts as the PDC for any existing BDCs.* If a domain contains any BDCs or client computers running Windows NT 4.0 and earlier, the PDC emulator functions as a Windows NT PDC. The PDC emulator replicates directory changes to any BDCs running Windows NT.

- *Manages password changes from computers running Windows NT, Microsoft Windows® 95, or Windows 98.* Active Directory writes password changes directly to the PDC emulator.

- *Minimizes replication latency for password changes.* The time that is required for a domain controller to receive a change that was made on another domain controller is called *replication latency*. When the password of a client computer running Windows 2000 or later is changed on a domain controller, the domain controller immediately forwards the change to the PDC emulator. If a logon authentication fails at another domain controller because of a bad password, that domain controller will forward the authentication request to the PDC emulator before it rejects the logon attempt.

- *Synchronizes the time on all domain controllers throughout the domain to its time.* The Kerberos version 5 authentication protocol requires the time on domain controllers to be synchronized to enable authentication. Client computers in a domain also synchronize their time with the domain controller that authenticates the user.

- *Prevents the possibility of overwriting Group Policy objects (GPOs).* By default, Group Policy reduces the potential for replication conflicts by running on the domain controller that holds the PDC emulator role for that domain.

Note For more information about managing time synchronization, see "What Is the PDC Emulator?" in Module 9 on the Appendices page on the Student Materials compact disc.

What Is the RID Master?

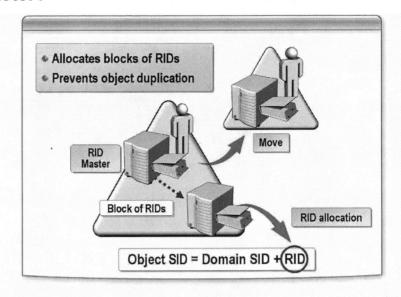

Introduction

The *relative ID (RID) master* is a domain controller that allocates blocks of RIDs to each domain controller in the domain. Whenever a domain controller creates a new security principal, such as a user, group, or computer object, it assigns the object a unique security identifier (SID). This SID consists of a domain SID, which is the same for each security principal that is created in the domain, and a RID, which is unique for each security principal in the domain.

How the RID master supports creating and moving objects

The RID master supports creating and moving objects as follows:

- *Creating objects.* To allow a multimaster operation to create objects on any domain controller, the RID master allocates a block of RIDs to a domain controller. When a domain controller requires an additional block of RIDs, it contacts the RID master, which allocates a new block of RIDs to the domain controller, which in turn assigns them to the new objects.

  If a domain controller's RID pool is empty, and the RID master is unavailable, you cannot create new security principals on that domain controller. You can view the RID pool allocation by using the Domain Controller Diagnostic utility (the **dcdiag** command).

  Note You can install the Dcdiag utility by installing the support tools, which are located in the \Support\Tools folder on the product compact disc.

- *Moving objects.* When you move an object between domains, the move is initiated on the RID master that contains the object. This way, there is no duplication of objects.

  If you moved an object, but no single master kept this information, you could move the object to multiple domains without realizing that a previous move had already occurred.

The RID master deletes the object from the domain when the object is moved from that domain to another domain.

What Is the Infrastructure Master?

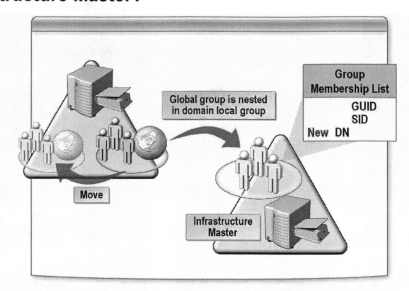

Introduction

The *infrastructure master* is a domain controller that updates object references in its domain that point to objects in another domain. The object reference contains the object's globally unique identifier (GUID), the distinguished name, and possibly a SID. Active Directory periodically updates the distinguished name and the SID to reflect changes that were made to the object, such as when you move an object within a domain or between domains or delete the object.

Group membership identification

If the SID or the distinguished name of a user account or group is modified in another domain, Active Directory must update the group membership for a group on your domain that refers to the changed user or group. The infrastructure master for the domain in which the group (or reference) resides updates the group membership by replicating the change throughout the domain.

The infrastructure master updates object identification according to the following rules:

- If the object is moved, its distinguished name changes because the distinguished name represents its exact location in the directory.

- If the object is moved within the domain, its SID remains the same.

- If the object is moved to another domain, the SID changes to incorporate the new domain SID.

- The GUID does not change regardless of location because the GUID is unique across domains.

Note In a single domain forest, there is no requirement for the infrastructure master to function because there are no external object references for it to update.

Infrastructure master and the global catalog

Do not make a domain controller that hosts the global catalog an infrastructure master. If the infrastructure master and the global catalog are on the same computer, the infrastructure master does not function because it does not contain any references to objects that it does not hold.

Periodically, the infrastructure master for a domain examines the references in its replica of the directory data to objects that are not held on that domain controller. It queries a global catalog server for current information about the distinguished name and the SID of each referenced object. If this information has changed, the infrastructure master makes the change in its local replica. It then replicates these changes to the other domain controllers within the domain.

Lesson: Transferring and Seizing Operations Master Roles

* Transfer of Operations Master Roles
* When to Seize Operations Master Roles
* How to Determine the Holder of an Operations Master Role
* How to Transfer an Operations Master Role
* How to Seize an Operations Master Role

Introduction

This lesson discusses the transfer and seizing of operations master roles. It explains how to determine the holder of an operations master role and how to transfer and seize an operations master role.

Lesson objectives

After completing this lesson, you will be able to:

- Explain the purpose of transferring an operations master role.
- Explain the purpose of seizing an operations master role.
- Determine the holder of an operations master role.
- Transfer an operations master role.
- Seize an operations master role.

Transfer of Operations Master Roles

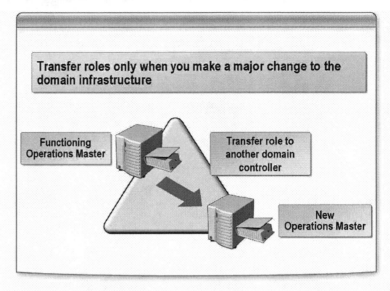

Introduction

You place operations master roles in a forest when you implement the forest and domain structure. Transfer an operations master role only when you make a major change to the domain infrastructure. Such changes include decommissioning a domain controller that holds a role and adding a new domain controller that is better suited to hold a specific role. Transferring an operations master role means moving it from one functioning domain controller to another. To transfer roles, both domain controllers must be up and running and connected to the network.

Implications of transferring a role

No data loss occurs when you transfer an operations master role. Active Directory replicates the current operations master directory to the new domain controller, which ensures that the new operations master has the most current information. This transfer uses the directory replication mechanism.

Required permissions   You must have the appropriate permissions to transfer an operations master role. The following table lists the groups that you must be a member of to transfer an operations master role.

Operations master	Authorized group
Schema master	The Change Schema Master permission is granted by default to the Schema Admins group.
Domain naming master	The Change Domain Master permission is granted by default to the Enterprise Admins group.
PDC emulator	The Change PDC permission is granted by default to the Domain Admins group.
RID master	The Change RID Master permission is granted by default to the Domain Admins group.
Infrastructure master	The Change Infrastructure Master permission is granted by default to the Domain Admins group.

Note   When a domain controller is demoted to a member server, it relinquishes any operations master roles that it held to other domain controllers arbitrarily. To control which domain controllers get the role, transfer the roles prior to demotion.

When to Seize Operations Master Roles

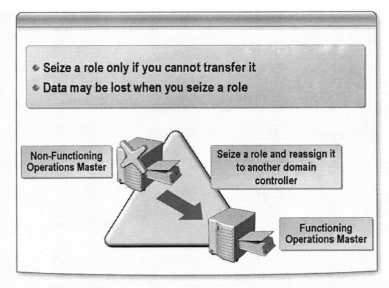

Introduction

Seizing an operations master role means forcing an operations master role on another domain controller, which cannot contact the failed domain controller when you seize the role. You must be a member of an authorized group to seize a role.

Implications of seizing a role

Seizing an operations master role is a drastic step. Do it only if the current operations master will never be available again and if you cannot transfer the role. Because the previous role holder is unavailable during a seizure, you cannot reconfigure or inform it that another domain controller now hosts the operations master role.

To reduce risk, perform a role seizure only if the failed operations master role affects the performance of Active Directory in an unacceptable way. Calculate the effect by comparing the impact of the operations master role being unavailable to the amount of work that you must perform to bring the previous role holder safely back online after you seize the role.

Important Before you seize a role, you must permanently disconnect the domain controller that holds the operations master role from the network.

If you do manage to repair the previous role holder and bring it back online after you seize an operations master role, the previous role holder waits until after a full replication cycle before it resumes the role of operations master. This way, it can determine if another operations master exists before it comes back online. If it detects one, it reconfigures itself to no longer host the role in question.

Active Directory continues to function when the operations master roles are unavailable. If the role holder is offline for a short time only, it may not be necessary to seize the role. The following table describes the risks and consequences of returning an operations master to service after the role is seized.

Operations master role	Consequence if role is unavailable	Risk of improper restoration	Recommendation for returning to service after seizure
Schema master	You cannot make changes to the schema.	Conflicting changes can be introduced to the schema if both schema masters try to modify the schema at the same time. This conflict can result in a fragmented schema.	Not recommended. Can lead to a corrupted forest and require that you rebuild the entire forest.
Domain naming master	You cannot add or remove domains from the forest.	You cannot add or remove domains or clean up metadata. Domains may incorrectly appear as though they are still in the forest.	Not recommended. Can require that you rebuild domains.
PDC emulator	You cannot change passwords on client computers that do not have the Active Directory client software installed. No replication occurs to Windows NT 4.0 backup domain controllers.	Password validation can randomly pass or fail. Password changes take much longer to replicate across the domain.	Allowed. User authentication can be erratic for a while, but no permanent damage occurs.
Infrastructure master	Delays displaying updated group membership lists in the user interface when you move users from one group to another.	Displays incorrect user names in group membership lists in the user interface after you move users from one group to another.	Allowed. May affect the performance of the domain controller that hosts the role, but no damage occurs to the directory.
RID master	Eventually, domain controllers cannot create new directory objects because each of their RID pools is depleted.	Duplicate RID pools can be allocated to domain controllers, which results in data corruption in the directory and can lead to security risks and unauthorized access.	Not recommended. Can lead to data corruption that can require that you rebuild the domain.

How to Determine the Holder of an Operations Master Role

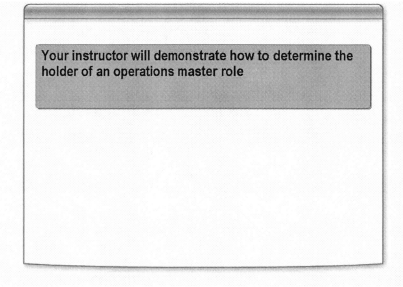

Your instructor will demonstrate how to determine the holder of an operations master role

Introduction

Before you consider moving an operations master role, determine which domain controller holds a particular operations master role. Only authenticated users have the permission to determine where the operations master roles are located. Depending on the operations master role, use one of the following Active Directory snap-ins:

- Active Directory Users and Computers (PDC, RID, and infrastructure master roles)
- Active Directory Domains and Trusts (domain naming master role)
- Active Directory Schema (schema master role)

Procedure for determining the RID master, the PDC emulator, and the infrastructure master

To determine which domain controller holds the RID master role, PDC emulator role, or infrastructure master role, perform the following steps.

1. Open Active Directory Users and Computers.

2. In the console tree, right-click the domain for which you want to view operations masters, and then click **Operations Masters**.

3. On the **RID**, **PDC**, or **Infrastructure** tabs, under **Operations master**, view the name of the current operations master.

Procedure for determining the domain naming master

To determine which domain controller holds the domain naming master role, perform the following steps:

1. Open Active Directory Domains and Trusts.

2. Right-click **Active Directory Domains and Trusts**, and then click **Operations Master**.

3. In the **Change Operations Master** dialog box, view the name of the current domain naming master.

Procedure for determining the schema master

To determine which domain controller holds the schema master role, perform the following steps:

1. Register the Active Directory Schema snap-in by running the following command:

   regsvr32.exe %systemroot%\system32\schmmgmt.dll

2. Click **OK**.

3. Create a custom Microsoft Management Console (MMC) console, and then add the Active Directory Schema snap-in to the console.

4. In the console tree, expand and right-click **Active Directory Schema**, and then click **Operations Master**.

5. In the **Change Schema Master** dialog box, view the name of the current schema master.

Note   To identify an operations master in a different domain, connect to the domain before you click **Operations Masters** in step 4. To identify the operations master in a different forest, connect to the domain by typing the domain name of the forest before you click **Operations Masters**.

How to Transfer an Operations Master Role

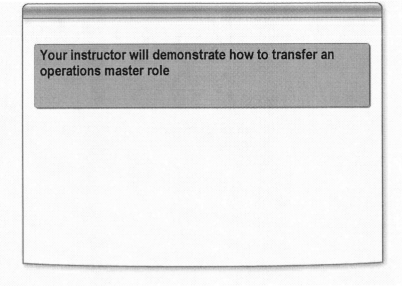

Your instructor will demonstrate how to transfer an operations master role

Introduction

You can transfer the three domain-wide operations master roles by using Active Directory Users and Computers. To transfer the domain naming master role, use Active Directory Domains and Trusts. To transfer the Active Directory schema master role, use the Active Directory Schema tool.

Procedure for transferring the RID master, PDC emulator, and infrastructure master roles

To transfer the operations master role for the RID master, PDC emulator, or infrastructure master, perform the following steps:

1. Open Active Directory Users and Computers.

2. In the console tree, right-click **Active Directory Users and Computers**, and then click **Connect to Domain Controller**.

3. In the **Or select an available domain controller** list, click the domain controller that will become the new operations master, and then click **OK**.

4. In the console tree, right-click the domain that contains the server that will become the new operations master, and then click **Operations Masters**.

5. On the **Infrastructure, PDC, or RID** tab, click **Change**, and then click **Yes**.

Caution Ensure that you do not transfer the infrastructure master role to a domain controller that hosts the global catalog.

Procedure for transferring the domain naming master role

To transfer the domain naming master role to another domain controller, perform the following steps:

1. Open Active Directory Domains and Trusts.

2. In the console tree, right-click **Active Directory Domains and Trusts**, and then click **Connect to Domain Controller**.

3. In the **Or select an available domain controller** list, click the domain controller that will become the new domain naming master, and then click **OK**.

4. In the console tree, right-click **Active Directory Domains and Trusts**, and then click **Operations Master**.

5. When the name of the domain controller that you selected in step 3 appears, click **Change**, and then click **Yes**.

Procedure for transferring the schema master role

To transfer the schema operations master role, perform the following steps:

1. Open Active Directory Schema.

2. In the console tree, right-click **Active Directory Schema**, and then click **Change Domain Controller**.

3. Click **Specify Name**, type the name of the domain controller that you want to transfer the schema master role to, and then click **OK**.

4. In the console tree, right-click **Active Directory Schema**, and then click **Operations Master**.

5. When the name of the domain controller that you typed in step 3 appears, click **Change**, and then click **Yes**.

Note   Before you open the Active Directory Schema, you must first use Regsvr32.exe to register the Active Directory Schema snap-in, Schmmgmt.dll, and then create a new custom MMC console.

How to Seize an Operations Master Role

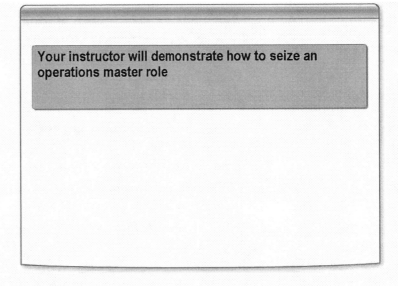

Your instructor will demonstrate how to seize an operations master role

Introduction

You can seize an operations master role by using the Ntdsutil command-line tool. The procedure varies slightly depending on the role that you seize. Because you can seize the PDC emulator and the infrastructure master roles without losing data, you can seize them by using Active Directory Users and Computers. To seize the other roles, use only the Ntdsutil utility to help prevent accidental seizing of these roles.

Recovery tasks

To recover from a failure of a RID master, schema master, or domain naming master, perform the following tasks:

1. Disconnect the current operations master from the network before you seize the role.

2. To perform the seizure, use the **ntdsutil** command.

3. Wait until all updates that the failed domain controller made have been replicated to the domain controller that is seizing the role.

4. Ensure that the domain controller whose role was seized is removed from the domain and never restored.

5. Before you reconnect that computer to the network, reformat the partition that contained the operating system files of the original operations master and reinstall Windows Server 2003.

Procedure for seizing a role by using Active Directory Users and Computers

To seize an operations master role for the PDC emulator or infrastructure master, perform the following steps:

1. Open Active Directory Users and Computers.

2. In the console tree, right-click the domain for which you want to seize an operations master role, and then click **Operations Masters**.

   It may take several seconds for the data to appear because Active Directory Users and Computers is waiting for a response from the current holder of the operations master role.

3. In the **Operations Master** dialog box, on the **Infrastructure, PDC, or RID** tab click **Change**.

4. In the **Active Directory** dialog box, click **Yes**.

5. When an **Active Directory** dialog box appears, indicating that this computer is a nonreplication partner, click **Yes**.

6. When an **Active Directory** dialog box appears, indicating a transfer is not possible, click **Yes**.

7. In the **Active Directory** dialog box, click **OK**, and then click **Close**.

8. Close Active Directory Users and Computers.

Procedure for seizing a role by using Ntdsutil

To use the **ntdsutil** command to seize an operations master role, perform the following steps:

1. In the **Run** box, type **cmd** and then click **OK**.

2. At the command prompt, type **ntdsutil** and then press ENTER.

3. At the **ntdsutil** prompt, type **roles** and then press ENTER.

4. At the **fsmo maintenance** prompt, type **connections** and then press ENTER.

5. At the **server connections** prompt, type **connect to server** followed by the fully qualified domain name (FQDN) of the domain controller that will be the new role holder, and then press ENTER.

6. Type **quit** and then press ENTER.

7. At the **fsmo maintenance** prompt, type one of the following commands to seize the appropriate operations master, press ENTER, type **quit** and then press ENTER.

   - **Seize RID master**

   - **Seize PDC**

   - **Seize infrastructure master**

   - **Seize domain naming master**

   - **Seize schema master**

8. At the **ntdsutil** prompt, type **quit** and then press ENTER.

Practice: Transferring Operations Master Roles

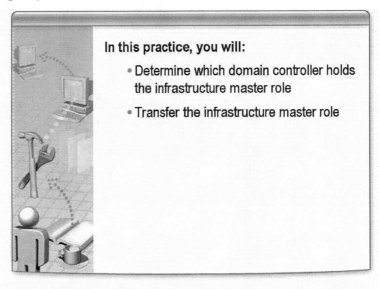

In this practice, you will:

- Determine which domain controller holds the infrastructure master role

- Transfer the infrastructure master role

Objectives

In this practice, you will:

- Determine which domain controller holds the infrastructure master role in your domain.

- Transfer the infrastructure master role to the other server in the domain.

Instructions

Work with a partner whose domain controller is in the same Active Directory domain as yours. This practice can only be performed on one server in the domain, so you must work together on a server.

Scenario

Northwind Traders is developing a disaster recovery plan. One important consideration is how the operations master roles will be distributed. The Active Directory implementation team has decided that they will place the infrastructure master role on a different server than the one that currently holds the role.

Practice

▶ **Transfer the infrastructure master role**

1. Log on as **Nwtraders***x******ComputerName***User** with a password of **P@ssw0rd**

2. Click **Start**, point to **Administrative Tools**, right-click **Active Directory Users and Computers**, and then click **Run as**.

3. In the **Run As** dialog box, click **The following user**, type **Nwtraders***x***\\Administrator** as the user name with a password of **P@ssw0rd** and then click **OK**.

4. In the console tree, right-click **nwtraders***x***.msft**, and then click **Operations Masters**.

5. On the **Infrastructure** tab, in the **Operations master** box, record the name of the current operations master, and then click **Close**.

_____

_____

6. In the console tree, right-click **nwtraders***x***.msft**, and then click **Connect to Domain Controller**.

7. In the **Connect to Domain Controller** dialog box, in the **Or select an available domain controller** list, select the server that does not currently host the infrastructure master role, and then click **OK**.

8. In the console tree, right-click **nwtraders***x***.msft**, and then click **Operations Masters**.

9. On the **Infrastructure** tab, click **Change**.

10. In the **Active Directory** dialog box, click **Yes**, and then click **OK**.

11. In the **Operations Masters** dialog box, notice that the operations master has been transferred to the selected domain controller, and then click **Close**.

12. Close Active Directory Users and Computers.

Lesson: Planning the Placement of Operations Masters

- Guidelines for Placing Operations Masters
- Guidelines for Placing the Schema Master
- Guidelines for Placing the Domain Naming Master
- Guidelines for Placing the PDC Emulator Master
- Guidelines for Placing the RID Master
- Guidelines for Placing the Infrastructure Master
- Guidelines for Seizing Operations Masters Roles

Introduction

This lesson explains the guidelines for placing and seizing operations master roles.

Lesson objectives

After completing this lesson, you will be able to:

- Explain guidelines for placing operations masters.
- Explain guidelines for placing the schema master.
- Explain guidelines for placing the domain naming master.
- Explain guidelines for placing the PDC emulator master.
- Explain guidelines for placing the RID master.
- Explain guidelines for placing the infrastructure master.
- Explain guidelines for seizing operations master roles.

Guidelines for Placing Operations Masters

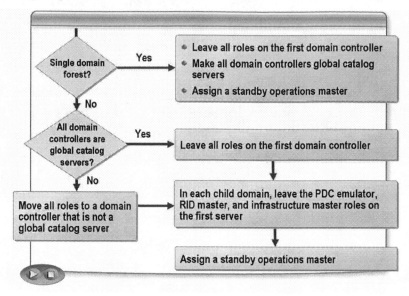

Introduction

Windows Server 2003 automatically places operations master roles on domain controllers. This placement works well for a forest that is deployed on a few domain controllers in one site. In a forest that has many domain controllers or multiple sites, however, you must plan the placement of operations master roles to maximize performance and minimize risk in the event of a loss of the domain controller.

Guidelines

Apply the following guidelines for placing operations masters:

- In a single domain forest, leave all of the operations master roles on the first domain controller in the forest. Designate each domain controller as a global catalog server, because the data in the global catalog contains only the domain data.

- In a multiple domain forest, use the following guidelines:

  - In the forest root domain:

    - If all domain controllers are also global catalog servers, leave all of the roles on the first domain controller in the forest.

    - If all domain controllers are not also global catalog servers, move all of the operations masters to a domain controller that is not a global catalog server.

  - In each child domain, leave the PDC emulator, RID master, and infrastructure master roles on the first server in the domain, and ensure that this server is never designated as a global catalog server.

- In each server that holds one or more operations master roles, make another domain controller in the same domain available as a standby operations master. The standby operations master should:

  - Not be a global catalog server except in a single domain environment, where all domain controllers are also global catalog servers.

  - Have a manually created replication connection to the domain controller that it is the standby operations master for, and it should be in the same site.

Guidelines for Placing the Schema Master

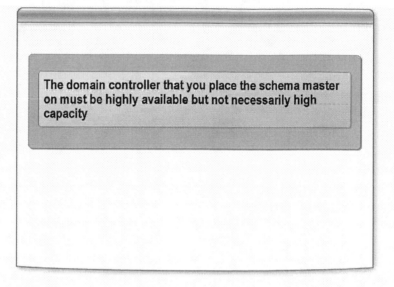

The domain controller that you place the schema master on must be highly available but not necessarily high capacity

Introduction

The schema master is a forest-wide operations master role. It controls all originating updates to the schema. If the schema master is unavailable, you cannot modify the schema. By default, the first domain controller of a new forest holds the schema master role.

Guidelines

Apply the following guidelines to determine the placement of the schema master:

- *Make a highly available domain controller the schema master.* Because the schema defines all of the objects that Active Directory can store, it is critical for Active Directory to record all changes that are made to the schema.

  A highly available domain controller is one that uses computer hardware that enables the domain controller to remain operational even during a hardware failure. For example, having a redundant array of independent disks (RAID) may enable the domain controller to keep running if one hard disk fails.

- *Do not require that the schema master be a high-capacity domain controller.* This requirement is unnecessary because schema changes are infrequent, the average server load is minimal, and the average replication traffic is not an overall concern.

  A high-capacity domain controller is one that has comparatively higher processing power than other domain controllers to accommodate the additional work load of holding the operations master role. It has a faster CPU and possibly additional memory and network bandwidth.

Guidelines for Placing the Domain Naming Master

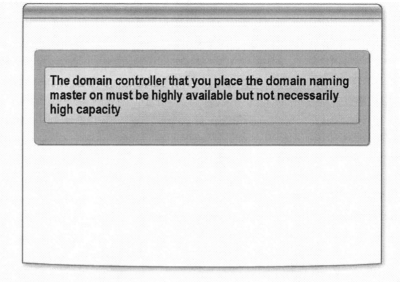

The domain controller that you place the domain naming master on must be highly available but not necessarily high capacity

Introduction

The domain naming master is a forest-wide operations master role. It controls the addition or removal of domains in the forest. By default, the first domain controller of a new forest holds the domain naming master role.

Guidelines

Apply the following guidelines to determine the placement of the domain-naming master:

- *Use a highly available domain controller as the domain naming master.* High availability is necessary when you add or remove a domain to or from the forest.

- *Do not require that the domain naming master be a high-capacity domain controller.* Adding and removing domains are infrequent tasks and the average server load is minimal.

Note If the forest is set to a functional level of Windows 2000 native, you must locate the domain naming master on a server that hosts the global catalog. If the forest is set to a functional level of Windows Server 2003, it is not necessary for the domain naming master to be on a global catalog server.

Guidelines for Placing the PDC Emulator Master

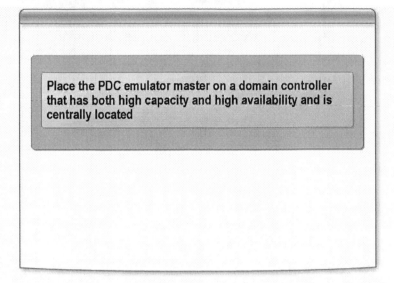

Place the PDC emulator master on a domain controller that has both high capacity and high availability and is centrally located

Introduction

The PDC emulator master is a domain-wide operations master role. It acts as a PDC in Windows NT to support any backup domain controllers (BDCs) running Windows NT in a domain that is set to the Windows 2000 mixed or Windows interim domain functionality. The first domain controller that you create in a new domain is assigned the PDC emulator role.

Guidelines

Apply the following guidelines to determine the placement of the PDC emulator master:

- *Use a highly available domain controller as the PDC emulator.* All domain controllers frequently access the PDC emulator for password changes, forwarding of mismatched passwords during logon, time synchronization, and support of BDCs and clients running Windows NT and earlier.

- *Use a high-capacity domain controller as the PDC emulator.* Because there is an increased load placed on this domain controller, do one of the following:

  - Increase the size of the domain controller's processing power.

  - Do not make the domain controller a global catalog server.

  - Reduce the priority and the weight of the service (SRV) record to give preference for authentication to other domain controllers in the site.

- *Do not require that the standby domain controller be a direct replication partner*. Seizing the PDC emulator role does not result in lost data, so there is no need to reduce replication latency for a seize operation.

- *Centrally locate this domain controller to accommodate the majority of the domain users*. Centrally locating this domain controller will reduce the amount of network traffic.

Note For more information about how to place the PDC emulator master and reduce the workload on the PDC emulator, see "Guidelines for Placing the PDC Emulator Master" in Module 9 on the Appendices page on the Student Materials compact disc.

Guidelines for Placing the RID Master

> - Place the RID master on a domain controller that is highly available but not necessarily high capacity
> - Place the RID master in a site that creates many security principal objects
> - Place the RID master centrally if a single site does not create many security principal objects

Introduction

The RID master allocates blocks of RIDs to each domain controller in the domain. Whenever a domain controller creates a new security principal, such as a user, group, or computer object, the domain controller assigns the object a unique SID. There is only one RID master in each domain.

Guidelines

Apply the following guidelines to determine the placement of the RID master:

- *Use a highly available domain controller as the RID master.* High availability is critical to the continued creation of security principals and to help prevent the necessity for seizing an operations master role.

- *Do not require that the RID master be a high-capacity domain controller.* Typically, you create security principals on an ongoing basis, which does not cause large peaks of CPU usage. Also, because RIDs are distributed in blocks of 500 to each domain controller, the average server load and the replication traffic are minimal.

- *Place the RID master in a site where you create a large number of security principal objects, such as user and group objects.* This placement is common when one group of administrators creates all user accounts for the organization because most of the user accounts are in the same location as the users, which reduces the potential effects of a network link failure.

- *Locate the RID master centrally in your network if most of the user accounts are not created in one site.* Placing the RID master centrally will reduce the amount of network traffic.

- *Configure the RID master as a direct replication partner with the standby or backup RID master.* This configuration reduces the risk of losing data when you seize the role because it minimizes replication latency.

Guidelines for Placing the Infrastructure Master

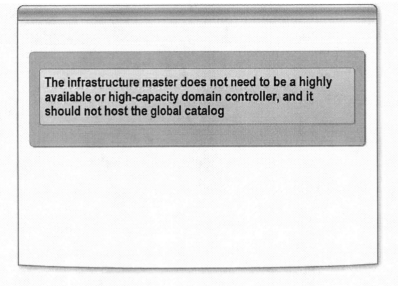

The infrastructure master does not need to be a highly available or high-capacity domain controller, and it should not host the global catalog

Introduction

The infrastructure master is responsible for making fast updates of cross-domain references, such as membership changes in a group that contains user accounts from other domains. There is only one infrastructure master in a domain.

Guidelines

Apply the following guidelines to determine the placement of the infrastructure master:

- *Do not require that the infrastructure master be a highly available domain controller.* There is no potential loss of information controlled by this operations master. In addition, the impact of the infrastructure master being offline for a short period of time is negligible because it does not affect end users.

- *Do not require that the infrastructure master be a high-capacity domain controller.* The infrastructure master does not use server resources intensively.

- *Avoid placing the infrastructure master role on a domain controller that hosts a global catalog.* If a domain controller that holds the infrastructure master role is also a global catalog server, cross-domain object references in that domain are not updated.

- *Locate the infrastructure master in the same site as a global catalog server.* The infrastructure master must communicate with a global catalog server to update its cross-domain references.

Guidelines for Seizing Operations Masters Roles

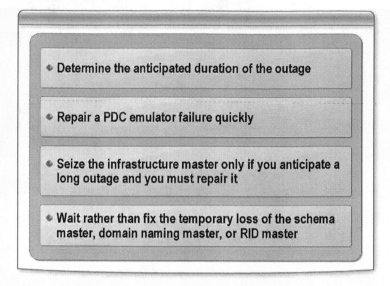

Introduction

Only seize operations master roles when you cannot restore the domain controller that supports the role—for example, when a domain controller is physically destroyed and cannot be restored from backup media. Before seizing an operations master role, physically disconnect the domain controller from the network.

Guidelines

Apply the following guideline to respond to operations master failures:

- *Determine the anticipated duration of the outage.* If you expect the outage to be brief, wait for the role owner to become available before you perform a role-related function. If the outage is longer, it may be necessary to seize the operations master role from a domain controller. This decision depends on the role and the expected length of the outage.

Apply the following guideline to seize a PDC emulator master:

- *Repair a PDC emulator failure quickly.* A user running Windows NT Workstation, Windows NT 4.0, Windows 95, or Windows 98 without the Active Directory client cannot change her password without her computer communicating with the PDC emulator. If her password has expired, she cannot log on. Seize the PDC emulator role from a standby operations master domain controller if the PDC emulator is offline for a significant period of time.

Apply the following guideline to seize an infrastructure master:

- *Wait rather than fix a temporary loss of the infrastructure master.* The temporary loss is not visible to end users or administrators, unless you recently moved or renamed a large number of accounts. Seize the infrastructure master role if you anticipate a long outage and you must repair it.

Apply the following guidelines for seizing the schema, RID, and domain naming masters:

■ *Wait rather than fix the temporary loss of the schema master, domain naming master, or RID master.* These roles are not visible to end users nor do they typically hinder your work as an administrator.

■ *Physically disconnect the domain controller from the network to ensure that its outage is permanent.* A domain controller whose schema master, domain naming master, or RID master role is seized must never come back online.

Multimedia Practice: Planning the Placement of Operations Masters

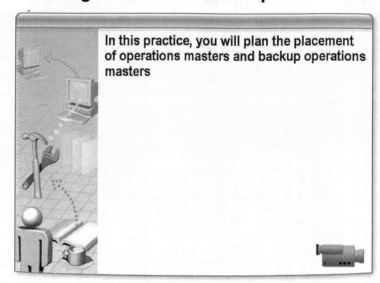

In this practice, you will plan the placement of operations masters and backup operations masters

---

File location

To view the *Placing Operations Masters* multimedia practice, open the Web page on the Student Materials compact disc, click **Multimedia**, and then click the title of the presentation. Do not open this presentation unless the instructor tells you to.

Objective

In this practice, you will plan the placement of an operations master.

Instructions

This activity includes multiple choice and drag-and-drop exercises that help you test your knowledge. Read the instructions, and then begin the practice.

Exercise 2
Transferring Operations Master Roles

In this exercise, you will transfer operations master roles to another server. The Northwind Traders IT team has decided to place the PDC emulator and the RID master roles on a server that does not hold the schema master and domain naming master roles. You must transfer the PDC emulator and the RID master roles to the other server.

Tasks	Special instructions
1. Transfer the PDC emulator role to the other server in your domain.	a. Log on as **Nwtraders*x**ComputerName*User** with a password of **P@ssw0rd** b. Click **Start**, right-click **Command Prompt**, and then click **Run as**. c. In the **Run As** dialog box, click **The following user**, type a user name of **Nwtraders*x*\\Administrator**, a password of **P@ssw0rd** and then click **OK**. ⚠ **Important:** Perform this task only on the server that currently holds the PDC emulator and RID master roles.
2. Transfer the RID master role to your server.	a. Log on as **Nwtraders*x**ComputerName*User** with a password of **P@ssw0rd** b. Click **Start**, right-click **Command Prompt**, and then click **Run as**. c. In the **Run As** dialog box, click **The following user**, type a user name of **Nwtraders*x*\\Administrator**, a password of **P@ssw0rd** and then click **OK**. ⚠ **Important:** Perform this task only on the server that does not hold the RID master role.
3. Use Active Directory Users and Computers to verify that the roles were transferred successfully.	⚠ **Important:** Perform this task on both servers in the domain.

Course Evaluation

Your evaluation of this course will help Microsoft understand the quality of your learning experience.

At a convenient time before the end of the course, please complete a course evaluation, which is available at http://www.CourseSurvey.com.

Microsoft will keep your evaluation strictly confidential and will use your responses to improve your future learning experience.

Microsoft®
Training &
Certification

Module 10: Maintaining Active Directory

Contents

Overview

- Introduction to Maintaining Active Directory
- Moving and Defragmenting the Active Directory Database
- Backing Up Active Directory
- Restoring Active Directory
- Planning for Monitoring Active Directory

Introduction

Information in the Active Directory® directory service in Microsoft® Windows® Server 2003 is stored in a transactional database, which makes it easy to maintain the integrity of the data in the event of a failure. A failure can include such things as hardware failure, software failure, and a complete system loss, such as in a fire.

The Active Directory database uses transaction log files to recover corrupted data in the local copy of the database. After Active Directory recovers this information, it uses replication to recover data from other domain controllers in the domain. The interactions of Active Directory components provide the basis for Active Directory to back up and retrieve information about corrupted data.

When domain controllers do not function because of hardware or software problems, users may not be able to access resources or log on to the network.

Objectives

After completing this module, you will be able to:

- Describe the relationship between data modification and maintenance of an Active Directory database.

- Move and defragment an Active Directory database.

- Back up Active Directory.

- Restore Active Directory by using the primary, normal, or authoritative restore methods.

- Apply guidelines for monitoring Active Directory.

Lesson: Introduction to Maintaining Active Directory

* ● Multimedia: The Active Directory Data Modification Process
* ● The Active Directory Database and Log Files

Introduction

Maintaining an Active Directory database is an important administrative task that you must schedule regularly to ensure that, in the case of disaster, you can recover lost or corrupted data and repair the Active Directory database.

Active Directory has its own database engine, the Extensible Storage Engine (ESE), which manages the storage of all Active Directory objects in an Active Directory database. By understanding how changes to attributes in Active Directory are written to the database, you will understand how data modification affects database performance, database fragmentation, and data integrity.

Lesson objectives

After completing this lesson, you will be able to:

* ■ Explain how data is modified in Active Directory, and how it affects database performance, database fragmentation, and data integrity.

* ■ Describe the Active Directory database and log files.

Multimedia: The Active Directory Data Modification Process

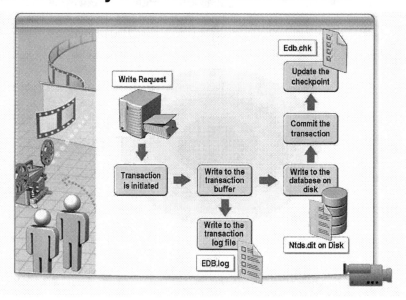

File location

To start *The Active Directory Data Modification Process* presentation, open the Web page on the Student Materials compact disc, click **Multimedia**, and then click the title of the presentation. Do not open this presentation unless the instructor tells you to.

Objectives

At the end of this presentation, you will be able to:

- Describe the data modification process.

- Describe how the data modification process affects database performance, database fragmentation, and data integrity.

Key points

The key points of Active Directory data modification process are:

- A *transaction* is a set of changes and the associated metadata.

- The basic data modification process consists of six steps:

  - The write request initiates a transaction.

  - Active Directory writes the transaction to the transaction buffer in memory.

  - Active Directory secures the transaction in the transaction log.

  - Active Directory writes the transaction from the buffer to the database.

  - Active Directory compares the database and log files to ensure that the transaction was committed to the database.

  - Active Directory updates the checkpoint file.

- Caching and logging improve database performance by enabling Active Directory to process additional transactions before writing them to the database.

- Active Directory automatically performs an online defragmentation as part of the garbage collection process at set intervals, which are 12 hours by default. Online defragmentation resolves performance issues, but it does not decrease the size of the database.

- The domain controller is not available to Active Directory when you perform an offline defragmentation. Perform an offline defragmentation only when you must decrease the size of Ntds.dit and you have resolved any problems that occurred by taking the domain controller offline.

- It is important to back up each Active Directory partition more frequently that the tombstone lifetime to preserve your data in the event of a network or hardware failure.

- When you back up Active Directory, Backup automatically backs up all of the system components and distributed services that Active Directory depends on. This dependent data is known collectively as the *system state data*.

The Active Directory Database and Log Files

File	Description
Ntds.dit	• Is the Active Directory database file • Stores all Active Directory objects on the domain controller • Use the default location *systemroot*\NTDS folder
Edb*.log	• Is a transaction log file • Uses the default transaction log file Edb.log
Edb.chk	• Is a checkpoint file • Tracks data not yet written to Active Directory database file
Res1.log Res2.log	• Are the reserved transaction log files

Introduction

The Active Directory database engine, ESE, stores all of the Active Directory objects. The ESE uses transactions and log files to ensure the integrity of the Active Directory database.

The files in Active Directory

Active Directory includes the following files:

- *Ntds.dit*. The Active Directory database, which stores all of the Active Directory objects on the domain controller. The .dit extension refers to the directory information tree. The default location is the %systemroot%\NTDS folder. Active Directory records each transaction in one or more transaction log files that are associated with the Ntds.dit file.

- *Edb*.log*. The transaction log file, which has the default transaction log file name of Edb.log. Each transaction log file is 10 megabytes (MB). When Edb.log is full, Active Directory renames it to Edb*nnnnn*.log, where *nnnnn* is an increasing number that starts from 1.

- *Edb.chk*. A checkpoint file that the database engine uses to track the data that is not yet written to the Active Directory database file. The checkpoint file is a pointer that maintains the status between memory and the database file on disk. It indicates the starting point in the log file from which the information must be recovered if a failure occurs.

- *Res1.log and Res2.log*. The reserved transaction log files. The amount of disk space that is reserved on a drive or folder for the transaction logs is 20 MB. This reserved disk space provides the transaction log files sufficient room to shut down if all other disk space is being used.

Lesson: Moving and Defragmenting the Active Directory Database

- How to Move the Active Directory Database and Log Files
- How to Defragment the Active Directory Database

Introduction

Over time, fragmentation occurs as records in the Active Directory database are deleted and new records are added. When the records are fragmented, the computer must search the Active Directory database to find all of the records each time the Active Directory database is opened. This search slows response time. Fragmentation also degrades the overall performance of Active Directory database operations.

Why defragment?

To overcome the problems that fragmentation causes, you defragment the Active Directory database. *Defragmentation* is the process of rewriting records in the Active Directory database to contiguous sectors to increase the speed of access and retrieval. When records are updated, Active Directory saves these updates on the largest contiguous space in the Active Directory database.

Why move database and log files?

You move a database to a new location when you defragment the database. Moving the database does not delete the original database. Therefore, you can use the original database if the defragmented database does not work or becomes corrupted. Also, if your disk space is limited, you can add another hard disk drive and move the database to it.

Additionally, you move database files in order to perform hardware maintenance. If the disk on which the files are stored requires upgrading or maintenance, you can move the files to another location temporarily or permanently.

Lesson objectives

After completing this lesson, you will be able to:

- Move the Active Directory database and log files.
- Defragment the Active Directory database.

How to Move the Active Directory Database and Log Files

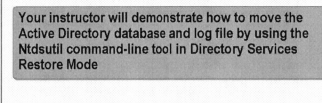

Your instructor will demonstrate how to move the
Active Directory database and log file by using the
Ntdsutil command-line tool in Directory Services
Restore Mode

Introduction

If disk space is low on the partition that stores the database, log files, or both, you must move the database and log files to a new location.

Why use Ntdsutil to move the database?

You use the Ntdsutil command-line tool in Directory Services Restore Mode to move the database from one location to another location on a disk. If the path to the database files changes after you move the files, you must always use Ntdsutil to move the files, instead of simply copying them. This way, you ensure that the registry key is updated with the path to the new location, and Active Directory restarts from the new location.

Procedure

To move the Active Directory database, perform the following steps:

1. Back up Active Directory as a precautionary measure.

   You can back up Active Directory while online if, in the Backup Wizard, you choose to back up everything on the computer or to back up only the system state data.

2. Restart the domain controller, press F8 to display the **Windows Advanced Options** menu, select **Directory Services Restore Mode**, and then press ENTER.

3. Log on by using the Administrator account and the password that is defined for the Local Administrator account in the Security Accounts Manager (SAM).

Note   This Administrator account is not the same as the domain administrator account. Restarting the domain controller in Directory Services Restore Mode causes the computer to load the user accounts from the local SAM hive of the registry. To verify that the computer is using local accounts, at the command prompt, type **net user**. Note that the local computer name rather than the domain name precedes the account name . Note also that the list of users does not match the users that you created in the domain.

4. At the command prompt, type **ntdsutil** and then press ENTER.

5. Type **files** and then press ENTER.

6. At the **files** prompt, after you determine a location that has enough drive space to store the database to be stored, type **move DB to** **<drive>:\<directory>** (where *<drive>* and *<directory>* are the path on the local computer where you want to place the database), and then press ENTER.

Note   You must specify a directory path. If the path contains any spaces, the entire path must be surrounded by quotation marks, for example, "C:\New folder."

The database named Ntds.dit is moved to the location that you specified.

7. Type **quit** and then press ENTER. To return to the command prompt, type **quit** again.

8. Restart the domain controller.

Note   You can also move transaction log files to another location. The **Move logs to** *<drive>:\<directory>* command moves the transaction log files to the new directory that is specified by *<drive>:\<directory>* and updates the registry keys, which restarts the directory service from the new location.

You must also perform a system state backup after you move the files to ensure that subsequent restores use the correct path.

How to Defragment an Active Directory Database

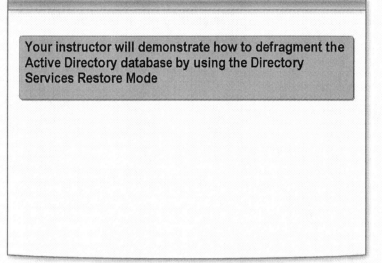

Your instructor will demonstrate how to defragment the Active Directory database by using the Directory Services Restore Mode

Introduction

Online defragmentation occurs automatically during the garbage collection process. You perform offline defragmentation manually.

Why perform offline defragmentation?

Offline defragmentation is necessary only if you want to create a new, compacted version of the original database file. Perform offline defragmentation only if you can recover a significant amount of disk space that you can use for other tasks. For example, if the domain controller was at one time a global catalog server for a multiple domain forest, you can free a significant amount of disk space by using performing offline defragmentation.

Disk space requirements

To perform defragmentation, the current database drive must have free space equivalent to at least 15 percent of the current size of the database for temporary storage during the index rebuilding process. Also, the destination database drive must have free space equivalent to at least the current size of the database for storage of the compacted database file.

Procedure

To defragment an offline Active Directory database, perform the following steps:

1. Back up the system state data.

2. Restart the domain controller, press F8 to display the **Windows Advanced Options** menu, select **Directory Services Restore Mode**, and then press ENTER.

3. Log on by using the Administrator account and the password that is defined for the Local Administrator account in the offline SAM.

4. At the command prompt, type **ntdsutil** and then press ENTER.

5. Type **files** and then press ENTER.

6. At the **files** prompt, type **compact to** *<drive>*:*<directory>* (where *<drive>* and *<directory>* is the path to the location) and then press ENTER.

   This step establishes a location that has enough drive space for the compacted database to be stored.

   Note   If the directory path contains any spaces, the entire path must be surrounded by quotation marks—for example, "C:\New folder."

   A new database named Ntds.dit is created in the path that you specified.

7. Type **quit** and then press ENTER. To return to the command prompt, type **quit** again.

8. Copy the new Ntds.dit file to the old Ntds.dit file in the current Active Directory database path.

9. Restart the domain controller.

Practice: Moving and Defragmenting the Active Directory Database

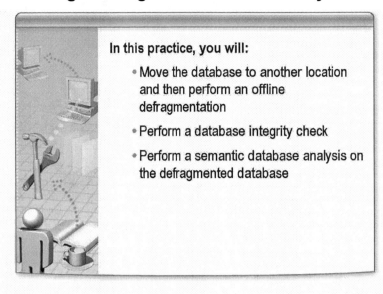

In this practice, you will:

* Move the database to another location and then perform an offline defragmentation

* Perform a database integrity check

* Perform a semantic database analysis on the defragmented database

Objectives

In this practice, you will move the database on your domain controller to another location and then perform an offline defragmentation. You will also perform a database integrity check and a semantic database analysis on the defragmented database.

Instructions

You will work with a partner in the Active Directory domain that contains your domain controller and your partner's domain controller.

Scenario

Northwind Traders defined a maintenance schedule to take domain controllers offline and perform a hard disk upgrade. After the upgrade is completed, you will move the Active Directory database to the new hard disk.

Practice

▶ **Move and defragment the Active Directory database**

1. Log on as **Nwtraders*x**ComputerName*User** (where *ComputerName* is the name of your computer) with a password of **P@ssw0rd**

2. Start a command prompt as **Nwtraders*x*\\Administrator** with a password of **P@ssw0rd**

3. At the command prompt, type **shutdown /r /d p:2:4** and then press ENTER.

4. Restart your domain controller in Directory Services Restore Mode.

5. Log on as **Administrator** with a password of **P@ssw0rd**

6. At the command prompt, type **ntdsutil** and then press ENTER.

7. At the **ntdsutil** prompt, type **files** and then press ENTER to specify the file maintenance mode for Ntdsutil.

8. At the **file maintenance** prompt, type **move db to c:\\moved-db** and then press ENTER to move the Active Directory Database to C:\\moved-db.

9. Defragment the moved database.

   a. At the **file maintenance** prompt, type **compact to c:\defrag** and then press ENTER.

   b. Use Windows Explorer to copy the defragmented database to the moved-db folder.

      Note that the file you are copying is smaller than the original.

   c. Delete \Windows\NTDS*.log.

10. At the **file maintenance** prompt, type **integrity**, and then type **quit** to perform a database integrity check.

11. Perform a semantic database analysis.

   a. At the **ntdsutil** prompt, type **Semantic Database Analysis**

   b. At the **semantic checker** prompt, type **Go**

12. Restart the domain controller.

Lesson: Backing Up Active Directory

- Components of the System State Data
- How to Back Up Active Directory

Introduction

Backing up Active Directory is essential to maintain an Active Directory database. You can back up Active Directory by using the graphical user interface (GUI) and command-line tools that the Windows Server 2003 family provides.

Why back up?

You frequently back up the system state data on domain controllers so that you can restore the most current data. By establishing a regular backup schedule, you have a better chance of recovering data when necessary.

To ensure a good backup, which includes at least the system state data and contents of the system disk, you must be aware of the tombstone lifetime. By default, the tombstone is 60 days. Any backup older than 60 days is not a good backup. Plan to back up at least two domain controllers in each domain, one of which is an operations master role holder. For each domain, you must maintain at least one backup to enable an authoritative restore of the data when necessary.

Lesson objectives

After completing this lesson, you will be able to:

- Describe the components of the system state data.
- Back up Active Directory.

Components of the System State Data

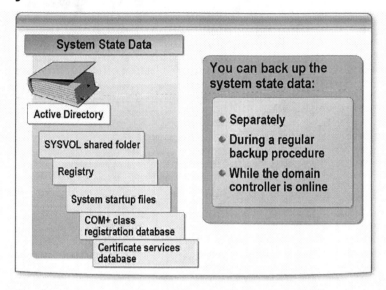

Introduction

Several features in the Windows Server 2003 family make it easy to back up Active Directory. You can back up Active Directory during your regular backup procedures without interrupting the network or the operation of the domain controller that you are backing up.

Components

The system state data on a domain controller includes the following components:

- *Active Directory*. System state data does not contain Active Directory unless the server on which you are backing up the system state data is a domain controller. Active Directory is present only on domain controllers.

- *The SYSVOL shared folder*. This shared folder contains Group Policy templates and logon scripts. The SYSVOL shared folder is present only on domain controllers.

- *The registry*. This database repository contains information about the computer's configuration.

- *System startup files*. Windows Server 2003 requires these files during its initial startup phase. They include the boot and system files that are under Windows file protection and are used by Windows to load, configure, and run the operating system.

- *The COM+ Class Registration database*. The Class Registration is a database of information about Component Services applications.

- *The Certificate Services database*. This database contains certificates that a server running Windows Server 2003 uses to authenticate users. The Certificate Services database is present only if the server is operating as a certificate server.

System state data contains most elements of a system's configuration, but it may not include all of the information that you require to recover data from a system failure. Therefore, be sure to back up all boot and system volumes, including the system state, when you back up your server.

When to back up the system state data

You can back up:

- The system state data by itself.
- The system state data as part of your regular backup procedures.
- The system state data while the domain controller is online.

How to Back Up Active Directory

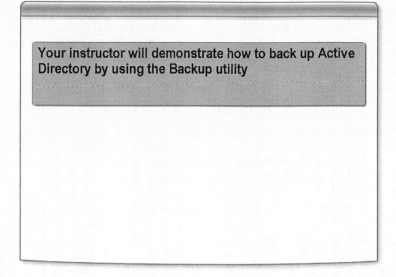

Your instructor will demonstrate how to back up Active Directory by using the Backup utility

Introduction

To back up the system state data, you must be a member of the Administrators or Backup Operators group on the local computer, or you must have been delegated the appropriate permissions. If the computer is in a domain, members of the Domain Admins group can perform this procedure.

You can only back up the system state data on a local computer. You cannot back up the system state data on a remote computer.

Procedure

To back up the system state data, perform the following steps:

1. On the **Start** menu, point to **All Programs**, point to **Accessories**, point to **System Tools**, and then click **Backup**.

2. On the **Welcome to the Backup or Restore Wizard** page, click **Next**.

3. On the **Backup or Restore** page, click **Backup files and settings**, and then click **Next**.

4. On the **What to Back Up** page, click **Let me choose what to back up**, and then click **Next**.

5. On the **Items to Back Up** page, expand **My Computer**, select the **System State** check box, and then click **Next**.

6. On the **Backup Type, Destination, and Name** page, click **Browse**, select a location for the backup, click **Save**, and then click **Next**.

7. On the **Completing the Backup or Restore Wizard** page, click **Finish**.

8. On the **Backup Progress** page, click **Close**.

You can use the advanced backup options in the Backup utility to set or configure parameters, such as data verification, hardware compression, and media labels. You can also set the backup job to be appended to a previous job or to schedule the backup to run unattended at another time. Data verification enables Backup to check for differences between the files that it backed up from the domain controller and those that it copied to the backup media. The Backup utility reports the results of the verification in Event Viewer.

Important   For full disaster recovery, back up all hard disks and the system state data. To perform this backup, run the Backup utility. On the **What to Back Up** page, select the **All information on this computer** check box.

Note   For more information about backing up the system state data by using the **Ntbackup** command-line tool, see "How to Back Up Active Directory" in Module 10 on the Appendices page on the Student Materials compact disc.

Practice: Backing Up Active Directory

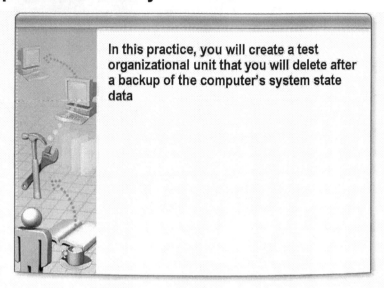

In this practice, you will create a test organizational unit that you will delete after a backup of the computer's system state data

Objectives

In this practice, you will create an organizational unit that you will delete after a backup of the computer's system state data.

Instructions

You will work with a partner in the Active Directory domain that contains your domain controller and your partner's domain controller.

Scenario

Northwind Traders has developed disaster recovery procedures. You must test the backup procedures to ensure that they are adequate before you implement them throughout the organization.

Practice

► **Back up Active Directory**

1. Log on as **Nwtraders*x****ComputerName*User** with a password of **P@ssw0rd**

2. Start Active Directory Users and Computers as **Nwtraders*x*\Administrator** with a password of **P@ssw0rd** by using **Run as**.

3. Create an organizational unit called **Practice***ComputerName***OU** in your domain.

4. View the properties of this object, and note the update sequence number.

_____

_____

5. Start the Backup utility as **Nwtraders*x*\Administrator** with a password of **P@ssw0rd** by using **Run as**, and then perform a system state backup.

6. Delete the **Practice***ComputerName***OU** organizational unit.

Lesson: Restoring Active Directory

* Multimedia: Active Directory Restore Methods
* How to Perform a Primary Restore
* How to Perform a Normal Restore
* How to Perform an Authoritative Restore

Introduction

In Windows Server 2003 family, you can restore the Active Directory database if it becomes corrupted or is destroyed because of hardware or software failures. You must restore the Active Directory database when objects in Active Directory are changed or deleted.

You can restore replicated data on a domain controller in several ways. You can reinstall the domain controller, and then let the normal replication process repopulate the new domain controller with data from its replicas, or you can use the Backup utility to restore replicated data from backup media without reinstalling the operating system or reconfiguring the domain controller.

Lesson objectives

After completing this lesson, you will be able to:

* Compare the primary restore method, normal restore method, and the authoritative restore method.

* Perform a primary restore.

* Perform a normal restore.

* Perform an authoritative restore.

Multimedia: Active Directory Restore Methods

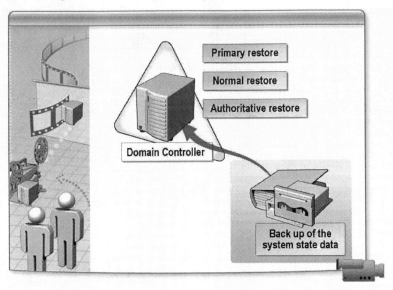

File Location

To start the *Active Directory Restore Methods* activity, open the Web page on the Student Materials compact disc, click **Multimedia**, and then click the title of the presentation. Do not open this presentation unless the instructor tells you to.

Objective

At the end of this activity, you will be able to decide which type of restore method to perform.

Instructions

Click the topics or subtopics on the left to browse to the required information. Each topic contains a brief animation and information. It may be necessary to scroll to see all of the information on a tab.

Key points

When you back up a domain controller, you back up all of the Active Directory data on that server in addition to system components, such as the SYSVOL directory and the registry.

When you restore Active Directory, you restore all of the backed-up data. This rollback to a previous state can affect Group Policy settings and the trust relationships between domains.

You can use one of three methods to restore Active Directory from backup media: *primary* restore, *normal* (*nonauthoritative*) restore, and *authoritative* restore.

- *Primary restore.* This method rebuilds the first domain controller in a domain when there is no other way to rebuild the domain. Perform a primary restore only when all the domain controllers in the domain are lost, and you want to rebuild the domain from the backup.

- *Normal restore.* This method reinstates the Active Directory data to the state before the backup, and then updates the data through the normal replication process. Perform a normal restore only when you want to restore a single domain controller to a previously known good state.

- *Authoritative restore.* You perform this method in tandem with a normal restore. An authoritative restore marks specific data as current and prevents the replication from overwriting that data. The authoritative data is then replicated throughout the domain.

  Perform an authoritative restore to restore individual objects in a domain that has multiple domain controllers. When you perform an authoritative restore, you lose all changes to the restore object that occurred after the backup.

Importance of tombstone lifetime

You cannot restore Active Directory from a backup that is older than the tombstone lifetime, which is 60 days by default. A domain controller keeps track of deleted objects for only this period. If there are multiple domain controllers, and the age of the backup is less than the tombstone lifetime, restore the backup that you have and then let the replication between domain controllers update Active Directory. If you have only one domain controller, you lose any changes that you made after the last backup.

How to Perform a Primary Restore

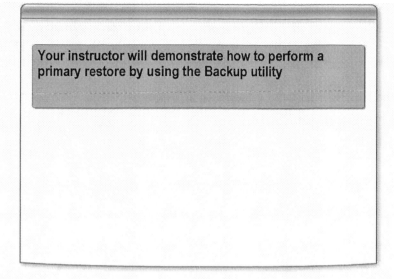

Your instructor will demonstrate how to perform a primary restore by using the Backup utility

Introduction

To perform a primary restore, you must be a member of the Administrators group on the local computer, or you must have been delegated the appropriate permissions. If the computer is in a domain, members of the Domain Admins group can perform this procedure.

Procedure

To perform a primary restore of Active Directory, perform the following steps:

1. Restart your domain controller in Directory Services Restore Mode.

2. Start the Backup utility.

3. On the **Welcome to the Backup or Restore Wizard** page, click **Advanced Mode**.

4. On the **Welcome to Backup Utility Advanced Mode** page, on the **Restore and Manage Media** tab, select what you want to restore, and then click **Start Restore**.

5. In the **Warning** dialog box, click **OK**.

6. In the **Confirm Restore** dialog box, click **Advanced**.

7. In the **Advanced Restore Options** dialog box, click **When restoring replicated data sets, mark the restored data as the primary data for all replicas**, and then click **OK** twice.

Important   Selecting this option ensures that the File Replication Service (FRS) data is replicated to the other servers. Select this option only when you want to restore the first replica set to the network.

---

8. In the **Restore Progress** dialog box, click **Close**.

9. In the **Backup Utility** dialog box, click **Yes**.

Note For more information about advanced options that are available for a primary restore, see "How to Perform a Primary Restore" in Module 10 on the Appendices page on the Student Materials compact disc.

How to Perform a Normal Restore

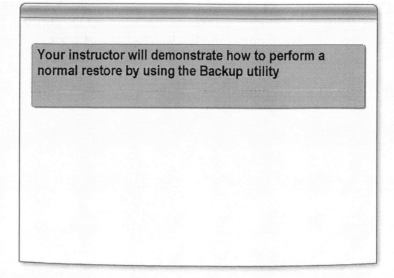

Your instructor will demonstrate how to perform a normal restore by using the Backup utility

Introduction

You can restore Active Directory nonauthoritatively when you replace a failed domain controller or repair a damaged Active Directory database.

Procedure

To perform a normal restore of Active Directory, perform the following steps:

1. Restart your domain controller in Directory Services Restore Mode.

2. Start the Backup utility.

3. On the **Welcome to the Backup or Restore Wizard** page, click **Next**.

4. On the **Backup or Restore** page, click **Restore files and settings**.

5. On the **What to Restore** page, under **Items to restore**, expand the list, select the **System State** check box, and then click **Next**.

6. On the **Completing the Backup or Restore Wizard** page, click **Finish**.

7. In the **Warning** dialog box, click **OK**.

8. In the **Restore Progress** dialog box, click **Close**.

9. In the **Backup Utility** dialog box, click **Yes**.

Warning When you restore the system state data, the Backup utility erases the system state data that is on your computer and replaces it with the system state data that you are restoring, including system state data that is not related to Active Directory. Depending on how old the system state data is, you may lose configuration changes that you recently made to the computer. To minimize this risk, back up the system state data regularly.

How to Perform an Authoritative Restore

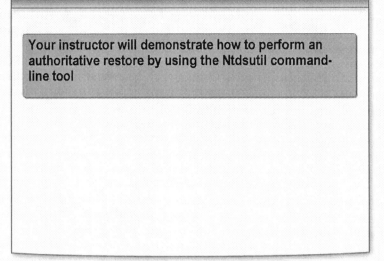

Your instructor will demonstrate how to perform an authoritative restore by using the Ntdsutil command-line tool

Introduction

Unlike a normal restore, an authoritative restore requires the use of a separate command-line tool, Ntdsutil. No backup utilities, including the Windows Server 2003 system utilities, can perform an authoritative restore.

Why use Ntdsutil for an authoritative restore?

The Ntdsutil command-line tool is an executable file that you use to mark Active Directory objects as authoritative so that they receive a higher version number than that of the current object. By marking objects, you ensure that recently changed data on other domain controllers does not overwrite system state data during replication.

Procedure

To perform an authoritative restore, perform the following steps:

1. Restart your domain controller in Directory Services Restore Mode.

2. Restore Active Directory to its original location.

3. If you must perform an authoritative restore on the SYSVOL folder, restore Active Directory to an alternate location by using the Backup utility, but do not restart the computer when prompted after the restore. If you are not performing an authoritative restore on SYSVOL, skip to step 4.

4. At the command prompt, run **Ntdsutil.exe**.

5. At the **ntdsutil** prompt, type **authoritative restore**

6. At the **authoritative restore** prompt, type
   restore subtree *distinguished_name_of_object* (where
   distinguished_name_of_object is the distinguished name, or path, to the
   object). For example, to restore an organizational unit called Sales, which
   existed directly below the domain called contoso.msft, type
   restore subtree OU=Sales,DC=contoso,DC=msft

7. Type **quit** and then press ENTER.

8. Type **quit** again, and then press ENTER to exit **ntdsutil**.

9. Restart the domain controller.

10. After FRS publishes the SYSVOL folder, copy the SYSVOL folder and only those Group Policy folders that correspond to the restored Group Policy objects from the alternate location to the existing locations.

11. To verify that the copy operation was successful, examine the contents of the SYSVOL*Domain* folder, where D*omain* is the name of the domain.

Note   For more information about distinguished user names, see Module 1, "Introduction to Active Directory Infrastructure," in Course 2279: *Planning, Implementing, and Maintaining a Microsoft Windows Server 2003 Active Directory Infrastructure.*

Practice: Restoring Active Directory

Objectives

In this practice, you will restore the most recent backup before you delete the test organizational units. You will also verify that the restore operation was successful by examining the authoritative data.

Instructions

You will work with a partner in the Active Directory domain that contains your domain controller and your partner's domain controller. Perform this procedure only on the domain controller that is designated as the restore server.

Scenario

Northwind Traders has developed disaster recovery procedures. You must test the restore procedures for an authoritative restore before you implement them throughout the organization.

Practice

▶ **Restore Active Directory authoritatively**

1. Restart your domain controller in Directory Services Restore Mode.

2. Log on as **Administrator** with a password of **P@ssw0rd**

3. Start the Backup utility and restore the system state data from the backup that you created in the Backing Up Active Directory practice.

4. At the command prompt, run **ntdsutil** in authoritative restore mode.

5. Mark the organizational units that you deleted previously as authoritative.

6. Restart the domain controller.

7. Log on as **Nwtraders*x**ComputerName*User**.

8. Verify that the organizational unit that you created in the Backing Up Active Directory practice has been restored.

9. View the properties of the organizational unit that has been restored and note the update sequence number.

Lesson: Planning for Monitoring Active Directory

* Overview of Monitoring Active Directory
* Events to Monitor
* Performance Counters to Monitor
* Guidelines for Monitoring Active Directory

Introduction

Monitoring the distributed Active Directory directory service and the services that it relies on helps maintain consistent directory data and the required level of service throughout the forest. You can monitor important indicators to discover and resolve minor problems before they develop into potentially lengthy service outages.

Most large organizations that have numerous domains or remote physical sites require an automated monitoring system, such as Microsoft Operations Manager 2002 (MOM), to monitor important indicators. By using an automated monitoring system to consolidate information and resolve problems promptly, you can administer Active Directory more successfully.

Lesson objectives

After completing this lesson, you will be able to:

* Explain why you must monitor Active Directory and which levels of monitoring are appropriate.

* Identify the events to monitor.

* Identify which performance counters to monitor.

* Apply guidelines for monitoring the health of Active Directory.

Overview of Monitoring Active Directory

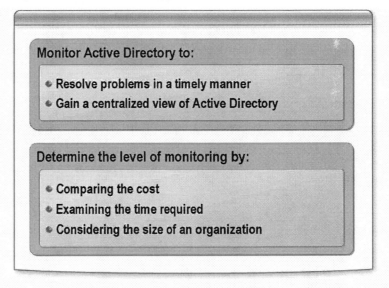

Monitor Active Directory to:

- Resolve problems in a timely manner
- Gain a centralized view of Active Directory

Determine the level of monitoring by:

- Comparing the cost
- Examining the time required
- Considering the size of an organization

Introduction

A cost-benefit analysis is a good method to determine the level of monitoring that is required for your environment.

Why monitor?

Monitoring Active Directory helps you resolve issues in a timely manner. Users experience improved reliability of applications that rely on servers, faster logon time, more reliable use of resources, and fewer calls to the Help Desk.

Monitoring Active Directory provides you with a centralized view of Active Directory across the forest. By monitoring important indicators, you can improve system reliability and better understand how the system operates. In addition, monitoring gives you greater schedule flexibility and helps you prioritize your workload, because you discover problems early and can resolve them before they become serious.

Monitoring Active Directory also assures you that:

- All necessary services that support Active Directory are running on each domain controller.

- Lightweight Directory Access Protocol (LDAP) queries respond quickly.

- Domain controllers do not experience high levels of CPU usage.

Levels of monitoring

You can typically monitor Active Directory at three levels:

- *Basic or a minimal monitoring* of events and performance counters.

- *Advanced monitoring* of the services that Active Directory relies on, domain controller response time, and forest-wide replication. Specialized scripts are typically required to provide these advanced monitoring levels.

- *Sophisticated monitoring*, such as what MOM provides, to enable enterprise-level monitoring. Sophisticated monitoring solutions collect and consolidate data by using agents or local services that collect and distribute the monitoring data.

   Sophisticated monitoring solutions also take advantage of the physical network topology to reduce network traffic and increase performance. In a complex environment, this sophisticated level of monitoring may be necessary to derive data that you require to make good decisions.

Windows Server 2003 provides a powerful set of interfaces and services that software developers can use to build sophisticated monitoring solutions.

How to determine the level of monitoring required

To determine the level of monitoring that you require, compare the cost of formalizing a monitoring solution with the costs that are associated with service outages and the time that you must spend to diagnose and resolve problems.

The level of monitoring required also depends on the size of your company and your service-level requirements. Organizations that have few domains and domain controllers or that must monitor only one computer may find the list of indicators to monitor in this module and the tools that Windows Server 2003 provides sufficient.

Larger organizations that have many domains, domain controllers, or sites, and organizations that cannot afford the cost of lost productivity from a service outage, may want to use a more sophisticated monitoring solution—by writing extensive in-house scripts, for example, or by purchasing a monitoring solution, such as MOM.

Events to Monitor

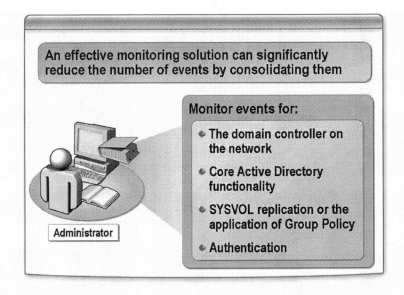

Introduction

A domain controller in a large enterprise typically generates hundreds of Active Directory-related events each day. An effective monitoring solution can significantly reduce the number of events by consolidating them on each domain controller and across several domain controllers. Although many of these events are not important enough to trigger an alert, they can be itemized in a weekly report.

Types of events

Basic monitoring may include the following events, which provide the best indicators of overall domain controller health.

Event	Description	Examples
Events for the domain controller on the network	These events indicate: ■ When the event log service started and shut down. ■ If a domain controller cannot register Domain Name System (DNS) name records. Use these events to determine when the system was running. DNS events indicate that the DNS name resolution is critically important in the environment.	6005, 6006, 11151, and 5773
Events for core Active Directory functionality	These events indicate problems with core Active Directory functionality.	Severity = error

(continued)

Event	Description	Examples
Events for replication	These events may indicate problems with SYSVOL replication or the application of Group Policy.	Severity = error, and User = System
Events for authentication	These events may indicate problems with the: ■ Maintenance of uniform time throughout the forest. ■ Kerberos version 5 authentication protocol. ■ Default authentication protocol. ■ Netlogon service and protocol that is required for proper domain controller functionality.	Severity = warning, Severity = error, and Report 11 weekly

Note For more information about advanced options that are available for a primary restore, see "Events to Monitor" in Module 10 on the Appendices page on the Student Materials compact disc.

Performance Counters to Monitor

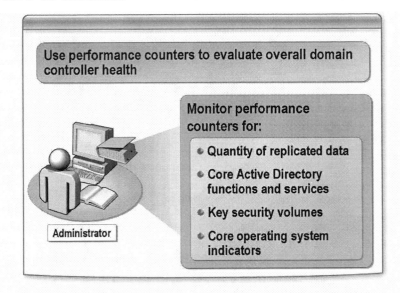

Introduction

When you perform basic monitoring, you also use performance counters to monitor overall domain controller health.

Types of performance counters

Basic monitoring includes the following types of performance counters.

Performance counter	Description	Examples
Performance counters to monitor the quantity of replicated data	Use baselines that you already established to determine thresholds for these performance counters, unless indicated otherwise.	DRA Inbound Bytes Compressed, DRA Outbound Bytes Compressed, DRA Outbound Bytes Not Compressed, and Outbound Bytes Total/sec
Performance counters to monitor core Active Directory functions and services	Establish baselines to determine thresholds for these performance counters, unless indicated otherwise.	DS Search sub-operations/sec, % Processor Time–LSASS, LDAP Searches/sec, Private Byte, and Handle Count–LSASS
Performance counters to monitor key security volumes	Establish baselines to determine thresholds for these performance counters, unless indicated otherwise.	NTLM Authentications/sec, KDC AS Requests/sec, and Authentications/sec
Performance counters to monitor core operating system indicators	Use these performance counters to monitor core operating system indicators; these performance counters have a direct impact on Active Directory performance.	Page Faults/sec, Current Disk Queue Length, Processor Queue Length, Context Switches/sec, and System Up Time

Note For more information about performance counters, their recommended intervals, threshold levels, and importance, see "Performance Counters to Monitor" in Module 10 on the Appendices page on the Student Materials compact disc.

Guidelines for Monitoring Active Directory

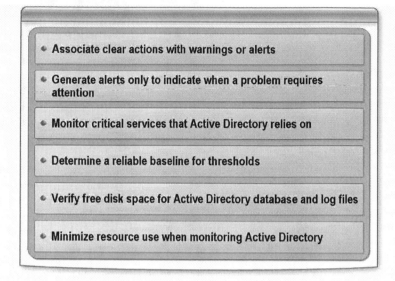

Introduction

Although each organization has specific monitoring requirements, you must be sure to follow general guidelines when you design a monitoring system.

Small organizations may find that the following guidelines, the utilities that are included with the Windows Server 2003 family, and some customized scripts are sufficient to deliver a reliable directory service. Larger organizations may require a more sophisticated monitoring solution that can provide a central-console view of many domain controllers, all of which are running agents or services that consolidate and filter events, counters, and indicators.

Guidelines

Apply the following guidelines to determine how to design and implement monitoring solutions:

- *Associate clear actions with all warnings or alerts that the monitoring system generates.* To maintain operational integrity of your Active Directory infrastructure, you must have a clear contingency plan to deal effectively with the various messages that Active Directory generates.

- *Generate alerts only to indicate a problem that requires attention.* The monitoring system must not generate unnecessary alerts that may overwhelm the operator who must resolve the problems.

- *Monitor services that Active Directory relies on.* Some services are critical to the proper function of Active Directory—services such as DNS, FRS, the Key Distribution Center (KDC), Netlogon, and Windows Time service (W32time).

- *Determine a reliable baseline for the thresholds that establish when to report warnings or alerts.* You must know the normal operational levels before you decide if any action is required. By establishing a baseline, you can gather enough data over time to make a decision about an action plan when unexpected conditions arise.

- *Verify free disk space for Active Directory database and log files.* The disk volumes that contain the Active Directory database file, Ntds.dit, and the log files must have enough free space for normal growth and operation. An alert must be generated if the free disk space falls below 50 MB or below 10 percent of the volume size. One hour is the recommended interval for monitoring disk space.

- *Minimize resource use when you monitor Active Directory.* Consider the following recommendations for minimizing resource use:

  - Monitoring must not consume so much memory that it diminishes system performance and core service delivery.

  - The computers that you monitor must not devote more than 5 percent of their total CPU usage to the monitoring solution.

  - The monitoring solution must generate a minimal amount of network traffic throughout the distributed environment.

  - The total number of performance counters and the frequency with which they are collected must be minimized. This way, you minimize the demands on the system, while still capturing relevant data in a timely manner.

  - Scripts must be run locally instead of remotely to reduce network bandwidth and latency.

Lab A: Maintaining Active Directory

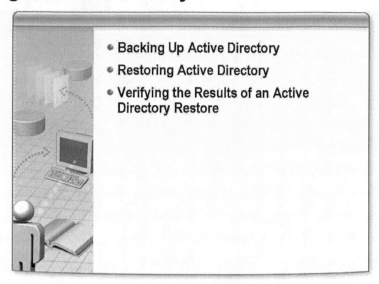

Objectives

After completing this lab, you will be able to:

- Back up an Active Directory database.
- Perform an authoritative restore of an Active Directory database.

Prerequisites

Before working on this lab, you must have:

- Knowledge of and experience with initiating Active Directory replication.
- Experience in creating Active Directory objects.

Estimated time to complete this lab: 45 minutes

Exercise 1
Backing Up Active Directory

In this exercise, you will create an organizational unit and a set of user accounts in the organizational unit. You will then back up the system state data on the domain controller, and then delete the organizational unit.

You will work with a partner in the Active Directory domain that contains your domain controller and your partner's domain controller. You will perform the following steps independently, and then verify with your partner that the backup includes the data that both of you created.

Scenario

Northwind Traders is opening a new division in the marketing department to promote environmental awareness throughout the organization. You must create the appropriate Active Directory object to contain the new division and five user accounts for the users who will work in the division. Northwind Traders has standardized on an initial password of St@rTr3k! for all new user accounts. You will disable the user accounts until Northwind Traders officially launches the new division.

Northwind Traders' management wants you to use this organizational unit to practice its disaster recovery procedure. After you create the supporting structure for the new organizational unit, you must delete the object and then verify that you can recover it by using the backup and restore procedures.

Tasks	Specific instructions
1. Browse to *Domain*.nwtraders.msft and then create an organizational unit.	a. Log on as **Nwtraders**x*ComputerName***User** (where *ComputerName* is the name of your computer) with a password of **P@ssw0rd** b. Create the following organizational unit: • **Lab**_ComputerName_**OU**

2. Create user accounts in the **Lab**_ComputerName_**OU** organizational unit.	▪ Create the following user accounts in the **Lab**_ComputerName_**OU** organizational unit:
	
	   • First name = *ComputerName*. Last name = User1. Logon Name = ComputerNameUser1
	
	   • First name = *ComputerName*. Last name = User2. Logon Name = ComputerNameUser2

3. Initiate replication with your partner's domain controller.	❶ **Note:** If your partner's organizational unit does not appear, perform the replication on the connection object from your partner's server again.
4. Back up your domain controller's system state data.	⚠ **Important:** Make sure that you set the backup to use detailed logging. ▪ Back up your system state date to the file named c:\MOC\2279\backup.bkf.

(continued)

Tasks	Specific instructions
5. View the log of the backed-up session.	▪ Note the files that make up the system state data and their location.
⚠ **Important:** Each student will perform the following tasks.	
6. Delete the organizational unit that you created earlier, confirm the deletion of both objects, and then force replication if necessary.	a. Delete the organizational unit that you created earlier. b. When prompted, click **Yes**.
7. Initiate replication with your partner's domain controller.	a. Log on as **Nwtraders*x*\Administrator** by using **Run as** with a password of **P@ssw0rd** b. Verify that the organizational unit that you created has been deleted.

Exercise 2
Restoring Active Directory

In this exercise, you will test disaster recovery capabilities by performing an authoritative restore of the organizational unit that you deleted in Exercise 1.

Scenario

While testing disaster recovery capabilities for Northwind Traders, you try to recover an accidentally deleted organizational unit and the user objects in the container.

Tasks	Specific instructions
1. Restart your domain controller in Directory Services Restore Mode.	a. Start a command prompt as **Nwtraders*x*\Administrator** by using **Run as** with a password of **P@ssw0rd** b. After restarting your domain controller, log on as **Administrator** with a password of **P@ssw0rd** c. When a message appears, indicating that Windows is running in safe mode, click **OK**.
2. Restore the domain controller's system state from the previous backup.	
3. Mark the organizational unit you have restored as authoritative.	▪ Use the organizational unit, **Lab***ComputerName***OU**.

Exercise 3
Verifying the Results of an Active Directory Restore

In this exercise, you will work with your partner to verify that the deleted objects have been restored and replicated to the domain controllers in the domain. Perform each step independently from your partner. Ensure that your partner has completed each exercise before you continue.

Scenario

You are in the final phase of the disaster recovery testing cycle. Now you must verify that the authoritative restore process works as expected. You will determine whether the recovered objects are now restored to the Active Directory database so that you can document the disaster recovery procedure for future use.

Tasks	Specific instructions
▪ Initiate replication with your partner's domain controller and verify that the organizational unit was authoritatively restored.	**Note:** If your partner's organizational unit does not appear, perform the replication on the connection object from your partner's server again.

Microsoft®
Training &
Certification

Module 11: Planning and Implementing an Active Directory Infrastructure

Contents

Overview

- Creating an Active Directory Implementation Plan for Tailspin Toys
- Implementing the Active Directory Infrastructure for Tailspin Toys

Introduction

In this module, you will apply the knowledge and skills that you learned in this course to plan and then implement an Active Directory® directory service infrastructure. You will implement Active Directory based on the business requirements of a fictitious company named Tailspin Toys.

Objectives

After completing this module, you will be able to:

- Review the Active Directory design and create an Active Directory implementation plan for Tailspin Toys.

- Implement the Active Directory infrastructure for Tailspin Toys.

Lesson: Creating an Active Directory Implementation Plan for Tailspin Toys

- Review of the Components of the Implementation Plan
- Introduction to Tailspin Toys
- Tailspin Toys Personnel
- Introduction to the Lab Environment

Introduction

This module presents a case study of a fictitious company named Tailspin Toys. The labs in this module focus on the company's efforts to plan and implement Active Directory within the company and with partners and service providers. In this module's labs, you will use an interactive lab application, called the Lab Browser, to analyze scenario-based information.

Lesson objectives

After completing this lesson, you will be able to:

- Identify the components of an Active Directory implementation plan.
- Describe the fictitious company.
- Identify the key personnel of Tailspin Toys.
- Describe the lab environment.

Review of the Components of the Implementation Plan

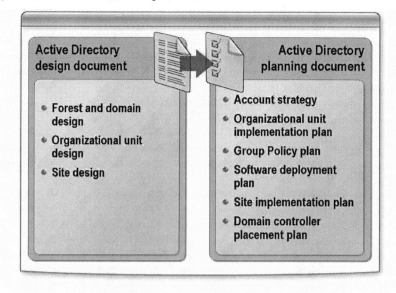

Active Directory design document

- Forest and domain design
- Organizational unit design
- Site design

Active Directory planning document

- Account strategy
- Organizational unit implementation plan
- Group Policy plan
- Software deployment plan
- Site implementation plan
- Domain controller placement plan

Introduction

The Engineering and Design team at Tailspin Toys has completed its review process of the company's business goals. The team has recommendations that affect the implementation of Active Directory. Review the design and planning documents and the recommendations, and then create an Active Directory implementation plan.

Active Directory design components

The design team created the following main components of the Active Directory design:

- The forest and domain design
- The organizational unit design
- The site design

Active Directory implantation plan components

The Active Directory implementation plan determines how Tailspin Toys implements the Active Directory design. Be sure to consider all the recommendations that the Engineering and Design team makes before you finalize your implementation plan. The Active Directory implementation plan should contain the following main components:

- Account strategy
- Organizational unit implementation plan
- Group Policy plan
- Software deployment plan
- Site implementation plan
- Domain controller placement plan

Introduction to Tailspin Toys

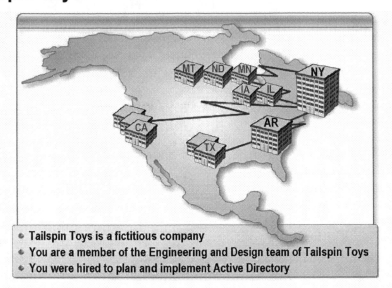

- Tailspin Toys is a fictitious company
- You are a member of the Engineering and Design team of Tailspin Toys
- You were hired to plan and implement Active Directory

Introduction

Tailspin Toys has headquarters in New York and 3,000 fulltime employees throughout the United States. Over the years, the company has expanded its business to include board games, an exclusive line of stuffed animals, building toys, dolls, and riding toys. To keep up with the growth of the company, it opened a production and distribution location in Fayetteville, Arkansas.

Future plans

To maintain pace with the competition from the electronic game industry, Tailspin Toys is acquiring two small manufacturers of electronic games, Contoso, Ltd and Wingtip Toys. Wingtip Toys, located in Houston, Texas, creates a successful line of robotic animal toys. It also maintains a production plant in Austin, Texas. Contoso, Ltd is located in Palo Alto, California. It markets a line of computer games for several gaming consoles. Contoso, Ltd maintains a research and development facility in San Ramon, California.

Two companies, Trey Research and A. Datum Corporation, will provide Tailspin Toys with electronic and packing supplies. Tailspin Toys will use these supplies to build and distribute its product line to new markets. Trey Research maintains headquarters in Helena, Montana and operates a factory in Fargo, North Dakota. A. Datum Corporation maintains headquarters in Davenport, Iowa and a factory in Eden Prairie, Minnesota. Both companies expect their workforces to increase 30-50 percent in the next three years based on the business plan that Tailspin Toys developed.

Tailspin Toys has decided to use an external vendor, Consolidated Messenger, to manage human resources (HR). Consolidated Messenger has headquarters in Chicago, Illinois and a branch office in La Jolla, California.

Tailspin Toys Personnel

Introduction

Labs A and B begin with a brief video presentation by several Tailspin Toys employees, who discuss Active Directory planning and implementation issues. The employees represent just a few of the roles that designers and implementers work with to create an Active Directory implementation plan for an organization.

Key personnel

You will hear from the following employees:

- *Jack S. Richins.* As the chief executive officer (CEO) of Tailspin Toys, Jack often provides business motivations for decisions.

- *Tad Orman.* As the director of new technology, Tad is responsible for ensuring that his team develops and implements an Active Directory design throughout Tailspin Toys, Contoso, Ltd, Wingtip Toys, its suppliers, Trey Research and A. Datum Corporation, and it external vendor, Consolidated Messenger.

- *Linda Meisner.* As the group manager for Engineering and Design, Linda has asked you to help plan and implement an Active Directory infrastructure in Tailspin Toys and its partner companies and suppliers. In the labs, you will obtain your instructions from Linda.

Introduction to the Lab Environment

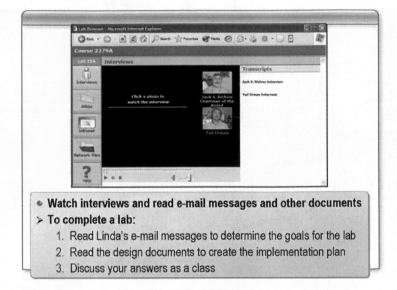

◆ Watch interviews and read e-mail messages and other documents

➤ To complete a lab:

    1. Read Linda's e-mail messages to determine the goals for the lab

    2. Read the design documents to create the implementation plan

    3. Discuss your answers as a class

Key points

To begin the lab, on the desktop, click **Internet Explorer**.

Each lab contains the following elements:

- *Interviews*. Company officials describe the scenario and recommendations to implement Active Directory at Tailspin Toys.

- *E-mail messages*. These messages contain detailed information for each lab scenario. The messages that you receive from Linda contain the goals.

- *Intranet*. Background information about Tailspin Toys, including company background, an executive organizational chart, and company locations.

- *Network files*. A file server that contains folders with relevant documents that you may require to complete a lab.

- *Help*. Instructions about how to use the Lab Browser.

▶ **Complete the lab**

1. Read Linda's e-mail messages in the lab to determine the goals for the lab.

2. Read the Active Directory design documents to create an implementation plan.

3. Discuss your answers as a class.

Lab A: Creating the Active Directory Implementation Plan for Tailspin Toys

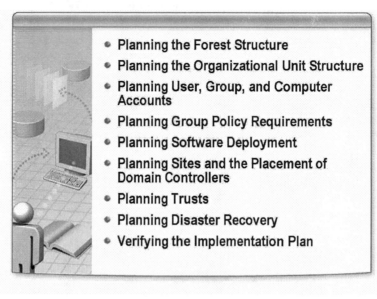

- Planning the Forest Structure
- Planning the Organizational Unit Structure
- Planning User, Group, and Computer Accounts
- Planning Group Policy Requirements
- Planning Software Deployment
- Planning Sites and the Placement of Domain Controllers
- Planning Trusts
- Planning Disaster Recovery
- Verifying the Implementation Plan

Objectives

After completing this lab, you will be able to:

- Create an Active Directory implementation plan for Tailspin Toys and its partner companies.
- Implement the Active Directory infrastructure in Tailspin Toys and its partner companies.

Prerequisites

Before working on this lab, you must have:

- An understanding of the components of Active Directory.
- An understanding of how Active Directory uses the Domain Name System (DNS) service.
- An understanding of Active Directory permissions and trust relationships.
- Knowledge and skills to create user accounts, group accounts, and computer accounts.
- Knowledge and skills to create and configure sites and site links.
- Knowledge and skills to place domain controllers.
- Knowledge and skills to implement Group Policy.
- Knowledge and skills to deploy software by using Group Policy.

Scenario

Tailspin Toys has hired you to develop its Active Directory implementation plan. Read this document before you begin the lab exercises. Then, see the Lab Browser to receive a briefing about the current business, the infrastructure, and the proposed design that is based on the recommendations of the Engineering and Design team.

Important   You can draw your diagrams on paper or use Microsoft® Visio® to document your solution.

Estimated time to complete this lab: 45 minutes

Exercise 1
Planning the Forest Structure

In this exercise, you will decide how to implement an Active Directory forest structure for the Tailspin Toys enterprise. Use information in the Lab Browser that the Tailspin Toys Engineering and Design team developed. Also use input from your colleagues to devise the implementation plan.

▶ **Document the plan for the forest structure**

■ Use the following table to help make your decisions.

Company name	Forest root domain	Additional domains	Number of domain controllers

Exercise 2
Planning the Organizational Unit Structure

In this exercise, you will decide how to implement an organizational unit structure for Tailspin Toys and its partner companies. Use the guidelines that the Engineering and Design team developed. Refer to the Lab Browser for the guidelines and other information that you require to make your decisions.

Scenario

Determine and then document an organizational unit structure for the Tailspin Toys enterprise. Because you will work in groups of four, you can use 16 charts to complete this task.

▶ **Document the plan for the organizational unit structure**

1. What approach will you use to implement organizational units in the enterprise? Document your decisions in the following charts.

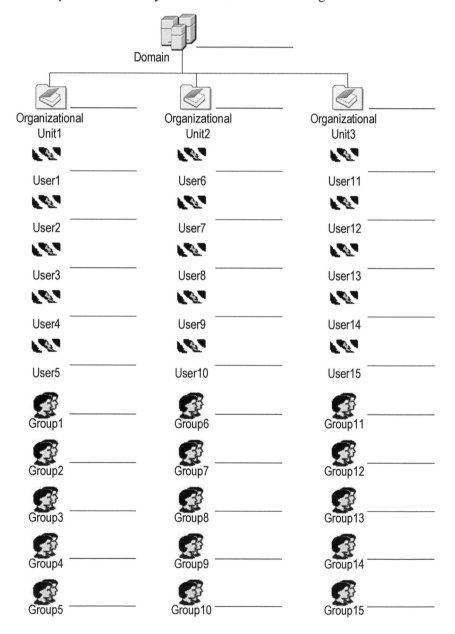

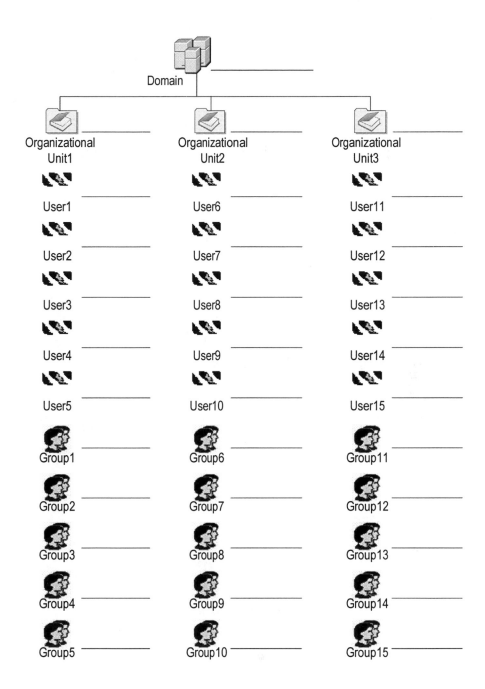

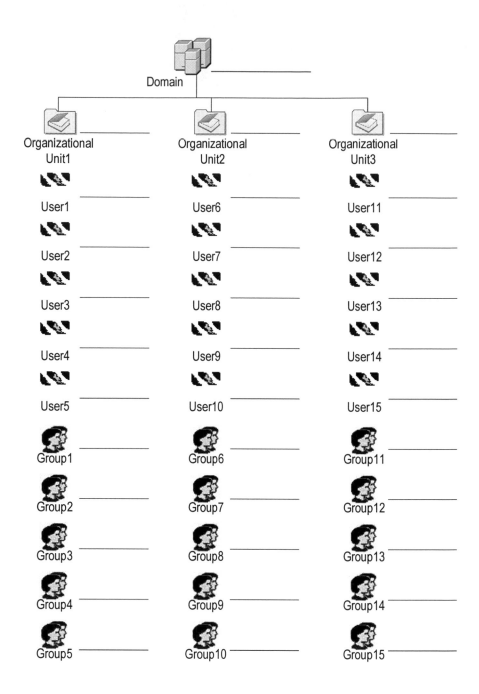

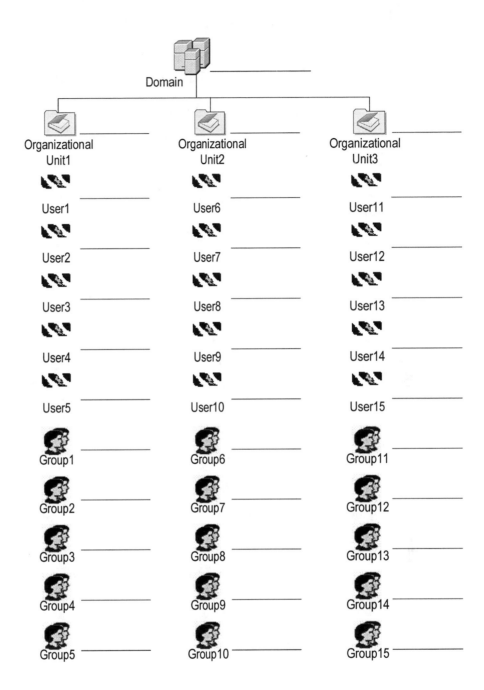

Exercise 3
Planning User, Group, and Computer Accounts

In this exercise, you will decide how to implement user, group, and computer accounts for Tailspin Toys and its partner companies. Consider standards that your decisions will set throughout the enterprise and what types of group account you must create. Use the guidelines by the Engineering and Design team. Refer to the Lab Browser for the guidelines and other information that you require to make your decisions.

▶ **Document the naming convention for user, group, and computer accounts**

■ What naming conventions will you use to create user, group, and computer accounts?

_____

_____

_____

_____

_____

_____

_____

_____

Exercise 4
Planning Group Policy Requirements

In this exercise, you will decide how to implement Group Policy in the Tailspin Toys environment. Consider the requirements of Tailspin Toys and its partner companies, including the guidelines by the Engineering and Design team. Refer to the Lab Browser for the guidelines and other information that you will require to make your decisions.

▶ **Document Group Policy requirements**

■ What elements will you implement by using Group Policy?

_____

_____

_____

_____

_____

_____

_____

Exercise 5
Planning Software Deployment

In this exercise, you will decide what software you will deploy in the enterprise's environment and how to best use the distribution methods that are available to you. Use the guidelines and other information in the Lab Browser to help you reach your decisions.

▶ **Document the plan for software deployment**

■ What software will you deploy in Tailspin Toys and its partner companies? How will you deploy the software?

_____

_____

_____

_____

Exercise 6
Planning Sites and the Placement of Domain Controllers

In this exercise, you will determine which sites, if any, you must create. You will also plan the distribution of domain controllers in the enterprise based on the roles that they perform. Use the guidelines that the Engineering and Design team created and other information in the Lab Browser to make your decisions.

▶ **Document site names and locations**

- Which sites will you create for the Tailspin Toys enterprise? Document your answers in the following table.

Site name	Location

▶ **Document the placement of domain controllers**

■ Where will you place domain controller roles in each company in the
Tailspin Toys enterprise? Document your answers in the following table.

Domain	Domain controller	Location

Exercise 7
Planning Trusts

In this exercise, you will decide what is the best approach to implement trusts. Use the guidelines by the Engineering and Design team. Refer to the Lab Browser for the guidelines and other required information. Based on the business scenario that the design team provided, decide the number and type of trusts to create in the enterprise. Consider the security implications of your decisions.

▶ **Document trust relationships**

■ What types of trusts will you establish for each company in the Tailspin Toys enterprise? Where will you create these trusts? Document your decisions in the following table.

Forest trust	Trust destination	Type of trust

Exercise 8
Planning Disaster Recovery

In this exercise, you will decide what is the best approach to use for planning disaster recovery. Use the design team's guidelines. Refer to the Lab Browser for the required information to make your decisions.

Scenario

Tailspin Toys requires a good disaster recovery plan. The enterprise must be able to recover quickly from potential data loss and catastrophic events that could disable data processing. Your team must devise a solution to meet these requirements.

▶ **Document the plan for disaster recovery**

■ What is the disaster recovery plan?

_____

_____

_____

_____

Exercise 9
Verifying the Implementation Plan

In this exercise, you will determine whether key components of the implementation plan work as expected for Tailspin Toys and its partner companies. Use the Engineering and Design team's guidelines. Refer to the Lab Browser for the guidelines and other information that you require to make your decisions.

▶ **Verify the implementation of Active Directory in Tailspin Toys**

- What parts of the implementation will you test? How will you test the implementation? Document your responses. You will use this test plan to verify the implementation at the end of Lab B.

_____

_____

_____

_____

Lesson: Implementing the Active Directory Infrastructure for Tailspin Toys

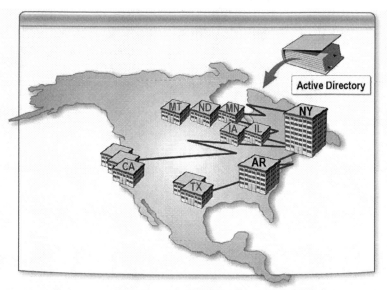

Introduction

In this lesson, you will implement a solution for Tailspin Toys based on the Active Directory implementation plan that you created in the lab in the previous lesson.

Lesson objective

After completing this lesson, you will be able to implement the Active Directory infrastructure for Tailspin Toys.

Lab B: Implementing the Active Directory Infrastructure for Tailspin Toys

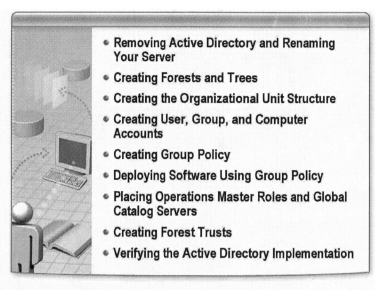

Objectives

After completing this lab, you will be able to implement the Active Directory infrastructure for Tailspin Toys.

Prerequisites

Before working on this lab, you must have:

- An understanding of the components of Active Directory.

- An understanding of how Active Directory uses the DNS service.

- An understanding of Active Directory permissions and trust relationships.

- Knowledge and skills to create user accounts, group accounts, and computer accounts.

- Knowledge and skills to create and configure sites and site links.

- Knowledge and skills to place domain controllers.

- Knowledge and skills to implement Group Policy.

- Knowledge and skills to deploy software by using Group Policy.

Scenario

Tailspin Toys has hired you to implement its Active Directory infrastructure. Use the Lab Browser to learn about the enterprise's current business, infrastructure, and proposed design, which is based on the recommendations of the Engineering and Design team. Complete the implementation plan before you begin these lab exercises.

Estimated time to complete this lab: 120 minutes

Exercise 0
Lab Setup

This section lists the tasks that you must perform before you begin the lab.

 Important: Configure the London server as authoritative for the .msft zone. This zone will be delegated to each student domain controller in the lab that is authoritative for its zone. Students will configure their computers to forward DNS requests to the London server in this lab.

Tasks	Detailed steps
▪ Configure the instructor computer to delegate DNS domains.	a. Click **Start**, point to **Administrative Tools**, and then click **DNS**.
	b. Expand **Forward Lookup Zones**, right-click the **msft** zone, and then click **New Delegation**.
	c. On the **Welcome to the New Delegation Wizard** page, click **Next**.
	d. On the **Delegated domain name** page, type **nwtraders_***x* (refer to the Domain column in the table in Exercise 2 to determine the value of *x*), and then click **Next**.
	Important! You must enter the name of only one server from each domain. Ensure that the server you choose from each domain is configured as the forest root domain controller in the lab.
	e. On the **Name Servers** page, click **Add**.
	f. On the **New Resource Record** page, type the server's fully qualified domain name (FQDN) and IP address, and then click **OK**.
	g. On the **Name Servers** page, click **Next**.
	h. On the **Completing the New Delegation Wizard** page, click **Finish**.
	i. Repeat steps b through h for each student domain in the configuration.

Exercise 1
Removing Active Directory and Renaming Your Server

In this exercise, you will remove the Active Directory installation on your computer in preparation for implementing the plan that you developed in the previous lab. You will then rename your server according to the role it will play in the implementation.

The following table lists the information about new server names.

Old name	New name
Vancouver	NYDC1
Denver	FYDC1
Perth	HODC1
Brisbane	AUDC1
Lisbon	PADC1
Bonn	SRDC1
Lima	HEDC1
Santiago	FADC1
Bangalore	DADC1
Singapore	EPDC1
Casablanca	CHDC1
Tunis	LJDC1
Acapulco	NYDC2
Miami	FYDC2
Auckland	HODC2
Suva	AUDC2
Stockholm	PADC2
Moscow	SRDC2
Caracas	HEDC2
Montevideo	FADC2
Manila	DADC2
Tokyo	EPDC2
Khartoum	CHDC2
Nairobi	LJDC2

Tasks	Specific instructions
1. Remove Active Directory from your domain controller.	▪ Log on to your domain as **Administrator**
2. Rename your server as shown in the previous table.	▪ Log on to your server as **Administrator**

Exercise 2
Creating Forests and Trees

In this exercise, you will use the implementation plan from Lab A to create the appropriate forests and domain trees.

The following table lists the six forest root servers and their corresponding domain names.

Forest root server	Domain
NYDC1	newyork.tailspintoys.msft
HODC1	houston.wingtiptoys.msft
PADC1	paloalto.contoso.msft
HEDC1	helena.treyresearch.msft
DADC1	davenport.adatum.msft
CHDC1	chicago.consolidatedmessenger.msft

The following table lists the six additional trees in the existing forests and the corresponding domain names.

Server	Domain
FYDC1	fayetteville.tailspintoys.msft
AUDC1	austin.wingtiptoys.msft
SRDC1	sanramon.contoso.msft
FADC1	fargo.treyresearch.msft
EPDC1	edenprairie.adatum.msft
LJDC1	lajolla.consolidatedmessenger.msft

The following table lists the additional servers and their corresponding existing domain names.

Server	Domain
NYDC2	newyork.tailspintoys.msft
FYDC2	fayetteville.tailspintoys.msft
HODC2	houston.wingtiptoys.msft
AUDC2	austin.wingtiptoys.msft
PADC2	paloalto.contoso.msft
SRDC2	sanramon.contoso.msft
HEDC2	helena.treyresearch.msft
FADC2	fargo.treyresearch.msft
DADC2	davenport.adatum.msft
EPDC2	edenprairie.adatum.msft
CHDC2	chicago.consolidatedmessenger.msft
LJDC2	lajolla.consolidatedmessenger.msft

Scenario

As a member of the Engineering and Design team, you must create the logical structure for Active Directory that you will use in the Active Directory implementation for Tailspin Toys.

Tasks	Specific instructions
1. Install Active Directory on the six forest root servers and then create domains.	■ Install Active Directory on the six forest root servers and then create domains based on the information in the first table in Exercise 2.
2. Install Active Directory to create the six additional trees in the existing forests and then create domains.	a. Install Active Directory to create the six additional trees in the existing forests and create domains based on the information in the second table in Exercise 2. b. Log on to your server as **Administrator** with a password of **P@ssw0rd** if you are not already logged on. c. Verify that the child domain controller has its DNS resolver pointed to the partner's forest root domain controller or to London.
3. Install Active Directory on the remaining computers in the classroom and configure each one as an additional server in the existing domains.	a. Install Active Directory on the remaining computers in the classroom and configure each one as an additional server in the existing domains based on the information in the third table in Exercise 2. b. Log on to your server as **Administrator** with a password of **P@ssw0rd** if you are not already logged on. c. Verify that the additional domain controller has its DNS resolver pointed to the domain controller for the domain it is joining or to London.

Exercise 3
Creating the Organizational Unit Structure

In this exercise, you will create an organizational unit structure according to your Active Directory implementation plan.

Tasks	Specific instructions
▪ Create the organizational unit structure according to your Active Directory implementation plan.	▪ Specify the name of an organizational unit from your plan in Lab A.

Exercise 4
Creating User, Group, and Computer Accounts

In this exercise, you will create user, group, and computer accounts according to the plan that you developed in Lab A. Use the Lab11users.csv file to import multiple accounts or create them manually. The import file contains 100 generic user and computer accounts and 50 generic group accounts that you can modify and then import into your Active Directory infrastructure.

Tasks	Specific instructions
▪ Create user, group, and computer accounts.	a. Log on as **Administrator** with a password of **P@ssw0rd** b. Use the CSVD file named Lab11users.csv located at C:\MOC\2279\Labfiles\Setup.

Exercise 5
Creating Group Policy

In this exercise, you will create Group Policy objects to configure Group Policy settings.

Tasks	Specific instructions
1. Open Group Policy Management.	a. Use **Run as** to open Group Policy Management. b. Use a password of **P@ssw0rd**
2. Browse to your domain and create a new policy.	▪ Select the appropriate settings for Group Policy based on the plan from Lab A.
3. Link the GPO to your domain.	

Exercise 6
Deploying Software Using Group Policy

In this exercise, you will create a software installation package to deploy Microsoft Office XP to a group in your domain.

Tasks	Specific instructions
1. Open Group Policy Management.	a. Use **Run as** to open Group Policy Management. b. Use a password of **P@ssw0rd**
2. Browse to the domain policy for your domain and edit the policy.	
3. Create a software installation package in order to assign Office XP to a group in your domain.	▪ Use the **Proplus.msi** package located on the instructor's software distribution point.

Exercise 7
Placing Operations Master Roles and Global Catalog Servers

In this exercise, you will transfer some of the operations master roles and enable the global catalog server.

Tasks	Special Instructions
⚠ **Important:** Perform the following task on NYDC2, FYDC2, HODC2, AUDC2, PADC2, SRDC2, HEDC2, FADC2, DADC2, EPDC2, CHDC2, and LJDC2.	
▪ Transfer the PDC, RID, and infrastructure master roles to the second server in each location.	▪ Log on to your server as **Administrator** with a password of **P@ssw0rd** if you are not already logged on.

Exercise 8
Creating Forest Trusts

In this exercise, you will raise the functional level of each domain and forest, and then create forest trusts.

Tasks	Special instructions
⚠ Important: Perform the following task on the first domain controller in each domain.	
1. Raise the functional level of each domain to Microsoft Windows® Server 2003.	▪ Log on to your server as **Administrator** with a password of **P@ssw0rd** if you are not already logged on.
2. On the root server of each forest, raise the functional level of each forest to Windows Server 2003.	
⚠ Important: Create a two-way forest trust between newyork.tailspintoys.msft and houston.wingtiptoys.msft. Create an additional two-way forest trust between newyork.tailspintoys.msft and paloalto.contoso.msft. Perform the following task on NYDC1, with the help of the administrators of HODC1 and PADC1.	
3. Create two-way forest trusts.	▪ On the **User Name and Password** page, have the administrator of HODC1 type a user name of **Administrator** and a password for the administrator of the houston.wingtiptoys.com domain.
⚠ Important: Create one-way trusts so that helena.treyresearch.msft, davenport.adatum.msft, and chicago.consolidatedmessenger.msft each trust newyork.tailspintoys.msft. Perform this task on NYDC1 with the help of the administrators of HEDC1, DADC1, and CHDC1.	
4. Create one-way forest trusts.	▪ On the **User Name and Password** page, have the administrator of HEDC1 type a user name of **Administrator** and a password for the administrator of the helena.treyresearch.msft domain.

Exercise 9
Verifying the Active Directory Implementation

In this exercise, you will verify the Active Directory implementation to ensure that the key components of the infrastructure work as expected.

Scenario

Now that you have completed the Active Directory implementation, log on as a test user to verify that the components of the implementation work as expected. Pay particular attention to resource access across forests or within domains if security plans call for that level of restriction. Also pay close attention to the inheritance of policy settings and to software deployment settings in Group Policy. Linda Meisner at Tailspin Toys is expecting a status report from you about these key implementation components. She has also asked your team to sign off on the functionality upon completion of the implementation plan. Linda has scheduled meetings to hand off the implementation to the operations team, which includes system administrators in the IT organization. Your team will remain on call for troubleshooting problems.

Tasks	Specific instructions
1. Log on as a user from Tailspin Toys.	
2. Verify resource access.	

Course Evaluation

Your evaluation of this course will help Microsoft understand the quality of your learning experience.

To complete a course evaluation, go to http://www.CourseSurvey.com.

Microsoft will keep your evaluation strictly confidential and will use your responses to improve your future learning experience.

Microsoft® Windows® Server 2003
Enterprise Edition 180-Day Evaluation

The software included in this kit is intended for evaluation and deployment planning purposes only. If you plan to install the software on your primary machine, it is recommended that you back up your existing data prior to installation.

System requirements

To use Microsoft Windows Server 2003 Enterprise Edition, you need:

- Computer with 550 MHz or higher processor clock speed recommended; 133 MHz minimum required; Intel Pentium/Celeron family, or AMD K6/Athlon/Duron family, or compatible processor (Windows Server 2003 Enterprise Edition supports up to eight CPUs on one server)

- 256 MB of RAM or higher recommended; 128 MB minimum required (maximum 32 GB of RAM)

- 1.25 to 2 GB of available hard-disk space*

- CD-ROM or DVD-ROM drive

- Super VGA (800 · 600) or higher-resolution monitor recommended; VGA or hardware that supports console redirection required

- Keyboard and Microsoft Mouse or compatible pointing device, or hardware that supports console redirection

Additional items or services required to use certain Windows Server 2003 Enterprise Edition features:

- For Internet access:
  - Some Internet functionality may require Internet access, a Microsoft Passport account, and payment of a separate fee to a service provider; local and/or long-distance telephone toll charges may apply
  - High-speed modem or broadband Internet connection

- For networking:
  - Network adapter appropriate for the type of local-area, wide-area, wireless, or home network to which you wish to connect, and access to an appropriate network infrastructure; access to third-party networks may require additional charges

Note: To ensure that your applications and hardware are Windows Server 2003–ready, be sure to visit **www.microsoft.com/windowsserver2003**.

* Actual requirements will vary based on your system configuration and the applications and features you choose to install. Additional available hard-disk space may be required if you are installing over a network. For more information, please see **www.microsoft.com/windowsserver2003**.

Uninstall instructions

This time-limited release of Microsoft Windows Server 2003 Enterprise Edition will expire 180 days after installation. If you decide to discontinue the use of this software, you will need to reinstall your original operating system. You may need to reformat your drive.

Notes

Notes

Notes

Notes

Notes

Notes

Microsoft® Windows® Server 2003 Enterprise Edition 180-Day Evaluation

The software included in this kit is intended for evaluation and deployment planning purposes only. If you plan to install the software on your primary machine, it is recommended that you back up your existing data prior to installation.

System requirements

To use Microsoft Windows Server 2003 Enterprise Edition, you need:

- Computer with 550 MHz or higher processor clock speed recommended; 133 MHz minimum required; Intel Pentium/Celeron family, or AMD K6/Athlon/Duron family, or compatible processor (Windows Server 2003 Enterprise Edition supports up to eight CPUs on one server)
- 256 MB of RAM or higher recommended; 128 MB minimum required (maximum 32 GB of RAM)
- 1.25 to 2 GB of available hard-disk space*
- CD-ROM or DVD-ROM drive
- Super VGA (800 × 600) or higher-resolution monitor recommended; VGA or hardware that supports console redirection required
- Keyboard and Microsoft Mouse or compatible pointing device, or hardware that supports console redirection

Additional items or services required to use certain Windows Server 2003 Enterprise Edition features:

- For Internet access:
  - Some Internet functionality may require Internet access, a Microsoft Passport account, and payment of a separate fee to a service provider; local and/or long-distance telephone toll charges may apply
  - High-speed modem or broadband Internet connection
- For networking:
  - Network adapter appropriate for the type of local-area, wide-area, wireless, or home network to which you wish to connect, and access to an appropriate network infrastructure; access to third-party networks may require additional charges

Note: To ensure that your applications and hardware are Windows Server 2003–ready, be sure to visit **www.microsoft.com/windowsserver2003**.

---

* Actual requirements will vary based on your system configuration and the applications and features you choose to install. Additional available hard-disk space may be required if you are installing over a network. For more information, please see **www.microsoft.com/windowsserver2003**.

Uninstall instructions

This time-limited release of Microsoft Windows Server 2003 Enterprise Edition will expire 180 days after installation. If you decide to discontinue the use of this software, you will need to reinstall your original operating system. You may need to reformat your drive.

Microsoft®